MW00609819

ARTHUR CARHART

Arthur Carhart

WILDERNESS PROPHET

TOM WOLF

To Ellen + Richard
Tom Wolf
2008

UNIVERSITY PRESS OF COLORADO

© 2008 by the University Press of Colorado

Published by the University Press of Colorado
5589 Arapahoe Avenue, Suite 206C
Boulder, Colorado 80303

All rights reserved
Printed in the United States of America

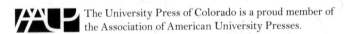 The University Press of Colorado is a proud member of
the Association of American University Presses.

The University Press of Colorado is a cooperative publishing enterprise supported, in part, by Adams State College, Colorado State University, Fort Lewis College, Mesa State College, Metropolitan State College of Denver, University of Colorado, University of Northern Colorado, and Western State College of Colorado.

∞ The paper used in this publication meets the minimum requirements of the American National Standard for Information Sciences—Permanence of Paper for Printed Library Materials. ANSI Z39.48-1992

Library of Congress Cataloging-in-Publication Data

Wolf, Tom, 1945–
  Arthur Carhart : wilderness prophet / Tom Wolf.
    p. cm.
  Includes bibliographical references.
  ISBN 978-0-87081-913-1 (hardcover : alk. paper) 1. Carhart, Arthur Hawthorne, b. 1892. 2. Conservationists—United States—Biography. 3. Environmentalists—United States—Biography. I. Title.
  QH31.C323W65 2008
  333.72092—dc22
  [B]

                                                                                2008003756

Design by Daniel Pratt

17   16   15   14   13   12   11   10   09   08   10   9   8   7   6   5   4   3   2   1

CONTENTS

v

ACKNOWLEDGMENTS

This book started with a Jackson Fellows Grant from the Southwestern Studies Program at Colorado College. I finished it with a grant from the Colorado Endowment for the Humanities. I wish to thank the staff of the Denver Public Library, especially John Irving, and the staff of the Pueblo Museum.

I had help from Doug Monroy, Bill deBuys, John Baden, Don Snow, Steve Jones, Ed Marston, Andrew Kirk, Andrew Gulliford, Mark Harvey, Curt Meine, Richard Etulain, Walt Hecox, Mark Smith, Jack McCrory, Patricia Marshall, Marjane Ambler, and Mike Smith (USDA Forest Service).

In Mapleton, Iowa, I received a gracious welcome from Keith Robinson. I thank Robert Hawthorn for reviewing the sections that pertain to his family.

My thanks to Christina Nealson, my beloved wife, for her support. And to my mother, Betsy Ross Wolf. Chris Webster and Carole Summer, Paul Thompkins and Emily Vardaman, and Steve and Susan McElmury provided me with writing sanctuaries.

ACKNOWLEDGMENTS

I respectfully dedicate this book to Emeritus Professor Denny Lynch (Colorado State University and USDA Forest Service):

I will not cease from Mental Fight,
Nor shall my Sword sleep in my hand:
Till we have built Jerusalem,
In Englands green & pleasant Land.

—WILLIAM BLAKE, *MILTON*

ARTHUR CARHART

IT'S OUR JOB, A JOB FOR ALL OF US

> Perhaps I do seem aggressively radical to many of them but it is because I
> have to scrap continually and in a somewhat radical fashion to get any con-
> sideration whatever. I am not done with recreation in National Forests when
> I leave. I will not be muzzled by censorship that exists in the department
> and while I am not going to do any "muckraking" I will be free to tell my
> ideas and views without restriction.
>
> —ARTHUR CARHART, 1921[1]

Arthur Carhart's centrist ideas about water and wilderness make him a good
guide for some of the choices ordinary citizens must make today. Conservation
politics have become polarized in ways that may benefit the blindly partisan
but that will only harm our public lands. As we look to a future where climate
change will dominate land management, we should give the past a vote by
examining Arthur Carhart's life. We should keep in mind Carhart's prophetic
way of linking water and wilderness.

Climate change is affecting our public lands—particularly the high-altitude
areas we have designated as Wilderness.[2] Which changes are good and which
are bad? We will lose many species and ecological communities permanently.
That is a great tragedy. But we are also gaining some surprises. Aspen (and
the rich ecosystem aspen supports) is appearing at timberline sites where aspen
did not exist in Carhart's time.[3] Meanwhile, lower-elevation aspen stands are
suddenly dying.

In a related development, the Trappers Lake watershed in northwestern Colorado, "the Cradle of Wilderness," burned in 2002. As precipitation patterns change and snowmelt occurs earlier and earlier, how will the 17,000-acre "Big Fish Fire" affect the ecological health of this hallowed watershed? Scientists are predicting a 50 percent reduction in stream flow by 2050 in western Colorado.[4] We will need to reconsider the tools we make available to land managers as we confront such changes. How can we learn to think beyond designated Wilderness to larger landscapes with buffer zones that will accommodate climate change?

One of the tools we need to reexamine is the Wilderness Act of 1964, which was not written in stone and genome. Partly with Carhart's help, it evolved over the decades since he took his courageous stand against roads and cabins at Trappers Lake in 1919. And it has continued to evolve since then, as Congress adds more wilderness areas and we learn more about managing wilderness. But now we are facing change on a scale that challenges many of our assumptions about what we are protecting as wilderness and why we are protecting it. As wilderness changes, so should the Wilderness Act.

"The first rule of intelligent tinkering is to save all the parts." Environmentalists are fond of quoting Aldo Leopold. As ecologists try to understand climate change, they are learning that Leopold's science has become outdated. Ecosystems often have redundancy built into them. Some parts are more important than others. As land managers deal with climate change, they need ecologists to guide them. Which parts are important and why?

Yet Leopold's wisdom endures in another way. Which values should we preserve? As we tinker with the environment, one intelligent thing to do is to recover some key "parts" from our past. That is my goal in this biography of Arthur Carhart, wilderness prophet. We ignore his life story at our peril. Carhart's thinking about wilderness offers a commonsense, nonpartisan, democratic approach to administering and—where necessary—changing the laws and the institutions that manage our natural resources. In 1961 Carhart wrote:

> Those who have been lumping all types and concepts of wildlands together and calling them all "wilderness," particularly those who insist that only where the natural environment is absolute, truly virgin, can there be "wilderness," may protest these listings [of wildland recreation zones]. To argue that "wilderness" is anything less than physically "virgin" may be heresy. If so, I am a heretic. I do not argue that there can be any gradations of virginity. I do argue that there may be gradations in the physical attributes representing the wildness of wildlands which, as in other areas of human experience, may be as gratifying to those associating with it as absolute virginity—perhaps even more so.[5]

Obscurity and ostracism became Carhart's "rewards" for questioning the environmental orthodoxy of his times. Carhart never lacked courage. And it took courage for the "father of wilderness" to withhold his support for a Wilderness Act that fell short, in his eyes, of what America needed.

In the decade before its final passage in 1964, the Wilderness Act (PL 88-577) went through sixty-six drafts and eighteen congressional hearings. President Lyndon B. Johnson signed it into law on September 3, 1964. As the horse trading progressed, Arthur Carhart became more and more dismayed with the results. There would be no buffer zones around wilderness, no attempt to place designated wilderness into a watershed-wide plan. Especially repugnant to him were the provisions that favored special interests, such as grazing and mining. Among many other problems, the final act compromised present and future wilderness designation, in Carhart's mind, because it allowed the continuation of existing grazing permits, regardless of ecological condition. It also gave the mining industry until 1983 to make claims and then develop them at its leisure. And it did not allow for the integrated planning that should include buffer zones around wilderness.[6]

Ironically, Carhart the centrist became a heretic in the eyes of many in the wilderness movement. Carhart's friend, Howard Zahniser of the Wilderness Society, had led the long, exhausting battle to hammer out a bill. In deference to many such friends in the wilderness movement, Carhart did not openly work against the final bill during the summer and fall of 1964. As the election campaign ground on, it became clear that a wilderness bill would help the Democratic Party. Ever the maverick, Carhart was supporting Republican Barry Goldwater in that campaign while backing the reelection of Democratic Congressman Wayne Aspinall of Colorado. Carhart felt Goldwater, as a fiscal conservative, would be less likely to pursue an expensive ground war in Southeast Asia and more likely to cut funding for the Bureau of Reclamation. Carhart knew that, when the time finally came, only Aspinall could deliver a wilderness bill that would have broad public support. Meanwhile, many conservationists were opposing Aspinall, who was present at the signing of the Wilderness Act along with Mardy Murie, Alice Zahniser, and Interior Secretary Stewart Udall.

The bill included wording by Zahniser that did not fit Carhart's sense of the place of humans *in* nature, *not* outside of nature: "A wilderness, in contrast with those areas where man and his own works dominate the landscape, is hereby recognized as an area where the earth and its community of life are untrammeled by man, where man himself is a visitor who does not remain." Carhart balked at this language because he knew too much about the place in nature that Native Americans had occupied. Zahniser's eloquence outlived its author. Exhausted, Zahniser had died four months before the bill was finally signed. Thus, he missed the signing event in the Oval Office, just as Carhart did.

Perhaps wilderness is best understood as the chief pillar of a secular twentieth-century religion, best articulated in Aldo Leopold's *Sand County Almanac.* The religious are quicker to punish heretics than they are to pursue unbelievers. Anonymity and suspicion have been Carhart's posthumous "reward" for a lifetime of conservation advocacy. The touchstone for wilderness history, Roderick Nash's *Wilderness and the American Mind,* has gone through many reprintings and four editions since its first appearance in 1967. Nash barely mentions Carhart. But Nash did go further in the Wilderness Society's magazine, acknowledging Carhart's true stature as a major conservation figure. Among environmental historians, Nash stands almost alone.[7] This book tries to explain why.

PERHAPS I DO SEEM AGGRESSIVELY RADICAL

Carhart is a good guide to such questions—not because he was always "right" but because his long career provides us with examples of how to change and how to learn. He was there at the beginning, after all, before the big dams arose, before the United States had a wilderness movement, and before we made the fateful, flawed choices that contribute to the degradation of both the environment and our politics.

Arthur Carhart (1892–1978) was one of the most significant conservationists of the twentieth century. Wallace Stegner said: "I have been convinced for a long time that what is miscalled the middle of the road is actually the most radical and the most difficult position—much more difficult and radical than either reaction or rebellion."[8] Carhart belongs in the company of such giants as Stegner and Aldo Leopold. That is why an interagency consortium still maintains the Arthur Carhart National Wilderness Training Center in Missoula, Montana, along with the Aldo Leopold Wilderness Research Institute.[9] And that is why Trappers Lake in northwestern Colorado and the Boundary Waters Canoe Area in Minnesota continue to inspire us. They should also inspire healthy debate about the idea of wilderness and the practice of wilderness management within the larger context of planning for America's wildlands.

As a lifelong moderate Republican, Carhart felt federal resource management bureaucracies were often the problem rather than the solution because they put their own welfare above the public good—and above the good of wildlife.[10] In contrast, Carhart's sensible, balanced approach locates planning and democratic institutions at the scale of an individual watershed, much as John

Wesley Powell recommended when he reported to Congress about the West.[11] Carhart wrote:

> The responsibility for water management rests in the hands of the fellow who puts a plow-share into the soil, and how he does it. It rests in the hands of the stockman—and he commits a crime against the community if in his greed he so over-grazes his range it becomes a tin roof to produce floods, mud and disaster below. Responsibility for sound water management also lies in the hands of the municipal water division of a community, in the city officials, in the chamber of commerce, in the national bodies of business and industry—it's our job, a job for all of us.[12]

Carhart wrote about conservation issues for many business-oriented publications, and he specialized in addressing business conventions. He thought Powell's ideas about watershed democracies should appeal to Americans of every stripe. In a 1952 talk, "The Future Course in Water Management," to the Annual Conference of the American Water Works Association, he said:

> I propose, now and here, that the organization directing inclusive management of the water wealth, and the soil wealth with it, should not be imposed from the top, but developed out of the minds and actions of those on the ground and in the field. I propose an organization of what might be termed a water resources planning and policy board, for every minor watershed in the nation—every creek, if you please. . . . Not an imposition of what to do from the top, but a development of policy and broad planning rising up from the grass-roots citizenry.[13]

Not everyone sees centrism when they look at Powell and Carhart. Donald Worster, Powell's most recent biographer, says:

> The Achilles heel of American environmentalism is the fact that, despite all their calls for government activism and regulatory power, environmentalists in their heart of hearts share the same ideology of liberty and self-determination that has created a degraded environment. The distance between the "wilderness freedom" of an Abbey or a Muir and the "economic freedom" of laissez-faire capitalism may at times not be very great. This confusing overlap of a liberty seeking ideology with its enemies may constitute the greatest embarrassment the wilderness movement has, one that even its most thoughtful philosophers have never fully addressed or clarified.[14]

Worster conflates environmentalists with wilderness advocates, a mistake Carhart taught us to avoid by insisting that wilderness management was only part of watershed-wide wildlands planning. Then Worster assumes that all environmentalists favor a strong regulatory role for the government, something Carhart warned against as early as 1922 when he was preparing to leave the Forest Service and begin his difficult relationships with the Bureau of Biological Survey and the Bureau of Reclamation. Finally, Worster caricatures liberty and self-determination, as if they inevitably lead to the excesses of capitalism and the degradation of the environment. But Carhart, who lived through the 1920s and endured the Depression and who actually worked in many different government bureaucracies, showed us how we might find a middle way.

One goal of this biography is to share with readers not just the social and political relevance of Carhart's conservationist conscience but also his homespun artistry and eloquence. More than any other twentieth-century conservationist, Carhart emphasized individual freedom and power within the rules of the game set by government to guide our conduct. His Iowa-based brand of rugged individualism may be repugnant to those who prefer restraint and humility based on knowing one's proper place—and for whom such individualism is dangerous, both morally and ecologically. Carhart's father wanted him to be an Iowa bookkeeper. It was his mother, an artist, who insisted that he be free to choose. He chose wilderness—and the West.

Where does a man like Carhart fit within the history of the West? Although he was one of the primary fathers of wilderness, Arthur Carhart was not a dour wilderness philosopher but an accomplished landscape architect and an artful storyteller. With a twinkle in his eye, he constantly shuffled the deck, reinventing himself and the idea of wilderness as the century advanced and environmental conditions changed. And yet his wilderness was always inhabited, a place both peopled and storied, not simply roadless and undeveloped.

Instead of the extremes represented by Edward Abbey and John Muir, Carhart bears comparison with Aldo Leopold. The two Forest Service employees met in Denver in December 1919. After Leopold had read of upstart Carhart's wilderness initiative at Trappers Lake, he rode the train north from Albuquerque to meet the Forest Service's first landscape architect, who bore the formal title "Recreation Engineer." The two Iowans shared their ideas, based on Carhart's remarkable proposal that the Forest Service should manage Trappers Lake for wilderness recreation instead of summer homes and the roads needed to access those homes. Both men shared a love for Teddy Roosevelt's way—for hunting and fishing in wilderness settings like Trappers Lake, playing within "the rules of the game and the laws of the land," as Carhart put it.

A few years later Carhart quit the Forest Service, disgusted with its failure to support adequate funding for recreation planning and its halfhearted effort to partner with local citizens' groups in watershed-based wildlands planning. In contrast, acting through federal fiat, Leopold helped create the first Wilderness Reserve on the Gila National Forest in New Mexico in 1924. And yet, as men of their time, both Carhart and Leopold struggled with deep ambivalence about the roles of predators and wildfires in wildlands management.

From his position outside the federal resource management bureaucracies, Carhart continued to fight for fifty years on behalf of watershed-wide management for places like Trappers Lake, Boundary Waters, and Echo Park. Over the course of a long life that was denied to Leopold, Carhart reinvented himself many times, for he wrote fiction, which Leopold did not.[15] He lived to see Echo Park saved, which Leopold did not, only to see Glen Canyon Dam truss up the wild Colorado River. He lived to witness the unruly spirit of wilderness bound within the Wilderness Act of 1964, which Leopold did not. And after half a century of wilderness advocacy, Carhart, the father of wilderness, could not support the Wilderness Act as it finally emerged. This book explains the many reasons why. From Carhart's populist point of view, the Wilderness Act was deeply flawed for yet another reason that grates on the ears of some environmentalists: the act rewards special interests at the expense of true public interest.

Carhart wrote for the common people. At the end of one of his many books about hunting, published in 1946 when soldiers were readjusting to civilian life, he addressed his readers: "It's something American that calls you back, the free America, where it is a birthright to bear arms, where you have the privilege of the sovereign to hunt without let or hindrance, except for the rules of the game and the laws of the land that you and your brothers have set up to guide human conduct. So you're going out next season again? Fine. I may see you out there. Good luck, and I hope you get your buck."[16]

As with his thinking about wilderness, Carhart's writing appealed to a broad, popular audience. He was a "populist" in the best sense of the term. He knew how to reach ordinary people with his conservation ideas. His numerous books and articles made him America's most widely read conservation writer in the mid-twentieth century.[17]

Part of Carhart's appeal to the common reader was that he pioneered a then-revolutionary aesthetic: if we plan and manage wisely, the beauty of America's wildlands will make us not just better individuals but also better members of our local community—and even better Americans. By this he meant independent people who do not rely on federal bureaucracies to subsidize their particular special interest, be it ranching or recreation. Seeking the middle way, so elusive today, Carhart knew when to compromise and when to take a hard stand, especially when it came to dealing with federal resource bureaucracies. Carhart's decision not to support the Wilderness Act is no mystery. After a lifetime of trying to work with federal bureaucracies, he felt the act favored the special interests that had learned to manipulate agencies like the Forest Service through congressional budgetary procedures. Thus, wilderness became whatever deal could be brokered among competing national interests. Carhart did not like generic, national approaches. He preferred the local.[18]

Although he considered reform of the Bureau of Reclamation a hopeless cause, Carhart tried, especially in his fiction, to imagine a better Forest Service that could be trusted to manage wilderness. In 1964, dismayed by the pro-grazing provisions of the Wilderness Act, he told his old friend and fellow Republican Joe Penfold of the Izaak Walton League:

> At the start, if you don't know already, I can state flatly that I have the most thorough dislike for "burocracy" that one can have. I've been inside and outside and I don't like the thing that is "burocracy." I've tried to analyze it, to get my own definition as to where that pertains. A bureau starts out to do a public service. For a time that spirit dominates. The intent of the organization's being is dominant in its actions. At some point the perpetuation of the bureau becomes the guiding spirit, and then we have "burocracy." Some day I hope to write a novel on this subject.[19]

Other aspects of the Wilderness Act that bothered Carhart were its failure to address the management of predators and wildfires. Carhart remained profoundly ambivalent about these difficult issues. He could remember the great fires of 1910, when smoke from burning national forests in Montana darkened the skies of Iowa. He had an ear for old songs, and he remembered this one in 1959:

> Run Boys, Run, there's fire in the mountains,
> Fire in the mountains, fire in the mountains!
>
> The song my father sang while I was still a little boy had folk ballad quality. It never was clear to me whether those lyrics commanded one to run from the fire or race to put it out. A touch of panic rode in the repeated phrase, "Run boys, run!"[20]

Similar ambivalence dogged Carhart's writing about predators. Carhart was not infallible regarding every conservation issue. Instead, he was right about his faith in our democracy's ability to experiment and to learn from the conservation failures he called "bunk." In 1929, Mary Austin sent Carhart her strongly positive review of his *Last Stand of the Pack*, a book about how the federal Bureau of Biological Survey had systematically exterminated the last wolves in the West. Boldly speaking for himself—and not his coauthor, Stanley P. Young—Carhart replied, "My sympathy too was with the old renegades; and I think the hunters felt somewhat the same way. Personally, I feel that we are floundering dangerously and ridiculously with our wildlife. A lot of so-called conservation is bunk."[21]

How do we know the "bunk" from the wisdom that will guide us to a modestly successful future in land management? Carhart's long career shows us how to learn new lessons and old—from others and from the land. He does what true conservation should do: he gives the past a vote.

Each of the chapters that follow begins with an introduction that summarizes the chapter's major themes. Subsequent sections examine those themes at greater length.

NOTES

1. The letters and most of the materials in the Carhart Collection at the Denver Public Library are arranged chronologically in the Conservation Collection. For the Finding Aid, see http://eadsrv.denverlibrary.org/sdx/pl/.

2. The best Rocky Mountain guide to climate change and its effects on wilderness areas is the Mountain Studies Institute in Durango, Colorado: http://www.mountain-studies.org/home.asp. See also Tom Wolf, "Climate Change and the Rockies," *Inside/Outside* (Spring 2007).

3. G. P. Elliott and W. L. Baker, "Quaking Aspen (Populus tremuloides Michx.) at Treeline: A Century of Change in the San Juan Mountains, Colorado, USA," *Journal of Biogeography* 31 (2004):733–745.

4. P. M. Brown and R. Wu, "Climate and Disturbance Forcing of Episodic Tree Recruitment in a Southwestern Ponderosa Pine Landscape," *Ecology* 86 (2004):3030–3038; Jonathan Overpeck, "Keynote Address: Global Climate Change, the West, and What We Can Do about It," San Juan Climate Change Conference, October 11, 2006. Available through the MSI Web site (note 2).

5. Carhart, *Planning for America's Wildlands* (Harrisburg: Telegraph Press, 1961).

6. For more background on the Wilderness Act, see the Wilderness Society, *The Wilderness Act Handbook: 40th Anniversary Edition* (Washington, DC: Wilderness Society, 2004). The 1964 act designated 9.1 million acres. "Since passage of the Wilderness Act, more than 105 million acres of public lands have been designated as Wilderness, about 4.4 percent of the entire United States. But as much as 200 million additional acres of federal public lands may be suitable for Wilderness, and so we and others continue the fight to win Wilderness designation for those lands—because once an area falls victim to roads or other destructive activity, that land is no longer eligible for Wilderness designation." Quote from the Wilderness Society's Web site: http://www.wilderness.org.

7. Roderick Nash, "Arthur Carhart: Wilderness Advocate." *The Living Wilderness* (December 1980): 32–34; Nash, *Wilderness and the American Mind* (New Haven: Yale University Press, 2001 [1967]), 185–186, 208.

8. Wallace Stegner, quoted in John L. Thomas, *A Country of the Mind: Wallace Stegner, Bernard DeVoto, History and the American Land* (New York: Routledge, 2000), 109. The context is Stegner writing about Joe Hill, the labor leader and Wobbly. The Ludlow Massacre (April 20, 1914) was fresh in Coloradoans' minds when Carhart

arrived in 1919. Concerned about steelworkers from Pueblo having access to the Sangre de Cristo Mountains, Carhart was convinced that the wilderness experience should be available to every potential Joe Hill. I am indebted to Richard Eutalain for the Stegner quote.

9. http://carhart.wilderness.net/.

10. See, for example, Michael Robinson, *Predatory Bureaucracy* (Boulder: University Press of Colorado, 2005).

11. See Wallace Stegner, *Beyond the Hundredth Meridian: John Wesley Powell and the Second Opening of the American West* (Lincoln: University of Nebraska Press, 1954).

12. Carhart, *Water or Your Life* (New York: Lippincott, 1951), 195.

13. "The Future Course in Water Management," speech given at the Annual Conference of the American Water Works Association, Kansas City, MO, May 3, 1952. Carhart Collection, Denver Public Library (hereafter CC, DPL).

14. Donald Worster, "Wild, Tame, and Free: Comparing Canadian and American Views of Nature," in Ken Coates and John Findlay, eds., *On Brotherly Terms: Canadian-American Relations West of the Rockies* (Seattle: University of Washington Press, 2002). See also Worster, *A River Running West: John Wesley Powell* (Cambridge: Cambridge University Press, 2002).

15. Leopold wrote a sort of fiction when he needed to make a point. He clearly fudged the chronology of his conversion from a wolf killer to a wilderness lover. See, among others, William deBuys, "Uncle Aldo: A Legacy of Learning about Learning," University of New Mexico School of Architecture and Planning: John Gaw Meem Lecture Series/Annual Aldo Leopold Lecture, March 9, 2004. Available from the author.

16. Arthur Carhart, *Hunting North American Deer* (New York: Macmillan, 1946), 277.

17. My pursuit of Carhart's middle way led me back to his boyhood roots in Iowa. At the University of Iowa I discovered among his papers a 1954 pitch to Alfred Knopf that he write a series of conservation-oriented boy's books of which *Son of the Forest* (already published in 1952) would be the first. Carhart proposed a novel on the planned Echo Park Dam: "My characters were to be the son of one of those men in Reclamation who question the wisdom of some of those gigantic dams." The manuscript for *Son of an Engineer* still eludes me; the son in the title was the son of William H. Wolf, associate chief engineer of the Bureau of Reclamation and chief design engineer for Glen Canyon Dam.

18. A good example occurred during the latest revision of the White River National Forest's plan. Responding to national money, Senator Ben Nighthorse Campbell (R-Colorado) monkey wrenched a painstaking planning process that had involved local and regional interests. Campbell was repaying a political debt related to funding for the Bureau of Reclamation's Animas-LaPlata Project, a pork project worthy of the great days of the 1960s. See Tom Wolf, "The Animas-La Plata Project," *The Los Angeles Times*, June 22, 1998; Wolf, "Why We Should Not Fund the Animas-La Plata Project," *Engineering News-Record*, June 1998.

19. Letter from Carhart to Joe Penfold, December 21, 1964, CC, DPL.

20. Carhart, *Timber in Your Life* (Philadelphia: Lippincott, 1955), 261.

21. Letter from Carhart to Mary Austin, January 14, 1930, CC, DPL, appreciating her review of *Last Stand of the Pack* in "The Saturday Review of Literature." Carhart wrote *Last Stand of the Pack* (New York: J. H. Sears, 1929) in collaboration with Stanley P. Young of the Bureau of Biological Survey.

CHAPTER ONE

LIFE WAS SURE RUGGED

Grandparents father's side, came from Cornwall, England, sailing vessel; mother's side, came from Maryland, covered wagon, both to western Iowa. Grandad Hawthorne was good friend of Sioux. Guess here's where I get restless foot, this pioneering stock.

ARTHUR CARHART TO MARY AUSTIN, 1929[1]

INTRODUCTION: LANDSCAPE MATERIALS FOR IOWA

In June 1978, as the eighty-five-year-old Arthur Carhart lay dying among the avocado groves in faraway southern California, the citizens of his hometown were holding the Centennial Celebration for Mapleton, Iowa. Couples danced to the music of an orchestra. At the intermissions, a barbershop quartet crooned the old tunes Carhart and his lifelong friend, Charles G. "Judge" Whiting, sang on their senior class day in 1910.[2] Thanks to the advent of the automobile and improved roads, young Carhart had witnessed many scenes like this Centennial Celebration. Between high school and the Great War, as he struggled to find himself, Carhart the professional musician had played barn dances, Chautauquas, and weddings throughout western Iowa, eastern Nebraska, and northern Missouri. Carhart would also have enjoyed the marching bands in that June 1978 Centennial Grand Parade. As late as 1977, he was revising and copyrighting marching music he had composed while serving in the U.S. Army sixty years earlier.

The people of Mapleton had much to celebrate in 1978.[3] While working some of the richest, deepest soils on earth, they had harvested so much wealth that they could afford to export restless progeny like Arthur Carhart, who brought to Colorado in 1919 a distinctively Iowan set of small-town, Republican, populist, rural values—and great expectations.

What were those values, and how did they influence Carhart's career? Those relating to family were as important in their own way as those relating to community. Having fallen under the spell of his reclusive mother's artistic talents, he resisted his gregarious father's desire that he finish his studies at business school. "My father was determined to make me a bookkeeper," Carhart wrote in his droll tone, "but I became far more interested in drumming than bookkeeping." He dropped out of business school and went to live for a year in Sioux City, where he anchored himself: "For several mid-winter months of 1911, I played trap drums in a three-piece orchestra holding forth in the 2-reeler movie theater on 4th Street in Sioux City. Then I joined up as trap drummer in a dance orchestra for greater pay."[4] The automobile offered new freedom. The dance orchestra went on the road:

> We'd gone from Mapleton to Hornick to play one of those 4-piece orches-
> tra Saturday night dance jobs; I played drums. Our deal was to play to
> midnight. The boys from the blue gumbo flats around there wanted more
> than that so they took up a collection and we finally played until 2 a.m.
> Then headed for home in the old, two-cylinder Maxwell that belonged to
> Henry Cook who, before becoming a horseless carriage tycoon[,] ran a
> saloon at 5th and Main in Mapleton. We got within 4 miles of Mapleton,
> the sun was coming up, and about the time we rolled down out of the "Big
> Cut" country, the danged Maxwell ran out of gas. Sunday, 4:30 or so a.m.,
> no gas, about 1911. We walked to town; the girl pianist curled up in the
> back seat and slept until Bill Cook, who drove the car, went back with a
> can of gasoline. Life was sure rugged in the valley of the Little Sioux in
> them days.[5]

Carhart got pneumonia playing a gig in Nebraska for the Winnebago Indians. While recovering at home, he read John Davey's popular book, *The Tree Doctor: A Book on Tree Culture.*[6] Fascinated by the possibilities of tree culture, he decided to go to Iowa Agricultural College in Ames. "My mother fostered this move; my father's brothers, being older, frowned on it. Vehemently and articulately. Be it credited to my mother that she set her face toward the goal of giving me such an education as I chose."[7] Arthur may have flunked his business school courses in "shorthand, bookkeeping, and mental arithmetic," he later recalled, but he seems to have learned enough to run his own numerous small and large businesses later in life. His choice of careers never translated into contempt for businesspeople. When he became a successful freelance writer, he did so in a most businesslike fashion.

No permanent father-son rift was hidden in this family tussle. The friendly George Carhart was a small businessman, a sometime farmer, a Republican, a Methodist, and a Mason. Somehow, he weathered the hard times of the 1890s, jumping back and forth between town and farm. In 1896 he sold his share of the furniture and hardware business he ran with his brother Steve, moving his family to an eighty-acre farm in the countryside near Mapleton that had once belonged to Ella's family.[8] That "tree claim" farm had been part of a failed federal program designed to encourage not just settlement but the planting of massive numbers of trees on the prairie—trees that were somehow supposed to ameliorate the climate and increase rainfall. That same year, 1896, George Carhart fortified his ties to the town by becoming Master of the Mapleton Masonic Chapter. This paternal agility stood Arthur in good stead. Although he was capable of the long periods of solitary labor that are the lot of the artist and freelance writer, Arthur Carhart had the natural bonhomie peculiar to those who genuinely enjoy the company of others. "Visiting," he called it. This made him a good storyteller and mentor for young people. His sociability certainly contributed to his success as a conservationist and as a fund-raiser for conservation causes. It served him especially well in mostly male settings, such as hunting and fishing camps, dude ranches, and the U.S. Army. He became an excellent outdoor cook and published widely on the subject. This was consistent with his conviction that humans were more than transient visitors to natural settings. People could and should be at home in nature.

On September 18 of each year, after the Great War and throughout the 1920s, Carhart's parents each wrote affectionate birthday notes to their only child. In 1920, George Carhart wrote to his son, then living in Denver:[9] "I was in the hardware business when you first saw the light and am in it now. A few years ago some sung 'I did not raise my boy to be a soldier.' Well, I never liked that song but preferred one something like 'I raised my boy to be a *man*,' and he has filled the bill to my entire satisfaction. What more could I ask? What more could I say? May you live to see many happy returns of the day. Love and best wishes to both of you."[10]

All of the Carharts liked to think of themselves as pioneering stock. Soon after this letter was written, George and Ella Carhart followed their son and his bride to start a new life in Colorado. George was seventy-one; Ella was fifty-five. Later, Carhart's loyalty to family values extended to taking his aged father into his own home for a decade after Ella's unexpected death in 1932.[11]

Young Arthur Carhart learned to express his community values in two ways. One was his lifelong membership in the Masons and the Republican

Party, from which he developed his mistrust of government bureaucracies and his respect for ordinary businesspeople as well as a sense of social obligation that ripened into his populist brand of conservationism. Unlike his strongly Methodist parents, Carhart was not formally religious until late in life, when he joined his wife, Vee, as an Episcopalian. But he was always an avid Mason. Carhart got his sense of humor from the Masons, including his good-natured ability to mock himself. By the late 1920s his personal stationery carried so many titles and affiliations that he referred to it as his "Mexican general" list. One of these stressed his Masonic affiliation, another his membership in the Republican Party. Much later, these affiliations would lead Carhart to support a fellow Mason, Barry Goldwater, for president in 1964.

Carhart's other community value, in a different sense of the term, was his conviction that he had a rightful place in nature, that leaving nature alone was not enough for a born tree doctor. As misguided as the tree claim farm might seem, the idea that trees came and went with climate changes had a basis in Iowa's ecological history. Carhart had grown up in a dynamic ecological community of enduring importance. When the first white settlers laid their hands on western Iowa's soils in the decades before the Civil War, they arrived at a moment in the region's ecological history that helped shape much of Carhart's long career as a writer, wilderness advocate, landscape architect, and city planner. These early pioneers plowed part of Iowa's wealth back into a superb education system. Carhart wrote of his education: "Eighth grade completed in the one-room, one-teacher country school, high school in a small corn belt town."[12]

Arthur Carhart benefited from a challenging high school education that featured writing, biological sciences, mathematics, music, and four years of Latin. All would prove useful when Carhart went to college at Ames, where the botanical precision of binomial nomenclature (for example, *Picea pungens* denotes genus and species, respectively) opened to the young man a brave new world of research and speculation about tree doctoring, about the place of humans in nature. Coupling new ideas such as the germ theory of disease and new technologies like the automobile, Carhart's pre–World War I Iowa seemed to put humans squarely in the driver's seat.

THE HUMAN FACE OF WESTERN IOWA IN CARHART'S YOUTH

Carhart was born at home in Mapleton in an Iowa of grasses and row crops, where before there had been trees. An only child, Arthur Hawthorne Carhart was born September 18, 1892, to George Carhart (1853–1941) and Ella Hawthorne (1869–1932). Young Arthur's parents left Mapleton when the boy was four. Arthur thrived in the country, where he had the solitude to read and the freedom to explore the countryside. At age eleven, he won a children's story contest with an article about the downy woodpecker that was published in *A Woman's Home Companion.* The magazine paid the budding author two dollars. The choice was a good one for a boy whose future lay in trees: the downy is the smallest of the woodpeckers, and it nests only in cavities it excavates in trees like the oaks, ashes, and maples Carhart loved.

In 1906, after their stint in the country, the family returned to Mapleton so Arthur could attend high school. The very name "Mapleton" is one of those touches of wishful thinking that endears to us his pioneering stock, for most of the region's trees (whether growing naturally or planted after settlement) quickly became ties for the Northwestern Railroad that literally put Mapleton on the map in 1877. The trees came and went from the landscapes of Carhart's youth. Perhaps George Carhart's tree farm experience gave Arthur his own deeply paradoxical feelings regarding trees. Misguided federal programs might put the wrong trees in the wrong place at the wrong time, but a tree doctor who practiced tree culture would design with nature. In his book on the national forests, published in 1959, Carhart looked back:

> You may regard me as rather tolerant toward the Timber Baron and his
> Paul Bunyan woodsmen. I have remarked that I had observed, as early as
> 1919, the aftermath of their invasion of the lake states pineries. Strictly as a
> feeling stemming from emotion I could throw my most scorching invective
> at them, and I would do so with far more background and feeling than most
> of those who flay yesterday's timber operators, considering it smart and
> somehow patriotic to damn their acts. Perhaps this is no valid reason for my
> having what seems tolerance towards the northwoods timbermen, but it was
> some Paul working for a Baron who logged the white pine that Valentine
> Smith nailed into one stout, Midwest-type frame house which faces on Sioux
> Avenue in Mapleton, Iowa. I was born in that house. It was a good shelter,
> and it housed a home. Although it was built in the 1880s, it still serves well
> as a family domicile.[13]

While the forests of western Iowa advanced and receded through millennia of relatively slow climate change, so did the humans and their fellow predators. Gone by Carhart's birth in 1892, along with fire and Native Americans, were the once-abundant wolves. One pre–Civil War Iowa legislator had wryly remarked that he represented more wolves than people.[14] Not for long. Monona County was organized in 1854. After the Civil War, it was split to create Onawa County. Early settlers and promoters drew these names from Henry Wadsworth Longfellow's long poem *The Song of Hiawatha* (1855). Monona means "peaceful valley" or "beautiful valley."

Carhart Home in Mapleton. Photo by C. Nealson.

Figures from the U.S. Census show how Monona County's population rose and then plateaued after the depression of the 1890s:

1860: 832
1870: 3,654
1880: 9,055
1890: 18,000
1900: 17,980

Early on, the railroads and the federal government conspired with speculators to encourage settlement, chiefly through the Homestead Act of 1862 and its successors, the Timber Culture Act of 1873 and the Desert Land Act of 1877. The latter lured Arthur Carhart's paternal grandfather to an unsuccessful land claim in Story, Nevada. Wood had become scarce and valuable in the prairie states. In response, the Timber Culture Act promised settlers an extra 160 acres of land beyond their original homestead if they would plant 40 acres to trees and maintain them for at least ten years. New stands of saplings nurtured the wonderful dream that forests would temper climatic extremes and increase rainfall. Abuses grew faster than tree plantations, however, and Congress repealed the Timber Culture Act in 1891.[15] The failure of these dubious federal programs to promote equitable property ownership is important in understanding Carhart's background.

Many pioneering families failed, but the individual successes were notable. Among the other families arriving in western Iowa between 1851 and 1861 were the aforementioned Whitings: Episcopalian businessmen, bankers, and lawyers who remained lifelong friends of the Carharts and extraordinarily generous benefactors of the region. The Whitings still fund a school and a library in Whiting, Iowa. They are also prominent philanthropists in today's Mapleton. Charles I. Whiting attended business school in Des Moines—as Carhart was supposed to do. His son, Charles G. Whiting, was Carhart's friend. One of their avidly shared interests was the breeding of prize iris, a species that adapted well to Colorado and remained a favorite in Carhart's professional and personal landscape designs. Charles G. Whiting was a graduate of the University of Iowa School of Law. He ran the bank in Mapleton, where he succeeded his father as chairman of the board. The Whitings and their irises were also a link for Carhart to another enduring friend, Jay Norwood "Ding" Darling (1876–1962). Puckish like Carhart, Darling, a famous cartoonist, served as chief of the Bureau of Biological Survey (BBS) in the 1930s and also worked for private conservation organizations.[16]

Old Mapleton was established in 1857 on the west side of the Maple River. New Mapleton appeared on the east side of the Maple River in 1877, anticipating the arrival of the Northwestern Railroad, part of the Union Pacific system. The new town incorporated as East Mapleton in 1878 and became simply Mapleton in 1896. Many of the newly thriving trees in and around the town were cut to furnish ties to the railroad. A nearby town called Tieville had a sawmill. The Mapleton Nursery was established in 1880, supplying hardy and adaptable stock for the town's attempt to become worthy of its ambitious name.

The Whitings and the Carharts/Hawthornes were friendly competitors during Mapleton's early years. In 1877, Whiting & Co. opened the first hardware store. Charles I. Whiting was one of the partners, along with his uncle, Baxter Whiting. In 1882 James B. Hawthorne (an uncle of Ella Hawthorne) bought a grocery store that became Martin & Hawthorne. In 1883 the Hawthornes sold to S. H. and G. W. Carhart (Arthur's uncle Steve and his father, George, respectively). Meanwhile, Baxter and C. I. Whiting established the Mapleton Bank in 1878, running it out of their hardware store until 1881, when they built the bank building. The Whitings had competition from the Monona County State Bank, established in 1889, with Stephen H. Carhart as a partner and officer.[17] As prosperity grew, so did the town's amenities. Permanent sidewalks arrived in 1910. Electricity appeared in 1916; a sewer system was added in 1919.

The Carharts were among the second generation of settlers in the Monona County area. The Carhart family itself has many branches in the United States and the United Kingdom.[18] In 1935, Carhart wrote to a relative in Great Britain:

"My father is living at 82, sitting before me here, and I will give you notes regarding our people as he gives them to me. Stephen Carhart, my grandfather, was born in Parish of St. Ervan, Cornwall, 1816." Stephen married Eliza Rundell on November. 20, 1841, and they came to the United States, first to Iowa and then to Platteville, Wisconsin, where there are Rundells still. Their children included Arthur's father, George, born at Platteville in 1853.[19]

Arthur Carhart's grandfather, Stephen, was born in Cornwall in Great Britain in 1816. He came to Wisconsin in 1842 and moved to Iowa in 1869 before attempting to homestead in Nevada. Then he returned to Iowa and settled in the Mapleton area. Both of Arthur's parents came from large families. George had three brothers and a sister. The Hawthorne/Carhart hardware and furniture store was the site where the first tree was planted in East Mapleton in 1878.[20] Treasured for years (and not suitable for use as a railroad tie), it was a box elder, a fast-growing, water-loving member of the maple family. Arthur's mother, Ella, had three brothers and two sisters. Originally from Ireland, the Boyds and Hawthorn(e)s moved from Maryland to Iowa in 1856, and in 1876 they settled in Monona County.[21]

LIFE IN A SMALL IOWA TOWN

When Arthur Carhart returned to Mapleton in 1964 and 1968 to pay his final visits to his home and to Judge Whiting, respectively, he tossed off some anecdotes for *The Mapleton Press*, all of them built around trees and on the perpetually muddy condition of the town's main streets.

> There was a row of boxelder trees on either side of the street, all the way up the main stem from the Northwestern Station that stood beside the board walk where kids dropped pennies, and very occasionally nickels. . . . But to get back to the trees. There were some left, all horse chewed and discouraged, after 1900. The last one, a landmark of its day, stood in front of the old Carhart Brothers hardware where the Mapleton Trust & Savings building now stands. It almost lasted, or did, until the new building was put up: a gnarled old trunk, scarred, often shooting water suckers, full of sparrows that twittered and built nests, and roosted, and sometimes dumped their young down on the heads of shoppers and others. That was probably the last homelike refuge of the whittling gang, the shade of that old tree. It was never the same after the tree was taken down.

Warming to his task, Carhart recalled the oak hitching posts and remembered irreverences:

> There used to be mud puddles on the crossings, mud a foot deep in the main block of the town, and women, in braided, tight waisted, very long skirted

Ella Carhart Artwork © 1910. Courtesy, Museum of American History, Mapleton. Photo by C. Nealson.

dresses[,] had the choice of lifting up their trains until some eagle-eyed loafer took time out from spitting tobacco juice to goggle at an ankle displayed, or the poor women let the trains drag in a mixture of dirt, water and horse traffic. Those crossings were like wading a good, rich barnyard.[22]

Another who remembered was 101-year old Elizabeth Durst, whom I interviewed in Mapleton in 2003, a year before her death. The Dursts lived next to the Carharts on Sioux Avenue, so the two families were neighbors until Elizabeth Durst married and left Mapleton in 1921, about the time George and Ella Carhart left for Colorado. Mrs. Durst's portrait of Carhart family life, undimmed by 90 years or so, rings true both in its vividly recalled details and in its harsh, small-town judgments. Those who wonder why sensitive, talented people like Arthur Carhart often leave small towns need look no further.

Ella was an artist, and that's all she ever did. She gave water color painting lessons to many of the women and girls in town. My older sister Hazel started out with Ella, and many of the elite in Mapleton took these lessons. Carharts' living room was where she gave her painting lessons.

I didn't want to go over there. I was scared because Ella was a Hawthorne and her brother was a banker. He had a daughter named Alice who came to Mapleton to finish high school. She was to stay with the Carharts. Ella would come over and see if I would play croquet with Alice. She offered me a quarter to play with Alice, but my mother said, "You do it anyway." Alice was a good singer, like Arthur.

I remember Arthur growing up. I don't know what they ate. They gave me quarters to stay the night when George was away at the farm. But Ella didn't have much to do with raising Arthur. She was an artist. He just grew up. He'd come around to our door and say "Hi." My mother would say "Hello," and he'd say, "It smells good." So she'd say, "Go home and get your bowl." My mother raised Arthur. Ella didn't know what day it was. Later, after Arthur went out West, he wrote my sister Eva's daughter a letter and told her how much he had loved my mother.

I never saw Arthur mow the lawn or sweep the sidewalk or do anything. He was nice looking, but he never did anything to make that muscle. What made him odd and different was that he was an only child and he didn't have any sisters. Ella was too busy painting, so they only had one child. Ella's paintings—people didn't buy them. Arthur was defensive about Ella's painting. Some of her students did become successful commercial artists, but she never did.

George and Ella were never seen out in public together. George did the yard work or worked at the store. Ella didn't help at the store. She was an artist! Arthur got what he wanted. He was kind of spoiled, and his dad provided for him. He just grew up like a dandelion. It must have been hard for him growing up alone, and his mother always so busy. My brothers were too young to be friends with him, but Charlie Whiting was his buddy in high school. I didn't know Arthur when he was in grade school because I was too young. Arthur never worked around the house or yard, and he didn't have a horse.

I never saw him with a girl. He didn't date in high school. I would have noticed, since I was 9 or 10. Finally, Arthur finished high school and went to Ames. When he came back, he had a maroon and gold blanket. He called it his "fussing" blanket. Arthur was interested in my sisters, especially Eva, but he couldn't get anywhere with them. They were older. And not interested in his blanket.

He went to Ames and came back with the idea that if you put tin cans in the hole when you plant roses, the cans will deteriorate, and so the rose bush will do better. That's all I saw him do—dig holes—besides his fussing blanket. His mother didn't do anything either.

George was short and a nice fellow, thoughtful and kind. He had a big black horse, and he'd let me exercise it. He and his brother Steve had a hardware store downtown. But George was very different from his brother. Steve had a cow, and I had to go get its milk when ours went dry. Steve gave me a glass of milk one day, and I went home and showed it to my dad and said, "He put something in it." Steve was always drinking, and I was banned from there. Steve's son was retarded. Steve's wife played cards. George was in charge of the store, and Steve spent most of his time in a bar.[23]

AFTER THE GOLDEN AGE

Arthur's own recollections were sweeter, especially late in life. In a 1964 piece for the local paper he wrote:

May Baskets were another [ritual]. Frilled boxes, decked with fancy tissue papers, filled with violets picked from the woods along the Maple River north of the old school house near the Cottonwood Grove. And with plum blossoms. Dogtooth violets and Dutchman's Breeches offered their blooms along the "gully" north of the school house. The unplowed meadow north of Heisler Creek, beside the railway, brought forth wild "sweet williams" and Turk's Cap lilies for Decoration Day. Drainage, wood cutting and cultivation have destroyed those wild flower gardens that bloomed around the town.[24]

In a 1957 letter to "Ding" Darling, Carhart remembered:

I was a kid in Center Township, Monona County, and the RFD [Rural Free Delivery] was instituted while we were on the farm there, and I was going to school in a one-room institution on the corner of our farm. It was painted white—of course. And a chubby, red-necked mailman named Hoadley used to bring the mail out from Castana, and we would look, as a first act of receipt of the mail, for your cartoon in the Journal. That period was a golden age, Ding.[25]

After high school, as war spread throughout Europe, young Carhart took a 1915 train trip to California with Judge Whiting. The travelers marveled at the forests—and the forest destruction—they saw along the way in the Rockies and the Sierras. Other than this trip, Carhart spent his early years in a place where trees played an important role in efforts to remake the scenery. Carhart's generation of midwestern landscape architects grew up under the influence of the Chicago Columbian Exposition of 1893, which featured the exquisite urban park landscaping of Frederick Law Olmsted Sr. The contrary midwesterners, however, were determined to adapt Olmsted's work to their horizontal setting. Jens Jensen, a Prairie School collaborator of Frank Lloyd Wright, modified Olmsted's compositions by using native plants where Olmsted often chose exotics. Chicago designer O. C. Simonds also influenced Jensen's taste for wide-open meadows and informal groupings of native plants and trees. In 1916 Simonds gave the young Carhart, fresh from Ames, his first job: installing a landscape design, including a pool, on the estate of a wealthy Chicago-area family. It was while working on this site that Carhart met his future wife, Vee.

He later wrote, "In early 1917, I became a probationer in the Chicago office of a famous landscape architecture firm."[26] Facing the draft, Carhart joined the U.S. Army as a musician. He soon returned to Chicago on leave. On August 16, 1918, in the residence of Episcopal Bishop Fallows of Chicago, Carhart married Vera A. Van Sickle of Aurora, Illinois. Simonds had promised him eighty-five dollars per month if he would come back to work after his military service. That did not seem like enough to Carhart, who had other ideas.

While serving in the military, Carhart—idealist and populist—decided that he wanted to use his skills not to gild the lilies of the wealthy but to improve opportunities for ordinary Americans to enjoy the natural beauty of public lands. Whereas Simonds and Jensen worked in both public urban settings and the cloistered estates of the Fords, Carhart aspired to work for the American people in the grander settings of the Rocky Mountain West. Some of these settings were urban, such as Denver's parks, where Arthur Hawthorn(e) Carhart showed his appreciation of Jensen's favorite tree, whose dark branches emerge at appealing angles from its sturdy trunk: the hawthorn.[27]

In 1961, near the end of his career as a planner and landscape architect, Carhart wrote: "The smartest landscape architect is the one who is clever enough to fit the use pattern deftly to the existing conditions with the least physical change needed to adapt site to use."[28] Characteristic of Carhart, the bold emphasis is on the *human uses* of an *inhabited* landscape, however deft the adaptations might be. His tree culture does not promote the unpeopled past or the paradisal illusion of effortlessness. To his teachers' great credit, Carhart learned at Ames that a judicious designer could improve the face of a landscape not just with a plow but also with trees. Young Carhart had only once traveled west of the Missouri River, but two Colorado-friendly spruces caught his attention as he finished his degree work in 1917: *Picea englemannii* and *Picea pungens*. The latter is the state tree of Colorado, and the former dominates high-country settings like Trappers Lake. Although it may seem odd to us today, the issue of the "right" trees for Colorado was a pressing one in 1919, when the Forest Service was still struggling to fulfill its original mandate: the reforestation and restoration of once-forested, badly burned, overgrazed watersheds.[29] This struggle would occupy Carhart until his dying day, showing how well his teachers at Ames had prepared him for a career in conservation.

One of the purposes of land grant schools such as the future Iowa State University was to support the federal government's plan for settling the new states, even if that meant spreading Iowa's wealth of graduates westward. Carhart obtained the first bachelor of science degree in landscape gardening ever granted at Ames in 1917; his thesis was entitled "Landscape Materials for Iowa." The challenge his professors posed to him was: "What introduced plants have proven 'hardy' and 'acceptable?'" The landscaping ornamentals that nurtured young Carhart's love of trees were two examples of pioneering stock from the very different plant communities of Colorado: the blue spruce and Englemann spruce.

In just five short years, those same professors, Frank Culley and Irvin McCrary, would join the migration westward to Colorado, following their prize student. Carhart, an adroit networker and horse trader, arranged for the Forest Service to hire Culley to landscape the first campground designed specifically for automobile-based recreation at Squirrel Creek near Pueblo in the San Isabel National Forest. Today, the Forest Service is renovating this historic site in partnership with the Frontier Pathways Scenic and Historic Byway and the El Pueblo Museum in Pueblo, Colorado. It was placed on the National Register of Historic Places in 2005.[30] In 1922, after Carhart left the Forest Service, he and Culley joined McCrary in Denver to form McCrary, Culley, & Carhart, one of Colorado's most influential landscape architecture and city planning firms. Among their specialties was landscaping the new city parks, civic centers, and college campuses that sprung up in a Rocky Mountain region where most people lived not in the federally owned, reforesting mountains but in cities and towns on the dry, mainly treeless plains.

WHAT INTRODUCED PLANTS HAVE PROVEN HARDY AND ACCEPTABLE?

Arthur Carhart and his partners were not mindlessly dedicated to recreating a golden age "Iowa" in the dry, high-altitude cities of the plains, such as Denver—and certainly not in the wetter, higher, colder mountains. But they brought a particular professional vision to the West: the conviction that humans should not simply be visitors to a place but should be at home in a worked, inhabited landscape. At Ames, Carhart learned a certain aesthetic: we create order wherever we look. Human perception has an organizing power that gives our spatial emotions force. Carhart thought people could and should organize these emotions in ways that make them not just better people but also better Americans. He was aware that wherever people go, they try to recreate an optimal environment. For him as an urban planner, that environment was a cross between the Iowa of his youth and Park Hill, the Denver neighborhood of his adult life, where the automobile did not yet dominate the landscape and landscape was more than shingles and streets.

Carhart and his colleagues based this picture of right relations between humans and nature on the vibrant ecological conditions they found at a particular time in Iowa's history: the period from 1850 through around 1915. Obviously, they did not see, as we can today, how radically humans could and would change the Iowa landscape—and yet how dynamic and even resilient environments can be over time. Nor did they share our modern view of limits related to the availability of water. They had little sense of the role of human-caused fire in maintaining grasslands. They knew little of the relationship between predators and the herd animals that depend on grasslands.

In all these ways, they were not duplicitous but merely ignorant and short-sighted, like almost everyone else in the West at that time, with the tragic exception of the lonely prophet bearing the resoundingly Methodist name John Wesley Powell (1834–1902).[31] In hindsight, we now can see what distinguished Carhart from most of his contemporaries: his treelike ability to endure and to learn from a new environment. Carhart not only came to appreciate Powell's vision of a West organized into watershed-based democracies; he was in a position to imagine them at work in a West where the role of the federal government might be considerably diminished from what it had been when he arrived in Colorado right after World War I.

As a young man, afire with an Iowa-based image of natural beauty, Carhart had little use for the dour Powell and much in common with the voluble William Gilpin (1815–1894). Gilpin had been Colorado's first territorial governor, as well as a shameless promoter of the same southern Colorado mountains and valleys where Carhart would make his mark as a landscape architect and recreation planner. Whereas Gilpin found mostly fool's gold in a destructive, extraction-based economy, Carhart saw the real gold that would drive Colorado's economy when the mines played out: natural beauty, recreation, wildlife, and the water that flows from healthy, well-maintained mountain watersheds to succor the development of the plains.[32]

Let us look more closely at the image of humans' relation with nature Carhart brought with him when he came west. The first European settlers arrived in western Iowa in the 1840s, during an era when relatively cooler, wetter conditions were luring forests west from their eastern refugia around the Mississippi River Basin to the Missouri River and beyond. The east-west ebb and flow of forests and grasslands through Iowa has tantalized moralists and ecologists ever since Lewis and Clark ascended the Missouri River in 1803 and reported back to President Thomas Jefferson about the richness of the land and the variety of Native Americans who lived on it. Today, the captains' names grace a state park along the floodplain of the Missouri west of Mapleton, while Sioux City, Iowa, and the Little Sioux River remind us of the Lakota the captains encountered. In the 1950s, Carhart fondly recalled the hunting and fishing lodge at Blue Lake that reminded Iowans of the lifeways of the Lakota who had been his Grandfather Hawthorne's friends. Yet the Lakota were also relative newcomers to the Missouri River Basin. They could not have told Lewis and Clark, as we know today, about the advances and retreats of the great ice sheets. They did not remember the mighty winds that helped form the region's deep loess soils.[33]

Nor would the Lakota have known that once the ice receded, spruce forests had flourished along the Iowa-Kansas border 18,000 years ago and that the spruce disappeared and returned again to thrive as far west as the Nebraska Sandhills 12,000 years ago. Until recently, no one knew that starting around 10,000 years ago, at least twenty-six different episodes of glaciation and re-afforestation occurred along the Missouri River Basin until finally the forest cover of the Great Plains receded as the climate dried and warmed into the nineteenth-century's conditions, where fine-rooted grasses could outcompete thicker-rooted trees for available moisture and nutrients. Among the "losers" in the years before the Civil War were the spruce. Among the new "winners" or dominants were big bluestem and switchgrass, the quintessential warm-season tallgrasses of the 1900s.[34]

What can we learn about Carhart's passion for trees from this picture of Iowa around 1915? When settlers entered this landscape, they suppressed both wildfire and their competing predators: Native Americans and wolves. One immediate result was a tremendous burst in the growth of trees, which soon fell to the needs of the settlers and the railroads. When this settler-railroad–fire suppression scenario was repeated a generation or two later in Colorado under very different soil, climate, and landownership conditions, federal agencies conducted extraordinarily thorough programs of fire and predator suppression. Ecologically, this resulted in small-diameter tree invasions, the proliferation of tree-dependent diseases and insects, and the buildup of fuel loads and elk populations to the catastrophic levels we know today in many Colorado forests. Carhart dubbed these failures "tin roof watersheds," a phrase that would resound throughout his entire career as a conservationist. Fire and grazing had destroyed the watersheds' ability to store water. They became conduits for floods like the one that struck Pueblo, Colorado, in 1921.

FROM BLUE GUMBO TO SPRINKLER IRRIGATION

What exactly did the western Iowa of Carhart's boyhood home, Monona County, look like? Fortunately, the Steele family in nearby Cherokee County, west of Larrabee, had been cutting prairie hay since 1880 on 200 black-soil acres. Today, their gift to us is known as Steele Prairie, one of the largest prairies remaining outside of the Loess Hills to the west. The mesic-wet prairie, sedge meadow, and marsh vegetation support a diverse array of prairie plants, including several rare species. The preserve is dotted with ant mounds and animal burrows, providing habitat for many species of birds, mammals, and butterflies. Since he grew up in such a setting around Mapleton, Carhart would have appreciated Steele Prairie's blue gumbo—a combination of black-soil prairie, sedge meadow, and marsh.

Before the advent of mechanized farming, much of western Iowa around 1900 was still recognizably big bluestem country. The blue gumbo bottomlands of the Little Sioux and its tributary, the Maple River, were too wet to plow with horses in the spring, and summer's heat rendered them too dry and hard. Farmers simply used the abundant wild hay to feed their many draft horses. Yet in addition to the coming tractor-drawn plows and related machines, another kind of change was pending that would propel Carhart into a rage over the foolishness of federal bureaucracies. For example, early settlers had originally patented much of this land under the Swamp Land Act of 1847, a predecessor of the Homestead Act and the Timber Culture Act. Gradually, federal help made it possible to set up the drainage districts that first dried out the gumbo bottomlands and culminated in many large dams and the channelization of the Missouri River. Both were part of the Pick-Sloan Plan, begun in 1944 by the Bureau of Reclamation.

Meanwhile, mechanization meant farmers could plow those formerly soggy bottoms and that hay was no longer needed for workhorses. By 1950, to Carhart's intense disgust, the former wetlands had dried out to the point where they had to be sprinkler irrigated with water obtained through a first-come first-served, prior appropriation-style legal system that had developed in dry states like Colorado. As a local history related without a trace of irony in 1982:

Drainage was still a problem, so the Little Sioux River was straightened, levies were heightened, and more lateral ditches were dug. It has taken over a half century to lower the water table to a respectable depth and to control the flooding to the extent that now cropping is almost a sure thing. In fact, today, much of this land has become so dry that overhead irrigation systems have been installed. One would never have guessed this in the 1920's.[35]

World War I brought prosperity and rising land and commodity prices to the Missouri River Bottom country. Land prices shot up, but by then George Carhart had sold his country property, so he and Ella did not share in the post-war boom. By that time, Arthur was married and living in Colorado. When he beckoned, his parents jumped at the chance to start anew with their son along the banks of the Arkansas River in Cañon City.

NOTES

1. Letter from Carhart to Mary Austin, September 29, 1929, Carhart Collection, Denver Public Library (hereafter CC, DPL).

2. The May 19, 1910, edition of *The Mapleton Press* gives the class day program for the high school's May 25 program: Music, Selected—Chas Whiting and Arthur Carhart. Song, "Anchored"—school.

3. When I first visited Mapleton in 2003, I received a gracious welcome from local historian and master teacher Keith Robinson, who provided many valuable sources. John Irwin of western Iowa and the Denver Public Library supplied me from his copious iowaiana. I also had help from a Carhart relative, Robert Hawthorn of Castana, Iowa.

4. Arthur Carhart, "This Way to Wilderness," unpublished manuscript, 1974, 6.

5. Letter from Carhart to Ding Darling, September 19, 1957, CC,.DPL.

6. John Davey, *The Tree Doctor: A Book on Tree Culture* (New York: Saalfield, 1904).

7. "Biographical Sketch," 1930, CC, DPL.

8. In "This Way to Wilderness," at an age when his memory might have been playing tricks on him, Carhart recounts boyhood experiences on his grandfather's Tree Claim Act homestead. He says his grandfather had sold the homestead to Newman, who later resold it to George Carhart. His boyhood "threshold" experiences included finding a pot belonging to a "woman of a native tribe." County chain of title records do not support Carhart's memory. A letter from Robert Hawthorn to the author dated August 29, 2004, says: "My understanding is that my great grandfather purchased the original eighty acre tract where I now live from the railroad. So far as I know, the Carhart name does not appear on any of the deeds of the present Hawthorn land holdings. The former Newman farm joins land we now own."

9. The 1920 census shows that Arthur and Vee were living in lodgings in Denver.

10. The correspondence between Carhart and his parents is in a separate "Mother/ Father" file, CC, DPL.

11. *The Mapleton Press*, July 3, 1941: "George Carhart Dies in Denver: Masonic Funeral Services Held Saturday for Former Resident."

12. "This Way to Wilderness," 6.

13. Arthur Carhart, *The National Forests* (New York: Alfred A. Knopf, 1959), 101.

14. Mapleton newspaper clippings, courtesy of Keith Robinson.

15. See Patricia Nelson Limerick, *The Legacy of Conquest* (New York: Norton, 1987), 61ff.

16. Darling was one of Carhart's links to Howard Zahniser, who worked for the BBS before taking over the Wilderness Society in 1945. Much later, Carhart became a trustee of the Ding Darling Foundation. The Whitings maintained the Maple Valley Iris Gardens in Mapleton. In 1950 the annual meeting of the American Iris Society was held in Iowa, and a hybrid named "Blue Rhythm," developed by Charles G. and Agnes Whiting, took the Dykes Medal, the highest honor an iris can receive. The Whitings also developed many other varieties, and Agnes published widely on irises. In March 1948, Carhart published an article about the Whitings and their iris gardens in *Nature* magazine. The Whitings were among the last Episcopalians in Mapleton (Trinity Memorial Episcopal Church). They donated the money for today's Mapleton library. The interesting former church is in the Gothic Revival/Romanesque style, with stained glass windows that came from an even older church in Sioux City. The last service was held in 1984: the funeral of Carhart's friend Charles G. Whiting, son of the original donor of the church, C. I. Whiting. Deconsecrated in 1988, the church now houses Keith Robinson's Museum of American History, which includes many Arthur Carhart–related materials.

17. *History of Monona County, Iowa* (Chicago: National Publishing Company, 1890).

18. See Mary E. Carhart Dusenbury, *A Geneaological Record of the Descendants of Thomas Carhart of Cornwall, England* (New York: A. S. Barnes, 1880). The obituary of Stephen Carhart appeared in *The Mapleton Press*, January 12, 1895.

19. On February 26, 1935, Carhart replied to a letter from a distant relative in England who had seen his stories; CC, DPL.

20. Steve and George's brother John had a son who was also named Arthur. John's sons founded the lumber businesses in eastern Nebraska that still operate under the Carhart name today. The family has no relationship to the Carhartt clothiers.

21. In 1976, Fred W. Hawthorn and his son Robert published *Idlewild Farm: A Century of Progress*. Robert Hawthorn told me in a 2004 personal communication that he did not know why Arthur sometimes spelled the family name with an "e." Idlewild was recognized as a Century Farm in 1976 at the Iowa State Fair. This farm remains in the Hawthorn family to this day.

22. "Spots and Splashes," *The Mapleton Press*, July 28, 1968, 13–14.

23. Elizabeth Durst interview, Mapleton, July 19, 2003.

24. "Spots and Splashes," 14.

25. Letter from Carhart to Darling, July 27, 1957, CC, DPL. That period on the farm also brought Carhart into contact with the genre of boys' books, including works

by G. A. Henty such as *The Heart of the Rockies*, which helped turn young Carhart's imagination westward. Carhart shared such tastes with Horace Albright.

26. "This Way to Wilderness," 6.

27. Robert Grese, *Jens Jensen: Maker of Natural Parks and Gardens (Creating the North American Landscape)* (Washington, DC: Johns Hopkins University Press, 1998).

28. Arthur Carhart, *Planning for America's Wildlands* (Harrisburg: Telegraph Press, 1961), 68.

29. See my treatment of Carhart in *Colorado's Sangre de Cristo Mountains* (Boulder: University Press of Colorado, 1995).

30. See "Corridor Management Plan," *Frontier Pathways Scenic and Historic Byway* (Pueblo, CO: Pueblo Museum, 1995). See also, U.S. Department of the Interior, National Park Service, *Squirrel Creek Recreational Unit* Registration Form (Denver: Colorado Historical Society, 2004). My thanks to principal investigator Jack McCrory for sharing his research about Carhart with me.

31. William deBuys, ed., *Seeing Things Whole: The Essential John Wesley Powell* (Washington, DC: Island, 2001).

32. Gilpin is the anti-hero of Wallace Stegner's *Beyond the Hundredth Meridian: John Wesley Powell and the Second Opening of the American West* (Lincoln: University of Nebraska Press, 1954). Carhart and Stegner became acquainted through Bernard DeVoto. Stegner competed with Carhart's more popular and commercially published fiction and nonfiction. The only correspondence between them dates from Stegner's days as assistant to President Kennedy's secretary of the interior, Stewart Udall. November 7 and 16, 1961, letters to Carhart from Stegner acknowledge Carhart's efforts to block the Bureau of Reclamation's plans for the Colorado River. Stegner wrote, "I'd like to talk policy with you, and some day will, but meantime all I can do is thank you and assure you that both your information and your opinions are going into the draft" (quote from the November 16 letter).

33. Today's *Mapleton Press* still advertises itself as "The Front Door to the Loess Hills." Carhart would have known Bohumil Shimek (1861–1937), a natural historian and geologist of western Iowa. Today's travelers can visit western Iowa via the Loess Hills Scenic Byway, part of the same federal system that covers Carhart's southern Colorado territory. The automobile-based aesthetics would have pleased Carhart. See Bill Witt, "Iowa's Last Wilderness" *The Iowan* (May-June 2001):30–41.

34. Stephen R. Jones and Ruth Carol Cushman, *Field Guide to the North American Prairie* (New York: Houghton-Mifflin, 2004).

35. *Monona County, Iowa* (Dallas: Taylor, 1982), 6.

CHAPTER TWO

ECONOMIC EFFICIENCY OF FOREST MANAGEMENT

The National *Forests* are set apart primarily for economic ends, and their use
for recreation is a by-product properly to be secured only in so far as it does
not interfere with the economic efficiency of the forest management. The
National *Parks* are set apart primarily in order to preserve to the people for
all time the opportunity of a peculiar kind of enjoyment and recreation, not
measurable in economic terms and to be obtained only from the remarkable
scenery which they contain.

FREDERICK LAW OLMSTED JR. (1916; ORIGINAL EMPHASIS)[1]

INTRODUCTION: "BO" CARHART

Carhart had a practical touch, a knack for fitting people and landscapes with
each other. He used basic sciences like bacteriology to improve this fit, not only
in 1917 with the U.S. Army but also in 1919 with the Forest Service, when he
discovered the shocking sanitary conditions at Squirrel Creek—future site of
the first Forest Service auto campground—and at Trappers Lake.

Carhart's solid education had prepared him to combine the visionary and
the practical. He provided this staccato version of his many activities during
wartime:

> Then enlisted as musician in army. Sent to Chickamauga Park, Ga.
> Headquarters Co. of old 6th Infantry, regiment which was reputed to be
> Geo. Washington's bodyguard. Call came for someone who knew bacteri-
> ology. Sgt. of Hdqrs. Co. 6th Inf. knew I had background to do this. Was
> transferred from Hdqrs. tho still as private to Base Hospital, Ft. Oglethorpe.

Starting doing commissioned officer's work fighting typhoid in German prison camp there. Then on water supply, milk, sewage disposal, etc. Transferred to Camp Greenleaf, there organized and directed first band of Med. Dept. of U.S. Army. Commissioned 1st Lieut. out of ranks, sent to Washington, there 10 days, sent to Camp Meade Md. Where took over running of water, milk, ice cream, supplies and sewage disposal from bacteriological control end. Promised us to go over [to the front in Europe] every few weeks. Ended war on this side.[2]

College life at Ames seems to have been a pleasant experience for Carhart. He thrived on the landscape architecture and city planning curriculum. He became so committed to his college fraternity, Acacia, that he organized its national meeting in Estes Park, Colorado, in 1927. Known to his fraternity brothers as "Bo," Carhart participated in many extracurricular activities relating to his musical talents, especially singing.

During his college years, Carhart seems to have spent summers and holidays helping his father in the hardware store when he was not traveling and playing music jobs. Times must have been relatively prosperous for the Carharts. Arthur was able to study one summer at the Shaw Botanical Garden in St. Louis, one of the world's finest herbaria. There was enough money for school and travel. A letter Charles Whiting later wrote to Carhart provides some of the flavor of their last fling before the Great War: "I ran across some pictures the other day taken when you and I were in Frisco and, believe me, they recalled many pleasant memories. We had a great time that summer, didn't we, old man, in spite of the fact that war was almost upon us. You remember that morning in Frisco when the extras announced the break between the U.S. and Germany."[3]

Ames had attracted some extraordinary faculty members to its new landscape architecture program. They prepared Carhart for the stunning leaps of imagination that followed soon after his arrival in Colorado in 1919. One teacher was Denver native Irvin McCrary, who brought a strong conservation commitment and Colorado connections.[4] After graduating from Princeton, McCrary had studied landscape architecture at Harvard. His special interest was in urban and regional planning related to water. Another teacher was Frank Culley of Marshalltown, Iowa, who had received his B.S. in landscape architecture from Massachusetts Agricultural College under Frank Waugh—the first contract landscape architect hired by the Forest Service.[5] Culley had earned an M.S. in landscape design from Harvard, where he worked under J. S. Pray. Pray later became Carhart's mentor in the American Society of Landscape Architects. Culley next went to Ames to set up the Department of Landscape Architecture with McCrary. They taught a vision of urban and regional planning meant to accommodate the automobile.

Culley was a crusader for the new National Park Service (NPS). When the Iowa Horticultural Society held its 1916 annual meeting in Des Moines, Culley and McCrary arranged for their prize student to present a paper entitled "A System of Parks, National, State, County and Municipal." This paper on prospects for the NPS and its allies might have led Carhart to a career with the fledgling NPS. But a flat job market and World War I intervened.

After graduating from Ames in 1916, Carhart found few prospects in his new profession. Finally, he took a job as a day laborer on a project at Iowa State under the direction of O. C. Simonds, a prominent Chicago landscape designer. Impressed with Carhart, Simonds hired him to execute a landscape plan at the estate of Senator Copley of Illinois. There he first met his future wife, Vera Amelia Van Sickle ("Vee"). Vee's maternal grandparents, the Boyds, were from Northern Ireland, and the Van Sickles had come from Toronto-Hamilton to the Chicago area.

Vera Amelia Carhart must have been a vigorous young woman. In just a few years she would accompany her husband to Colorado, where her new life included homemaking in isolated settings like Beulah (near Pueblo) and Westcliffe, at the foot of the Sangre de Cristo Mountains. Vee also rode with her husband on extensive backcountry horse packing trips, including a three-week trek through the San Juan Mountains in southern Colorado in 1922. It is no wonder Vee became a friend of another "wilderness wife," Mardy Murie, whose wildlife biologist husband, Olaus, was a friend of Carhart's (through the Bureau of Biological Survey, like Howard Zahniser) and one of the founders of the Wilderness Society.[6]

Carhart had tried to join the army at age twenty-five in a capacity that would use his skills as a planner. Frustrated, he interrupted his courtship of Vee to enlist as a musician, figuring that planning opportunities would appear. Carhart maintained contacts with his army buddies throughout his life. His commanding officer wrote him a glowing recommendation when he began his postwar job search in Washington, D.C.[7] At Ames, he had encountered the relatively new germ theory of diseases. As a budding city planner as well as a man familiar from boyhood with the filth and mud of Mapleton's streets, Carhart knew about horse manure and its associated flies as carriers of disease. That was just one of the reasons he and so many others welcomed the advent of the auto. Although still a private first class in October 1917, Carhart delivered a lecture on "City Planning & Camp Planning" to Medical Department officers at Fort Oglethorpe, Georgia. That talk got him promoted from the ranks to first lieutenant. Thus, it was as an officer that he went back to Chicago on leave to marry Vera Amelia Van Sickle on August 16, 1918.

48220 A

Vee Carhart, 1920. Courtesy, Forest History Society.

The newlyweds returned to Camp Meade, where Carhart became a victim of the deadly influenza epidemic. Later he wrote: "I suspect that I'd have died in that one if Vee hadn't been my new wife and nursed me instead of having to tough it out in the camp hospital."[8] Carhart's unit ended the war in Maryland. In late fall 1918 Carhart began to search for jobs, taking advantage of his Iowa contacts and his proximity to Washington and its burgeoning federal resource management bureaucracies.

TURF WARS

Through Culley and McCrary, Carhart had learned an Americanized version of the naturalistic aesthetics of John Ruskin.[9] One of Ruskin's most prominent U.S. disciples was Frank Waugh, whose ideas about ecological approaches to landscape gardening had influenced Carhart's choice of a senior thesis topic in 1917. Waugh agreed with the Forest Service's idea about its rightful role in managing public lands for many uses, including recreation. So it was not surprising when Chief Forester Henry Graves and Assistant Forester Edward A. Sherman hired Waugh, who was also Sherman's personal friend, on a contract basis in 1917 to tour the national forest system and make recommendations concerning its management. After five months in the field, Waugh reached many of the same conclusions Carhart would reach two years later after his tour of District 2, especially with regard to sanitary conditions at permanent camps and summer home communities. However, Waugh's hurried tour limited his focus to isolated projects and general prescriptions for the beautification of ranger stations through judicious use of decorative plantings. Waugh recommended that the Forest Service hire men "suitably trained and experienced in recreation, landscape engineering, and related topics,"[10] but he lacked Carhart's vision of watershed-wide, comprehensive planning for recreation. Consequently, his report delivered exactly what Graves and Sherman wanted: not a wide-ranging recreation plan for the national forests but simply ammunition to use in their budgetary wars against the new National Park Service.

The Forest Service had begun in 1897 with its own Organic Act. The Transfer Act of 1905 moved the new agency from the Department of the Interior to the Department of Agriculture. It also transferred the Forest Reserve from Interior to Agriculture. Under its founder, Gifford Pinchot, the Forest Service took such a strong utilitarian approach to public lands management that it caused the reaction that resulted in the formation of the NPS in 1916. Congress located the NPS in the Department of the Interior.

Waugh delivered his reports and returned to academe. Had Graves and Sherman been serious about actually implementing comprehensive recreation planning, they would have hired someone of Waugh's stature (i.e., full membership in the elite American Society of Landscape Architects [ASLA]) to lead the effort. Later, Waugh saw the limits of his approach and applauded Carhart's broader efforts. Meanwhile, not to be denied their piece of the budgetary pie, Stephen Mather and Horace Albright at the Park Service proceeded with their own version of planning. They hired the first NPS landscape architect, Charles Pierpont Punchard, in July 1918. Although interesting in terms of catering to the tastes of tourists, Punchard's plans differed from Carhart's in that they had no ecological basis in watersheds.

Based on his planning work for the army, Carhart became an associate member of ASLA in 1919. By 1920 he was a full member. None of this impressed the utilitarians in the Forest Service, who actively opposed management for recreation. Arguably, this group represented the majority opinion in the Forest Service until the 1980s. Just as Carhart tended to make lifelong friends, so did he accumulate lasting enemies. The utilitarians' leader, Leon Kneipp, became Carhart's permanent Forest Service adversary. As assistant chief of the Lands Office under Sherman, Kneipp's disdain for landscape architecture undermined Carhart's efforts, both during Carhart's service and after his departure into private practice. Much later, in the 1950s and 1960s, Kneipp still dogged Carhart's steps, especially with regard to the Boundary Waters Canoe Area. Carhart's portrait of Caverley, the quintessential bureaucrat and a thinly disguised Kneipp, in his novel *The Ordeal of Brad Ogden* (1929), returned the favor.

With the deck stacked against him, why did Carhart choose the Forest Service? As Culley's protégé, Carhart initially went to see Stephen Mather, the charismatic founding director of the NPS. Bull Moose Republican, patrician, and Sierra Club member, the volatile Mather had made a fortune by creating a national market for 20 Mule Team Borax, which was mined in and around today's Death Valley National Park. Mather was determined to sell parks as successfully as he had sold Borax. His goal was to have the NPS manage all outdoor recreation in the country, regardless of jurisdiction. That meant war, open or undeclared, with the Forest Service, including raids on lands under Forest Service jurisdiction. The home front for this war was Washington, D.C. The battle front was Colorado. In 1916 the Forest Service had been deeply alarmed and offended when Mather attempted to "steal" 200,000 acres from Pike National Forest and the Colorado State Forest to add to Rocky Mountain National Park in northern Colorado.

One aspect of this conflict involved the burgeoning numbers of automobile tourists. As Carhart had learned at Ames, it was important for the NPS to cater not just to railroad tourists but also to auto tourists by building appropriate roads and facilities. Mather "began a program to link the western national parks with a 'park-to-park' highway, acquired new national monuments to break up the long stretches between existing national parks, and received a congressional allotment for road building in the national parks."[11]

In contrast to the more single-minded Park Service, many in the Forest Service resisted management for recreation. Only a few saw the mounting value of income from the popular summer home permit fee program. Even fewer glimpsed a future of congressional funding for Forest Service recreation. Almost no one envisioned a postwar future of scenic roads that would lead auto tourists to Forest Service campgrounds and trail systems that were part of integrated, watershed-wide planning. One of these visionaries was E. A. Sherman, a complex and sympathetic man to whom Chief Graves had assigned the role of countering the perceived threat from the Park Service.

Carhart was finishing his junior year at Ames when the April 1916 issue of *Landscape Architecture* magazine appeared, featuring a special series of articles on parks. In his utilitarian contribution, Sherman pointed to examples of management for recreation on the Oregon and California national forests, adding: "Great as is the economic importance of the National Forests as sources of timber supply, water supply, and forage production, it is not improbable that their value as playgrounds for the public will in time come to rank as one of the major resources. The Forest Service is giving due consideration to this fact."

In that same issue, Frederick Law Olmsted Jr., the national leader in the field, took Mather's side in an article entitled "The Distinction between National Parks and National Forests." Brushing aside Sherman's slippery phrasing ("it is not improbable") and his utilitarian argument ("their value as playgrounds"), Olmsted made his case in a way that defied Forest Service founder Gifford Pinchot. Years earlier, Pinchot had promised a doubtful Congress that the Forest Service would actually return money to the federal treasury from its efficient management of public lands. By 1916, Mather and his allies were directly appealing to Congress for funding for the public good, regardless of monetary returns. Olmsted's 1916 statement represents one of the early examples of the extremism and polarization Carhart rejected (see the epigraph at the start of this chapter).

MR. CARHART GOES TO WASHINGTON

Seeking to exchange one uniform for another but hardly naive about interagency conflicts, Carhart traveled to Washington and asked to see the formidable Stephen Mather, nicknamed "Bulldog." Fatefully, Mather was away from his office. Happier hobnobbing in the field, the mercurial Mather suffered from depression so deep that he spent most of his time incommunicado and away from Washington, leaving his assistant to manage the new NPS.[12] So Carhart talked to the friendly Horace Albright, who gently told Carhart that he already had a landscape architect and doubted he needed another one.[13] Over the course of many years, Carhart and Albright would cultivate a friendship. Things worked out less well between Carhart and Mather. Carhart must have looked crestfallen when he heard what Albright had to say. But then Albright made a suggestion that radically altered the way recreation policy would develop in the United States. Rising above the fray, he sent Carhart to Edward A. Sherman.

Sherman was an early graduate of the forestry school at Ames and was also a Mason. At their first interview in December 1918, Carhart and Sherman took a liking to each other that would endure some radical ups and downs. Tough, shrewd, and cultured, the model of a Progressive bureaucrat, Sherman was the kind of agency mentor Carhart was looking for. Carhart thought Sherman looked like Lincoln. Sherman was committed to the Forest Service and to the procedures of the Civil Service system. Further, he told Carhart that his first hiring priority was to welcome back former Forest Service employees who had been on military duty. Sherman was also a shrewd judge of people, and he saw in Carhart the same potential Culley, McCrary, and Albright had seen.

Sherman made Carhart aware of the threat to Forest Service power posed by Mather's ambitious plan to take over all planning and management of recreation on all public lands. He also reminded Carhart that Waugh's report, *Recreation Uses on the National Forests,*[14] had said the Forest Service needed a full-time landscape architect.[15] Jumping at the chance, Carhart asked Sherman to help him navigate Civil Service hiring procedures. The canny and diplomatic Sherman reminded Carhart that all candidates had to follow the same regimen, but he also told Carhart in a letter that he would design the Civil Service exam to fit Carhart's qualifications. If Carhart scored high enough to be among the top three candidates on the post-exam list, Sherman would appoint his fellow Iowan to the job. He added, "I apprehend that you have sufficient sporting blood to run the risk of being one of the three topnotch men on the list."[16]

Meanwhile, though still on active duty, Carhart sent letters of application to all the district foresters. By the end of the year, he had some interest from a man in Denver (the headquarters of District 2, which included Colorado, Wyoming, Nebraska, South Dakota, northern Michigan, and Minnesota) who became a key figure in wilderness history: Assistant District Forester Carl J. Stahl.[17]

Stahl acknowledged Carhart's application and wanted to know if he had any experience in "hydro-electric engineering, or highway engineering." Stahl's reply was more positive than those from other districts. Carhart replied to

Stahl on January 7, 1919. He admitted that he had no hydroelectric training but expressed willingness to "assist materially" in road and highway engineering.

On January 19, Carhart mustered out of the army. He and Vee returned to Mapleton, where they lived with his parents. Sherman must have smiled when he read his young protégé's banter: "Of course there is little chance of rushing a matter of this kind but there are so many good outlooks for me at the present I would dislike to turn any position down while waiting for things in the service to adjust themselves." Carhart pointed out to Sherman that four of the six Forest Service districts had expressed interest in him, remarking: "The West looks good to me after the East. It surely is the place to live."[18]

On January 27, Stahl wrote to Carhart, offering him an as yet undefined job. After some dickering, Carhart accepted Stahl's offer of $1,800 in salary per year, promising to report for duty in Denver on March 1. He would travel at his own expense, and he believed that he would best the competition in the upcoming Civil Service exam.

When Carhart received his official pending-hire letter from District Forester Smith Riley on February 11, 1919, he learned the details of what Sherman had worked out for the new "recreation engineer" (Carhart's formal title). Sherman had closely followed Waugh's recommendations, as Riley's letter made clear:

> [A]mong your duties will be such as general sanitation work in the National
> Forests with special reference to ranger stations, simple highway landscape
> improvement, and improving the present layout plans for as many of our
> permanent ranger stations as you can personally visit during the field sea-
> son. As the library in this office on such subjects as these is rather limited,
> it would be well for you to bring with you any publications which you may
> now have and which will be of service to you in your work.[19]

Sherman was not about to turn Carhart loose in District 2 without further preparation for the exam, which would be given in Denver. He kept drilling Carhart by letter about his qualifications, and the young man rose to the challenge. "That makes a total of 13 months actually in landscape operations," he told Sherman, relating that the army had bounced him back and forth between planning and sanitation work, punctuated by periods in the band and work on insect control. He added: "You are right in your surmise that I am willing to take whatever chance there may be. If anyone or any three beat me out in the examination it is altogether right and fair that they be given the place. I am game on that count." Carhart told Sherman that his only regret was that he must reject three offers from commercial firms, "each of which is as attractive in point of salary and opportunity for advancement as is that I accept in the

Forest Service. I am glad to say that one of the firms is the one with which I was formerly associated."[20]

These claims about Carhart's marketability as a landscape architect and planner proved prophetic. A few years later, Carhart's former Iowa professors would invite him to join them as a partner in McCrary, Culley, & Carhart. While Carhart's years with the Forest Service have received some scholarly attention, from a broader perspective they appear as an interlude in the arc of his growth as a planner and writer.

Carhart still faced the Civil Service exam. Mr. and Mrs. Arthur Carhart boarded the train in Mapleton on February 27, 1919, heading west. The first handwritten notes from his mother, Ella, soon followed "my dear big boy."[21] These proud, loving, emotional notes are a good index of Ella's character and its influence on her son. She showered Arthur and Vee with the kind of divine invocations Arthur himself would use later in his life, when formal religion became more important to him. A few days later Ella wrote again to tell Arthur how happy his father was to have had him home: "I was glad you could be with him so much. It did his heart good—put new life in him—to have you enter in the business with him." She added a mother's touch: "You will surely enjoy a work that will eventually lead to even bigger things and *now you are capable of bigger things.* I look for you to do in the future as you have done in the past. *Go ahead! You will make it win!*"[22]

Thanks to his mother, the drive to build a New Jerusalem in Colorado came naturally to Arthur Carhart.

NOTES

1. Frederick Law Olmsted Jr., *Landscape Architecture* VI, no. 3, April 1916.

2. Paul Sears, "Timber in Your Life," *Saturday Review* (January 1955).

3. This letter, written on March 20, 1927, on Mapleton Trust and Savings Bank stationery ("established 1878: Capital and Surplus $90,000.00), is signed "Chuck" (Charles G. Whiting) and addressed to "Bo." Carhart Collection, Denver Public Library (hereafter CC, DPL).

4. McCrary (1885–1971) stayed in practice as a landscape architect after Carhart left to pursue his writing. The Denver Public Library has 653 of McCrary's architectural drawings in its collection, including landscape plans for residences, schools, universities, parks, subdivisions, and public buildings such as the residences of John Evans, L. C. Phipps, and George Cranmer; the Wellshire subdivision in Arapahoe County; and St. John's Cathedral (where Arthur and Vee were parishioners). McCrary and Carhart were still corresponding in September 1963.

5. Culley moved to southern California in the 1930s. He and Carhart conducted a long correspondence that culminated in Carhart's decision to leave Colorado and settle

in California after Vee's death. On April 15, 1957, Irvin McCrary wrote to Carhart, responding to his query about land near McCrary's home around Vista, California. McCrary regaled Carhart with stories about growing avocados on his land, telling him a house with half an acre of avocados was available at $33,000. But he added, "California has its drawbacks, as Frank Culley so well found out." Letters from Culley and McCrary to Arthur Carhart, CC, DPL.

6. The Muries were frequent visitors at the Carharts' home in Denver during the 1930s. Mardy Murie helped Carhart with the Conservation Library during the 1960s.

7. Major Charles Hyde, Sanitary Corps, Office of the Surgeon General, wrote this letter on May 17, 1919; CC, DPL.

8. Letter from Arthur Carhart to Horace Albright, December 28, 1957, CC, DPL.

9. The subjects of the sublime and the beautiful are too large for the present context. U.S. landscape architects of this period may have belonged in some sense to the British Arts and Crafts Movement, but the lines of influence seem blurry to me. Carhart's writing about applied aesthetics relies heavily on threshold experiences of the sort the British might call "sublime," but the contexts are often so pedestrian (in every sense of the term) that it seems more accurate to attribute these influences to a general concept like the Zeitgeist.

10. Frank Waugh, *Recreation Use on the National Forests* (Washington, DC: Government Printing Office, 1918), 37.

11. Hal K. Rothman, "'A Regular Ding-Dong Fight': The Dynamics of Park Service–Forest Service Controversy during the 1920s and 1930s," in Char Miller, ed., *American Forests: Nature, Culture, and Politics* (Lawrence: University of Kansas Press, 1997), 112–114.

12. Horace Schneck and Marian Albright Schenck, *Creating the National Park Service: The Missing Years* (Norman: University of Oklahoma Press, 1999).

13. Later, while Carhart was with the Forest Service and Albright had become superintendent of Yellowstone National Park, the two men cooperated on interagency plans for the Yellowstone area. Like many who went west to work for the Forest Service (such as C. J. Stahl), Charles Pierpont "Punch" Punchard suffered from tuberculosis. He died soon after he and Carhart toured Wyoming sites together in 1920. The Park Service had hired him in 1918. His immediate successor was Daniel Hull. See Linda F. McClelland, *The Historic Landscape Design of the National Park Service, 1916–1942* (Washington, DC: National Park Service, 1998).

14. Waugh, *Recreation Use on the National Forests.* Waugh had been at the University of Massachusetts before going to Dartmouth as head of the School of Landscape Engineering.

15. Sherman may have implied that Carhart might eventually head a Washington-based branch of landscape architecture. Much later, Carhart would hint at this, but no proof of such an offer exists, and Sherman seems far too shrewd a man to have made such an offer to the young Carhart.

16. Letter from Sherman to Carhart, February 8, 1919, CC, DPL.

17. Letter from Stahl to Carhart, December 30, 1918, CC, DPL. The Forest Service did not change its official names for administrative units until 1929, when districts became regions and forests were subdivided into districts.

18. Letter from Carhart to Sherman, January 24, 1919, CC, DPL.

19. Letter from Riley to Carhart, February 11, 1919, CC, DPL.

20. Letter from Carhart to Sherman, February 12, 1919, CC, DPL.

21. Letter from Ella Carhart to Arthur Carhart, March 1, 1919, CC, DPL.

22. Ibid., (emphasis in the original).

CHAPTER THREE

ULTIMATELY TO PERFECT THE SCENE

And did those feet in ancient time,
Walk upon Englands mountains green:
And was the holy Lamb of God,
On Englands pleasant pastures seen!

And did the Countenance Divine,
Shine forth upon our clouded hills?
And was Jerusalem builded here,
Among these dark Satanic Mills?

Bring me my Bow of burning gold:
Bring me my Arrows of desire:
Bring me my Spear: O clouds unfold!
Bring me my Chariot of fire!

I will not cease from Mental Fight,
Nor shall my Sword sleep in my hand:
Till we have built Jerusalem,
In Englands green & pleasant Land.

Would to God that all the Lords People were Prophets!

—WILLIAM BLAKE, FROM THE PREFACE TO *MILTON*

Ella Carhart's ardent ambitions for her son quickly bore fruit. As the Carharts' speeding train brought the Rocky Mountains ever closer, it seemed to become a chariot of fire. Such feelings only intensified when Arthur Carhart realized that Colorado was heavily industrialized and urbanized and that its once-forested watersheds were devastated. Who were the warriors who could restore the watersheds and their people to health?

"Would to God that all the Lords People were Prophets" (Blake, *Milton*). Public lands recreation would make men and women to match the mountains. Carhart, a professional singer, knew the uplifting, populist power of the old Wesleyan hymns.

The cool, secular Frederick Law Olmsted Sr. saw in scenery solely "a peculiar kind of enjoyment and recreation." In contrast, when the fervent Carhart left Denver for his first assignment as a recreation engineer in 1919, he saw along the Arkansas River at Pueblo the dark Satanic mills of Colorado Fuel & Iron (CF&I). Yet the landscape vibrated with place names that suggested redemption. There they beckoned, out to the west, at the foot of the celebrated Sangre de Cristo Mountains—the inviting Wet Mountains, where Carhart and his allies in Pueblo and the Forest Service would attempt to build a new Jerusalem in the New World. Could it be an accident that Arthur and Vee would soon be living in the idyllic, biblically resonant hamlet of Beulah? Following his mother's Methodism, the recreation engineer seized his two-edged sword and joined the fight. The older Carharts were Social Gospel Methodists. They applied Christian principles to problems like the mistreatment of CF&I workers. There would be no Second Coming until Colorado rid itself of its social ills. Justice and beauty for all!

But first, a few practical matters needed attention. While Arthur and Vee were living as lodgers in downtown Denver near Forest Service District headquarters (which were in *The Denver Post* building), Carhart took and passed the Civil Service exam. By April 1919, just a month into his new job, Carhart was already making Edward A. Sherman proud. The Sunday *Denver Post* for April 20, 1919, ran a big spread featuring Carhart's photo and "Development of Resorts to Attract Many Tourists" as the headline. The rest of the photo spread showed Carhart looking dapper in his Forest Service uniform, very much the ladies' man. Indeed, the scenic shots taken by his new friend and Forest Service colleague Wallace I. Hutchinson featured bevies of girls picnicking in carefully tended woods where flies, fires, floods, and fierce animals seemed like things of the past. "Hutch" understood right away that the new man at District 2 was as mediagenic as he was charismatic. The interview shows Carhart at his beguiling best:

> There are a number of small areas in the national forests where the scenic attractions are exceptional, which ultimately will be platted and cataloged and designated as scenic spots. Such a place, for instance, is "the Narrows" on the Poudre River. This is without value as homestead, grazing, mineral or timber land, but is rich in scenic attractions. These places will not be designated as scenic spots when such designation will interfere with their utilitarian value.

After the plot is designated, individuals will not be permitted to erect structures of any kind which will mar the beauty of the place. This should not be taken to mean that summer resorts in the vicinity will not be permitted. On the contrary, this is the desire of the service—to encourage such resorts nearby, to make the beauty spots more accessible to the public.

The next step will be to develop the scenic possibilities of the place. It may be that trees spoil the view from the best scenic vantage point. In such a case, the trees will be removed. Or if a landslide or fire has caused an ugly scar which mars the view, trees will be planted, ultimately to perfect the scene.

It may be that the place is rather inaccessible. In that event trails will be constructed from the nearest road.[1]

AMONG THESE DARK SATANIC MILLS

Building on such modest beginnings, Carhart would become big and bold when he traveled to Pueblo. There, the interrelated social and environmental ills of the times were closely and dramatically linked. It was already clear to Hutchinson and Stahl where Carhart could have the quickest impact: the watershed of the Arkansas River, where the newcomer marveled at the worn-out, overgrazed, beautiful Sangre de Cristo Mountains and their subrange, the Sierra Mojada—the Wet Mountains—both part of the San Isabel National Forest. Hutchinson had been San Isabel supervisor in 1914–1915, taking over from James A. Langworthy, who served from 1908 to 1914. Al Hamel succeeded Hutchinson, serving from 1915 to 1924. The Langworthy and Hamel families intermarried. And they all worked for Carl Stahl, who had run the San Isabel in 1906–1907.[2] All of these men knew the Forest Service had chosen the name "San Isabel" to suggest that each new arrival was a Columbus sailing to the New World.

Ever the performer, Carhart tight-roped the Forest Service's utilitarian party line while at the same time striking his own rapidly changing and developing balance for scenic beauty. Before the advent of the national forests around the turn of the twentieth century, the first and second generations of Coloradoans had engaged in a vast tragedy of the commons that had practically denuded public lands like the San Isabel National Forest.[3] It was the Forest Service's messianic calling to restore those damaged, flood-prone watersheds. A quick study who tempered the idealistic with the practical, Carhart saw right away that the task of restoring the scenic beauty of public lands was part of a larger task of restoring healthy watersheds—a task that would also have to involve nearby communities, especially in terms of cost-sharing.

In those postwar days, booming Pueblo rivaled Denver as a source of wealth and jobs. While the new federal bureaucracies were centered in Denver, the steel industry chose Pueblo, which had nearby sources of the wood and coal needed to smelt local iron ores. The Rockefellers founded CF&I in 1872. They were not only the largest employer in the region but also the most environmentally destructive and ruthless in dealing with widespread labor unrest. The Ludlow Massacre of 1914 and the local Communist Scare of 1919 were fresh in the minds of civic-minded Coloradoans. These moderates deplored the butchery of Rockefeller's agents, who machine-gunned men, women, and children. Cooler heads sought temperate, balanced ways to address the injustices and environmental devastation that radiated out from Pueblo and into the public lands of the Arkansas River watershed. Among their leaders was Albin Hamel, supervisor of the San Isabel National Forest, who knew how to prick the Rockefellers' corporate conscience.

Enter the fiery new recreation engineer, full of the kind of Methodist-style enthusiasm that also seems to have characterized the ultimate watershed planner, John Wesley Powell.[4] Ella Carhart's effusive aestheticism and social justice–style Methodism had profoundly influenced her son, even if he did not yet express his feelings as openly as she did. Also following his father's Masonic concept of civic duty, he believed strongly in what he called "service," meaning his duties to help all Americans fulfill their right to have beauty in their lives, both natural and artistic. Carhart's populist sympathy for working people and his revulsion at the brutal methods of both the Rockefellers[5] and the Communists were the foundations for his efforts to "Americanize" recent immigrants through recreational opportunities.

It was Carhart's good timing to step into the growing competition for tourists and recreationists between Pueblo and Denver as well as between the Forest Service and the Park Service. It was also good timing to propose a Jeffersonian solution to Colorado's labor problems. Carhart thought of the national forests as democratizers, as extensions of the concept that every American should have access to the public's wildlands, just as every American should have the right to own guns and hunt on public lands. Carhart arrived in Colorado along with numerous first-generation Americans, many from urban settings in Central Europe. He believed they had the same right he did to enjoy public lands.

Colorado's first and second generations had come and gone, retreating to cities and leaving public lands in ruins. The Colorado the Carharts found in the spring of 1919 had been among the most urban U.S. states since at least 1890, when the U.S. Census showed around 75 percent of Colorado's residents were concentrated in urban areas. By comparison, the Iowa of Carhart's childhood was relatively rural. In 1890, the United States as a whole was only 22 percent urban. Similarly, as the century turned and World War I came and went, Colorado had more people working in industry than in agriculture and more railroad employees than farmers. Around 25 percent of the state's residents were defined as foreign-born, double the figure for the United States as a whole. Immigrant populations ran as high as 50 percent, especially in the southern part of the state east of the San Isabel.

Around the turn of the century, the establishment of national forests under President Theodore Roosevelt and the advent of the Forest Service had seemed to check and even reverse the tragedy of the commons. The Forest Service made real progress in watershed restoration up until the advent of World War I. However, war-related resource panics wiped out much of that progress, and the watersheds Carhart encountered in 1919 were worthy of the derisive name he chose for them: "tin roof watersheds." Pueblo suffered a disastrous flood in 1921. The immediate cause of that flood was an intense thunderstorm not far upriver from the city, which lies at the junction of the Arkansas River and Fountain Creek. But the poor condition of the entire watershed allowed the flood to reach disastrous proportions. With over 200 fatalities (concentrated among poor immigrants), this flood remains the worst natural disaster in Colorado history. Similarly, war-related resource panics and overstocking of the watersheds led to another tragic flood in 1947. This flood destroyed one of Carhart's finest legacies, Squirrel Creek Campground west of Pueblo.

The Forest Service's post–World War I response to these discouraging conditions was threefold: (1) cultivation of newly replanted forests, coupled with complete fire suppression—the goal was sustainable timber production; (2) cultivation of public land ranchers and hunters as political allies, especially in an all-out campaign to exterminate wolves—the goal was regulated grazing; and (3) cultivation of the tourism and recreation industries, especially those that were automobile-based—the goal was to compete with the Park Service for recreation-related congressional appropriations. Meanwhile, other federal agencies, such as the Bureau of Reclamation and the Army Corps of Engineers, aggressively pursued engineering solutions to the state's watershed problems. As Carhart pointed out to Denver's city fathers in 1924, Denver was second only to Washington, D.C., in the number and size of resident federal bureaus.[6]

QUEEN CITY OF THE PLAINS

Carhart made a wise professional choice in coming to District 2, where District Forester Smith Riley had begun planning for automobile-based recreational developments as early as 1917.[7] Riley had promoted Wallace Hutchinson from supervisor of the San Isabel to head of the Information and Education Branch of the District Office. Hutchinson was well aware of the need to popularize the national forests, given the conflict with the Park Service and the recreational needs of laborers and auto-borne tourists. In particular, the clever Hutchinson knew how to exploit the rhetorical split between "the rich man's Park Service and the poor man's Forest Service."

Wide-open Denver was already a mecca for landscape architects and city planners. Reinhard Schuetze had become the city's first landscape architect in 1893, when Denver committed itself to develop an exemplary park system. Schuetze rebuilt City Park and designed many others. In 1904 Mayor Robert W. Speer supported a "City Beautiful" effort in Denver, just as the City and County of Denver received a new charter that would enable it to implement City Beautiful standards.[8] These farsighted men had their work cut out for them. Denver's population had grown from 4,759 in 1870 to 106,713 in 1890. Denver had started its urban park system in 1881 with Curtis Park and then City Park (near Carhart's future home in Park Hill), followed by Montclair Park farther to the southeast in 1886. In 1898, Cheesman and Washington parks were laid out closer to the downtown area. By 1910, the city's population was 213,381. In 1911, the city began its Civic Center and Pioneer Monument.[9]

Before the Great War, booming Denver did not wait for the Forest Service to wake up to the need for nearby, auto-based recreation opportunities in the watersheds that fed its municipal water system. In 1912, getting the jump on Pueblo, Denver hired Frederick Law Olmsted Jr. to design its mountain park system, including Red Rocks, Buffalo Bill's Grave, Chief Hosa Lodge (finished in 1918), the Genesee Mountain bison herd enclosure, and Summit Lake near Mount Evans.

LEAD, FOLLOW—OR GET OUT OF THE WAY

Would the Forest Service lead or follow these ambitious local efforts to link the mountains with the cities of the plains? As he learned the institutional and geographic lay of the land, Carhart wanted his new employer to lead, not just locally along the Front Range but also nationally in the increasingly heated competition with the Park Service for more federal money and power. Carhart realized that he needed to act quickly. He sought a forest where he could experiment with his new ideas about public lands recreation, hoping to create a model the Forest Service could apply nationwide.

Carl Stahl was Carhart's immediate superior. Having come to Colorado to recover from tuberculosis in 1904, he may have seemed reserved to some, but Carhart found him warm-hearted and sensitive. Carhart shared an office with Stahl. The floor below housed Hutchinson in public relations—in close striking distance to *The Denver Post* reporters on the ground floor.

Having started his own career on the San Isabel, Stahl understood more than most its potential for recreation. Stahl knew Carhart should leave the Denver office soon to develop a feel for his new territory. But first the green-horn had to see that Colorado was no untouched paradise. Picking the aptly named Clear Creek, one of the most spectacularly plundered watersheds on the Front Range, Stahl took Carhart on a long driving tour. Later, Carhart wrote, "I had always carried an image of a solid stand of mature, first-growth trees, stretching without a break to the horizon. . . . My first field trip to acquaint me with the forests of the region began with a chilly, fog-blinded ride in an old-time open touring-car up the canyon of Clear Creek west of Denver. Next morning the cloudless sunrise revealed fire-scarred ridges and slopes where early miners had burned off timber in order to locate ore veins more readily." Everywhere he went he saw "the pattern of cut, slash, and burn, which characterized the operations of most lumber companies during the nineteenth century."[10]

Meanwhile, Hutchinson helped Carhart improve his writing skills. Carhart's first official publication introduced him and his projected work to District 2. He remarked, "Not a surprising lot will be accomplished this season perhaps but the important thing, the beginning of a full utilization of Forest Recreation, commenced."[11] Hutchinson's influence on Carhart was obvious in this article. Hutchinson also included in the bulletin his own article announcing Carhart's appointment and asking line officers to send Carhart information about beautiful spots with recreation potential. Hutchinson added, "He is a good fellow, knows his business and is enthusiastic."[12]

Carhart let communities know he was available to develop recreational opportunities that would connect them with their watersheds by way of mountain parks. Hutchinson arranged for Carhart to publish a series of articles on the subject. The first appeared in July 1919: "Municipal Playgrounds in the Forests."[13] The others appeared throughout 1920 in the magazine *American Forestry*.[14] One of Carhart's selling points was an appeal to the tourist industry to support the Forest Service in developing a system of automobile-based camps that would serve not only locals but also vacationers from afar, a point Sherman had suggested during their first meetings. Both Iowans knew the Midwest's hot, muggy summers would drive people west to the Forest Service's cool, mountainous domain.

Carhart spent early April 1919, his first week on the job, studying the office records and making a preliminary survey of district-wide recreational needs. The auto trip up Clear Creek Canyon followed. Then there was the successful debut interview with *The Denver Post*. In the last half of April, Carhart took the train south to Colorado Springs, where he toured the Pike National Forest with

Ranger Roy Truman of the Manitou District. Carhart proved his worth to the veteran by quickly designing a footpath that connected the popular Barr Trail to the summit of Pike's Peak.

AL HAMEL, PUEBLO, AND SIPRA

The Barr Trail also linked Carhart to Al Hamel. Albin Gustave Hamel was an American-born Swede from Nebraska. Before taking over the San Isabel, he had earned a degree in forestry at the University of Nebraska and conducted ecological studies at the Fremont Experiment Station on Pike's Peak, where the Forest Service was trying to restore the distressed municipal watershed above Colorado Springs.[15] Later, in his guidebook to Colorado, Carhart wrote: "Here some ten million forest trees have been grown and planted on the fire swept slopes of Pikes Peak and other old burns. Normally after one fire goes through a forest country there are enough seed trees left to start a new forest. Where the burning is repeated neither seed nor seed tree is left. That is what happened on these hills in the early days."[16]

Stahl sent Carhart farther south to Pueblo, telling him to use the San Isabel as "a good pilot project" for his larger assignment of "making a master recreation plan" for all the national forests in District 2.[17] Carhart had been in Colorado two months before he saw an old-growth forest to match his preconceptions—and that was on the steep slopes of the San Isabel.[18] Carhart had a Forest Service–issue 115-A Kodak camera. He took around 2,000 pictures with it during his travels in the summers of 1919 and 1920, an invaluable baseline against which to measure Forest Service accomplishments. Hutchinson was conducting a region-wide camera contest to encourage field personnel to document their work and develop an appreciation for aesthetics. Perhaps because of a scarcity of competitors, Carhart won first, second, and third place.

An adept student of the new communities along the Front Range, Hamel wanted the Forest Service to lead in a new way—he wanted it to partner with neighboring communities on a watershed-by-watershed basis that gave due weight to tourism and recreation as well as to traditional resource extraction. In Carhart, Hamel found someone who could not only articulate ideas about beauty but could also sell them to "buyers" or shareholders, ranging from executives at CF&I to the auto parts dealer who was a member of the local Masonic lodge. Like a good preacher, Carhart had the knack for speaking and writing simply about what he saw—and what he could help others see. In particular, he was curious about the Spanish and Mexican aspects of the Sangre de Cristos' history, an interest that would lead him a few years later to write some of his best historical fiction. Later, Carhart wrote: "The San Isabel is first of all a watershed forest. . . .The San Isabel is one of my favorite national forests. . . . I like the Cristos for their sharp, incisive forms, their positive rhythm and lack of confusion. They also intrigue me with history that is laced all over their slopes."[19]

The tenderfoot Carhart must have made a strange travel companion for the more experienced Hamel, but that does not seem to have bothered the older man. As clean-living as he was high-thinking, Carhart did not chew or smoke tobacco or drink coffee or liquor.[20] He took Postum (a coffee substitute) with him on trips. Hamel and Carhart rode out one fine May morning in an automobile. Ten years later, in his auto-oriented guidebook, Carhart wrote: "I am going to take you over the North Hardscrabble highway into the Wet Mountain Valley because that is the trail Al Hamel, Forest Supervisor, chose for introducing me to the Sangre de Cristos."[21]

Floods had destroyed earlier railroad and wagon routes (such as those up Grape Creek) into the Wet Mountain Valley. So the men drove up the new North Hardscrabble Highway through the Wet Mountains to a point east of present-day Silver Cliff. Here the foreground presented images of mining-related desolation, but the soaring peaks of the Sangre de Cristos drew the eye to the horizon. As Carhart later wrote, "One evening at sunset, with a ghostly light on the peaks, Al Hamel and I sat in his old roustabout car out near Bull Hill and counted fifty-two peaks in sight that were certainly over 12,000 feet above sea level."[22]

During this tour, Carhart met Rangers Paul Gilbert and Karl Gilbert.[23] Enriched by the Gilberts' working knowledge of the region, Carhart and Hamel's tour led to a report titled *General Working Plan, Recreational Development of the San Isabel National Forest, Colorado*, which Carhart drafted over the summer and produced in December 1919. He dubbed it "the San Isabel Playground."

At the end of this trip, upon their return to Pueblo, Hamel introduced Carhart to the members of the fledgling San Isabel Protection and Recreation Association (SIPRA). Carhart knew how to motivate the businessmen Hamel had recruited to serve Pueblo's recreation needs. Later that year, on November 6, 1919, SIPRA filed its nonprofit papers: "Its objects and purposes being to develop the recreation possibilities in and adjacent to the San Isabel National Forest in the State of Colorado; to own, hold and sell real estate, and to own, operate or lease hotels, stores, camp colonies, places of entertainment, stage lines, roads, trails, and to engage in all kinds of publicity and similar activities."[24]

SIPRA's clever founders divided their capital stock of $100,000 into $5 shares, which they successfully offered to the public. With Carhart's help, they also struck a cooperative agreement with the Forest Service whereby their funds were dedicated solely to SIPRA's specific purposes. Thereafter, SIPRA began to undertake all kinds of forestry work, with Hamel's approval, for "beautifying" the San Isabel.

War-related hysteria had forced Hamel to increase stocking rates of sheep and cattle on the San Isabel to levels that destroyed the rehabilitation efforts Stahl, Hutchinson, and others had begun after the founding of the San Isabel Forest Reserve in 1903. If future forest supervisors were to resist such political pressure, they would need broad public support for forceful, logical, comprehensive policies that integrated recreation into the pantheon of more traditional extractive uses through watershed-wide planning.

Hamel knew he urgently needed more than just beautification in the name of restoration. He needed to address multiple recreation needs, not only for automobile-borne tourists from nearby states but also for the burgeoning local labor force. While the wartime sanctions and shortages might have temporarily quieted labor unrest, the end of the war meant a revolution of rising expectations among southern Colorado's workers, who had more free time, money, and cheap transportation in the form of the automobile. And, like Carhart, many had experienced a wider world through military service, including outdoor experience, which they felt entitled them to the use of public lands—especially for camping but also for hunting and fishing.

Around 1900, CF&I's regional employee base had been 15,000 (comprising thirty nationalities and almost as many languages). By 1915, the number had risen to 30,000. By the time Hamel and Carhart teamed up, CF&I employed 7,000 people in Pueblo alone. Another 10,000 labored in the coal camps near the southern end of the San Isabel around Walsenburg and Trinidad. Yet another 10,000 were working along the Arkansas River from Pueblo up to Florence and Cañon City.[25] Extensive rail lines linked Pueblo to mines like the Orient on the west side of the Sangres near today's Valley View Hot Springs. Little foothills communities like the well-named Beulah (where the Carharts lived in the summer of 1920) bore the brunt of demand for recreation from these users, especially around watercourses where the more desirable and typically private lower-elevation lands blocked access to the higher public lands. Summertime also meant the Wet Mountains behind Beulah were the nearest refuge for tourists from the sweltering states to the east.

Even if potential recreationists could reach public lands, the national forests had few roads; they also had few suitable trails, campgrounds, or picnic areas. Frustrated visitors parked, trespassed, and polluted with abandon. They also cut and burned what vegetation they could access. In 1916, short-sighted local officials made things worse by surfacing a twenty-six-mile road leading from Pueblo directly to Beulah and ending at Squirrel Creek Canyon and the

San Isabel National Forest boundary. In 1919 and 1920, Carhart photographed Squirrel Creek's piles of trash and human waste, and Hamel told him that the barren slopes above the creek had lost their ability to absorb potential floodwaters. Hamel did not need to tell the former U.S. Army sanitation engineer about the health risks to downstream communities posed by human waste.

In the winter of 1919–1920, when Carhart finally had the time to formalize his plans for dealing with the recreation needs of workers, part of his solution was to create company town–like camps, where workers loyal to company and nation would be rewarded with free or low-cost stays. In California, the Angeles National Forest was already running such camps, charging families $11.25 for two-week visits. Carhart wrote:

> There is a chance in this sort of camp to teach better Americanization of the people of foreign blood now living in our midst. . . . [We need] a system of camps for the industrial population of this portion of the state. The thousands of citizens of foreign birth or of foreign extraction found residing near the borders of the Forest and now never realizing anything from this proximity, will through cooperation of the Forest and with the Industrial Companies, come to know the hills and by means of camps where it will be possible to live as cheaply or even at a more reasonable rate than in town, these people will become better citizens and far less open to insidious suggestions of the radical agitator to strike at this land they have come to know and love.[26]

PLANS MUST BE BIG AND BOLD

Carhart returned to Denver and to Vee for a short visit in late June 1919. Then, working alone, he spent two weeks hiking and surveying the glacial basins east of Mount Evans to see if the area was of national park quality. A solo climbing accident nearly cost him his life, as he was unprepared for the lightning that accompanies summer thunderstorms. Shaken, he returned to Denver on July 10. He concluded that Mount Evans should remain under Forest Service administration, since an extensive road system made it not of park caliber.

In July–August 1919, Stahl accompanied Carhart on the first leg of a tour of the rest of their huge district. Traveling through Wyoming by train and auto, they visited the Washakie and Big Horn national forests on their way to the Shoshone National Forest near Cody, where Carhart met his Park Service counterpart, landscape architect Charles Punchard. The men traveled up the North Fork of the Shoshone River to Yellowstone National Park, agreeing on the need to cooperate to preserve this important scenic corridor.

Carhart then left Stahl and took the train east from Cody, stopping at the Black Hills National Forest in South Dakota and the Nebraska National Forest.

From there, Carhart went to the Superior National Forest in Minnesota, where he first saw the lakes in late July 1919. The lakeshores were rimmed with private cabins, which alarmed Carhart. He wrote a report for Stahl recommending against construction of a controversial road that would have allowed the erection of cabins to follow wherever logging roads might lead. Stahl pulled funds for the road out of a pending budget. He was beginning to sense Carhart's potential as a bold visionary who could make a place for recreation in large regional plans.

Perhaps this relatively small episode also demonstrated the difference between Waugh's status as a contractor and Carhart's as a staff employee. Carhart was learning to think and act with a vision broader than Waugh's focus on mere beautification of isolated sites. Profoundly impressed with the beauty and the potential for beauty in the vast District 2, Carhart was beginning to formulate the comprehensive approach to planning he would spell out that winter in his *General Working Plan*:

> There is one principal, one fundamental truth that must be recognized. That is, in order to fully utilize the possibilities of any forest and in order that we keep our recreational development in proper perspective with the size of the forests, plans must be big and broad. There should be no great building of isolated improvements small in size but rather a recognition that any camp, or summer home site has direct relation to all other uses and improvements in that region and plans should be shaped to meet those conditions. The bigger the plan on which improvements are built the greater the total return will be to the service and to the public.[27]

Blake's hymn in the epigraph at the start of this chapter calls it "mental fight." Carhart was learning the martial arts. Surely, it was not lost on Ella Carhart's son that he and Vee were pioneering in Beulah, whose beguilingly biblical name points to the idealism of the frontier and its promise of a Jerusalem rebuilt in the New World. But would there be room for wolves? Like Aldo Leopold at about this same time in 1919, Carhart was learning that mental fight had little value in a landscape that had lost its wolves. Without wolves to rival humans, former Ute Indian territory like the Sangre de Cristos and Trappers Lake were diminished things. Could the wild and the wilderness be different? What would the Utes say? If there was a good answer to these questions, it awaited Carhart at a Ute sacred site: Trappers Lake.

NOTES

1. Forbes Parkhill, "Development of Resorts to Attract Many Tourists," *The Denver Post*, April 20, 1919. This excerpt is from an interview with Carhart.

2. See Tom Wolf, *Colorado's Sangre de Cristo Mountains* (Boulder: University Press of Colorado, 1995), 305, n. 12.

3. Ibid., 199–206.

4. The Greek roots of "enthusiasm" mean something like "seized by the divine." Although Powell scholars like Donald Worster and William deBuys play down this side of the great man's character, perhaps it deserves greater attention. Today the mills stand silent, but one cannot help but think of Pueblo when one sings Blake's great Wesleyan hymn.

5. Much later, Carhart would sit on the boards of Rockefeller-funded foundations. He also received Rockefeller money for various conservation causes.

6. "Street Traffic and the Business District," a Report to the City Planning Association, Denver, Colorado, April 1924, McCrary, Culley, & Carhart, City Planners, Denver.

7. Donald Baldwin, *The Quiet Revolution: Grass Roots of Today's Wilderness Preservation Movement* (Boulder: Pruett, 1972), 12.

8. See the magazine *Denver Municipal Facts*, published by the city from 1909 to 1931, which covers the City Beautiful movement. See also Thomas J. Noel and Barbara S. Norgren, *Denver: The City Beautiful* (Denver: Historic Denver, 1987).

9. During Carhart's long life, planners and developers would struggle to keep up with growth. Carhart was frequently involved in these efforts, such as the East High School building and Esplanade in 1925. By 1930, the city's population was 287,861. In 1932, the City and County Building rose to the west of the capitol. In 1950 the population had reached 415,786. By 1970 it had grown to 514,678. Carhart lived to see the High Line Canal Greenway (Carhart and Vee are buried in nearby Fairmount Cemetery), developed in 1974, and the 1975 Four Mile Historic Park.

10. Arthur Carhart, *The National Forests* (New York: Alfred A. Knopf, 1959), 5.

11. Arthur Carhart, "Your Scenic Attractions," *The Bulletin, District 2* (Denver: USFS III, May 1919).

12. Ibid.

13. "Municipal Playgrounds in the Forests," *Municipal Facts Monthly* 2 (July 1919).

14. "Recreation in the Forests," *American Forestry* 26 (May 1920); "The Department of Forest Recreation," *American Forestry* 26 (September 1920); "Vacation Opportunities in Your National Forests," *American Forestry* 26 (September 1920); "Auto Camp Conveniences," *American Forestry* 26 (September 1920); "What Is Recreation's Next Step?" *American Forestry* 26 (October 1920); "Live Game and Forest Recreation," *American Forestry* 26 (December 1920).

15. In 1925, Hamel became superintendent of the Pike National Forest west of Colorado Springs.

16. Arthur Carhart, *Colorado: History, Geology, Legend* (New York: Coward-McCann, 1932), 134.

17. See the December 6, 1920, memo Carhart ghost-wrote for Stahl in the Carhart Collection, Denver Public Library.

18. Carhart, *The National Forests*, 5–6.

19. Ibid., 174, 176. Carhart's photos of subjects like the Penitentes are in the Western History Collection, Denver Public Library.

20. The only mention of liquor I found in the entire Carhart Collection is in a January 25, 1959, letter schmoozing an industry pulp man: "Hey, if you're not doing anything truly important, let's get together with Mr. Schlitz and some Silverfield cheddar, and scramble up some ideas."

21. Carhart, *Colorado*, 159. Carhart added: "Of all the mountain ranges in the state this is perhaps [the] most cloaked in early Spanish romance" (159).

22. Ibid., 161.

23. From these brothers' families came many prominent Colorado recreation planners, including Douglas Gilbert of Colorado State University.

24. These papers are signed by District Forester A. S. Peck for the Forest Service and P. A. Gray for SIPRA. They also wisely provide for SIPRA's demise. Gray was secretary of the Pueblo Commerce Club.

25. H. Lee Scamehorn and Lee Scamehorn, *High Altitude Energy: A History of Fossil Fuels in Colorado (Mining the American West)* (Boulder: University Press of Colorado, 2002).

26. "San Isabel Forest Recreation Plan," 1919, 14. Document on file at the Pike–San Isabel headquarters in Pueblo. See also my discussion of "Carhart in the Sangres" in *Colorado's Sangre de Cristo Mountains*, 199ff.

27. Arthur Carhart, *General Working Plan: Recreational Development of the San Isabel National Forest*, 14. Carhart's internal memos often appear in this breathless style. He dictated such work to a stenographer, often not even pausing to proofread. Nevertheless, one can see here the beginnings of his later prose style.

CHAPTER FOUR

TRAPPERS LAKE, CRADLE OF WILDERNESS

But when it comes to the actual work of pioneering, the one big element
involved is good old style—I will be polite and conservative and say "nerve."
. . . All "frontiers" are comparative anyway. If you think of "frontier" as a
place of danger and yearn to meet it, just make a trail to that great plateau
region of northwestern Colorado, outfit at some good town and hit out on
your own particular brand of trouble-trailing.

—CARHART, *COLORADO* (1932)[1]

In 1919, Arthur Carhart's imagination and foresight helped make Trappers
Lake "the cradle of wilderness," as Roderick Nash has said. In 1975, fifty-six
years later, Congress designated the Flat Tops Wilderness, including Trappers
Lake. In 2002, the Big Fish Fire burned all the timber around the lake, consum-
ing 17,000 acres of the watershed. In 2005, the Colorado Division of Wildlife
started reintroducing Colorado River cutthroat trout to Trappers Lake as part
of a new management plan that begins at the top of the watershed.[2]

Trappers Lake has a history as checkered as the concept of wilderness itself.
Can it be true, as Donald Worster suggested, that the concept of wilderness con-
tains within itself the seeds of wilderness destruction?[3] If we forfeit the style and
nerve that spell "frontier," have we given up wilderness? The answers may lie in
the young Carhart's experience at Trappers Lake in the fall of 1919. Or in the
young Leopold's similar experience on the Gila National Forest in 1909, when he
was fresh from Yale Forestry School: "We reached the old wolf in time to watch a

fierce green fire dying in her eyes."[4] As with Aldo Leopold, for Carhart the concepts of wilderness and the wild clashed for a lifetime. Both men followed a trail that always led to the wolf, but it did so through a maze of fact and fiction.

Can there and should there be wilderness without predators and without natural processes like periodic wildfires? Was it the wolf that spoke to Arthur Carhart at Trappers Lake? Was it a Ute spirit? Carhart would not be alone among American nature writers in flailing at the ineffable when he tried to represent the wilderness and the wild. The experience at Trappers Lake led to Carhart's historic meeting with Aldo Leopold. But it was only the beginning. For both men, the tension between the wild and the wilderness would hang high like a glacial lake: power poised on a precipice. Nevertheless, Trappers Lake inspired Carhart and Leopold to imagine a better Forest Service: one that might yet learn to manage for many values, including wilderness and wildfires and even wolves, within a watershed context.

Carhart learned that wilderness planning served the public interest best if it represented a vision broader than simply balancing special interests—including the special interests of federal bureaucracies. Remember that Carhart had formulated his grand recreational plans for the San Isabel in the winter of 1919–1920—*after* his experience at Trappers Lake and after he met Leopold. And while Carhart and Leopold went on to make grand plans, others did so as well. The Bureau of Reclamation blocked wilderness designation for Trappers Lake for fifty-six years. By 1922, all of Colorado's wolves were dead at the hands of killers who worked for another federal agency that had big and bold plans of its own—the Bureau of Biological Survey. So, do our problems with wilderness and the wild lie with rugged individualists or bland bureaucrats? Carhart the die-hard maverick would have liked the phrase "predatory bureaucracy" Michael Robinson uses to describe the Bureau of Biological Survey.[5]

Many have tried to trail Carhart to the "cradle of wilderness" at Trappers Lake. No one has ever completely succeeded in understanding what happened to him there.[6] Now that Carhart has ceased to be, some context and chronology may help those who value wolf lore and wilderness lore—those who wish to understand before Carhart's trail cools beyond recognition. As Carhart later despairingly put it, "Civilization of the white man has almost covered the West."[7] Or has it? Renegade wolves are again returning to the rangelands of Colorado's national forests, working their way south from Yellowstone, following the deer Carhart loved to hunt. In ways that baffle many literal-minded wilderness lovers, Carhart always insisted that wilderness experiences, like wolves, are where we find them. Perhaps, like the elusive wolves, Carhart covered his trail so thoroughly that readers are well advised to visit Trappers Lake for their own wilderness experience.[8]

In 1957, Carhart described Trappers Lake in geophysical terms, ending with the phrase "natural dam," which must have amused his enemies in the Bureau of Reclamation. Like any good writer, Carhart reveled in paradox and metaphor. "Natural dam" is Carhart's version of Wallace Stegner's "angle of repose," a civil engineering term used to describe earth-fill dams. Both metaphors present the clash, the "mental fight," between the physical and the spiritual that makes wilderness so important.[9] Carhart wrote:

> Trappers Lake is the second largest natural body of water in Colorado. It is not well known, but the lake and its setting are very scenic. Eons ago the shrinking earth pushed up a gigantic block of crust, thousands of feet thick, to form the White River Plateau. Lava flows spread over this flat-topped tableland and later ice sheets slid across it, thrusting tongues over the vertical sides. One of these tongues dug a straight-walled valley. It pushed debris down the wide gorge to form a moraine, which is the natural dam holding back the waters of Trappers Lake.[10]

The concept of wilderness is one of North America's finest contributions to world history, as Roderick Nash has shown. Wilderness speaks in many tongues. It shape-shifts: now a place, now a spirit, now an animal, now a feeling. Never still. In the rest of this chapter, I consider Carhart's changing concepts of wilderness over the years.[11]

THIS WAY TO WILDERNESS?

Throughout the summer of 1919, Carhart traversed the hard-used forests of District 2. Although Vee again had to wait alone in Denver, Carl Stahl gave Carhart his final assignment of the field season: go to Trappers Lake and plan a Park Service–style automobile loop. Survey a through road around Trappers Lake. Then locate spots for 100 summer homes, two commercial sites, and a marina. Come back with a plan to build all this as soon as Congress funds it.

A few years prior to Carhart's time, as part of its campaign to cultivate an auto-based recreation constituency, the Forest Service had encouraged yet another version of the old Homestead Laws designed to dispose of public lands. In 1915, Congress authorized the Forest Service to grant permits to "[r]esponsible persons or associations to use and occupy suitable spaces or portions of ground in the national forests for the construction of summer homes, hotels, stores, or other structures, needed for recreation or public convenience."[12]

By 1919, the San Isabel Protection and Recreation Association (SIPRA) was preparing to operate under some provisions of this law. Meanwhile, up north on the White River National Forest, less happy aspects of the law had generated a noisy, unruly backlog of applicants for long-term leases at the choicest spots on federal lands.[13] On the Superior National Forest, as Carhart had seen for himself earlier in the summer of 1919, zealous bureaucrats were already implementing the law: they were not only aggressively marketing the summer home program but also promising to lease waterfront sites in locales as aesthetically and environmentally sensitive as Trappers Lake.

Carhart's travels around District 2 stimulated his imagination. He saw that with luck and pluck he might develop a policy for what he called "pure type recreational service." Was this what we today mean by "wilderness?" Perhaps, but the concept and associated language of wilderness are at their mysterious best when they keep evolving in tandem with a protean wilderness itself. As for the word "wilderness," Carhart rarely used it during his time with the Forest Service, whether in official documents or personal correspondence. Like peering through a telescope the wrong way, placing too much emphasis on what we today call "wilderness" can distort our perception of how Carhart's sensibility was changing during the years 1919–1922. One bit of continuity is clear: Carhart always placed humans squarely in the midst of any landscape he planned or imagined. That was one reason he was so interested in the Indian and Spanish history of the Sangre de Cristo Mountains. Carhart never valued uninhabited wilderness after the fashion of his Wilderness Society friends such as Howard Zahniser or the Muries or even Aldo Leopold. This was consistent with his well-earned reputation as a nonconformist. Over the years, as "wilderness" became a rolling bandwagon, more and more revisionists clambered aboard and fought over the reins. Carhart was not above fighting over the paternity of wilderness, especially later in life, but he was just as likely to shove a stick in the self-serving spokes of the official wilderness movement as he was to criticize the Forest Service for its unimaginative, generic product. Carhart detested "burocracies," whatever their stripe.

In his imagination, and also with Vee and their Forest Service friends, Carhart kept revisiting both the (increasingly mythical) Trappers Lake of 1919 and the actual lake as it evolved over the years under Forest Service administration. The orthodox story is that a Moses-like Carhart descended from on high, bearing the wilderness commandment inscribed on a tablet of stone. And so Trappers Lake somehow became the "cradle of wilderness," with the Forest Service naming the trail around the lake after Carhart in 1985.[14] The real story is different, although not without prophetic resonance. As he recedes in time and grows to biblical proportions, Carhart resembles the prophet Elijah much more than the lawgiver Moses.

Carhart returned to Denver from Trappers Lake and recommended to Carl Stahl that it be preserved rather than developed. His recommendations threatened so many fiefdoms within the Forest Service, though, that actual implementation, however imperfect, took many years.[15] Carhart spent the next half century or so harrying the Forest Service about Trappers Lake, calling attention to the chronically substandard condition of the resort, as well as of its parking, camping, and sanitation conditions, and formally objecting as late as 1965 to Regional Forester Dave Nordwall's plans for expanding the parking lot and campground. After four singled-spaced pages of fulminations, he finally ended his letter to Nordwall, showing that he still vividly recalled the lake's mountainous setting: "That's all, Dave. This is my last comment on Trappers. If the people want a chair lift to the top of Amphitheatre Mountain, and a two-hump camel concession to take them to the top of Shingle Peak, and you figure the USFS [U.S. Forest Service] should meet this 'demand,' you issue the permits. I'll not lift my voice."[16] But he did continue to lift his voice, in the 1970s cajoling some well-meaning Forest Service historians into paying him to record his memories of what had happened at Trappers Lake in 1919.

Meanwhile, the "burocracy" took its sweet time. Four of the six cabins that were at the lake in 1919 remained standing until 1929, when the Forest Service burned them down, leaving two to molder on into the twenty-first century, when the Big Fish Fire consumed everything. Jealous of its prerogatives in the face of criticism from the National Park Service and a nascent Wilderness Society, the Forest Service administratively declared the Flat Tops a "primitive area" on March 5, 1932. This declaration, however, specifically withdrew from "primitive" Trappers Lake and all the lands surrounding it for a quarter of a mile: a total of 1,160 acres. The reason? The "natural dam." On April 4, 1927, while the Forest Service dallied, the Bureau of Reclamation preemptively selected Trappers Lake as a potential hydropower and water storage site, pointing to some easily engineered "improvements" to the outlet. It took to 1964 for the Bureau of Reclamation to decide that Trappers Lake leaked too much to qualify as a storage site. Designation as official wilderness did not follow until 1975. Well aware of the Bureau of Reclamation's zeal and the Forest Service's deviousness, Carhart followed this grim game with bemused disgust.[17]

WE POETS IN OUR YOUTH BEGIN IN GLADNESS
BUT THEREOF COME IN THE END DESPONDENCY AND MADNESS

Ten years after his experience at Trappers Lake, Carhart was still wrestling with its hold on him, much like one of his four-legged renegades struggling in the wolfer's trap. Mary Hunter Austin told him to throw government reports into the fire and listen to his gods.[18]

It was Carhart's ambition to write about inhabited wilderness poetically, the way Mary Austin thought he should. But would that writing be fact or fiction? Later in life, as his artistic talent blossomed, Carhart found one solution to this "or" in his historical novels. Other solutions appeared in his boys' books and his sportsmen's books. As an old man, Carhart desperately wanted his story told. He felt his contributions to conservation remained chronically undervalued. Given such vanity and personal twists, it is not surprising that Carhart warily approached the baited wolfer trap of fact, just as Austin said he should. He was an artful dodger who wrote and rewrote his personal history.

Let us start at the end and consider the twilight debut of Old Man Colby. In 1974, when Carhart was eighty-two, there appeared in his official, Forest Service–commissioned history of his time at Trappers Lake a garrulous Civil War veteran who waylaid visitors plodding along the fishermen's trails around the lake—trails slated to become a road. Carhart, a future master fisherman, had been so busy in that summer of 1919 that he had not yet wet a line in trout country. A fisher of men, like Saints Peter and Paul, Colby talked to the credulous young Carhart about the profound simplicity of fishing, giving the Iowa bass fisherman advice about fly patterns for the Colorado River cutthroat. Only two were needed to catch big trout at Trappers Lake: the #10 Royal Coachman and the Grey Hackle Peacock.

This old-young scene occurred along the trail leading from Old Man Colby's cabin to the lake. Immediately after this encounter, Carhart wrote in 1974, he had the kind of threshold experience familiar from British Romantic poetry and codified in Victorian aesthetics. This was the kind of "halt, traveler" moment of enlightenment that animates literary history from Saint Augustine to Wordsworth (another lake poet) to Yeats to the present.[19]

What "really" happened to Carhart at Trappers Lake in 1919? The rational Carhart was refining his watershed approach to land-use planning by adding the concept of zoning by use. However, at Trappers Lake he had an experience that defied Forest Service demands for the analytical, the sequenced, and the pragmatic. Students of the sublime know that some experiences are simply ineffable—leaps of faith, beyond words—and so we who wish to appreciate Carhart should warily follow historicity as far as we can while not deceiving ourselves about narrowing the gap between facts and imagination. Rather than re-fight old wilderness paternity battles, it seems better to consider Carhart's many revisions in the context of his development as an imaginative writer. Carhart's colleague Aldo Leopold never openly became a fiction writer, although toward the end of his life he was not above tampering with the facts to adorn his morality tales about wolves and wilderness.[20]

Old Man Colby stands at the top of the White River watershed at Trappe Lake. Long and winding is the river of traps that leads from the original 191᷍ experience to the 1974 Old Man Colby version. Here, in rough chronological order, are Carhart's versions of his experience at Trappers Lake.

1919—MEMO FOR MR. LEOPOLD

Carl Stahl's counterpart in District 3 was Aldo Leopold. Leopold had just rejoined the Forest Service after an unsuccessful stint with the Albuquerque Chamber of Commerce, and his stature within his district may not yet have been firm. Stahl circulated Carhart's unusual recommendations in late fall of 1919 throughout all the Forest Service districts. Carhart's thinking caught Leopold's attention, and Leopold was soon on the train north from Albuquerque. Leopold had been forest supervisor on the Carson National Forest in northern New Mexico, so along with his own emerging views about wilderness and wolves, he shared with Stahl and Carhart an interest in the Sangre de Cristos, which stretch from Salida in Colorado south to Santa Fe, New Mexico.

The three men met in Denver on December 6, 1919, for a daylong conference. Knowing nothing could happen in the Forest Service without an official memo of record, Stahl and Leopold arranged for their junior colleague to write a summary account.[21] Leopold was familiar to his Forest Service colleagues as a writer, especially through internal publications, so it seems odd that he did not write this memo himself. Whatever the case, authorship fell to Carhart, who produced a four-page "Memorandum for Mr. Leopold, District 3" on December 10.

Carhart first posed a rhetorical question: "How far shall the Forest Service carry or allow to be carried man made improvements in scenic territories, and whether there is not a definite point where all such developments, with the exception of perhaps lines of travel and necessary sign boards, shall stop." In answer to his own question, after lamenting the passing of the frontier, Carhart wrote in cadences reminiscent of the mature Leopold's polished, balanced prose: "There is a limit to the number of lakes in existence; there is a limit to the mountainous areas of the world; and . . . there are portions of natural scenic beauty which are God made, and . . . which of a right should be the property of all people."

Carhart mentioned Paul Rainey (a sportsman he had met at Trappers Lake) and Theodore Roosevelt as examples of those who crave "undeveloped country." Then he laid out his personal contribution, the zoning approach to comprehensive, watershed-wide planning for recreation: "There is no question in my mind but that there is a definite point in different types of country where man made structures should be stopped."

Carhart asked whether the Forest Service should define these stopping points and preserve them on its own initiative. He stressed the need for immediate attention to the problem, concluding: "[T]he question of how best to do this is perhaps the real question, rather than shall it be done." In this part of the memo, Carhart asked disingenuously whether the Forest Service should consider working with land-use professionals, such as landscape architects, outside federal agencies.[22]

1920—SWEETWATER

Apparently pleased with Carhart's summary of their meeting with Leopold, Stahl next asked him to apply the same concepts to Trappers Lake.[23] Carhart wrote: "There are a number of places with scenic values of such great worth that they are rightfully [the] property of all people. They should be preserved for all time for the people of the Nation and the world. Trappers Lake is unquestionably a candidate for that classification. . . . If Trappers Lake is in or anywhere near in the class of superlatives, it should not have any cabins or hotels intruding in the lake basin."

He added, citing his own experience from the fall of 1919, that Trappers Lake was such a "smashing climax" that "if it were continually in view . . . the very intensity of it would make it displeasing to the individual." As a solution, Carhart called for an answer typical of his thinking about inhabited wilderness—placing summer homes out of sight but within easy walking distance of the lake, leaving the lakeshore for all to enjoy.[24]

The next step in the chain of command included Assistant District Forester Fred Morrell. Encouraged by Stahl, Carhart approached Morrell and District Forester Allen Peck with an eleven-page memo designed to introduce them to the lake and to elaborate on his plans for its development.[25] Neither man had seen Trappers Lake, so Carhart described it for them and their superiors. He advocated excluding from the shore of the lake "all man made buildings with perhaps the exception of one publicly owned building such as the Fish Hatchery from the immediate lake basin." As at Squirrel Creek on the San Isabel, the populist Carhart suggested substituting for some or all of the summer cabins "a good large public camp" along the stream below the outlet of the lake.

Carhart had found concessionaire Scott Teague's "shack-like tent houses" aesthetically offensive. His original mission at Trappers Lake had been to survey sites for more than enough summer homes to overwhelm the lake's ability to deal with human waste. His superiors never seemed to have thought of such impacts, so it was up to Carhart, bacteriologist and Beauty Doctor, to emphasize the reality of poorly planned recreation development at the head of a key watershed. Even more offensive were the existing sanitary facilities. The more he thought about limiting development at Trappers Lake, the more Carhart found that his rapidly developing new ideas about zoning for "wild lands" were consistent with the Forest Service's original mandate to manage for healthy watersheds, beginning with the most basic water quality issues. Perhaps Carhart even knew the lake's early Ute name: Sweetwater. He was certainly aware that the lake is the North Fork of the headwaters of the White River (a major tributary of the Colorado River) and that the White River National Forest is, like the San Isabel, first and foremost a watershed forest.

Carhart's prescient ability to think in terms of entire watersheds would distinguish the rest of his career at least as much as his ideas about zoning public lands. Years later, when he was writing his guidebook to Colorado and again when he was in charge of reintroducing beaver to Colorado's trapped-out, cow-burned watersheds, Carhart would remember the furry origins of the name Trappers Lake.[26]

In 1919, thanks to the automobile and ambitious road building, more and more people could access public lands. Carhart put his developing skills as a writer to graphic use:

> The worst condition in the camp was with reference to the provision of human offal. The privies supplied were indescribable. There was no attempt to keep them flyproof nor adequately house the seats. The construction was a mere board with holes in it placed over a pit and around this was a structure made of poles and gunny sacking with some building paper for the roof and sacking for a door. One of these dilapidated things was designed to serve the entire camp. As a result many of the men took to the woods. At one point I counted at one time eighteen stools of human feces within less than 150 feet of the lake and so situated that they would have been washed directly into the lake by a hard rain fall. The water of the lake and outlet stream is used for domestic purposes. The guests of the camp could not be blamed for using the great outdoors when the privy supplied was so filthy and inadequate.[27]

In an undated series of notes pinned to these memos, Carhart claimed that Morrell and Stahl had already approved his plans. In his retaliatory note to Peck, Morrell quickly rose to the bait: "I think Mr. Carhart has unconsciously overstated my agreement. I felt that homes should be always screened from the lake, but not certainly out of sight so that the dweller could not get a view except by leaving his premises."[28] In spite of such reservations, Peck's reply expressed tentative approval of Carhart's plans, leaving the junior recreation engineer in a jubilant mood as he prepared for a 1920 field season that would send him south again to the San Isabel.

None of Carhart's dreams for Trappers Lake could come to pass without sufficient funding—and without passing through the proper chain of command. After the 1920 field season, Peck asked Carhart to compose a memo to the new chief of the Forest Service, William Greeley, about the dilemmas White River National Forest Supervisor James Blair faced with regard to Trappers Lake.[29] The officialese may seem dry, and it is certainly lengthy, but Peck had to make the case to Congress for money to fund Carhart's plans. He and Carhart also had to convince Edward A. Sherman and the skeptical Leon Kneipp. One can sense everywhere the spirited presence of the recreation engineer:

> Supervisor Blair spoke of the desirability of building a trail or road. In my opinion, the best plan would be to end the automobile road some little distance from and out of sight of the lake, and then build a trail around the lake just inside the timber, with spurs running out to the various points where a person can step out now and then to get a view from the water's edge. Blair spoke of the pressure which is being brought to bear on him by people who desire summer sites at Trappers Lake. He seems to think that under the present plans, it will be necessary to wait for a couple of years before he can begin issuing permits: since he tells me that it would take a full season's work or more to make a complete survey of all the sites.
>
> It is easy to give people the locations they wish at this stage of development, but, if this course is followed, it will ruin any opportunity for a complete and adequate artistic development of this lake. In order to hasten this work and to eliminate the rather caustic criticism of our delay, and as early as possible put this land into good shape for the particular use to which it is so well fitted—recreation—there should be an allotment for study and direction of development here of not less than $600 during the fiscal year of 1922.
>
> The Recreation Engineer spent four weeks in this region on preliminary study during 1919, and the general policies regarding the protection of the scenic beauty of this region are well fixed. There is a general scheme of development which needs further study and work to make it operative.
>
> However, it is well settled that there should be a trail out from the basin of Trappers Lake to the top of Amphitheatre Mountain and to Wall Lake and return. . . . With proper plans in existence for the summer home and hotel use of this lake, private investments would probably total not less than $12,000 in the first two years, and in order to make the regional wholly usable after this investment has been made, it will be necessary to start this trail work and follow it up with other trail work and camp developments at a later date.[30]

Simultaneously, in a series of articles for *American Forestry* that he must have written during the winter of 1919–1920, Carhart shared with his readers a scene at Trappers Lake involving an early version of 1974's Old Man Colby: a pipe-smoking character he called "the Traveler":

> Purple-gray shadows crept into the lake basin. Dusk's domain was invading the land that a moment since had been gorgeous with the flash of the sun's rays the instant before he climbed down behind Marvine peak. In silence the Traveler and I sat while he smoked his pipe and dreamily watched deep black shadows come up out of the depths of the lake to hide under the over-hanging spruce trees until next day's sun should drive them back to watery fastnesses behind deep reefs in the lake.[31]

Not lost in Carhart's poetic prose was another point the Traveler made about watchable wildlife. In this same article, Carhart put a $500 value on the experience of sighting bighorn sheep in their native habitat at Trappers Lake.

1922—"BUROCRACY"

Carhart's next comments on Trappers Lake came in November 1922, when he was preparing to quit the Forest Service in despair over what he would later call "too much burocracy." His parting-shot–style memo noted that the issue had deteriorated from aesthetics to logistics. Should the highway encircle the lake or just access it?

> It is inevitable that some people with selfish motives will try to force this road around the lake so that they may have their own individual wishes gratified. Such a forgery of the road would be a decided calamity. . . . If this road must be pushed on any further it should if possible swing to the westward and if these people must have a lake to look upon from a highway, it may be possible to bring it to Big Fish Lake where the scenic qualities are not so high as at Trappers Lake.[32]

1927—MURDERED IN ONE BREATH

Like Al Hamel, Fred Morrell maintained his friendship with Carhart when Morrell moved north from Colorado to Minnesota, where he became district forester for the newly constituted Northern District, which included Hamel's Superior National Forest. Recalling their days together in Denver, Morrell asked Carhart for input on road issues, knowing Carhart was involved as a private citizen in the fight over the Boundary Waters Canoe Area.[33] Carhart replied:

> I assure you one of my virtues, which some other people I am sure think are flaring faults, is a tendency to be what might be called non-conformist. So

you may find my stuff a little off the usual beaten path. The recreative value
of that lake [Trappers Lake] lies in its wilderness soul which would be mur-
dered in one breath if the road were to encircle it and bring tincanners and
cottages to litter the shore. There is something in the old man that is within
us that demands such restful escape from the squirrel cage of modern city
life and when we bring all of the flivver and jazz stuff of the city into such a
setting it destroys the very thing we go after.[34]

1932—PRESERVE IT IN ITS UNSCARRED BEAUTY

Carhart's next "say" was in his guidebook to Colorado,[35] where he introduced
Trappers Lake by sympathetically portraying the Ute Indians, to whom Trappers
Lake was (and is) a sacred site.[36] He continued:

> The road up the north fork of the White River reaches within three-eighths
> of a mile of Trappers Lake. Oliver P. Wiggans, who came west with Kit
> Carson, was the first white man to see this lake. It was alive with beaver.
> Elk were everywhere and unafraid.
>
> It was laborious work to reach Trappers Lake then; now, by highway
> and motor, it takes but a few hours; yet it is still much as it was in the early
> days. A few years ago an attempt was made to build a road around it and
> give over its shores to private summer homes. But the U.S. Forest Service
> with rare foresight realized that this would ruin its finest charms and
> stopped the road just short of the lake. Trappers is a lake well worth every
> ounce of protection to preserve it in its unscarred beauty.
>
> This White River Plateau is pack territory. This is where President
> Roosevelt hunted big game years ago. A trail up over the "tops" [Flat Tops]
> from Trappers leads to Marvine Lakes, the south fork of the White, by a
> number of high lakes; or another branch takes you to the Derby Lakes, one
> of the wildest of all sections of Colorado.
>
> My trail to the Flat Tops came in 1919. For about a month we were
> camped at the lower end of the lake. At that time, Paul Rainey, famous
> African hunter, and his party were at this camp with a pack of hounds hunt-
> ing bear.
>
> Trappers is as much of a scenic climax as that last blaring theme of the
> Pilgrim's Chorus is a climax of music. Do not miss Trappers Lake. It is one
> of Colorado's finest, probably the equal of any lake in the world.[37]

Carhart's second trip into the Flat Tops had been in 1928, when he and
Wallace Hutchinson revisited Trappers Lake with their wives on a long horseback trip that took them up and over from the Marvine side (by way of the
South Fork of the White River) of the Flat Tops to Trappers. At the end of his
1932 guidebook, although he substituted coyotes for wolves, Carhart portrayed

his understanding of a wilderness trip: "[A] coyote choir yapped crazily, suddenly hushed their chorus as though echoes of their own yammering flung back, had scared them, then started again their wild, blood-stirring chant of back country; of wilderness."[38]

Carhart went on to tell his readers what they would need to bring on a real pack trip to Trappers Lake—including a list specifically for women: "I've been on all kinds of pack trips and my idea is to enjoy the trip; not make it an ordeal. And do it with a minimum of comforts."[39] Carhart "completed" his guidebook by admitting he could not complete it, just as he could never complete his account of what happened to him at Trappers Lake in 1919.

> Far beyond the rim of the cañon gouged through this tableland, is cow country, or the ragged unwashed sanctuary where men can hide from super-civilization and rediscover themselves.
>
> Trails are there; trails that reach beyond the end of today's last tenuous highway that links you back to [the] city.
>
> You find liberty, my friend, if you follow the trail past that rainbow on the ridge. No, I realize now, I cannot tell you of this country. The winds tell me tales as I ride Colorado's far trails. But what they whisper to me is sacred. They have cast a spell on my vocabulary. I try to tell you what they say but their message to you is for you alone. These songs are lost for all time if you do not catch them as they are sung.
>
> It's West. And it is almost untouched West. In some spots there is still pioneering, even exploring to do. And in it all there is a rich empire awaiting the day when a greater population will demand resources locked away in this great northwest Colorado empire. This was frontier. . . . It was unconquered wilderness. . . . It is still unconquered West; a true frontier.[40]

1950—ONE FISH PER MINUTE

Carhart's next rendition of conditions at Trappers Lake in 1919 came in a casual aside in his book *Fishing in the West*. The tone is one of camaraderie with Rainey and McFadden. According to this version, young Carhart in 1919 was doing as much fishing as he was surveying and talking. As fish stories go, this is an interesting one, for it explains why early game managers used Trappers Lake as an egg source for Colorado River cutthroat trout. McFadden bet Rainey he could catch a fish per minute. McFadden lost, getting only fifty-one in an hour, but that was only because the weather changed. Carhart described the drop-off shelf at Trappers that characterizes so many glacial lakes. Cast beyond that steep shelf, every angler learns, and you will catch fish. But he never mentioned wilderness here, saying only that the road ended four miles below the lake in those days.[41]

1955—"AREN'T YOU A BIT ASHAMED OF WHAT YOU'RE DOING?"

In *Timber in Your Life*, in a chapter titled "With No Ax Swinging," Carhart wrote:[42]

Three men—Carl J. Stahl, Paul Rainey and William McFadden—deserve credit for their part in this—the first actual studied application of protected wilderness as such within the national forests.

Scott Teague, a pioneer dude wrangler, had set up a tent camp with log sidewalls right in the center of the great view from the outlet of the lake. His guests were brought in from the end of a rough wagon road several miles down the north fork of the White River, which has its source in Trappers Lake.

I found bed and board at Teague's camp, and began surveying the spruce-covered benchland between the lake and the tapestry-covered cliffs surrounding that lovely basin. At the camp were two sportsmen, William McFadden, from Oklahoma, and Paul Rainey, who brought back the first wild animal movies from Africa. They observed the project on which I was working, but held their peace for a week or more.

As I roughed out the survey on which access roads would be located and cottage lots plotted, I began to feel uneasy. The place was getting a strange hold on me. I experienced a quality of peace, exhilaration at being a part of it. The spirit and values of wilderness would be ruptured and rent when the lake was girdled with little buildings, autos rambled back and forth on a shoreline road and motor boats chattered across the lake. I liked Trappers without these distractions.

But I had orders; to draw plans for just such a use of this basin.

The three of us were sitting in one of the tents the night Rainey and McFadden jumped me.

"Aren't you a bit ashamed of what you're doing?" one of them slapped me with that blunt question.

They gave me no moment to get set for their attack.

"There are a hundred or more lakes in this region anyone can reach by auto," said McFadden. "Only a few left not overrun with cars, cottages and tin-can tourists. Can't you fellows leave one lake unmolested?"

"Keep Trappers as it is," put in Rainey. "Keep it for people willing to make a little effort to enjoy a place like this. You'll ruin it if you let a flock of shacks come in here!"

There was another side to the argument, and I presented it; the hours of pleasure the cottagers would find here, the great numbers of them privileged to dwell on the lake and observe all its moods and tempers.

"They'll not find what they think they want with all the cabins, cars, and the motor boats coming in," declared Rainey. "It will be just like dozens of other places over-run by vacationers."

"Trappers is priceless, don't mess it up," McFadden demanded.

It was midnight before that session adjourned. I argued, but they fiercely countered my points. The nebulous feeling of unrest that had haunted me, the feeling of something of high worth being jeopardized by the summer home project, became a solid conviction that evening. That conviction grew as I prowled spruce thickets along the lake, listened to the singing of brooks racing to find rest in Trappers, watched the changing lights on the lake and the cliffs that were streaked with the soft, glowing colors of a Persian rug.

I finished the survey as directed. A month later I laid the topographic sketches before Carl Stahl.

"There's our data; we can lay out lots and roads on those sheets," I reported. "But I'm against the scheme—the whole business. Against a lot of cabins along the lakeshore, the roads, that circle highways that would put Trappers on a tourist merry-go-round."

Carl Stahl listened as I presented the case for preserving Trappers Lake and its basin in its natural state. He was an old-timer in the Forest Service. I hadn't worked with him long enough at that time to fully realize his fierce love of the outdoors. He sat with steady, blue eyes boring at me, no flicker of what his thoughts might be showing in his expression.

"What sort of use do you propose at Trappers?" His query was flat and challenging.

"Anyone capable of taking the auto trip to the lake can walk a quarter of a mile," I stated. "There's a good turn-around and campground that distance below the lake. Stop the highway at that point. Put in fireplaces, safe water supply, toilets, garbage pits, maybe some picnic tables there. Plan a resort development a few hundred yards down the new road for those who don't want to camp. Let the summer home builders have sites at other places. Keep Trappers for those who will walk the little distance from the turn-around— so they'll come up to that smashing view from the outlet and find all the rest of the natural beauty there as God made it.

"Look," I persisted, as Stahl said nothing, his eyes probing, "unless we save some places like this where people can really escape to the fullest the grind of routine living, we're just not going to have any such outdoor sanctuaries left. Trappers is one such area we should protect."

Probably Stahl was sitting there remembering the host of places he had known that had been filled with solitude but were now being overrun with "development." He didn't speak for several long moments.

Finally he said rather sharply, "Maybe you've got something. Let's think it over."

There was no fanfare; no press releases announcing a new idea in action. Carl Stahl simply moved quietly after he'd "thought it over"; perhaps he had discussed this shift in policy with other Regional Office men who also were infused with a deep love of the hushed places. The "circle trip" road that would have put the lake on a tourist route, and the cottage settlement were abandoned quietly. The campground and turn-around and the resort were installed. The temporary tent camp on the lake was moved out after it had had reasonable time to pay a profit to the operator.

We had no name for this policy at that moment. It was, however, a recognition of the fact that if sanctuaries of natural wilderness were preserved they would achieve their greatest usefulness to human beings as places of complete escape from high-velocity living. Not as many people might reach these areas, but those who did would realize greater value per hour if the original, peaceful, wild country surrounded them.

That incident was the prelude to a much larger, more positive application of the policy which recognizes special possibilities for popular use of the wilderness.[43]

1964—A PIONEERING OFFICIAL OF THE FOREST SERVICE

In a letter about the Wilderness Bill to New Mexico senator Clinton Anderson,[44] Carhart retold the familiar Trappers Lake story, casually dropping a remark that an assistant had accompanied him at Trappers Lake as he worked on the topographic maps. This person has never been identified. Carhart also told Anderson more about Carl Stahl, who had been a "high level assistant to executives in U.S. Steel, had contracted tuberculosis, had come west to become a pioneering official of the Forest Service."

1965–1972: DONALD BALDWIN

In 1972, Donald Baldwin's *The Quiet Revolution* appeared posthumously.[45] As a graduate student at the University of Denver, Baldwin had befriended Carhart and written a 1965 Ph.D. dissertation on the wilderness concept. Baldwin was a dream come true for Carhart. He used the Conservation Collection at the Denver Public Library exactly as Carhart wished: to further the causes of conservation and of Carhart. Baldwin was a bright and feisty scholar with a wry sense of humor. His untimely death robbed Carhart of the son he and Vee never had.

Baldwin's close relationship with Carhart may help shed light on a few of the mysteries that enshroud Trappers Lake. Baldwin had a broad understanding of the history of the White River watershed. He even planned to write a book about the larger subject of watersheds once he was finished with the subset of wilderness issues. Baldwin was not a naive researcher and was certainly not simply Carhart's captive. He was a fervent advocate for wilderness who found himself in the midst of an often unseemly post–Wilderness Act struggle, in which various parties tried to take credit for the beginnings of the concept of wilderness. Baldwin recognized that political victory in the wilderness wars also meant the end of a more or less united front among wilderness lovers. A kindly man, he could not stand by as Carhart's enemies unleashed the snarling dogs of nastiness, which were free to snap at heretics and then to fight among themselves over the question of who deserved credit. Carhart's own pettiness and his reticence about the final bill left Baldwin in an unenviable position.

Baldwin decided to set the record straight. He had been a special investigator for the U.S. Air Force during the Korean War, so he could hitchhike on air force planes to do research in Albuquerque, Washington, D.C., Milwaukee, and Duluth; he could also use records at the Federal Center in Denver. As Carhart said, "He was a man who was thoroughly trained in the methods of securing basic data."[46]

Baldwin and Carhart persuaded former Secretary of Agriculture Orville Freeman to contribute an introduction to Baldwin's book. Freeman told Baldwin: "You will note, I am sure, that I have taken this occasion to set the record straight a bit on some of the things that actually happened during my administration where the Forest Service and wilderness areas are concerned. There has been some cruel and ill-founded criticism of Ed Cliff and the Forest Service in recent years as emotional environmentalism has taken over with a vengeance. Hence, my specific references to Chief Cliff and his administration."[47]

Just before his untimely death, Baldwin wrote to Carhart on the occasion of Carhart's eightieth birthday: "Had I written the Introduction myself I could not have done as well. Mr. Freeman did a fabulous piece of work. I like particularly the last paragraph on page 2 where at last you are given the long-overdue credit for your pioneer role; it's about time that 'a new and authentic hero' emerges." The book is dedicated to the person most worthy of it: Arthur Hawthorne Carhart.[48]

Although Baldwin's book quickly received positive attention from Roderick Nash, it suffered from overstatements in several areas, such as Carhart's role in the Boundary Waters controversy. Had Baldwin lived to defend his views, he would clearly have become a major environmental historian.

1974: I MAY BE THE ONLY ONE STILL ALIVE

After passage of the Wilderness Act in 1964, the Forest Service decided to rewrite its own history, recruiting Carhart to help.[49] By the time a deal could be struck, Carhart had left Colorado for southern California, where he finagled an open-ended contract to deliver this work at some future date. After many false starts, Carhart hired a stenographer, Helen Hoag, to help him. But he could not get beyond 1919. Finally, the perplexed Hoag wrote to the Forest Service historians who were paying her salary: "As is, every time he gets first section, he drops last part and revises first section again."[50] Finally, Carhart produced a short manuscript titled "This Way to Wilderness," which he built on the traditional Romantic metaphor of a walk:

> This is a friendly invitation for you to walk beside me along a trail of memories. Although I traversed this trail a half century ago, recollections of moments, places, and persons along the pathway are vivid and enduring. So, come with me as we stroll through these pages that follow.
>
> Along our main trail are detours and byways where we may loiter or stop. At such points we may become more acquainted with those who were important in the struggle of wilderness as sanctuaries versus fatter pocketbooks of exploiters.
>
> I may be the only one still alive of those in the ranks that, because of our convictions, joined battle against those seeking to make these easy dollars.[51]

Perhaps with tongue in cheek, Carhart said, "Memories that are 51 years old cannot be accepted as flawless."[52] Flawless or not, Carhart remembered that some of those with claims for sites had already moved into finished cabins around the lake. One was Jo Neal, president of the First National Bank in Meeker—the town nearest the lake—and also president of the Colorado Livestock Association. Carhart recalled that some wealthy Denverites, such as the Bosworths, had also established themselves at the lake.

As he now recalled, a reluctant young Carhart checked out a plane-table surveying kit and an alidade telescope (suitable for rough topography) and took the train to Yampa. From there, it was eighteen miles by horse to Trappers Lake. Carhart described Teague's special use permit and his ramshackle resort in detail, recalling that it was located on the moraine below the lake's outlet. At this point Old Man Colby appeared, and then:

> Here, as I loafed along the trail, was a place, a moment, when one could explore his thoughts. In the hour, these surroundings, my thoughts were troubled.
>
> Suddenly a strange sibilance filled the basin. I halted, I listened. The soft eerie whispers came clearly through the sun drenched air. I glanced in all directions, hoping to discover their source. I failed.
>
> Silence returned quickly.
>
> Abruptly the strange sound returned, increased, dimmed, and in a moment was gone.
>
> The little noises of undisturbed wilderness came trooping back. A wayward breeze lisped among the needled twigs of lakeside spruce and fir trees. The lap-lap of pigmy waves ruffled along the lake's shoreline. A gray squirrel scolded me for intruding.

As I have looked back along many trails, I recognize that incident at Trappers Lake was in truth a moment when I stepped across a threshold.

I discovered true wilderness and reached the conviction that without the sanctuary found in our wildlands, without the experience of living as a part of it, this nation might perish from the earth. That statement I mean literally, and I ask you to continue along with me until, together, we face stark truths of our need for protecting enough physical wilderness to supply the life of the nation, community, individual, all three.[53]

A long characterization follows of a man in the mold of Carhart's much-admired Teddy Roosevelt, Paul Rainey.[54] Rainey had just returned from Africa, where he had trained a pack of dogs to track lions and other African cats. He had brought back a fearless wirehaired terrier named Frisky from that pack, and Frisky was with him at Trappers. Teague had a two-year-old bear cub in camp, tethered to a chain fifty to seventy feet long. Frisky and the cub played during interludes when Rainey was not using the cub to train sixty-six pure-bred hounds to follow bear scent until they treed their prey.

Like Leopold, Carhart was often simply a man of his times. Both men loved to hunt. And, also like Leopold, Carhart sometimes soared above his beginnings into the brave new world of wilderness.

NOTES

1. Arthur Carhart, *Colorado: History, Geology, Legend* (New York: Coward-McCann, 1932).

2. http://wildlife.state.co.us/NR/rdonlyres/4A73E0F5-B864-4E74-B8C0-/0/TrapperMgmtPlan3b.pdf.

3. David Worster, Wild, Tame, and Free: Comparing Canadian and American Views of Nature," in Ken Coates and John Findlay, eds., *On Brotherly Terms: Canadian-American Relations West of the Rockies* (Seattle: University of Washington Press, 2002).

4. Aldo Leopold, *A Sand County Almanac* (New York: Oxford University Press, 1966), 138.

5. See Michael Robinson, *Predatory Bureaucracy* (Boulder: University Press of Colorado, 2005), 403, n. 31, for a review of the status of the Colorado wolf population in 1920. District 2 Forester Smith Riley collaborated with the Bureau of Biological Survey's extermination efforts.

6. Donald Baldwin and Roderick Nash are examples of those who have tried.

7. Arthur Carhart, *Colorado: History, Geology, Legend* (New York: Coward-McCann, 1932), 282.

8. I thank Professor Andrew Gulliford of Fort Lewis College for one of the best guesses about the nature of Carhart's experience. The lake was sacred to the Utes, and a Ute spirit visited Carhart there in a form he later described as "the voice of the

wilderness." Gulliford believes Carhart never acknowledged this visitation for reasons of his own. See Andrew Gulliford, *Sacred Objects and Sacred Places: Preserving Tribal Traditions* (Boulder: University Press of Colorado, 2002).

9. Wallace Stegner, *Angle of Repose* (New York: Penguin, 1971). Stegner's hero, Lyman Ward, fails at dam building. Then the Bureau of Reclamation shows him how to build a dam. Like Carhart, Stegner was Iowa-born. He received his Ph.D. from the University of Iowa. Stegner got caught in a snare of his own making when heirs of Mary Hallock Foote claimed he had fictionalized the facts of her letters without acknowledging their source.

10. Arthur Carhart, *Timber in Your Life* (Philadelphia: Lippincott, 1955), 137.

11. I quote long passages to give readers direct access to Carhart's words about wilderness. Many of these sources are out of print or inaccessible. They appear here as a convenience to ordinary readers who may wish to ponder the original texts.

12. Public Law 63-293, approved March 4, 1915.

13. My grandfather, George Wolf, was an (ultimately unsuccessful) applicant for one of these ninety-nine-year leases. As with most land giveaways, this one was subject to abuses. Politicians and powerbrokers moved to the head of the line.

14. See, for example, the Web site for Colorado Wilderness: http://www.coloradowilderness.com/wildact.html. There are photos on this Web site, possibly from the 1880s, of extensive buildings at the outlet of Trappers Lake.

15. Carhart's role in the evolution of the wilderness concept remained controversial within the Forest Service and its satellite organizations. Retired Region 2 assistant regional forester Fred Johnson lived a block from Carhart on Eudora Street in Park Hill. He based his support for Carhart's pioneering role in wilderness work on his official Forest Service field diary. In a 1958 letter to Carhart, Johnson reminded him that the Forest Service had finally burned the shacks at Trappers Lake in 1929.

16. Letter from Carhart to Regional Forester Nordwall, September 6, 1965, Carhart Collection, Denver Public Library (hereafter CC, DPL).

17. My personal introduction to Trappers Lake came on Bureau of Reclamation reconnaissance missions with my father during the late 1950s and early 1960s. By then, Trappers was so easily accessible that it was fished out. We went over the Flat Tops for better fishing in the Marvine watershed.

18. Letter from Austin to Carhart, September 23, 1930, CC, DPL. See p. 174.

19. See Tom Wolf, "Literary Tradition on a Walk in Colorado's Sangre de Cristo Mountains," *The Walking Magazine* (Spring 1986). See also Jeffrey Robinson, *The Walk* (Norman: University of Oklahoma Press, 1989). Lovers of poetry will recognize in Old Man Colby Wordsworth's Leech Gatherer from his 1802 poem "Resolution and Independence."

20. As William deBuys shows, Leopold manipulated the chronology of his famous encounter in which he watched "the green fire die" in the eyes of a wolf he had just shot. See William deBuys, "Uncle Aldo: A Legacy of Learning about Learning" (University of New Mexico School of Architecture and Planning: John Gaw Meem Lecture Series/ Annual Aldo Leopold Lecture), March 9, 2004. See also Michael Robinson's discussion of Leopold's "challenge of fang against bullet" in *Predatory Bureaucracy*, 102.

21. Carhart and Leopold had little contact after this meeting. The next time Leopold appeared in Carhart's world, it was related to controversies around the Boundary Waters in 1926, after Leopold had left the West and settled in Wisconsin. See Aldo Leopold, "Report on D-1 Trip June 15–July 23, 1926. Aldo Leopold, Associate Director, Forest Products Laboratory," CC, DPL. It seems probable that Al Hamel, supervisor of the Superior National Forest, asked Leopold for this nineteen-page review. On pp. 7–8, Leopold dances around the issues that involved Carhart and Hamel. The point Leopold makes is about using the waterways to drive logs: "Driving wastes not only timber, but other forest values. It deteriorates the recreational value of streams, especially where splash dams are used. It means dams on lakes and partial to complete deterioration of their recreational value. Streams and lakes are the heart of any country, and their sacrifice, even for the sake of getting out timber, is ultimately a matter of consequence. This region has not yet felt the effects of crowding in the use of recreational resources. . . . Possibly this question strikes very near the heart of our present problem. Possibly the inevitable pre-occupation of products men with the immediate job of analyzing economic conditions prevents us from thinking far ahead in terms of management plans." Leopold was in Colorado Springs in 1939 and in Colorado again in 1941, but he and Carhart did not meet. Leopold's father had wanted him to go to Ames, and his mother wanted him to go to Yale. His mother prevailed.

22. Arthur Carhart, "Memorandum for Mr. Leopold, District 3," December 10, 1919, CC, DPL.

23. Memorandum (L Uses) from Stahl to Leopold, White River, District 2, USFS, Denver, Colorado, February 1, 1920, CC, DPL.

24. Ibid.

25. Carhart Memorandum (L Uses), White River, District 2, USFS, Denver, Colorado, April 7, 1920, CC, DPL.

26. Early trappers reported taking 800 beaver from the lake and the rest of the watershed in 1856–1858. See Baldwin's note 22 on p. 253 of *The Quiet Revolution: Grass Roots of Today's Wilderness Preservation Movement* (Boulder: Pruett, 1972).

27. Carhart Memorandum (L Uses).

28. Memorandum from Morrell to Peck, April 9, 1920, CC, DPL.

29. December 6, 1920, memo over Peck's signature but obviously written by Carhart, CC, DPL.

30. Ibid.

31. Carhart, "Live Game and Forest Recreation," *American Forestry* 26 (December 1920):723.

32. Carhart memo, November 22, 1922, CC, DPL. Much of this memo is virtually incoherent.

33. Letter from Morrell to Carhart, February 28, 1927, CC, DPL.

34. Letter from Carhart to Morrell, March 5, 1927, CC, DPL.

35. Carhart, *Colorado*, 264.

36. For a guide to the way historians and others should treat Native American sacred sites, see Gulliford, *Sacred Objects and Sacred Places*.

37. Carhart, *Colorado*, 269–270.

38. Ibid., 271.

39. Ibid., 275.

40. Ibid., 282.

41. Carhart, *Fishing in the West* (New York: Macmillan, 1950), 75–76.

42. Carhart, *Timber in Your Life* (Philadelphia: Lippincott, 1955).

43. Ibid., 144–145.

44. Letter from Carhart to Anderson, January 16, 1964, CC, DPL.

45. Donald Baldwin, "Historical Study of the Western Origin, Application and Development of the Wilderness Concept," Ph.D. dissertation, University of Denver, 1965; Baldwin, *The Quiet Revolution.*

46. Letter from Carhart to Joseph Fisher of Resources for the Future (RFF), March 17, 1969, CC, DPL. At the time, Carhart was also trying to get RFF to hire him to write his wilderness memoirs.

47. Letter from Freeman to Baldwin, August 22, 1972, CC, DPL.

48. Letter from Baldwin to Carhart, September 14, 1972, CC, DPL.

49. On October 13, 1972, Frank Owsley, director, Forest Service History Program, delivered a paper at Yale to the Western History Conference titled "Opportunities in Forest Service Historical Research." He said, "Stirrings of interest in a better organized history effort in the Forest Service began in the 1960's, when Arthur H. Carhart started the Conservation Library, and came to Washington to ask that the Forest Service begin to send papers and documents to the Conservation Library." Out of this cooperation came Carhart's contract to tell his side of the early Forest Service history at Trappers Lake.

50. The correspondence relating to "This Way to Wilderness" is in Box 2:100, CC, DPL.

51. Carhart, "This Way to Wilderness," 11.

52. Ibid.

53. Ibid., 2–3. The best study of this inspiring phenomenon, known as "the correspondent breeze," remains M. H. Abrams, *Natural Supernaturalism* (New York: Norton, 1973).

54. Ibid., 35. Paul Rainey died of a heart attack at age forty-six in 1923. Among his holdings were wetlands in Louisiana that his sister gave to the Audubon Society as a memorial. The 26,000-acre Paul J. Rainey Sanctuary became controversial in the 1950s when oil and gas production started there. By some estimates, the Audubon Society has earned at least $25 million from this development. Has the development damaged the wetlands? For differing views, see Pamela S. Snyder and Jane S. Shaw, "PC Oil Drilling in a Wildlife Refuge," *Wall Street Journal*, September 7, 1995. The Audubon Society's rejoinder can be found on its Web site in a statement dated January 19, 2001: www.audubonsociety.org. As a conservationist who usually worked well with industry interests (and never met a dollar he did not like), Carhart would have relished Audubon's squirming.

CHAPTER FIVE

PLANS MUST BE BIG AND BOLD

You have every reason to feel jubilant over what you have accomplished in launching the recreation associations of the San Isabel. To say that I am more than delighted is putting it mildly.

E. A. SHERMAN TO ARTHUR CARHART, 1920[1]

INTRODUCTION: THE MORAL BENEFITS ARE ALL POSITIVE

After his month or so at Trappers Lake, Carhart returned to Denver and Vee in mid-October 1919. There is no record of his homecoming after such a long absence or of their domestic relations during this period. During this time, however, Ella Carhart started weaving grandmother-in-waiting hints into her letters to Arthur and Vee.

For the time being, there was apparently more exhilarating work: Carhart was writing. In addition to the spate of wilderness-related memos mentioned in earlier chapters, he also wrote an essay for his colleagues titled "Landscape Appreciation." This is the sort of aesthetic effusion Aldo Leopold produced for the edification of his colleagues on the Carson National Forest—the kind of work that must have made Leon Kneipp and his fellow timber beasts guffaw: "Get a good draft working in your nostrils, smell the hot sun on the pine needles, the tangy odor of the sage, the scent of the fire weed in full bloom.

. . . Brush the dust of habit away from your eyes and see the lacery of the pine needles, the vivid coloring of the cliff or wild flower, the majesty of the peaks. In other words, take stock of the world in which you live."[2]

Along with his work on recreation plans for the San Isabel, Carhart spent the rest of the winter writing an influential series of articles (under Wallace Hutchinson's direction) for *American Forestry*. Carhart had little time for writing during the field season, so this series is a good indicator of his state of mind immediately after Trappers Lake. His prosaic side dwelt on sanitation. His poetic side teetered on the perilous passage from aesthetics to morality that is so familiar in Leopold's writing. When Carhart talked about public health, he meant both spiritual and physical health, and he thought of "recreation returns" both in dollar and unquantifiable terms. These pieces appeared throughout 1920. They must have set alarm bells ringing at the National Park Service. Speaking of forest recreation, Carhart said: "The moral benefits are all positive. The individual with any soul cannot live long in the presence of towering mountains or sweeping plains without getting a little of the high moral stand of Nature infused into his being."[3]

The question of competing with the National Park Service for funding always hung fire. Did Sherman and Kneipp really support Carhart strongly enough to champion his requests among so many competing demands? Would Congress fund Carhart's work? Quite naturally for someone who was "writing for his life," Carhart praised the Forest Service for employing landscape architects. The readers and editors of *American Forestry* must have liked his work, for the magazine began to publicize the value of recreational opportunities on the national forests as never before.[4] In the September 1920 edition, Carhart called attention to Squirrel Creek Campground on the San Isabel. Photos celebrated the San Isabel Protection and Recreation Association's (SIPRA's) pioneering work in providing camping for automobile-borne tourists.[5] Carhart detailed the rapid advance of auto-based tourism, and he praised both the National Park Service and the Forest Service for their foresight in accommodating such tourists' needs.[6]

Carhart even advocated consolidation of the recreation resources of the National Park Service and the Forest Service (and states and counties) under the guidance of a commission run by the American Society of Landscape Architects. He pumped the recreation value of both game and nongame species, making his claim for watchable wildlife by drawing on the figure of the Traveler at Trappers Lake.[7] The stage seemed to be set for Sherman to make the case to Congress for funding Carhart's work. Only Leon Kneipp and Stephen Mather stood in the way.

THE CASCADE TRAIL DESERVES SPECIAL MENTION

As he approached the 1920 field season, Carhart was riding tall in the saddle. Perhaps as a sign of his euphoria, Carhart arranged for Vee to spend the summer with him in southern Colorado while he fleshed out the San Isabel Recreation Plan he had begun during the winter. The Carharts left Denver on April 1, 1920. They moved to the pleasant town of Beulah on the east slope of the Wet Mountains, about twenty-five miles west of Pueblo. In those times, the headquarters of the San Isabel National Forest were still farther west in Westcliffe, between the Wet Mountains and the Sangre de Cristos.

Carhart started work in the Wet Mountains, conducting a survey of recreation opportunities on the highest peak in that range, Greenhorn Mountain (13,347 feet). He also needed to be close to Pueblo and the Pueblo Municipal Parks system, where he had arranged for SIPRA to hire Frank Culley to begin work on nearby Squirrel Creek Campground and the Cascade Trail. As Carhart summarized his work in December 1920, "It was thought expedient, and was approved heartily by the Directors of the association, to hire a talented landscape architect to assist the Recreation Engineer." Thinking watershed-wide, he added: "The association eventually intends to interest the citizens of all of the towns of the Arkansas valley."

Carhart was aware that he was breaking new ground. His discussion of Squirrel Creek also mentioned the Cascade Trail: "The need is for short foottrails and lines of hiking traffic to take the people out of the congested area in the floor of the canon [sic]. . . . The Cascade Trail deserves special mention. It is a trail of [a] different type from any that is in existence on any National Forest. It is a recreation trail of the pedestrian class, and, so far as known, the only one which is exclusively developed from this standpoint."[8]

In Beulah, the Carharts first stayed at the Signal Mountain Hotel, then in May they rented a cabin. Toward the end of the field season they moved to Westcliffe, where Carhart could work with Hamel. In her annual September birthday letter to her son, Ella Carhart wrote: "I'm glad to know Vera is with you and that you are both happy." She mentioned a set of dishes she would send along with her son's furniture whenever the young couple was ready, adding, "I think your children will like it."[9]

Carhart and Sherman maintained a personal correspondence. In late September, Carhart reported on his progress to Sherman, who sent this slightly sobering reply: "Your letter of September 28 is extremely interesting both in its showing of actual accomplishment and in its indication of the practically unlimited possibilities for recreational development in the National Forests. At present this work is in the pioneer stage and pioneer development is . . . subject to all of the disappointments and delays which you have experienced. . . . While I do not desire to add to your heavy burden of work, I will appreciate other reports."[10]

In early October 1920, a year after Trappers Lake, Stahl arrived in West-cliffe with a reward for the Carharts: an Indian summer tour of southern Colorado. Stahl's devotion to wild places had a profound effect on the Carharts. The three drove south along the Sangre de Cristo Mountains by way of Gardner and the Huerfano River to Walsenburg, then over La Veta Pass to Conejos in the southern San Luis Valley, near where Zebulon Pike had built his stockade in February 1807.[11] This trip was the Carharts' first exposure to the Indian and Hispanic cultures of southern Colorado and northern New Mexico, including the fascinating cult of the Penitentes.[12] The Carharts would eventually buy property in the area near Coyote, New Mexico, and spend a great deal of creative time there that would lead to friendship with Santa Fe's Mary Hunter Austin, at that time the dean of southwestern writers. Vee developed expertise in Navajo jewelry and blankets. Later, she ran a small business linking artists in New Mexico and buyers in Denver.

The Carharts and Stahl went to the Conejos area to check out Dr. Henry W. Taylor's proposed Conejos Rainbow Trout Lodge.[13] At the camp they ran into Bert Edwards, a Biological Survey predator hunter who headquartered there. Edwards's stories around the campfire introduced Carhart to the real-life drama of exterminating the last wolf in Colorado.[14] Later, Carhart named this old female "the Greenhorn Wolf" after the mountain he had just surveyed—and after Cuerno Verde, the Comanche chief whose exploits seized his imagination.

Their work in Conejos done, Stahl and the Carharts horse-packed for two weeks through the San Juan Mountains and across the Continental Divide before returning to Denver in November 1920. There the Carharts moved back into lodgings in downtown Denver. Arthur spent most of the time until the following April working on the San Isabel Recreation Plan,[15] taking time off for a fateful January trip back to Iowa that would largely determine the rest of his career.

In the meantime, back in Washington, Leon Kneipp replaced Sherman as head of the Branch of Lands and Recreation. One of his first initiatives was to send out a memo directly questioning the assumptions behind Carhart's thinking.[16] Kneipp's strategy was to draw a sharp line between recreational work on the one hand and utilitarian protection/regulation on the other. Whereas Carhart looked at entire watersheds and saw recreation, protection, and regulation as complementing each other, Kneipp looked at budgets and saw competing needs—especially when Congress was generous with money for the extensive

Carhart at Forest Service Camp, 1920. Courtesy, Forest History Society.

road building that was popular on its own terms and that could also be directly related in the public mind to the equally popular missions of fire suppression and predator extermination.

SIPRA AND THE SQUIRREL CREEK RECREATION DISTRICT

During the summer of 1920, Carhart and Culley worked on their showpiece campground in the Wet Mountains. Looking back fifty years later, Carhart astonished Forest Service historian Frank Harmon by claiming that part of Culley's design at Squirrel Creek had actually "tuned" Cascade Falls after the fashion of Italian water-garden designers. Harmon asked Carhart (who may have been pulling the agency's leg) whether Culley "made the water 'shawl' (spread) over rocks on one side of the falls, and 'plunge' free in a small steam into the pool on the other side—instead of having a 'pouring' waterfall. You say 'all falls were *tuned* to make water motion sounds.' Do you mean that he actually diverted or reconstructed the waterfall so as to change the way the water fell from the way he found it naturally?"[17]

Carhart and Culley were not working alone. Responding to the challenge from Denver's tourist industry and to local demand, the city of Pueblo had received 600 acres of state land on the forest boundary at Squirrel Creek near Beulah in 1919. While SIPRA was still in its formative stages in 1919, the Pueblo Commerce Club had taken the lead in providing labor and $1,200 for the project. By early summer of 1919, SIPRA was off and running. And by August 1919, thanks to Wallace Hutchinson's internal selling skills at District 2 headquarters, Chief Forester Henry Graves himself had visited Squirrel Creek Canyon, followed by a luncheon address to the Pueblo Commerce Club. Hutchinson may have written both the chief's speech and the *Pueblo Chieftain's* banner headline: "Pueblo to Get All the Forests She Wants Declares Visiting Head of Forests." Graves told the assembled businessmen how impressed he was with the diversity of plant species at Squirrel Creek. Some botanically literate soul (perhaps Carhart) had adorned the camp with Forest Service signs sporting both the common and scientific names of the tree species.[18] By 1919, Squirrel Creek Canyon already had ten campsites, two shelters, twelve fireplaces, two spring developments, three chemical toilets, three garbage pits, and three footbridges. According to the National Register of Historic Places, "These improvements were the first known campsite improvements placed in the San Isabel National Forest."[19]

By the end of 1920, the city of Pueblo had spent around $8,000 on recreation-related developments at its municipal sites in the watershed. Carhart succeeded in meshing this beginning effort with Culley's SIPRA work on Forest

Service land, helping to open coordinated public access to the jointly planned and managed lands that came to be known as the Squirrel Creek Recreation District.[20] Well aware that his work was pioneering, Carhart set out to make the recreation district a reality. Whether as a city planner or a landscape designer, Carhart tried to see the lay of the land in regional watershed terms, dividing the sometimes arbitrary administrative entity of a national forest into units according to topography and access. Then he linked all elements (such as timber, grazing, fire suppression, transportation, sanitation, recreation, and wildlife) in his watershed-wide plan. Another innovation was to figure out the sources of recreation traffic, then analyze the distribution points for this traffic as it impinged upon the forest. He next designed a network of primary and secondary roads to distribute use evenly and equitably, concentrating recreation in places where scenic and wildlife values were highest and providing for the tent camps, auto camps, lodges, and hotels that would feed sightseers onto recreation trails.

Looking beyond this single recreation district to the entire San Isabel, Carhart developed a firm planner's sense of how to zone the land for distinct uses. As he and Hamel developed their comprehensive plans for the San Isabel, they worked out five levels of human use ranging from Culley's intensive development at Squirrel Creek to wildlands higher up in the watershed, such as those in the towering peaks and glacial lakes above auto-accessible Alvarado Campground in the Sangre de Cristos.

The key was the automobile. At Squirrel Creek, Carhart started with the circulation and dispersion of vehicular and pedestrian traffic. While Culley's efforts progressed on the campsites in Squirrel Creek Canyon, Carhart saw to it that the work on the access road begun in 1919 would continue until it was finally finished in 1922, forming a loop tour along with two other scenic roads appropriate to the relatively gentle terrain of the Wet Mountains.

In the early summer of 1920, Carhart followed up on the chief's groundbreaking 1919 visit with the help of Culley and SIPRA. As 1920 progressed, the new recreation district sprouted forty-five fireplaces, two shelters, seven toilets, and twelve footbridges, along with signs and garbage pits. SIPRA had raised another $6,000 by late summer, so Carhart and Culley made plans for a small resort lodge or community house and for construction of the Cascade Trail.

This experiment in recreation improvements was as successful with the public as it was with Chief Graves. It seemed to be an ideal match: SIPRA provided the money, and the Forest Service provided the expertise. Carhart noted later in 1920 that on one Sunday in August, 700 cars had visited the new campground.[21] Yet he had to ask himself: Would congressional funding be a better alternative than local funding? How could a federal planner meet both national and local demand, especially in a setting where the present funding source was predominantly local and municipal land was adjacent to federal land? Taken aback by the overwhelming volume of traffic and people, Carhart also worried about issues of fairness: some local groups and families sent advance squads to the campground on Friday afternoons to stake out space for the weekend. Carhart planned to deal with the burgeoning demand for recreation by distinguishing between "picnic arrangements" and "auto camps," hoping the former would adequately serve local people while the latter would serve those who came from farther away and for longer stays. But where would the money come from?

BREAKING NEW GROUND

Because it represents the Forest Service's first foray into campsites for auto-based recreation, Squirrel Creek deserves a closer look. Carhart and Culley designed Squirrel Creek Campground to serve automobile-borne recreationists, especially local picnickers who flocked to the Squirrel Creek Recreational Picnic Shelter (built in 1919 and modified in 1927). Squirrel Creek Campground is twenty-six miles southwest of Pueblo and two miles west of Beulah. True to his promise to Stahl that he could design roads, Carhart collaborated on the design of the access road with District 2 Engineer James Brownlee. To accommodate modestly powered vehicles, the rise from 6,500 feet to 8,500 feet never has more than a 7 percent incline. Carhart had a hand in the design of bridges and overlooks (which focused on waterfalls). The precedent-setting road design also featured flexible culverts, many bridges, and guardrails.

Amid the duff and undergrowth, today's researchers have identified the vestiges of thirty-eight campsites at Squirrel Creek Campground. No two are more than forty feet apart, and there are no remaining natural barriers or shrubs, so it seems Carhart and Culley's design intentionally left campsites open to each other's view. The clusters include three to six campsites, a latrine, an in-ground garbage can, and a well with a hand pump. The "sanitaries," as Carhart called them, had one hole and were at least fifty feet from the creek. There were separate facilities for men and women. Wire mesh vents provided ventilation and dealt with the fly problem.

Distances of 400 to 1,800 feet separated the camping clusters, all of which were sited within a few feet of the stream. (This is less obvious today because Squirrel Creek has changed its course over time.) Campers parked their cars in designated pullouts—not adjacent to campsites: "The most striking design aspect of the Squirrel Creek campground is the close proximity of campsites to one another. This important design feature distinguishes an early 1920s developed campsite or campground from the campgrounds built beginning in the mid-1930s."[22]

Were campers of those days afraid of the wild? Very little wildlife was left on the San Isabel in the 1920s, except for the Greenhorn Wolf.[23] Or did family and ethnic group structures welcome more proximity? Whatever the case, Squirrel Creek was such an important trendsetter that the public reacted negatively in the 1930s when the Forest Service began placing individual campsites more than 100 feet from each other.[24]

What did pleasure seekers do once they arrived? Cascade Trail was three-quarters of a mile long. Connecting the lodge with the campground, it featured stepping stones, retaining walls, hanging bridges, and metal handrails. The aesthetic climax of the Cascade Trail was Squirrel Creek Lodge, also known as Squirrel Creek Community House. It was based on designs done by Carhart in 1920 and located at 7,800 feet atop Squirrel Creek Hill, a promontory that overlooks Squirrel Creek Gorge. Carhart and SIPRA squabbled over the best location—SIPRA preferred the more easily accessible base of the hill, but Carhart prevailed. The lodge was built in 1923–1924. It was 88 feet by 20 feet, with a central hall and two angled wings. There were two stories with two large fireplaces, a kitchen, and a dance floor. In back of the lodge, a set of steps followed switchbacks to descend 100 feet down to the water.

In the 1940s the lodge housed forest workers. However, SIPRA's right to perpetual use of the lodge became moot in June 1947, when a flash flood forced the Forest Service to permanently close the Squirrel Creek access road. A 1979 fire destroyed what remained of the lodge. Today, a large stone foundation is all that is left.

There is no record of Carhart ever returning to Squirrel Creek after he left the Forest Service. Reasonable people can disagree about whether the San Isabel's ambitious recreation program ever progressed beyond the caretaker stage.

By 1925, SIPRA and the Forest Service had constructed more than thirty developed campgrounds and 225 miles of scenic recreation roads in the San Isabel. By 1922, the San Isabel had become the first "recreational" forest in the National Forest System.[25]

SIPRA's heyday ended around 1930. The association would live to collaborate with the Civilian Conservation Corps in 1941 to build cabins some distance from the main lodge at Squirrel Creek. And it would participate in the recreation-related development of nearby Lake San Isabel. But SIPRA and the Forest Service never rose to the level of Carhart's challenge to integrate recreation into long-term, comprehensive plans that could withstand the demands of depressions, financial panics, and wars. Hamel and Carhart and Stahl all knew that incoherent resource management could never resist special interest greed when it took the form of war profiteering. Sadly, no one ever successfully addressed the degradation of the San Isabel's recreation resources and watersheds that was repeated during World War II, when once again vast numbers of sheep joined too many cattle on the San Isabel, undoing much of Hamel's careful restoration work. In 1947, a flood roared through Squirrel Creek Canyon, destroying Culley's artful falls and many of the pioneering recreational facilities. The flood also annihilated State Highway 76, formerly the route for recreationists into the Wet Mountains and beyond into the Wet Mountain Valley from Pueblo.[26]

COMMUNITY-BASED CONSERVATION

SIPRA remains an interesting example of a cooperative partnership between the Forest Service and nonprofit organizations.[27] Among other things, Carhart's and Hamel's support for SIPRA shows how government employees can play an important role in nurturing the development of their nonprofit partners. When all the smoke cleared, Carhart was only asking Congress for $12,000 for recreation planning for the San Isabel. Yet SIPRA raised more than that for the San Isabel alone. SIPRA's Carhart-designed campgrounds on the Wet Mountain Valley side of the Sangres included those at Comanche, Lake Creek, and Alvarado. Although chronically overwhelmed, under-funded, and under-maintained, all of these campgrounds are still in use today, serving as access points to the Sangre de Cristo Wilderness.

Carhart knew that SIPRA and the Forest Service remained behind a very large eight ball. As he noted in the fall of 1920, in 1919 the forests of District 2 had counted 1,223,544 recreation visitors, an increase of 17 percent over 1917. By 1925 the Forest Service was projecting 2.35 million annual visitors, for whom there was little in the way of recreation facilities, to say nothing of fire protection and sanitation.

Closer to home, the San Isabel had 64,183 recreation visitors in 1919. That might have seemed like a small number, but Carhart pointed out to Stahl and Sherman that almost all of them were "concentrated in restricted regions because of the lack of adequate recreation development." Carhart remained frustrated by the fact that the Forest Service failed to deal with the consequences of its ambitious road-building programs. He wrote: "A count one Sunday in August 1919 disclosed that 700 automobiles entered in Squirrel Creek Canon. This camp area was developed by the City of Pueblo, in cooperation with the Forest Service, so that it could comfortably take care of 125 recreation visitors." Those 700 autos carried 2,500 people. Nearby South Hardscrabble was just as crowded, and auto-borne crowds also overwhelmed Alvarado at the base of the Sangre de Cristos. Carhart tried to make SIPRA and the Forest Service understand that roads reaching farther west and up into the steep Sangres would have to end with the kinds of facilities Carhart supported. Ghost-writing again for his superiors in the spring of 1922, Carhart halfheartedly wrote: "Through the efforts of your Association, a substantial amount of the 651,200 acres within the San Isabel National Forest has during the past year been made usable through road construction, water development and the installation of sanitary and camp equipments not only for the people of Colorado, but for the tourists generally, and there is no charge whatever to anyone for camping, wood, fuel or use of the conveniences installed."[28] Carhart also wryly noted that more than $75,000 had been expended on the roads leading to and within the San Isabel National Forest.

SIPRA was not Carhart's only success. Carhart's services would soon be in demand throughout the district, including with many SIPRA-like organizations along the Front Range, at the Mount of the Holy Cross, and at the Spanish Peaks in the southernmost part of the San Isabel. In western Colorado, Charles K. Collins nurtured a version of SIPRA on the Uncompahgre National Forest in the 1930s.

ANOTHER KIND OF WATERSHED

Although he could not have known it at the time, the summer of 1920 was a watershed time for Carhart. Vee Carhart's presence in the field seems to have invigorated her husband as much as the opportunity to work with Frank Culley and Al Hamel. Squirrel Creek was also not Carhart and Culley's only accomplishment.[29] Culley supervised a crew of Boy Scouts who built campgrounds at South Hardscrabble Creek and at North Creek, both in the Wet Mountains near Beulah. Facilities included seventy-five camp units, twelve toilets, and fourteen footbridges. Somehow during that busy summer, Carhart also found time to make sure inappropriate roads did not penetrate the Sangre de Cristo Mountains and the adjacent Great Sand Dunes National Monument:

> In the summer of 1920 I accompanied James Brownlee, then in the
> Engineering Department of USFS Region 2, on a preliminary scouting of
> a road over Mosca Pass; along the lines of the old road then being pushed
> by Pueblo, Colo. As a shorter route into the San Luis Valley, it was blocked
> by Walsenburg interests. They did not want a road that would by-pass
> their town. Luckily, the road was not built. But now, I've learned, it is being
> boomed by some interests, Pueblo and San Luis Valley. It poses a serious

threat. . . . The tender wildland is the east edge of the monument land and that whole "waist" area of the San Isabel's Sangre de Cristos. A highway of any sort over any one of three passes between the upper Huerfano river drainage and the dunes would bring in the horde.[30]

PITFALLS IN THE PATH OF RECREATION DEVELOPMENT

At Stahl's urging, in late 1920 Carhart summarized their conversations during the 1919 and 1920 tours. The point of the memos Carhart wrote was to create a paper trail. In the case of the Conejos Rainbow Trout Lodge, for example, this paper trail would allow Stahl to formally alert his superiors to a potential role for the Forest Service in promoting fishing-based recreation, which Carhart understood as "pure type recreational service," perhaps along the lines of his thinking for Trappers Lake. Carhart's foresight was also preemptive. Given soaring demand, he said, the Forest Service should work with private interests before inappropriate developments (especially in the many private inholdings within Forest Service boundaries) degraded the common recreation experience.

Such an opportunity was at hand on the watershed of the Conejos River as it drains into the southern San Luis Valley before joining the Rio Grande. A wealthy medical doctor wanted to invest in a lodge that would prosper better if its offerings were coordinated with the Forest Service's recreation planning. Sounding like a populist, Carhart lauded the doctor's "practical altruism," hoping it would serve as an example that could spread throughout the "entire western portion of the Grand Regional Plan."[31] As Carhart thought about such examples, he took a hard look at the problems that might accompany the kinds of monopolistic concessions the National Park Service was developing at places like Yosemite. There, Stephen Mather had a conflict of interest that Horace Albright took great pains to disguise, fearing it would compromise the National Park Service's competing requests for recreation funding. Mather was directly involved in the chosen concessionaire's business dealings. In discussing the Conejos proposal, Carhart showed his awareness of such potential problems relative to an associated pack outfit and hunting concession—the same one that had carried him, Vee, and Stahl through the San Juans after the 1920 field season was over.

Carhart's comments proved prophetic. Before his death in 1978, he would see the owners of private in-holdings within officially designated wilderness in Colorado extort huge sums for government buyouts by threatening inappropriate development. He would also see, as Mather and Albright learned, monopolistic concessionaires deliver substandard, amusement park–style services unless contracts were carefully drawn. And so he added a comment based on his exposure to helter-skelter Park Service planning in Yellowstone:

> An earlier part of this forest plan for the Grand Region of the Southwest included a brief discussion of the production of recreation of pure type. It was stated that a unified, typical, harmonious development of trails, roads and hotels making possible the offering of a dominant type of play produced the greatest and best recreation from any given area. This is in special contrast to the present systems in vogue in our "resort" areas where a great many types of unrelated play are indifferently offered in the same territory and by the same public service organizations. Theoretically the best sort of recreation service would be governmentally owned transportation and residential facilities suited to the area to be developed.[32]

Carhart was becoming aware that complete government ownership and management of all recreation (as proposed by the Park Service) might not be desirable, even if it were feasible. As he stated:

> Obviously the next best thing when public ownership is not possible is to get some altruistic organization interested in the development of play facilities in outdoor places. If such a company could be formed which would put back into development of further public service of harmonious type a goodly share of profits instead of putting it into the pockets of stockholders, that company would be doing a great public service. It would step in and in a measure do exactly what the Government should do but which is impossible under present circumstances.[33]

In the same memos, Carhart also offered Stahl ideas about how to approach the "problem" of profit. Regarding SIPRA, he said:

> The policy has been followed that the association will not enter the commercial field unless forced to by unsatisfactory service or the charging of exorbitant rates by hotels, stores or transportation companies. In the case of such a practice being followed on Forest land, the Service could act to prevent price-gouging; but, when such an activity is carried [out] on private lands, it is then up to the association to see that a good service at a fair profit is maintained.

In contrast, SIPRA charged a reasonable commercial rate that included a profit. Although SIPRA had nominal stockholders, profits went back into further development of recreation for the region. Carhart pointed out that the Conejos Rainbow Trout Lodge proposal was as ambitious as SIPRA, since it encompassed the entire Conejos River watershed and addressed much more than just fishing:

The residential service is equally typical of a sportsman's area. Comfortable lodges form the base camps. They are not hotels in the generally accepted term in that they are free from the artificiality of the typical "resort" hotel. Beyond the lodge types and reached by typical traffic of the region are chalets serving as satellite camps. Even beyond this there is opportunity for temporary residential arrangements in tents, this giving the most direct touch with the outdoors. Throughout, the housing and service are based on the fundamentals of clean, comfortable beds, adequate shelter and whole-some, tasty, clean food. This is the foundation for the typical use of the region and is embodied in the plans of the Rainbow Trout Lodges approved by the Forest Service.[34]

THE WRITER VS. THE WRITER OF MEMOS

The ebullient Carhart and the laconic Stahl must have made curious office mates. Back in Denver in the early winter of 1920–1921, Stahl turned Carhart loose on the great question that faced them both. Dream as they might, they still had to jump through the internal hoops that stood between their needs at the forest level and the Forest Service's politically driven budget requests to Congress. As he composed his summary memos for Stahl, Carhart tested his wings as a writer. Carhart also spent considerable time during the winter drafting revisions of the recreation sections of the Forest Service Manual—the agency's Bible.

Carhart's growing talent and ambition continually probed the limits of acceptable bureaucratic behavior. Because he typically ghost-wrote memos for the steely Stahl, Carhart had to respect the fact that those memos were the basis for budget requests. They were also the basis for much of Stahl's evaluation of Carhart and for the Forest Service's evaluation of Stahl. As he approached the end of his second year with the Forest Service, Carhart did the reasonable thing: he completed his Forest Service assignments with verve and gusto. And he looked to the future, carefully cultivating professional and personal contacts inside and outside the Forest Service. Further, he used his position to develop his talents as an imaginative thinker and writer, not just a note taker. Viewing Carhart's brief four-year tenure with the Forest Service this way makes more sense than the peevish, truncated judgment that Carhart was a quitter. The Forest Service years were part of his development as an independent planner, a private landscape architect, and a freelance writer.

Carhart's writing was beginning to improve beyond stilted bureaucratese. He was developing a broader view of his conservation goals and how he might use his writing skills to move Americans toward those goals. He was groping his way toward the style that would make him one of mid-century America's most popular conservation writers. Further, he was also probing the limits of nonfiction and exploring the different standards demanded by fiction.

Carhart's writings for Stahl took different forms. One example was a December 3, 1920, "digest" of "problems and needs" directed to Colonel Peck, the new district forester. This digest served as an executive summary of a forty-eight-page report (also ghost-written by Carhart) to the chief that went out under Peck's signature on December 6, 1920. Carhart wrote it in a somewhat detached manner. The report followed the digest's outline form, but its prose became more pressing and urgent. Consider this passage from "Stahl's" December 6, 1920, memo to the chief of the Forest Service, in which Carhart was literally writing for his professional life:

> The San Isabel has received more attention from the Recreation Engineer than all other Forests of the Districts combined. Still, there is need of further planning than has been done and there is even more need of proper supervision of the construction work so it will conform to the general plan and be of good quality in the details. Plans for work that should be carried out next in the program of general development here will be made this winter and, it is hoped, this will cover a three year program of recreational development.[35]

Carhart, Stahl, and Peck were jointly seizing this opportunity to spell out their understanding of how the Forest Service could and should compete with the Park Service before Congress for funding for recreation. Even referring to Sherman's personal letter to Carhart of October 23, 1921, the digest was a typical Carhart effort: "There has been no attempt to compile a statistical report. It is felt preferable to cover the field of recreational use in an informal way."

Carhart began the digest: "The recreational use of National Forest territory has always existed, even before those areas were set aside as National reservations." He continued:

> Previous to the last decade, the major use of the Forests for recreation was by those people who have the habit of invading unsettled country for the experience of being in lands where few have before passed. In other words, the visitors were those who are explorers in a minor way and pioneers in vacation country, and sportsmen hunters.
>
> These two uses still remain in a very much increased form, but recently there has been added a great mass of use by the large body of the population which is today traveling to the woods and park lands to satisfy a normal demand for vacation and recreation. . . .
>
> Ten years ago, recreation in the Forests was no more than a recognized minor use incidental to other uses. Today it stands as the most direct

and personal use made by people who utilize the Forests. This increase has
been so rapid that the Forest Service in this District has been confronted
by a large, insistent demand for development and policies governing recreation in the Forests to meet the recreation needs, almost before it was
realized this need was present in any large degree. It is confronted with the
urgency for policies to be tried out in situations which were not existing a
month since, and is facing a real problem in building up a staff of competent
men to handle the work of development and the direction of recreation in
the Forests.

In the same digest, Carhart detailed the causes of this increase in demand,
highlighting the war factor, the return of veterans, increasing prosperity,
and the advent of the automobile.[36] Broadening his scope to all of District
2, Carhart stressed the numbers of people coming to the Superior National
Forest from all over the nation and the world. This was his way of leading into
the subject of community-based conservation. He said local support groups
were appearing not just on the Superior and the San Isabel but also in many
Colorado communities, where citizens had asked "that they be assigned a piece
of recreation territory to develop." Then Carhart proceeded with a history of
SIPRA's formation, fund-raising, and achievements. Although Carhart knew
the Forest Service would primarily serve automobile-borne tourists, he did not
leave out the railroads, especially the ones whose lines ran east-west along the
Arkansas River (from Pueblo to Salida) or over La Veta Pass to the south (from
Walsenburg to Alamosa).[37]

Carhart then made his case for "a comprehensive recreation plan," including numerous lodges and hotels. Not forgetting revenue streams, he showed
how the Forest Service could develop 1,000 summer home sites in District
2—but only in appropriate locales. In 1921, they already had applications for
200 such leases on the San Isabel alone. Having brought up the sensitive issue
of how recreation might generate revenue, Carhart then turned to Trappers
Lake. He and Stahl knew that however much Congress might like to hear about
the revenue-producing potential of the national forests, politicians were happy
to quietly subsidize special interests when it served their mutual political ends.
Seizing this bull by the horns, Carhart acknowledged in the digest that there
were already a score of applications

> for summer home sites near the lake. Some lots were laid out by the regular
> forest force, but these were not used because they did not properly fit in with
> plans and policies which are governing the summer home locations in this
> District, and those plans and policies which have been especially established
> for Trappers Lake. The whole scheme should be thoroughly planned and the
> construction here adequately supervised by a competent landscape archi-

tect, so there will be the best arrangement existing. It is essential that the best plan be applied in such places as Trappers Lake for the reason that the scenic values are such here that any poor arrangement would do irreparable damage. So rather than accommodate the wishes of these score or more of applicants and spoil scenic values of exceptional worth, it has been necessary to withhold all areas for which applications have been made. An appropriation which will provide for an adequate and properly trained field force would allow this office to put competent men in there to lay out several hundred lots, and thus satisfy this demand without dissipating any of the beauty found there.

Carhart next shifted his argument back to SIPRA and the San Isabel: "The Forest Service, representing the Government in the matter, has been in the regrettable position of accepting a great amount of charity [i.e., SIPRA money] in this matter of funds used in building recreation utilities." Then Carhart, knowing that his work would percolate throughout the bureaucracy, went directly at Kneipp and other internal enemies: "The men in the field are neither capable of handling landscape work, which demands a special training and experience, nor have they the time to give it without slighting other activities." As Carhart would soon learn, such comments were not lost on Kneipp.

PLANS FOR 1922, SHOULD FUNDS BECOME AVAILABLE

Continuing his discussion in the digest, Carhart cut to the chase in all caps. He was still making the $1,800 per year he and Sherman had agreed on as a way to get Carhart's foot in the door. Now ready to shoulder the door wide open, Carhart said: "There are several factors limiting this answer. One is the feature of being able to get competent landscape architects as recreation engineers at the salary now offered by the Service. Inquiry has shown that the best students leaving colleges and universities are able to command a salary of $2000 per year in the professional landscape field."

Carhart pointed out that the sum of the needs detailed for District 2 alone exceeded the total national amount requested in the current Forest Service budget. Stressing the need for the Forest Service to take the initiative in comprehensive regional planning, he estimated that SIPRA and others would have spent $35,000 from 1919 through 1921. He said the Forest Service should match that sum or at least put in $8,000 to pay "the salary and expenses of a competent landscape architect as recreation engineer and one or two student assistants." Sensitive to the need to keep a federal focus, he made the case that the rest of the federal money should go to developing trunk line trails that would serve all Americans, not just the citizens of the adjacent towns.

Carhart presciently noted the recreation potential of the Vail/Aspen/ Crested Butte area. Then (still in the digest) he returned to the issue of Trappers Lake, referring to the difficulties encountered by the local forest supervisor on the White River National Forest:

> Supervisor [James] Blair spoke of the desirability of building a trail or road. In my opinion, the best plan would be to end the automobile road some little distance from and out of sight of the lake, and then build a trail around the lake just inside the timber, with spurs running out to the various points where a person can step out now and then to get a view from the water's edge. Blair spoke of the pressure which is being brought to bear on him by people who desire summer sites at Trappers Lake. He seems to think that under the present plans, it will be necessary to wait for a couple of years before he can begin issuing permits: since he tells me that it would take a full season's work or more to make a complete survey of all the sites.
>
> It is easy to give people the locations they wish at this stage of develop- ment, but, if this course is followed, it will ruin any opportunity for a com- plete and adequate artistic development of this lake. In order to hasten this work and to eliminate the rather caustic criticism of our delay, and as early as possible put this land into good shape for the particular use to which it is so well fitted—recreation—there should be an allotment for study and direction of development here of not less than $600 during the fiscal year of 1922.

This long memo shows how far the Forest Service still was from having a "wil- derness" management plan for Trappers Lake. Carhart continued:

> However, it is well settled that there should be a trail out from the basin of Trappers Lake to the top of Amphitheatre Mountain and to Wall Lake and return. . . . With proper plans in existence for the summer home and hotel use of this lake, private investments would probably total not less than $12,000 in the first two years, and in order to make the region wholly usable after this investment has been made, it will be necessary to start this trail work and follow it up with other trail work and camp developments at a later date.

After further reviewing the recreation needs of the Wyoming and Minnesota forests, the digest asked for the same amount of money for the Superior as for the San Isabel ($12,000). And it promised that Carhart would work on the Superior in the summer of 1921. The total recreation budget request was $56,000, much of it for study and planning.[38] The memo closed by asking for additional funding for hiring five recreation engineers as soon as possible. One of these engineers, he said, would accompany Carhart to the Superior in the spring of 1921. Thereafter, this new man would stay in Minnesota to finish the work under Carhart's supervision.

THE CURE FOR TOO MUCH ROOF

Full of great expectations, the Carharts were learning to love Colorado. The field seasons must have been wonderful times for them. The wintertimes in Denver were harder, as they worried over professional prospects. Carhart began to sketch two designs. One was a home and garden for himself and Vee. Another was a very large commercial greenhouse.

Restless, Carhart was thinking along these lines: "The cure for 'too much roof' is the great outdoors and if we are going to effect the cure we must intelligently plan and direct it."[39] Accordingly, he drafted some memos, allowing himself the luxury of distinguishing the recreational planning efforts of the National Park Service from those of the Forest Service. To his mind, the basic difference was helter-skelter amusement parks versus comprehensive, watershed-based regional planning driven by the concept of zoning. The most radical distinction was a new kind of zone—what Carhart during those times called "pure type recreational service" and what we today might call "wilderness." Interestingly, it was in the digest of the longer report of December 3, 1920, that Carhart used the word "wilderness" under the heading "Recreation has always existed on National Forests." The word did not appear in the longer report and was used only once more in the digest: "[p]ast use . . . by hardy, amateur explorers and seekers of recreation in wilderness settings."

In retrospect, we can see that Carhart's ideas about recreation management were gaining a small but influential national audience. Not only had he become the editor of *American Forestry*'s section on recreation, but the magazine also paid him for his submissions—even though he was a Forest Service employee writing on government time. Thanks to his Forest Service accomplishments, Carhart became a full member of the American Society of Landscape Architects. He saw not only that he had professional prospects outside the Forest Service but also that he could make money as a writer and speaker. Further, based on his successes with business groups like SIPRA, Carhart was beginning to understand that he could do something that had always eluded the more aloof Leopold. He was beginning to feel his oats as a fund-raiser and an organizer—someone who could help ordinary Americans articulate their longing for the right to recreate on public lands and who could organize them politically to defend their interests.

Meanwhile, wanting to participate in Colorado's postwar economic boom, the Carharts kept their eyes open for business prospects that would utilize Arthur's botanical and horticultural skills. New roads seemed to converge, along with existing rail lines, on the little town of Florence. After their summer spent in the promising new towns of the Arkansas River Valley, Arthur and

Vee were beginning to think about business schemes that would unite their families by drawing their parents to Colorado. But where would the capital come from?

On January 1, 1921, George Carhart sent his son a typed, formal accounting of the family business, asking Arthur for help with income taxes. While the business owed a bank $3,300, it also maintained a positive balance of $10,000. George's handwritten note said, "I think we are holding our own."[40] However, it was becoming clear to all the Carharts that the business would probably not break even in 1921. For "pioneering stock" like the Carharts, that bleak prospect suggested it was time for a change.

Meanwhile, although clearly concerned about his family's future, Arthur Carhart did not passively await his fate at the hands of Congress. He knew through Sherman that his most ferocious opponent outside the Forest Service was Stephen Mather. As the year turned, Carhart was preparing for a round or two with Mather. The fateful clash would occur at a January 1921 meeting in Iowa (right after Carhart had visited Mapleton for a family conference).

Around the turn of the new year, Carhart produced three remarkable draft memos.[41] One was about "Pure Type Recreational Service." The next was titled "Outdoor Recreation in the United States and the Need for Organization." Carhart's most ringing theoretical work to date, this latter draft reads like a keynote speech he was composing for a grand national conference on recreation, possibly to be announced in a few weeks at an upcoming meeting in Iowa and to be held sometime in 1922. Obviously, Carhart was dreaming that Congress would fund all of District 2's requests in a way that would propel him to the leadership of recreation planning in the Forest Service—if not the nation. Matching his rhetoric to his aspirations, Carhart was learning to let his writing crescendo:

> The turning of the population to the outdoors is a fundamental movement. There is so much of the outdoors in all of us that there is no escaping the forces that make us seek play in the open places. Recreation is a complement of work. It is recuperation from toil. It is as necessary as work for the best effort cannot go on without some compensating recreation.
>
> Recreation or play came before work. And through nearly 2000 centuries men played outdoors. They lived outdoors. Through inheritance they came to be so much at home in outdoor places that they now turn from city conditions seeking their old habitat that was the place of their abode for so many centuries.
>
> Therefore, there is no transitory movement that is taking people to our greater open places but a genuine expression of a necessity. People go to the outdoors because it is a fundamental need of their existence, there to get the

force and vision necessary to go back into the artificialities of the civilization and meet the demands of modern business.

Unlike Aldo Leopold and other future founders of the nascent Wilderness Society,[42] Carhart saw himself writing and speaking to and for common Americans, especially with regard to the new freedoms that came with the automobile. Reveling in the free space of a budding writer, Carhart grandly reviewed history in a fate-tossed but America-centered way:[43]

> The cure for "too much roof" is the great outdoors and if we are going to effect the cure we must intelligently plan and direct it.
>
> But the people have already demonstrated that if they are given half a chance they will turn naturally to the outdoors for the recreation that they need so much. The last few years, through the agency of the automobile, practically the whole nation has been able to get into the outdoors and get some of the benefits to be had with association with outdoor places.
>
> This recreational use has not been that of the more artificial city parks and playgrounds. It has been a use that has demanded great stretches of open country. All outdoor life has felt the force of this movement and even in our outdoor games of the city play places there has been added impetus. But the great basic foundation of such a use is imbedded in the hunger of modern man for associations with his racial environment the great outdoors.

Carhart then reviewed the increasing recreation uses of the national parks, showing how the Forest Service lands could complement Park Service offerings. Claiming increased use from 1910 to 1920 of between 1 and 5 million people on Forest Service lands, he said this "tremendous activity lacks coordination and direction." He blamed this failing on the misguided federal policy of maintaining the Park Service in the Department of the Interior and the Forest Service in the Department of Agriculture. Asking pointed rhetorical questions about this fragmented approach to recreation, Carhart said, "And if there isn't a unified, correlated public opinion[,] shouldn't we have it right now or at least start towards reaching a clear understanding of what is needed to bring order out of this chaotic disarray?" He also reached out to many different constituencies, including state foresters, state parks, and wildflower lovers.

Carhart hit on the idea of a federation of all outdoor clubs—something like the structure of today's National Wildlife Federation, with strong state affiliates informing a national leadership that would take its marching orders from the field.[44]

Draft 3 of this pioneering document has "Return to Carhart" written in his hand on the cover, suggesting it was circulated around the District 2 office. It is titled "A Federation of Outdoor Clubs, By Arthur H. Carhart" and is dated only 1920.

Carhart started with a disclaimer, saying that all his thinking-at-the-typewriter was merely "informal." That freed him to soar: "[T]he members of the universal outdoor fraternity have come to the conclusion that there is to be a central organization where [there] will be common meeting ground." Carhart envisioned an elaborate weaving together of many recreation concerns, united by a common interest in fighting wildland fires and predators. The core of the group, as he saw it, would consist of foresters and game protectors. He proposed to call the group "the Federated Outdoor Clubs of America," saying, "This Federation will be in politics but not a political machine if it is to do its most good."

Foreshadowing his later work with the Conservation Collection at the Denver Public Library, Carhart closed with these thoughts:

> The Federation has been pointed out as an ideal medium of exchange of ideas. Its bulletins or publications should always carry either a digest of all of the best articles, reports or pamphlets issued by various outdoor agencies or at least a list of such articles. The relationship to other fields of activities touched by such articles should be noted in the list or digest through cross reference so each one interested in a particular field may know what is doing in another field.
>
> Here's wishing the Federated Outdoor Clubs a big success. May they join in the advancement of outdoor interests on a platform of "All for one and one for all."

Carhart would soon learn some hard lessons about the distance between dreams and politics. Clearly, some in the Forest Service were thinking of birthing the "Federated Outdoor Clubs" as a way of consolidating Forest Service power.[45] Although more of a dreamer than a schemer, Carhart was one of these optimists. With such high hopes, Carhart boarded a train in Denver in January 1921 and headed home to Iowa—and to his fateful confrontation with "Bulldog" Mather.

NOTES

1. March 12, 1920. Sherman mentioned in the letter that the local "Commercial Club" from the Superior National Forest had come to Washington to request Carhart's help in starting a SIPRA-like organization.

2. *The Bulletin, District 2* III (November 1919).

3. Arthur Carhart, "Recreation in the Forests," *American Forestry* 26 (May 1920): 268.

4. Arthur Carhart, "Vacation Opportunities in Your National Forests," *American Forestry* 26 (September 1920):552–553.

5. Arthur Carhart, "Auto Camp Conveniences," *American Forestry* 26 (September 1920).

6. Arthur Carhart, "What Is Recreation's Next Step?" *American Forestry* 26 (October 1920).

7. Arthur Carhart, "Live Game and Forest Recreation," *American Forestry* 26 (December 1920).

8. Carhart memo to Morrell, December 6, 1920, Carhart Collection, Denver Public Library (hereafter CC, DPL).

9. Letter from Ella Carhart to Arthur Carhart, September 14, 1920, CC, DPL. This is the only reference to children in all of Carhart's correspondence.

10. Letter from Sherman to Carhart, October 9, 1920, CC, DPL.

11. This trip provided Carhart with material for his novels *Drum up the Dawn* and *Cattlemen of the C Bit Brand.*

12. Carhart's photos of the Penitentes are in the Western History Collection, DPL.

13. Still open for business: rainbowtroutranch@earthlink.net.

14. Arthur Carhart, "This Way to Wilderness," unpublished manuscript, 1974, 55.

15. December 16, 1974, report to Frank Owsley, Box 2:100, CC, DPL.

16. Leon Kneipp memo, December 3, 1920, CC, DPL. Meanwhile, Frank Waugh's praise for Carhart's work provided a stark contrast. See his letter to Carhart, October 18, 1920, CC, DPL.

17. Letter from Frank Harmon to Carhart, August 8, 1973, CC, DPL.

18. *Pueblo Chieftain*, August 24, 1919, 3.

19. National Register of Historic Places, Section 8, 27.

20. My thanks to Carhart scholar Jack McCrory; this section includes some of the details from his account of the construction of Squirrel Creek written for the National Register of Historic Places. Formal designation followed in 2006.

21. Arthur Carhart, "Digest of L, Recreation Letter, December 3, 1920," 13, Box 1:100, CC 88, DPL.

22. National Register, 37.

23. See my discussion of fluctuating regional wildlife populations in Wolf, *Colorado's Sangre de Cristo Mountains* (Boulder: University Press of Colorado, 1995).

24. Terence Young of the Department of Geography and Anthropology, California Polytechnic Institute; cited in National Register, p. 28.

25. National Register, 29. Carhart was extremely proud of his precedent-setting work, for he hoped someday the Forest Service would see things his way. That day seemed to arrive in 1960, when Carhart found himself deeply involved in the generation of the Multiple Use–Sustained Yield Act. An alarmed Carhart got word that the Lewis and Clark National Forest was trying to take credit for the first cooperative recreational development. On November 6, 1960, Carhart wrote to the district forester to set things straight. *Colorado's Sangre de Cristo Mountains* chronicles my interpretation of Congress's never-ending failure to fund recreation management on the San Isabel

National Forest. Carhart returned to other areas of the San Isabel later in his career to try to restore its chronically abused watersheds (especially the Upper Huerfano above Gardner) through the reintroduction of beaver. In the 1990s, San Carlos district ranger Cindy Rivera (whose training was in recreation planning) instituted an ecosystem management plan for some of the watersheds of the Sangres, such as the Upper Huerfano. Her successor, Paul Crespin, has expanded this work into fire management. Throughout all these changes, the San Carlos District has benefited from the continuity provided by Mike Smith.

26. The Forest Service has adopted Squirrel Creek as part of its "New Century of Service" project celebrating the agency's 100th anniversary. After the 1947 flood, engineers abandoned the old Highway 76. Now Highway 78 goes over Twelve Mile Road to Colorado 165. Volunteers for Outdoor Colorado, the latest successor to SIPRA, are renovating Squirrel Creek Campground, including some of the old campsites and half a mile of the Cascade Trail.

27. In the years 2003–2005, I was project forester and ecologist for one such effort in the Pot Creek watershed on the Carson National Forest near Taos, New Mexico. This was part of the Community Forest Restoration Project funded by Congress in 2001. In the 1990s I also participated in cooperative projects that partnered the San Isabel National Forest and the private, nonprofit Sangre de Cristo Mountain Council.

28. See SIPRA's Board of Directors Report to Stockholders, March 18, 1922, CC, DPL.

29. Robert W. Cermak, "In the Beginning: The First National Forest Recreation Plan," *Parks & Recreation* 9, 11 (November 1974):20–24, 29–33.

30. Carhart to Arthur Greeley, deputy chief of the Forest Service, November 29, 1964, CC, DPL. He and Greeley were corresponding about Carhart's role in the early history of wilderness. Harold Schaafsma, superintendent of Great Sand Dunes National Monument, supported wilderness designation for the monument in 1964, and he turned to Carhart for help when local interests "boomed" a road instead. Carhart told Greeley that the dunes themselves could take the increased pressure, but he opposed wilderness designation. Instead, he proposed "interlocking forest and monument in a roadless wildland with recreational values in the class I call 'dominant use.' And I'd not make it too restricted." Carhart sent copies of his letter to Greeley to Schaafsma, Dave Nordwall of the Forest Service, Estella Leopold of the Wilderness Society, and Joe Penfold of the Izaak Walton League. Federal acquisition of the Baca Ranch in 2004 turned the monument into a national park.

31. These early December 1920 memos are filed chronologically in the CC, DPL. Especially with drafts, I have corrected spelling errors. Carhart's spelling could be idiosyncratic. Further, he clearly dictated most of these memos to a stenographer.

32. Ibid.

33. Ibid.

34. Plans for the Conejos Rainbow Trout Lodge went awry when the Forest Service refused to request money from Congress.

35. The report, the digest, and associated draft memos are all in the 1920 Correspondence, CC, DPL. This series has all the early San Isabel recreation plans and photos plus Carhart's revisions to the Forest Service Manual.

36. 1. War Factor.

    a. The Army introduced a large number of the male population of the country to outdoor life and physical exercise in the open. Once the taste for outdoor life is acquired, it is hard to lose. A yearning for a few days each year in camp will remain throughout life with those men who have been in the military service. They will take with them friends and relatives who will acquire the taste for camping and outdoor life from direct association with vacation activities. . . .

    b. The war, with the intense training periods and grueling work, taught the Nation, as nothing else would, that there must be a time for play if the highest efficiency is to be attained.

    c. A third factor growing out of the war is the keeping of the American touring public away from the beaten paths of European tourist lands and forcing them to become acquainted with the recreation resources in America. . . .

2. Disappearing Local Camping Areas.

3. Increase of Wealth among Large Bodies of Citizens.

4. "See America First" is really what many do before they go to the more established European and other foreign tourist centers, and they are doing so, not because they cannot afford to go to the other lands, but because of a certain belief and pride in what America has to offer.

5. Automobiles. Probably no other one factor is so great as this one.

6. Good Roads.

(Digest, p. 6).

37. Carhart reported: "The Missouri Pacific has sent a special party into the San Isabel Forest during the summer and has secured about 4000 feet of motion picture film and several hundred still pictures for publicity purposes" (digest).

38. "There is one important work, however, that the Service must keep in hand and to which it must allot funds, and that is the planning of these areas so that they will fit in with other uses of the Forests and so that they will fully utilize, without waste and lost motion, the areas which can be turned over wholly or in part to a recreational use" (digest).

39. Carhart memo of December 3, 1920, CC, DPL.

40. George Carhart's note is in a special file dedicated to Carhart family correspondence, CC, DPL.

41. These memos can be found under the year 1921 in the chronological sequence of the CC, DPL. They read like drafts of articles or speeches.

42. See Paul Sutter's discussion of the early wilderness movement's defensive disdain for the democratizing effects of the automobile: *Driven Wild: How the Fight against Automobiles Launched the Modern Environmental Movement* (Seattle: University of Washington Press, 2002).

43. "Babylon, Egypt, Rome, Athens and many other older civilizations have reached a high point of organization and then have fallen to pieces. The artificial conditions that they built up around their cities lowered their vitality and with the vitality

of the individual lowered the whole nation lost its ruggedness and was conquered or fell to pieces because of the forces within it. It is not inconceivable that we are at the present time moving rapidly towards over organization which will in time so lower the 'punch' of our people that they will disappear from the face of the earth as have the older races. This thought is worth grave consideration. And if the people of the United States can look it straight in the eye and recognize its dangers and what is more important, the cure, then there is some chance of our keeping our national life in a strong progressive state for many centuries beyond what it would otherwise be" (1921 Carhart draft memos).

44. "So that the great field of this meeting is to organize the layman public so it can see the needs in the various fields, recognize the chaotic conditions existing in handling this utility in all of our public properties and then after thorough study and consideration of all angles, say to our governmental officials just what they consider the rational, sane, efficient method of getting the greatest service from the human use of our outdoor areas. A national federation of all outdoor clubs cannot help but move towards a goal of ultimate success and to a great service of great good if they will but consider the present needs in this field and then move sanely to meet them by well directed, cooperative effort" (1921 Carhart draft memos).

45. Carhart's dream of a big conference did not come to pass until 1924. The First National Conference on Outdoor Recreation convened in Washington, D.C., on May 22–24, 1924. The "permanent" association that emerged lasted on paper until July 1929, when Congress terminated it. Perhaps fulfilling Carhart's doubt that Congress would ever support recreation on a par with other uses, it was not until 1964 that Congress funded a Bureau of Outdoor Recreation as part of the Land and Water Conservation Fund legislation signed in September during the Johnson-Goldwater presidential campaign.

CHAPTER SIX

MY DISAPPOINTMENT COMES
FROM EXPECTING TOO MUCH

At the start, if you don't know already, I can state flatly that I have the
most thorough dislike for burocracy that one can have. I've been inside and
outside and I don't like the thing that is burocracy. I've tried to analyze it, to
get my own definition as to where that pertains. A bureau starts out to do a
public service. For a time that spirit dominates. The intent of the organization's being is dominant in its actions. At some point the perpetuation of the
bureau becomes the guiding spirit, and then we have burocracy. Some day I
hope to write a novel on this subject.

—CARHART TO JOE PENFOLD, DECEMBER 21, 1964

INTRODUCTION:
THE STUDY AND DEVELOPMENT OF LAND SURFACES FOR HUMAN USE

Carhart spent December and early January preparing for the National Conference on Parks, set to be held in Des Moines, Iowa, on January 11–12, 1921.
As a native Iowan and the Forest Service's sole recreation engineer, Carhart
was an understandable choice to represent the Forest Service, however unof-
ficially. James Good, chair of the House Appropriations Committee, had been a
Republican congressman from Iowa since 1909, so he was a lobbying target for
Carhart and his allies in state and federal forest agencies.

After a brief visit with his parents in Mapleton, Carhart continued his
homecoming campaign by returning to Ames, where on January 7 he addressed
the Iowa Conservation Association, whose president was L. H. Pammel, chair
of the Botany Department, and whose secretary was G. B. McDonald, professor of forestry. The next day the recreation engineer addressed a student

group of would-be landscape architects. Carhart told his former professors that he planned on attending the conference in Des Moines. He asked them why the agenda was limited to national parks instead of covering broader national recreation problems. Pammel and McDonald agreed that Forest Service recreation also deserved a spot on the agenda. Pammel suggested that Carhart should speak about forest recreation during the session he was to chair.[1]

Earlier that winter, as Carhart prepared for the National Conference on Parks, he had ghost-written an internal memo[2] from District 2 Forester Col. Allen Peck, drawing Chief Greeley's attention to the recent "action of the American Society of Landscape Architects [ASLA] in modifying the duties of the standing committee on National Parks, so it is now the Committee on National Parks and National Forests. This action has been brought about through the interest of Prof. J. S. Pray of Harvard, who has been corresponding with our Recreation Engineer, Mr. Carhart."

The memo went on to say that this action by ASLA represented a chance for the Forest Service and the National Park Service to cooperate. "Peck" urged Greeley to write to ASLA president Frederick Law Olmsted Jr.[3] The memo closed with a recommendation that the Forest Service should hire more ASLA members as consultants—such as Frank Culley at Squirrel Creek.

I DID NOT SAY ONE WORD AGAINST THE NATIONAL PARKS

As soon as he returned to Denver from Iowa, Carhart wrote a memo for Peck detailing his version of what had happened at the conference. Newspaper accounts about his clash with Stephen Mather were already circulating nationally. The January 12, 1921, headline in *The Des Moines Register* was "Forest and Park chiefs clash," and the *Rocky Mountain News* picked up the story immediately. Like the clash itself, the memo gave Carhart the opportunity to test his wings—and to demonstrate his growing narrative skills.

Carhart's "L Supervision Memorandum for the Forester," dated January 17, 1921,[4] details that he went to Des Moines merely to find out "whether it was in effect not so much a conference on Parks as a conference on outdoor recreation of National scope." Professors and others in attendance assured him it was the latter and urged him to speak about "the extent of recreational use in the Forests." However, he had still demurred, remarking that if the conference really were to be about parks only, he would sit in only as an interested landscape architect. During the roll call, Carhart identified himself as a member of the Forest Service who was also representing the Colorado Mountain Club.

I took the opportunity to say only a few outstanding things regarding the National Forests. I then endeavored to show where the National Forests fitted into a big, comprehensive, recreational scheme and used several parables in this connection. I stated that the National Parks were the big outstanding jewels of the recreation system in the Nation, and that the National Forests were the great setting for these gems of scenery; that the National Parks, because of this unusual beauty, were the aristocracy of the scheme, while the National Forests were the common folks in the scheme of recreation; and that the National Parks were the delicacies in the scenic and recreation offerings, while the National Forests were the meat and bread of the recreation system. I finished with a statement that the National Forests were the property of the people of the United States and everyone was welcome to come and visit them. (p. 2)

Other attendees pressed Carhart to say more. By chance, an opening occurred in the program for the next day. Herbert Evison of the Park Service handed the session chair, Everett Millard, a note requesting that Millard call on Carhart. Carhart detailed the increased recreation uses on the national forests, especially the San Isabel. He also pointed out "that while there were no National Parks east of the Mississippi River, there were several National Forests which could be used for outdoor recreation; emphasized the fact that everyone was welcome in these Forests" (p. 3) Carhart told his superiors, "I endeavored to commend the National Parks in every way. I wish to emphasize this point—that I did not say one word against the National Parks" (p. 4) He continued, writing as he would in his later fiction about the Forest Service, describing a bureaucratic showdown:

Before I had time to reach my seat in the convention, Mr. Mather was on his feet. In substance he said: He wished to dissipate any possible inference that the people might derive from my speech that the National Parks were not made for poor people and that they were developed only for the aristocrats. He said he was sure that I had not meant to create such an impression, to which I at once agreed that it had not been my intention whatever. I am certain that no one who attended that meeting had received that impression; but Mr. Mather, after this original statement, very evidently let his grip slip as far as his temper was concerned, and he continued, saying that it made his blood boil to see a fine lithograph posted any place which said: "The National Forests—The People's Playground." He then continued to state, with some heat, that the National Forests should not try to develop the recreation use; that it was not their business to do this; that they were duplicating the work of the National Park Service; that he had talked personally with Congressman Good, head of the Appropriations Committee, and that Mr. Good was distinctly opposed to the use of Forest Service

moneys in making recreation developments. He further stated that the
Forest Service should depend upon local support only, in this development
within the National Forests, and that all National funds should go to the
National Parks for recreation development.

It is evident in these words that Mr. Mather somewhat lost control of
himself. . . . Further, it is evident . . . that he does not consider the cooperation between the Forest Service and the Park Service, in recreational
development, to extend beyond the passive cooperation of the Forest Service
with the Park Service; and that whenever the Forests are mentioned for recreation, it is not proper cooperation on the part of the Forest Service. (p. 4)

This internal memo helps show why Carhart began to hate "burocracies."
It must have made interesting reading for Carhart's friends and enemies within
the Forest Service. And it also showed Carhart's ability to judge character,
for he correctly divined the secret Horace Albright and others were hiding:
Mather suffered from a severe manic-depressive condition. If the facts about
his instability became public, they might jeopardize the very existence of the
National Park Service.[5]

According to Albright, Mather saw in Carhart a threat to his agenda for
the National Park Service.[6] This master of bureaucratic infighting saw that
Carhart's fund-raising accomplishments with the San Isabel Protection and
Recreation Association (SIPRA) could serve as a two-edged sword. Congress
might match SIPRA's efforts. Or Congress might ask why it should fund Forest
Service recreation if local organizations were willing to do so.

Thanks to Colorado-based informants like Enos Mills, Mather was fully
aware of what Wallace Hutchinson, Carhart, and others were doing in District
2—including some moves that must have seemed provocative to Mather, such
as the adverse report Carhart had filed on Mount Evans's suitability as a
national park. In addition, after Carhart's visit to Yellowstone and its surrounding national forests in 1919, Hutchison had distributed the poster that raised
Mather's ire. The offending artwork pictured Square Top Mountain in Jackson
Hole, with the caption: "THE NATIONAL FORESTS—THE PEOPLE'S PLAYGROUND!"

Carhart's superiors must have been amused when he continued his grip-
ping narrative in his January 17, 1921, memo to Peck, adding some flourishes:
"As Mr. Mather finished, I asked for the floor. The chairman stated that he
believed there was no more time for discussion of this subject, but I remained
standing and he asked me if I had something to say: whereupon I made the following statement" (p. 5). Carhart told his audience that users were already on
the forests:

They must be taken care of. And, second, that as long as the National
Forests are the people's property and the recreation use of these areas offers

a greater aggregate return to these people through this use, it is the duty of the Forest Service to consider this demand and make this return to the public. I offer these points only for consideration.

Immediately after the meeting, I met Mr. Mather in the entrance room to the Convention Hall. He came over and shook hands with me, stating that he wished me to understand that there was no personal feeling in this matter, to which I readily agreed. Following this, Mr. Mather, still with no small amount of heat in his statements, started to berate the Forest Service for endeavoring to duplicate the National Park Service in the recreational use of the forests. (p. 6)

Mather repeated to Carhart what he had said on the open floor about Congressman Good:

His whole attitude towards me, at this time, was that of trying to browbeat me into an admission of the impropriety of the Forest Service in engaging in this activity. Naturally, I stood my ground, merely reiterating the two points that I had made. . . . Happily, I may state that during this entire time, I did not lose control of myself, nor did I make any unwarranted statements; although I feel that there was plenty of provocation for some pretty sharp rejoinders to Mr. Mather's assertions. (p. 6)

Carhart had not seen *The Des Moines Register* headline when he arrived for the second day of the convention. Other attendees wanted to censure the paper for sensational, misleading reporting. They also asked for a resolution supporting Forest Service recreation. But Carhart was determined not to stir Mather up again: "I considered this merely the writings of a rather inaccurate reporter who had a decided thirst for bloodshed" (p. 6). Carhart admitted that he tried to get through a resolution supporting the Forest Service recreation program.

Mather was not the only one looking for a fight in Des Moines. Peck, Carl Stahl, and others in the Forest Service had probably set this intrigue in motion. When the session opened on January 10, the chair asked for any written revisions to the proposed agenda. Carhart was ready: "Gentlemen: May I suggest that in your deliberations, you consider the recreational use of National and State Forest lands" (p. 6). For some reason, Carhart's recommendations did not reach the policy committee. As the convention was coming to a close, an alarmed Carhart took his concerns to a friend of Frank Waugh's, Harris Reynolds of the Massachusetts Forestry Association. They drafted a resolution that might make their point without detonating Mather:

Whereas Forest Lands, wherever located, offer an opportunity for recreation without any serious destruction of their economic values; and whereas, at the present time, millions of people annually receive this return from National, State, County, and municipal Forests; therefore, be it resolved that this conference, recognizing the fundamental value of Forest recreation, recommends the establishment of other publicly owned Forest lands and the correlation of the recreational use on these lands with similar activities on other publicly owned areas. (p. 7)

This motion upset both Mather and Albright, especially when it received several strong seconds and enthusiastic support from Walter Filley, the Connecticut state forester. Discussion was hot and heavy: "Mr. Filley concluded his endorsement of this resolution and was followed by Mr. Bade, President of the Sierra Club of California, who was sitting next to Mr. Mather and had been conversing with him a moment before. Mr. Bade belittled the Forests as much as possible" (p. 7). Eventually, in spite of Mather's furious coaching of the Sierra Club president (who was leading the opposition to Carhart's resolution from the floor), the state forest representatives supported Carhart's resolution, and it finally passed.

On January 20, 1921, Carhart wrote another memo titled "On the National Conference on Parks Jan 11–12 in Des Moines." Carhart revealed that he had attended the meeting at Stahl's suggestion. Stahl's idea was to prepare for "a similar conference in which the Forest Service will take active part" (p. 1). (This must have been the proposed National Conference on Outdoor Recreation mentioned at the end of Chapter 5.) Carhart also provided more detail. Mather had "stated that the National Park system has not in mind the control of all recreation in the Nation which would point to the recognition by that Service of National Forest recreation territories" (p. 1). He added that Mather seemed to include state and county recreation systems in his plans but not the national forests.

Could Mather be trusted? Could he be consistent? Mather made many presentations at Des Moines. Even Albright must have quailed when Mather said

he would assist all local agencies in securing legislation to have areas taken from remaining public lands to be made into state parks. (It is my [Carhart's] understanding of this statement, by Mr. Mather, that he would, under all circumstances, assist states, counties and municipalities in the West in securing lands from public domains, and probably from National Forests, to be given to these local bodies for their use. I believe this statement especially significant to Forest men.) (p. 1)

Mather was not the only obstacle Carhart encountered in Des Moines. He scolded some of the biggest names in his profession, and he saw potential allies in women's clubs. Carhart was thinking about his own proposed conference, built on his idea for "a Federation of Outdoor Clubs." Obviously, he thought the "human use of recreation areas" conference he was planning could do better than the one in Des Moines. Here, in the same memorandum, we get a glimpse of Carhart's problems with the 1964 Wilderness Act:

> The program presented at this conference, with a few exceptions, constituted more of a mutual admiration society than an attempt to press forward constructive work. There was a decided atmosphere of fanaticism along certain lines, which did not take into consideration the human use of recreation areas whatever. Birds, flowers, animals and rocks received more consideration in the discussions than did underfed children or working people craving outdoor recreation. The entire attitude of some devotees of certain lines was that nothing mattered so long as the birds were protected or some wild flowers were allowed to bloom in native settings.
>
> Mr. Jensen, landscape architect of Chicago (and he should know better), spent the entire time during his address in harping upon the destruction that economic development of farm lands had wrought in native flower and shrub life of the prairies. The geologists at the meeting were entirely centered on geological formations, and the other devotees of particular lines were equally self-centered. As a result, there was no real effort towards rational organization in presenting these elements of landscape to human users, which should have been one of the objectives of this meeting. (p. 2)

There were exceptions to this dreary litany, and Carhart named them, emphasizing the final conference session on "methods for handling the recreational use of public lands . . . methods and policies for handling the human use of recreation areas" (p. 3) Carhart concluded that a plenary annual meeting on national recreation needs should be held that would focus on comprehensive planning:

> [What is needed is the] correlation of landscape elements to produce a rational human use—rather than a discussion of these elements without particular regard for [their] general relation to human beings. In other words, the entire convention was dominated by several groups of ardent naturalists and scientists who were very self-centered. The proper program for such a meeting would not eliminate these groups, but would give more consideration to the relation of the human family to recreation grounds. (p. 3)

Carhart knew emancipated and enfranchised women could play an important role in building a constituency for comprehensive recreation planning. In his memo, he mentioned an attendee at the Des Moines convention who had impressed him. Mrs. Florence Whitley of Webster City, Iowa, was the conservation chair of the General Federation of Women's Clubs. These clubs were interested in forestry and forest recreation. They were also a great national contact for "putting over a National Forestry program." Carhart indicated that he also spent time at the Des Moines gathering hobnobbing with advertising men and with convention and tourist bureau men.

He ended his memo with a plea for direct Forest Service participation in his proposed conference: "It will be necessary for more people being present who are actively interested in the adaptation of land surfaces to human use" (p. 4). Here are more seeds of Carhart's objections to the 1964 Wilderness Act. Are we part of nature or just visitors? Humans always stood at the center of his plans for wildlands. Real conservationists would "counteract the undesirable influence of a too one-sided outlook which is prevalent among the scientists and other people interested in only one phase of outdoor life" (p. 4). In particular, Carhart hoped for attendance from "all Forest men interested in game and flower preservation and the human use of Forest lands" (p. 4).

While Carhart was serving on the front lines, Wallace Hutchinson was leading District 2's lobbying efforts back in Washington, where both Mather and Leon Kneipp had their knives poised at Carhart's back. On February 10, 1921, Hutchinson warned Carhart that Kneipp was on the warpath against recreation interests: "[T]he least they [Forest Service officials] could have done was to have handed you some form of meager compliment on the way you answered Mather." Underestimating Mather, Hutchinson reassured Carhart that "we have nothing to fear in the future from him; also that there will probably be a new head of the parks under the coming administration."

Hutchinson gave Carhart a worldly explanation for Good's favoritism: "Mr. Good spent last summer in company with the Director of the Parks on a grand vacation tour throughout the West." Hutchinson added: "However, the point is that folks in this office have 'laid down' completely as far as pushing the recreation game goes. It seems like the same old story of frigidity of the pedal extremities. So marked is this reaction that we are not to be allowed this year to even run a recreation picture on the front of the *Yearbook*. Under such a handicap, how can we expect to ever secure any results?"[7]

SO—WHAT'S THE VERDICT?

In the 1960s, Carhart was working on a history of recreation planning with Samuel T. Dana of the University of Michigan. Their effort was part of a larger campaign, headed by Carhart's unlikely friend and ally, Democratic congressman Wayne Aspinall of Colorado, to finally make national planning for recreation as big and bold as Carhart had always thought it should be.[8] Laurence Rockefeller chaired the Outdoor Recreation Resources Review Commission (ORRRC). Carhart wanted to be sure ORRRC had its history straight, beginning with his dogfight with Mather. So Carhart provided Dana with an interesting version of the Des Moines conference:

> As I finished, Mr. Mather shot up from where he sat in the audience. He flayed me. He said the forests were for growing wood, supplying forage; the NPS [National Park Service] was the outfit to supply recreation. I got up and restated—the people were coming to the forests and something must be done to meet problems created. He lost his temper, got on his feet again, and let me have it. I got up, perhaps bewildered, maybe hurt by a man I had so much regard for, and the chairman said he thought we had discussed this problem enough. . . . I was laid low by the whole incident.

I might say, I never lost my admiration for Mr. Mather. And in perspective it's greater today than forty years ago.

Yet, here it is most certainly, an untold but powerful interlude with impacts in the entire recreational field; it explains a number of phases that are evident but their genesis and relationships unclear. I can give this a once-over story of off-hand handling, skip it and let someone who might prowl my papers in the Conservation Library Center some years hence, find the facts "hitherto unreported," and gather stature as a researcher thereby, or tell the facts, as stripped of personality and impulses as possible, doublestripped with your help, and say, in effect "This is historical fact of importance" and let chips fall. Certainly I can't be accused of any adverse feeling toward NPS and the parks; I've fought, sometimes pretty much alone, for Dinosaur, Teton, against Yellowstone dams, as early as 1920 for the Great Sand Dunes. So—What's the verdict?[9]

THE GREAT PUEBLO FLOOD OF 1921

In spite of the promising beginnings in 1919–1920, reasons were proliferating in 1921 for planners and landscape architects to avoid southern Colorado. One of these was the growing realization that, in spite of the Forest Service's valiant restoration efforts, abused watersheds were compromised more seriously than anyone dared admit. Carhart left Denver for St. Paul, Minnesota, on May 2. On June 3, following heavy rainstorms throughout the upper Arkansas River watershed, a massive flood inundated Pueblo, followed by a declaration of martial law and the deployment of federal troops. Amid concerns about an epidemic and a complete lack of drinking water, Supervisor Al Hamel had to face the fact that Congress's failure to fund recreation was part of a larger failure to fund the sort of comprehensive planning that would restore resiliency and absorptive capacity to the "tin roof watershed" of the Arkansas River's headwaters.

Instead of working slowly and painstakingly on watershed rehabilitation, short-sighted federal planners had sought a quick, cheap solution. Engineers had built a system of levees that the floodwaters easily obliterated. One of the letters Carhart received at Ely, Minnesota, when he emerged from his long canoe trip was Al Hamel's account of the great Pueblo flood: "Thank God the Forest Service people and their families were all safe after the flood, which is the worst thing that I have ever seen. Newspaper accounts cannot exaggerate it in any way. When I tell you that the water was 8 feet deep at the Federal Building and 16 feet deep at the Vail Hotel and 14 feet at the Union Station, you can get some idea of what conditions were like."

When the flood hit Pueblo, Hamel rushed back from his fieldwork, fording flooded streams like the St. Charles River near Squirrel Creek. Hamel looked beyond his Forest Service duties to the public good. Hamel told Carhart: "The big loss will be from the foreign population who refused to move when ordered. I see where the San Isabel can play a big part in this relief work and no doubt many will want to get out of here and camp in the hills until conditions become better established. Pueblo will be no place for children to be in for sometime."[10]

The worst natural disaster in Colorado history killed 200 people and destroyed 50 percent of Pueblo's businesses. The "foreign population" from southern and eastern Europe and Mexico suffered the most.[11]

BOUNDARY WATERS CANOE AREA

Carhart was depressed. Field season was his cure for too much roof—and too much "burocracy." Vee's feelings during this long separation remain unknown, except that she was corresponding with her mother-in-law on subjects that included nest building. The spring and summer of 1920 had been glorious for the young couple. During the spring of 1921, however, Vee stayed in Denver, living in rented rooms, where she received her husband's letters about his adventures—some addressed to her alone, some to "Dear Wife and Folks." Many of the letters are in longhand, but when Carhart briefly returned to Ely, Minnesota, on May 29, he wrote: "Guess that I had better get to the Corona for this for if I keep at the writing by hand it will never be read by you."[12]

The daily clatter of Carhart's Corona typewriter soon became more familiar to Vee. A month after writing the May 29 letter, after plunging again into the maze of lakes and burned-over, cut-over forests, Carhart was facing the reality of his professional future, weighing his post–Forest Service options. He wrote to Vee alone about taking "the folks and you" to see some of his work near Boulder.[13] Money was obviously tight. Carhart got a summer suit at a good price in Minnesota, hoping to stretch its light wool to make do in warmer Denver until he could afford a winter-weight suit. He affectionately kidded Vee about "bargain chasing again." Aware of the dangers of his forays into wild country, he reassured her that he had put "33 dollars into insurance."

The Forest Service provided expense money for fieldworkers. Carhart hoarded his, also mentioning how glad he was to have the monthly *American Forestry* check for his series of articles.[14] The couple was saving to buy a home in east Denver. Carhart believed, "If we are careful we can have a cool thousand in the bank by the end of the year." He added:

> What I would like to do would be to have about say $1500 to put on a house
> if we find one that suits and get a little more definite idea of what is going
> to happen to us in the next three years. One thing is certain: my stay in D-2
> is not more than two years from next March or perhaps Jan. 1 1924. By that
> time they should know what they want to do in the way of a real salary and
> whether they want me to take charge of the entire service or not. Anyway
> that is two and a half years away and we will not worry about it but get the
> extra $500 where we can use it when needed with some surplus left when
> the time comes. . . . And it is about 30 days until I will be with you. Little
> over four weeks! Heaps of love, yours.

Another entry in this series of letters, dated May 22, 1921, reveals Carhart's practical state of mind: "There is an island in the lake I may try to buy if the price is right, it is about ¼ mile long and has been cut over." The source for this real estate tip was a versatile, thirty-year-old Finn named Mat Sodobaker. "Mat is a Forest Guard, a canoe man of exceptional ability, and good company. Equipment includes a camera, a six-shooter and grub for 10 days." Sodobaker knew all about land prices (ranging from $2.50 to $10 per acre), and Carhart added: "It will be a very desirable point for a canoe camp club." The twenty-acre island was near Basswood Lake, about twelve miles from Ely. The Carharts never developed their speculative purchase. They sold it in the late 1920s.[15]

Carhart covered between 300 and 400 miles during his five-week voyage. He mapped many of the routes that would become the Boundary Waters Canoe Area in 1930. As always, the Forest Service faced the challenge of restoring lands that had been cut, burned, or both. And as always, Carhart faced proposals to build dams in places where he felt they would damage recreation values. A prolific photographer, he took many pictures that he sent to headquarters along with his recommendations for protecting and promoting recreational values.

When he emerged from the backcountry in late June, he wrote to Vee on June 26, "It should make a pretty good story." It did. And it continued to do so as Carhart elaborated his role over the years. In his zeal to celebrate Carhart's contributions to conservation, Donald Baldwin raised many hackles among wilderness partisans. He plainly overstated Carhart's role in the planning of Boundary Waters. Carhart himself did his reputation no good when he chronically misrepresented his original proposal as consistent with the ideas of other wilderness advocates of the time. Yet Carhart did glimpse something on the Superior that he had seen earlier on the San Isabel. That something went beyond the drive to find and protect pristine wilderness. Carhart was learning about ecological change and resilience. He saw the restoration potential of cut-over and burned-over lands as departure points for nurturing a wilderness experience. One of Carhart's strengths as a planner was his visionary ability to blaze a trail from the blackened stumps of the present to a future with wilderness qualities. His gift lay in transitions, in transporting visitors to emotional, aesthetic, and physical thresholds where they might soar into wilderness. Carhart saw that some of the waterways could serve as "highways" into the wilderness. He was not above recommending that some of these "highways" be improved, even suggesting that highway funds should be used to develop an interrelated system of roadways and waterways.

The Forest Service spent years trying to digest (or avoid) Carhart's recommendations. The continuity was Carhart's friend and admirer Al Hamel. Ultimately, the Forest Service did not adopt Carhart's plan for Quetico-Superior, instead choosing one designed by Ernest Oberholtzer. This plan finally became reality with the Shipstead-Nolan Act of 1930.

After he left the Forest Service in 1922, Carhart stayed involved in the Boundary Waters battle in many ways. Working with landscape architect and planner Paul B. Riis, Carhart served as a conduit between friends like Hamel in the Forest Service and conservationists. This role led some in the Forest Service, especially Kneipp, to impugn Carhart's motives in ways that exasperated Donald Baldwin: "It should be emphasized that Carhart's motives were unselfish, above reproach, and his actions reflected profound loyalty to his fellow man and to the Nation. He sought neither monetary reward nor personal gain."[16]

A more systematic planner than Carhart, Oberholtzer, along with Benton MacKaye, helped form the Regional Planning Association of America. MacKaye and Oberholtzer then joined Leopold, Bob Marshall, and others in founding the Wilderness Society. Oberholtzer's scheme followed Carhart's in many ways, including measures to increase fish and game production, as well as some logging and a system of hotels and chalets. The main difference was in scope— Carhart's strategy was more restricted.

In Carhart's mind, time seemed to enhance the value of what he had done in 1921. In 1955, Carhart published his universally acclaimed *Timber in Your Life*, with a glowing introduction by Bernard DeVoto. Looking back, he wrote of his Boundary Waters adventures:

At the time I was making the study of the Superior forest, with recommendations for its best type of development, it was all just a job to be done. Looking back and referring to the report containing my recommendations for public use of this Lakeland, I have a feeling of having had guidance of some sort beyond my actual abilities and perceptions. For what the report proposed was the retention of as much as possible of the forest as primitive canoe country.[17]

Perhaps trying to settle old scores, Carhart (unwisely) gave more credit to Stahl and to Paul Riis than to others. Then he made a peculiar claim (which slipped by both DeVoto and reviewer Paul Sears).[18] He somehow conflated Trappers Lake with Boundary Waters, thereby confusing everyone:

> While I was still writing my report on the Superior, Aldo Leopold, then Regional Forester at Albuquerque, visited the Denver headquarters. As we talked for several hours we discovered [we] both had arrived at conclusions that were almost identical. Leopold was particularly interested in saving the best of the remaining wilderness areas. I talked of the dominant use principle, and wilderness set aside to preserve its values as an application of that principle.
>
> Soon Leopold began to preach the need for retaining primitive lands we still had in the nation for the type of recreational use they supplied. He did great service in developing this idea into positive action.
>
> Actually, both the "wilderness idea" and the allotting of land units to any defined type of recreational use is [sic] analogous to zoning practices in city planning.[19]

Rather than stir these muddy waters further, it seems more fruitful to relish Carhart's descriptions of what he saw and did on his 1921 canoe trip. Carhart meticulously cataloged the wildlife, especially game birds such as the partridge, and he took particular care to record each moose sighting. He was also very good at describing the fishing and the lay of the land in ways that would make sense to hunters and fishermen. Not every day was devoted to professional pursuits. Like errant adolescents, the two men chased a cow moose and tried to catch her calf. Some of the land they paddled by had recently been timbered, often illegally, which might account for the sparse descriptions of the vegetation. And Carhart recorded a new phenomenon: a Forest Service fire lookout: "This whole country was burned over in the Hinkley fire of 1900 or 1890 but it now has some jack pine 5 to 8 inches big on it." In spite of Sodobaker's familiarity with the waterways, he and Carhart had a hard time finding lakeside land that had not been burned over. Taking many pictures, Carhart expressed wonder at the restoration contributions of the numerous beaver.

In the June 26 letter to Vee, Carhart said, "Must ring off and talk to Mat. It's lonesome as the devil out here. The nearest white folks we know are 20 miles away." Carhart and Sodobaker encountered many Indians during their travels. They saw some Indians in a canoe netting game fish illegally. They also witnessed Indian families coming from a dog feast. Carhart caught his first lake trout—a thirty-two-incher. Sodobaker introduced Carhart to the fighting pike—and to camp cooking so bad that Carhart resolved to do better. He spent a few days sick in his tent, where at least he could escape mosquitoes, sand flies—and Finnish camp cuisine.

When the two returned briefly to Ely to reprovision, they witnessed a Decoration Day (our contemporary Memorial Day) program that stirred their patriotism. Carhart noticed that Ely's economy was not taking advantage of being near the lake. But he liked Ely and compared it to Mapleton: "The younger generations are mixing up in pretty good shape and making a really American body in the town. Another factor along that line is that boys of every group went to the war together."

Carhart ended his homespun account in the June 26 letter to Vee: "My Dear: This will finish that compendium of thrilling adventures of the good ship USFS canoe that we brought to a close on last Friday night by arriving in here from Perry portage at the upper end of Basswood Lake."

YOUR WAIL OF JULY 5 IS RECEIVED

On his return to Ely, Carhart found a letter from Stahl asking him to visit the Minnesota National Forest before leaving for home. Looking to his future, Carhart also set up a meeting with the Midwest chapter of ASLA. But once he was out of the field and back within the Forest Service bureaucracy, he realized how unhappy he had become. While Carhart was paddling a canoe, Kneipp and E. A. Sherman had visited District 2 and the San Isabel—and Kneipp carried the day. Unburdening himself, Carhart injudiciously wrote Stahl on July 5. Stahl replied on July 9:

> Your wail of July 5 is received. . . . When you get over your bilious attack you will probably look at it differently. I will admit you have had a dose of the same medicine that each of us has had. You would be in about the same boat that I was if they had taken part of your salary and part of your expenses away, and told you to go on and do your work. . . . I believe that if you will just keep in good spirit you will be about as successful [as I have been] when the right time comes.
>
> After talking with Colonel Greeley and Mr. Sherman who was recently here, I am convinced that the Forester will never ask for enough money for Recreation to enable the Service to go ahead and put up the sort of constructions that we need to carry out such plans as you have been formulat-

ing. That is not his notion at all, neither is it Mr. Kneipp's. By the way, Mr. Kneipp said, after seeing the San Isabel, that all those developments we showed him were just about what he thought ought to be done in the way of recreation developments in the National Forests, and that he had never seen any recreation development in the Service which pleased him more or seemed more appropriate than those. He doesn't think much of the Eagle Creek or many of the California improvements, but he does feel that communities ought to bear the expense of the improvements which they principally will utilize. The Forester believes that we ought to have some money for recreation improvements, but wants to confine them to what will largely be protection against fire and protection of the public health. I believe that his notion is fairly sound. I don't mean by that that I fall for District 6's scheme of going out and begging [for] money, but if a community wants to develop a recreation center, we will make them a plan and supervise the improvements, hold the ground for them from other appropriations and use, and let them put up the money, because they are going to profit by the improvements.[20]

Stahl did not stop there. Not mentioning the recent Pueblo flood, he noted that SIPRA had failed to meet its most recent funding matches with the Forest Service. Yet Stahl was fond of Carhart, and he tried to encourage him as best he could. Perhaps Stahl knew Hamel was bound for the Superior, for he asked Carhart to warn James Dahlgren, at that time head of the Superior, "that this [recreation] is his business as much as claims or selling timber." Further, Stahl encouraged Carhart about the Conejos fishing lodge scheme. He closed: "For heaven's sake cheer up before you get to the Minnesota and put some life into Marshall. You will have to be optimistic though, if you do."[21]

CARHART AND THE AMERICAN SOCIETY OF LANDSCAPE ARCHITECTS

Everyone in District 2 must have known that their ambitious $56,000 budget request was a long shot. Even before the Des Moines meeting, it was probably already clear to Kneipp, Sherman (now assistant chief), and others in the chief's office that the Park Service had long since gained the ear of Congressman James Good of the Appropriations Committee.[22] Perhaps that is why Carhart was the only Forest Service representative at Des Moines.

Carhart's uncertain situation led him to redouble his efforts to make sure SIPRA was headed in the right direction. SIPRA's accomplishments were his showpieces as he contemplated a move into the wider professional world of landscape architecture. In 1921, SIPRA was planning to continue the development of Squirrel Creek, and Carhart wrote to Hamel: "With the completion of this program the San Isabel National Forest will afford greater conveniences, greater scenery and greater inducements for tourists than any section of the West."[23]

For some months Carhart had been conducting a warm correspondence with Professor James Sturgis Pray, McCrary's mentor and chair of the School of Landscape Architecture at Harvard. Pray was trying to find an alternative to Olmsted's absolutism regarding agency roles. Pray could afford to be more of a gentleman than Carhart. He had turned down an earlier offer, conveyed through Culley, to work on Squirrel Creek, claiming insufficient remuneration. Yet Carhart's articles in *American Forestry* had impressed Pray, as had accounts of the pioneering designs at Squirrel Creek. He pumped Carhart for news from the West. He sent Carhart scurrying to find summer Forest Service jobs for his son, Benjamin, and for his students. And he made noises about coming out west for a tour of District 2 that he expected Carhart to lead.

An anxious and increasingly disappointed Carhart bombarded Pray with letters throughout the spring of 1921, while Congressman Good's committee was going through the motions of deciding the fate of Carhart's recreation proposals. Clearly thinking of Trappers Lake, Carhart was especially concerned about the threat of federal water developments to recreation planning. He sent Pray photos of water features on the national forests. But the die was cast.

On April 23, 1921, after the bad budget news broke, Pray finally sent a sympathetic response, remarking that the Forest Service might have succeeded if it had relied more on ASLA and other friends for support. This was too little and too late. But Carhart must have already been looking beyond the Forest Service to private employment as a landscape architect. The professor's somewhat Olympian attitude shows in a letter he wrote to Carhart in the fall of 1921, in which he promised to "whisper something in Colonel Greeley's or Mr. Sherman's ear, so to speak, about the urgent necessity of your making a trip East to study Eastern recreation facilities."[24]

By the time he left for the 1921 field season, Carhart had apparently seen the writing on the wall concerning his future with the Forest Service. About to leave for a major tour of the threatened Superior National Forest's Boundary Waters, Carhart redoubled his requests for Pray's help in getting ASLA behind a campaign to protect all water features on the forests—ranging from Trappers Lake to the Boundary Waters.

Pray mentioned that he remained in touch with Sherman, who, at Carhart's instigation, had enlisted ASLA's help in salvaging something from the failed budget request. Pray summed up his own concerns: "First, the formal adoption of general plans for the National Forests in which, along with other use districts, those in which recreation is the dominant function shall be clearly marked; and, Second, an exemption of these recreation areas from the application of the Federal Water Power Act."[25]

Carhart responded to Pray's request for an account of how landscape architects had behaved at the Des Moines conference. Carhart's populist emphasis on economics and human use is notable.[26]

> Although there were probably more landscape architects present than any other profession or group they received far less consideration in discussions and on the program than any other major interest present. Mr. [Jens] Jensen and Mr. [O. C.] Simonds both spoke. Mr. Jensen taking rather a radical attitude relative to farmers cutting out the hedge rows and plowing up natural meadows. As far as I am personally concerned, I would like nothing better than to see the entire country [be] one great park but economics demand that we have production of food and it is useless to storm against necessity which demands that fields shall be plowed up in order to sustain our population. There is another point which to my mind is worth consideration and that is that well ordered and well cultivated fields are in themselves beautiful. Mr. Simonds gave his usual good plea for the native naturalistic developments.
>
> Perhaps the best result out of the meeting is the amount of enthusiasm it stirred up, but this enthusiasm will surely be directed towards service to birds, service to fossil rocks, to wild flowers, and not service to poor, underfed youngsters. Sentimentalism is a great and good principal [sic] when well directed, but I do think that this conference could have done a great service through more of a discussion of human service than was present. Perhaps I expected too much real discussion of broad policies, of systems of doing things, of fundamental ways in which problems were studied and disposed of, and that my disappointment comes from expecting too much. I had hoped for a big, broad, constructive nation-wide policy regarding recreation from this conference but nothing approaching this, other than the good sentiment embodied in their one set of resolutions, came of it.

While Carhart was in Minnesota that summer, Pray shared Carhart's private remarks about Mather with others in ASLA. Pray's betrayal of privacy and his failure to support Carhart's work must have seemed crushing. Because Carhart was in the field, he did not discover Pray's indiscretion until July 1—too late to do anything about the resulting gossip and bad blood. Somehow, Carhart and Pray overcame this breach of confidence. On July 19, Pray sympathized:

> I can understand and am not surprised by your heart-sinking over the recreation situation in the National Forests. Under all the circumstances—not only the failure of the appropriation but the lack of full sympathy in certain desirable quarters—your discouragement is not to be wondered at. I know the situation is discouraging, and this is due in part to a very unhappy

current materialistic tendency in our country, a sort of a reaction from the wonderful spirit which, during the war, lifted the country as a whole high above the petty and selfish and merely commercial. But there is bound to be a return wave. Meanwhile, don't let go of the job; keep up your excellent propaganda in the magazine, "American Forestry"; and, above all, keep up a stout heart.[27]

Carhart kept a stout heart by pouring his feelings into his writing—both to Pray and to the public. Pray finally came to Colorado to visit Carhart and see some of Carhart's work in August 1921. He was too busy to go to the San Isabel, but the two men did ascend Pike's Peak, where the professor could see Carhart's design for the Barr Trail and they could discuss watershed-wide planning and the aesthetics of the glaciers that were at the head of many Rocky Mountain watersheds.[28] Both men were still disturbed by the Pueblo flood in the spring of 1921. Pray suggested that Carhart start writing for other "parks and recreation" outlets about watershed health's relationship to urban planning. Carhart responded quickly with an article about St. Mary's Glacier: "Denver's Greatest Manufacturing Plant."[29]

More cold comfort arrived for Carhart at the end of November, when his friend and ally from the Des Moines conference, Harris Reynolds of the Massachusetts Forestry Association, wrote to say that the state foresters were opting to "tour the European forests" the following summer rather than visit SIPRA's work on the San Isabel.[30]

Carhart also sought counsel from Frank Waugh, who praised his younger colleague's work and asked many questions about the San Isabel, SIPRA, and the effects of the Pueblo flood on living conditions for working people.[31] Carhart replied to Waugh on December 12, 1921, at a time when his moods were alternating between extremes.[32]

FAMILY MATTERS

Like his son, George Carhart was comfortable at a typewriter. He wrote his annual birthday letter to his son on the stationary of "G. W. Carhart, Hardware & Furniture, Mapleton, Iowa":

> Little did I know 29 years ago when you came to live with us what was in store but you sure started out strong in stature and lungs and have gradually and continuously grown in all desirable ways till at the present time you are not only our joy and our pride but the pride of a great many who know you.
>
> You have climbed step by step until you now hold an enviable position with prospects for greater achievements. You are now an authority in your

line, a distinction that might be the envy of many who had better chances than you.

I love you and hope for the very best for you that could be wished for.[33]

Ella Carhart's birthday letter followed a few days later. She referred to a letter she had received from Vee and mentioned sending Vee money to buy Arthur "a house jacket," gently adding that she was sure Vee was happier now that Arthur would be home more. Providing her son with images of contented domesticity, she told of putting up jams and jellies. And she spoke of going with women friends to see a movie, *Birth of a Nation.*[34]

George Carhart added a note to his wife's letter. Referring to their son's contemplated job change, he cautioned, "It is my opinion that so long as you are drawing so good a salary as you are and at the same time getting a greater reputation that you had better be sure of something good and lasting before you make the change."

NOTES

1. Carhart's January 17, 1921, memo to District 2 forester Allen Peck, Carhart Collection, Denver Public Library (hereafter CC, DPL).

2. Carhart memo, December 3, 1920, CC, DPL.

3. Ibid. Carhart wrote: "This move is no small accomplishment, for it puts an official stamp of recognition on the recreational field in the National Forests which no other organization could so well do. It is worth noting that this society is very conservative and slow to take any action without being very thoroughly acquainted with relative facts. Most of the men of the Society are constantly being called upon to talk to the public on landscape art, and if, through the work of this Committee, all members can become as familiar with the recreational use of the National Forests as they are now with the National Parks, it will be no small source of help in having the recreation features of the Forests presented to people of culture and influence in a good manner by an authority. The Forest Service is endeavoring to cooperate to the fullest extent with the Park Service. Here is surely a meeting ground where a third group of people, with only the interests of the public and art at heart, may be able to help each Service in getting closer cooperation and correlation with the other. Furthermore, this group will be trained to look at the problems of recreation in the National play areas from the standpoint of trained men, familiar with the study and development of land surfaces to human use" (p. 3).

4. In the correspondence file for 1921, CC, DPL.

5. See Horace Albright and Marian Albright Schenck, *Creating the National Park Service: The Missing Years* (Norman: University of Oklahoma Press, 1999).

6. The conflict between these agencies remains alive today. It was important when Congress was considering ORRRC's recommendations in the 1960s. Letter from Carhart to Samuel T. Dana, February 2, 1962, CC, DPL. Horace Albright tells how he covered up Mather's manic-depression in ibid.

7. Letter from Hutchinson to Carhart, February 10, 1921, CC, DPL. Mather remained head of national parks until 1929, when his illness forced him to hand over power to Albright. Mather died in 1930. Carhart and Albright remained friends for the rest of their lives.

8. Carhart had written to Joe Penfold for Penfold's version of who had the original idea for ORRRC. In a February 16, 1962, letter to Carhart, Penfold credited Aspinall (CC, DPL). Carhart's loyalty to Aspinall began with ORRRC. By 1962, although there is no evidence for such a claim, Carhart was telling Dana that Mather had passed him over in favor of Punchard in 1919.

9. Letter from Carhart to Dana, February 2, 1962, CC, DPL.

10. Letter from Hamel to Carhart, July 7, 1921, CC, DPL. Hamel's legacy continues. On May 2, 1996, I interviewed his son and members of the Bosanko family, who are involved in parks and open space activities in Minnesota.

11. The Historic Arkansas River Walk in today's Pueblo shows the history of the flood. In 1922 engineers relocated the Arkansas River into a manmade flood control channel through Pueblo. In 1998 they moved the river back to its original channel. See www.puebloharp.com.

12. Letter from Arthur Carhart to Vee Carhart, May 29, 1921, CC, DPL.

13. Letter from Arthur Carhart to Vee Carhart, June 26, 1921, CC, DPL.

14. Although the Forest Service exercised its right to approve the content of these articles, there was no objection to Carhart keeping the payment. For example, a March 3, 1922, letter from the assistant district forester said his glaciers article "has been approved for publication, with compensation, in some standard magazine"; CC, DPL.

15. On July 19, 1928, Hamel replied to Carhart's query about the direction of local land values. He advised Carhart to hold on to his island. Hamel's letter is in the CC, DPL.

16. Donald Baldwin, *The Quiet Revolution: Grass Roots of Today's Wilderness Preservation Movement* (Boulder: Pruett, 1972), 202.

17. Arthur Carhart, *Timber in Your Life* (Philadelphia: Lippincott, 1955), 145.

18. Reviewed in *The Saturday Review of Literature* in January 1955 by Paul Sears of Yale: "Thus it is that when an author undertakes to tell, in the words of his publishers, 'the full story of the uses and misuses of one of our most crucial natural resources' he is tackling a man-sized job. Bless his soul, Arthur Carhart has brought it off. From now on, whenever I am asked, as often happens, 'Where can I find out about forests and forestry in a way I can understand?' there will be no problem. 'Timber in Your Life' is the answer. I have caught no important aspect of the subject which has been forgotten, nor have I detected any unfairness, despite the author's strong convictions, in his presentation of hot controversial issues—notably the current attempt to wrest control of grazing on national forests and other public lands from those charged by law with conserving them. Mr. Carhart has done an imposing piece of research and translated it into good readable vernacular." See also p. 231.

19. *Timber In Your Life*, 147.

20. Letter from Stahl to Carhart, July 9, 1921, CC, DPL.

21. Ibid.

22. Oddly, Good resigned his position in June 1921, but by then the damage to Carhart's cause had been done. Good served for a few months as President Hoover's secretary of war. He died in November 1929.

23. Letter from Carhart to Hamel, October 10, 1921, CC, DPL.

24. Letter from Pray to Carhart, October 11, 1921, CC, DPL.

25. Ibid.

26. Carhart told Pray: "The recreational resources in National Forests can be utilized without interference with the economical production and as an added return to the Nation from their properties, and that it is the duty of the Forest Service, acting as the Agent of the people[,] to make the greatest return possible from the Forests and to do this they necessarily must develop the recreation use. I then sat down. Afterwards Mr. Mather stopped me in the hall way and practically re-stated his speech of the afternoon in a manner which appealed to me as being very much that of a scold. I am thankful that Mr. Mather has come into the open and shown his true colors. . . . Some time in the future I hope that all nature lovers, and I mean by this everybody, may meet in a conference which will be so comprehensive and so broad that only fundamental, basic policies will be considered . . . and that out of this will grow the big, constructive, universal movement and basic plan I had hoped might develop in the Des Moines Meeting." This quotation and the extract in the text in letter from Carhart to Pray, October 14, 1921, CC, DPL.

27. Letter from Pray to Carhart, July 19, 1921, CC, DPL.

28. Carhart's articles about the St. Vrain Glacier in Colorado appeared in *The Denver Post* and the *Rocky Mountain News* on August 25, 1921.

29. *Municipal Facts Monthly* IV, August 1921.

30. Letter from Reynolds to Carhart, November 25, 1921, CC, DPL.

31. "In particular I would like to know if it will be possible to revise in 1922 the plan for a municipal health camp in Pueblo." Letter from Waugh to Carhart, November 12, 1921, CC, DPL.

32. "I am just starting on a regional plan for a portion of the Rio Grande. Things are booming and I am going to have more than I can do to clear up the program for this winter season. The big things on hand now are the Superior plan, a plan of the glacier area, and this section of the Rio Grande. We have organized a fourth recreation association at Boulder. A fifth is being talked of at Fort Collins. Both of these will operate in the Colorado National Forest. I don't believe I can give you any official dope on the health camp at Pueblo. My impression is that the Forest Service was not in a position to talk real business which is necessary when you start dealing with Pueblo and they have made a camp of their own on County owned property just outside of the Forest. I don't think it is good business to suggest anything to these fellows out here unless you are ready to do work for when they get a notion out in this section of the country they go." Letter from Carhart to Waugh, December 12, 1921, CC, DPL.

33. Letter from George Carhart to Arthur Carhart, September 14, 1921, CC, DPL.

34. Letter from Ella Carhart to Arthur Carhart, September 18, 1921, CC, DPL.

HOG WILD ON RECREATION

Other districts, I am told, consider this one "hog wild" on recreation. And all we are trying to do is to get a regional plan started before there is necessity of doing any work. Just the other day the District Forester told me that he was certain that if I was turned loose on this work without the restraint imposed by the foresters of the organization that I would run riot on recreation and carry it far beyond any reasonable bounds.

Perhaps I do seem aggressively radical to many of them but it is because I have to scrap continually and in a somewhat radical fashion to get any consideration whatever. I am not done with recreation in National Forests when I leave. I will not be muzzled by censorship that exists in the department and while I am not going to do any "muckraking" I will be free to tell my ideas and views without restriction.

—ARTHUR CARHART, 1922[1]

INTRODUCTION: THE QUITTER?

Carhart's stint in the U.S. Army showed that he could serve a cause. His later federal work showed that he could function in a bureaucracy, although never smoothly. After he left the Forest Service, he spent the next fifty-six years serving the cause of conservation with honor and distinction—and a fierce sense of independence. As George Carhart had warned his son, leaving the Forest Service would exact a pound of flesh. Carhart paid this price in terms both emotional and financial. The Carharts, for example, did not move into their own house in Park Hill until June 1927.

Always mercurial, Carhart began his final year with the Forest Service by exploring other ways to serve the cause of conservation. A return to private practice in landscape architecture seemed to offer the best possibilities, and Carhart's correspondence with American Society of Landscape Architects (ASLA) dignitaries like James Pray took on a tone at once personal and professional. Sensing that he could no longer trust Carl Stahl or E. A. Sherman, Carhart sought mentors in Pray, Irvin McCrary, and Frank Culley. After some agonizing, he found what he was looking for at the end of 1922, when he resigned from the Forest Service to become the junior partner with the new landscape architecture firm of McCrary, Culley, & Carhart.

In the meantime, Carhart had to manage his transition out of the Forest Service. It was not easy, for both Carhart and his Forest Service colleagues nurtured an ambivalence that lasted more than half a century. Toward the end of Carhart's career, when the doctrine of Multiple Use had come under fire and the Forest Service found it expedient to write its own history to counter critics, Forest Service historian Frank Harmon recruited the eighty-one-year-old Carhart to the cause. Donald Baldwin's book had just appeared, and Harmon gave a copy to former Forest Service chief Richard McArdle, who said:

> I suppose I should enter a protestation of my own. I knew and liked Art
> Carhart. We first met in 1935 when I moved to Colorado. We continued
> our friendship over the years. Carhart quite the FS [Forest Service] after
> about 3½ years because he was impatient with official acceptance by the FS
> of all his ideas and proposals. He wanted immediate action, now, at once
> and no quibbling about it. I never heard any disagreement in the FS about
> Carhart's ideas or philosophies but I can understand why the FS could not
> immediately and at once drop everything else and put all of these into effect
> everywhere. For one thing there was neither money nor legislative author-
> ity for recreation. There were other obstacles. When I was in the FS I never
> could do all the things I knew should be done as quickly as possible. We did
> do most of them eventually. Carhart was never vindictive. He maintained his
> good relations with FS people. But I often wondered how much more would
> have been done and how much faster recreational use would have developed
> if Carhart had curbed his impatience and stuck with the job. He quit just
> as the times began to be on his side. Which I always thought was a loss to
> Carhart as well as to the FS.[2]

I FEEL IN NEED OF ADVICE AND GRAVE COUNSEL

Carhart spent the winter of 1921–1922 working on his comprehensive recreation plans for the Superior National Forest. He was also heavily involved in
planning a national recreation conference, partly on behalf of the Forest Service
and partly on his own time and letterhead, working with Culley and Pray. One
of their goals was to develop model legislation for a uniform state parks act, a

move that may have reflected a general professional disenchantment with the infighting between the National Park Service and the Forest Service.

One conference took place in St. Louis, another in New York City. Kept on a short leash by Stahl, Carhart dragged through both. He found them disappointing in terms of his Forest Service goals but promising in terms of his contemplated career change. More contact with Pray at the conferences led to an intensification of their correspondence. Carhart poured his heart out to the older man, who found himself on the receiving end of some brilliant ideas—and some intemperate remarks. Carhart suggested to Pray that ASLA support an effort to transfer the National Park Service to the Department of Agriculture. An alarmed Pray warned Carhart that such a move was inadvisable, referring him to the seminal 1916 issue of *Landscape Architecture*. Pray had ASLA send Carhart a copy. He added a remark that showed much more concern about inappropriate water developments than about automobile incursions: "Certainly whatever the present shortcomings in Park Administration and the present excellences in the Forest Administration, particularly with respect to your Department, there would be in the long run far more danger that forests would be open to appeals for exploitation for irrigation and hydro-electric power and in general engineering undertakings."[3]

Pray was in touch with Sherman in Washington. The professor shared Carhart's contempt for Leon Kneipp's and Sherman's plans to train foresters to be landscape architects. Pray warned Carhart that the Forest Service was going to ask its junior recreation engineer to conduct this misbegotten training. Then Stahl gave Carhart his field assignments for 1922: train foresters to become landscape architects in two-week sessions. And complete the kinds of summer home designs for most of the forests of District 2 that the Forest Service had rejected at Trappers Lake. Carhart was both angry and hurt. The extremes of his feelings appeared in his rejoinder to Pray, a seven-page, single-spaced screed marked "CONFIDENTIAL."[4] At Carhart's request, Pray had started marking his letters to Carhart the same way. He told Carhart he admired the younger man's work so much that he had ordered a complete set of Carhart's San Isabel photos and the accompanying recreation report for the Harvard library.[5]

Although still officially muzzled, Carhart opened fire:

> The recreation situation in the National Forests is rapidly nearing a show-down. I have felt it since last fall more acutely than ever. When I came out here I thought that there was a magnificent opportunity to do a work that would be of national importance and of magnificent scope. The opportunity still exists but until there is a very definite change in conditions the opportunity might as well be buried at the bottom of the sea.

I have definitely decided that unless things change very materially by the first of the year in the way of support of recreational development in the National Forests that I will leave the Service and the foothold that landscape architecture has in this work will either have to be held by some other man or it will be lost. I simply will not battle against the situation alone longer without getting results.[6]

Pray had sent Carhart a copy of Sherman's official reply to ASLA.[7] Warming to his task, Carhart put his finger on the primacy of timber production that would dominate Forest Service planning throughout his life:

They simply will not countenance the intrusion of the aesthetic use of forests until the foresters' ideas of what a forest should be is met. This means, if followed to ultimate conclusions, that recreation will never be adequately handled by the Forest Service.

There has grown up a distinct idea in this district that the foresters have been neglecting forestry proper in favor of other uses of forests. There is a very determined move to get back to the idea of growing timber and doing that first. It has resulted in a sentiment that recreation especially should be chucked in the discard so to speak. It is perhaps true that foresters in the past have neglected to sell the idea of forestry for wood's sake to the public and have paid too much attention to the aesthetic idea. But it should not go to the extent of eliminating the inevitable functions of the forests when it is produced such as recreation, game production and other by-products of timbered lands which are of exceptional value. Alone against such a sentiment, founded in fundamental training, I will be helplessly buried.

Carhart detailed how many districts, given half an opportunity, had put other kinds of engineers in charge of recreation, often with unfortunate results. He saw this sort of juggling as a typical bureaucratic ploy, remarking of such docile men, "They will stand hitched." Then he turned to his own experience. Carhart told Pray he wanted to be "a doer" and not a "teacher of the field force." He continued:

They seem to think that by mixing with these men that I can teach them the fundamentals of landscape architecture like one learns the multiplication table or which plant is poison to cattle.

Another slant on this idea may be found in the questions and situations such as these: "What is there so mysterious about this landscape planning. You have the field men so scared that they will do something wrong they will not go ahead. Can't you open up and give them enough of it so they can go ahead." I have specifically been instructed to avoid giving the field man an idea that planning of summer home lot arrangement is anything but applied common sense and good taste.

Screeds have a momentum of their own. Carhart next turned to the Des Moines conference, where he felt his worm had turned:

> Personally I think that the opposition of the park people is the greatest
> stumbling block in the way of an adequate development of recreational use
> on the National Forests. RECREATION WILL NEVER REACH A STANDING IN A
> FOREST ORGANIZATION WHERE IT WILL BE GIVEN PROPER WEIGHT IN PLANNING,
> ADMINISTRATION OR APPROPRIATIONS.
>
> Finally, I do not think that the people in Washington have had what
> constitutes the recreation landscape design that is needed on every Forest.
> They have little conception of just what a landscape architect of standing
> would do in planning a forest. They have never asked me anything about
> this phase. Whenever I have met them they have lectured me as to what I
> should and shouldn't do and have not attempted to get ideas from me. On
> the other hand the District Forester and Mr. Stahl and Supervisor [Al]
> Hamel of the San Isabel all appreciate just what the regional planning of a
> forest for human use mean. I know that I have gone so far that I have been
> gently reprimanded on some occasions [emphasis in the original].

A composed gentleman like Pray found this sustained howl discomfiting. The normally genial Carhart did not often resort to such bitterness, such irony, such exaggeration. Before closing with the news of his resignation, Carhart told Pray that if the Forest Service did not hire 50–100 landscape architects in the near future:

> WE ARE GOING TO LOSE NATURAL BEAUTY THROUGH INADVISED PLANNING WHICH
> IN THE AGGREGATE WILL FAR SURPASS IN TOTAL QUALITY AND QUANTITY WHAT
> WE HAVE NOW IN THE NATIONAL PARKS. Would not the landscape men and
> nature lovers in general get right into their fighting clothes with blood
> in their eye if the entire National Park system were to be abolished? The
> situation in the National Forests with regard to natural beauty and human
> usability is just as serious and ultimately as far reaching as that would be.
> But there is no organized sentiment to force the protection of our forest
> treasures of scenic worth [emphasis in the original].

In the light of Pray's earlier indiscretion, it seems remarkable that Carhart would trust the professor with this confidence. On the other hand, perhaps he wanted Sherman to hear such news from someone of Pray's eminence. Having signaled his resignation, Carhart added that he might be persuaded to stay if two conditions were met: (1) if Congress were to appropriate adequate money for comprehensive recreation planning, and (2) "The other is such a salary that I will stay purely out of consideration for the remuneration—and that would have to be pretty substantial I assure you to keep me identified with a partially strangled, undernourished, somewhat forlorn cause."

Finally, he reached his main point.

> If you have any idea where I could get into similar work that promises the
> opportunity to actually see your plans at least partially carried out, even if
> the remuneration is not more than I am getting here, I will appreciate your
> telling me. . . . I feel in need of advice and grave counsel. I feel that in the
> position I am now in I have a great amount of responsibility to the profes-
> sion and more so to the future of America. . . . If there is a way to bring the
> great human use of the National Forests through to a real glorious service
> built on sound principles before the scenic, aesthetic and other human use
> values are ruined, I want to do what I may to aid.

Carhart closed: "Either there must be the organized support on the part of the
men of the profession and that in a militant form backed by an aroused public
sentiment, or recreation is going to be in the hands of the foresters to make
it wholly subservient to producing wood. I hope I haven't bored you. This is
pretty vital to me. I certainly will appreciate your reply."

CONSIDERED CRAZY BY THEIR ASSOCIATES

Pray did not reply until April 21, 1923, almost a year after Carhart begged
him for help. Perhaps he was taken aback by Carhart's vehemence. Meanwhile,
Carhart left Vee once again in Denver, setting out for Wyoming's Washakie
National Forest, the first assignment of his last field season with the Forest
Service. This time, however, Vee had something to look forward to. Her husband promised to take her on a valedictory tour of the Colorado forests later in
the summer. Meanwhile, on June 15, 1922, McCrary invited Carhart to partner
with him in private practice. Carhart had already talked to Culley about such a
firm, which they planned to headquarter in Denver.

Carhart kept peppering Pray with letters from the field. As with other
letters he wrote to various correspondents during that unhappy summer, they
referred to his plight with phrases such as "breach of promise" and "breaking
of faith."[8] Carhart told Pray what he had learned from the supervisor of the
Washakie—simultaneous with Carhart's departure from Denver, a letter had
gone out telling all District 2 forest supervisors: Do not work on any recreation
improvements this year.[9]

Sick at heart, and perhaps as bewildered by his friends as by his enemies,
Carhart turned to Sherman. But now he marked his letters "PERSONAL," assail-
ing Sherman with a four-page, double-spaced missive he obviously intended for
wider circulation. Later, after Carhart left the Forest Service, Sherman tried to
circulate this letter throughout the entire organization:

I am positive that recreation is fundamentally a part of the values present in every forest, that it is of national importance and that unless the Forest Service handles it properly in National Forests from now on that it will some day have to explain why it did not at least show proportionally as aggressive an attitude towards a national program of outdoor recreation as it is showing in the National Forestry Program which is almost exclusively timber production. I know I am considered "hog wild" on recreation by some eminently practical men with viewpoints different from mine. But there are several thousands of people before me that were considered crazy by their associates that afterwards were given revised ratings.[10]

When Carhart returned to Denver and Vee later in the summer, his friends at District 2 must have sympathized with his unhappiness, or perhaps they wanted to entice him into staying with the Forest Service—or maybe just to get rid of him for awhile. Carhart must have kept his impending resignation to himself, for this was not the kind of investment in departing personnel any organization would make.

Whatever the case, Stahl sent the Carharts on a three-month tour of the southern Colorado forests they had not visited previously. Carhart was working on his final contribution to comprehensive planning: a recreation-oriented map of the major watersheds of all the national forests of southern Colorado, with special emphasis on the San Juan Mountains. Carhart had his hands full, checking the connectivity of a complex series of trails, roads, and rail lines.

Although not without rigors, the extended idyll resonated through the years for the Carharts, forming the basis for many books, including both novels and short stories set in southern Colorado and also his first major travel guide, *Colorado*. For example, Labor Day 1922 found the Carharts traveling south by horseback with Supervisor Agee of the Cochetopa Forest from the narrow-gauge railway station at Salida. They crossed from the Arkansas River watershed to the Rio Grande near today's Poncha Pass and stayed overnight at the ghost town of Bonanza in the upper San Luis Valley. Their second night found them at the Hispanic ranching town of Saguache. From there the Carharts stayed with District Ranger Tibo Gallegos at the Carnero Ranger Station. Ranger Gallegos and his wife provided models for many positive fictional portrayals of Hispanics in the years to come. After Agee returned to Salida, the two couples took to their horses again, riding over Half Moon Pass into the La Garita Range and staying overnight at Wheeler National Monument. The Gallegoses returned to the eastern side of the range, and the Carharts went on alone, crossing over the Continental Divide to Cathedral Creek on the Gunnison National Forest, where the local district ranger met them. Finally, they descended Slumgullion Gulch to Lake City, then mostly a ghost town like Bonanza. Carhart capped this part of the trip with a solo ascent of Uncompahgre Peak, a fourteener. The ranger at Ouray welcomed them, and they rested up at McElmo Hotel. The twenty-five-mile route demanded two nights camping out in the snow.[11]

The Carharts stayed out in the backcountry of the San Juan Mountains until October 20, when they ended up far to the west at the mining town of Telluride. From there, the narrow gauge took them to the headquarters of the Montezuma National Forest at Mancos, where they met Arthur Hoffman, a former Acacia fraternity brother from Ames, who took them on a tour of Mesa Verde that deepened Carhart's understanding of pre-settlement Indian culture. The trip ended in the little timber town of South Fork on the Rio Grande. After a look at the mining town of Creede, they took the railroad back to Denver.

Back in Denver, Carhart went into mop-up mode. He completed the map of his summer travels throughout Colorado. Then he turned to a series of memos intended to sum up his tenure with the Forest Service. By 1922 things had worsened at Trappers Lake. At Thanksgiving, Carhart submitted a part-ing-shot–style summation of what was really happening at Trappers Lake.[12] Incoherent and even hysterical, the memo did not mention "wilderness" at all. A disgusted Carhart felt the issue had deteriorated to the point that the only decision that remained was whether the highway would encircle the lake or just access it.[13] If he was disgusted with what he perceived as Forest Service malfea-sance at Trappers Lake, Carhart was alarmed and angry when he discovered late that fall what the Forest Service had in mind for the Superior National Forest, where plans were afoot that would have severely compromised his rec-ommendations for recreation development.

Although Carhart, as a staff officer, was out of the line of formal author-ity that determined action on the Superior, he was so disturbed by these plans that he quietly wrote to conservationist Paul Riis, who was very concerned about the fate of the Superior. Carhart had acted within his authority when he advised Riis on setting up the Superior National Forest Recreation Association (SNFRA). But SNFRA did not yet enjoy a partnership with a forest supervi-sor of Al Hamel's caliber. Instead, Riis found himself at odds with Supervisor Richey, and he took a much more adversarial position—at least until Carl Stahl wisely transferred Hamel to the Superior in 1926.

Carhart formally submitted his resignation to Stahl on December 10, 1922, effective December 31, 1922. Starting after Thanksgiving, he was already oper-ating out of a private office at 900 Exchange Building in downtown Denver—the future home of McCrary, Culley, & Carhart.

PERHAPS MY BOMBARDMENTS HAD BEEN TOO MUCH

Pray's reply to Carhart's spring 1922 cry for help did not arrive in Denver until late April 1923. By then, Carhart had hit the ground running in this new phase of his career. He seemed pleased with himself when he replied to the tardy Pray:

> I had come to think that perhaps my bombardments had been too much. I'm surely happy to hear from you again. The Forest Service situation is all history so far as my connection with the work is concerned. But I am out now where I may say just what I think and when I think. I'll not have to pussy-foot any more thank goodness. The Superior deal was most trying, illuminating and finally gratifying. I am certainly happy to see it turn out as it has. Now there is to be formed an association to stand guard over it as you probably have heard from Dr. Riis.[14]

Paul Riis had become an important figure in Carhart's new life. Free from the strictures of the bureaucracy he loathed, Carhart sharpened his pen and his tongue—and became the fighting conservationist he would remain for the rest of his life. Typically, Carhart expected that SNFRA, the organization he and Riis had formed to fight for the Superior, might "go national." And just as typically, he assured Pray that although he was busy with more professional work than anticipated, he would be happy to work on conservation issues from his post as a member of ASLA's Forests and Parks Committee.

NOTES

1. Letter from Carhart to Pray, June 12, 1922, Carhart Collection, Denver Public Library (hereafter CC, DPL).

2. Frank Harmon wrote to Carhart on November 11, 1973, detailing McArdle's response: "We showed him Baldwin's book and he borrowed it to read, and was much interested in it. We asked him to write us his comments on the book for use in our quarterly newsletter, *History Line,* which he did. A copy is enclosed for your information" (CC, DPL). Historian Harold Steen provided a less varnished version in an e-mail to me in December 2000. Recalling a dinner conversation with McArdle, he said the chief called Carhart "a quitter."

3. Letter from Pray to Carhart, May 27, 1922, CC, DPL.

4. Letter from Carhart to Pray, June 12, 1922, CC, DPL.

5. See also James Sturgis Pray, "Danger of Over-Exploitation of Our National Parks," *Landscape Architecture* 6(3):11 (n.d.).

6. Letter from Carhart to Pray, June 12, 1922, CC, DPL.

7. Carhart added: "The reply that Mr. Sherman made to you I think gives you a very clear insight into the attitude of the Forest Service with regard to this work. They

consider it a very minor value in the forest and everything of economic importance must be considered before the recreation work is taken up. I have talked with a number of foresters in the district in the last few weeks and they have in nearly every case taken a very antagonistic attitude on one ground or another against recreation in our forests. They all admit that recreation comes when there is green timber produced but they almost all say that it is not a thing that a forester should bother his head about."

8. Letter from Carhart to Pray, June 17, 1922, CC, DPL.

9. Ibid.

10. Letter from Carhart to Sherman, June 29, 1922, CC, DPL.

11. Carhart described this trip a few years later in *Colorado: History, Geology, Legend* (New York: Coward-McCann, 1932), 184.

12. Carhart memo, November 27, 1922, CC, DPL.

13. Ibid. "It is inevitable that some people with selfish motives will try to force this road around the lake so that they may have their own individual wishes gratified. Such a forgery of the road would be a decided calamity. . . . If this road must be pushed on any further it should if possible swing to the westward and if these people must have a lake to look upon from a highway, it may be possible to bring it to Big Fish Lake where the scenic qualities are not so high as at Trappers Lake."

14. Letter from Carhart to Pray, May 12, 1923, CC, DPL.

CHAPTER EIGHT

THAT THREADBARE THEORY "LEAVE NATURE ALONE"

I guess I told you once what Stahl said to me one day when talking of
the Superior and our work for it. He said, "Well, if I had to do this over
again I don't think I'd play with you fellows at all. I think I'd tell you to
go to hell." And then went on to read me a bitter lecture on my near
"treachery" because I wrote you the menace to the Superior in confidence
two months before the time I resigned from the Service. In other words,
should have "stood hitched" and as that was one thing which I would
not do I deemed it best to get out where I could be an entirely free
agent, stating my views as I saw them.

—CARHART TO PAUL RIIS, 1926[1]

INTRODUCTION: I'D A DARNEDSIGHT RATHER GO FISHING

Carhart once wrote: "And sometimes I wonder why in the devil I'm driven to
be three men: landscape architect, greenhouse executive and key pounder! I'd a
darnedsight rather go fishing!"[2] Conservation advocacy was an important part
of Carhart's key pounding. He was beginning to see that the writing skills he
had developed while in the Forest Service might not only serve the cause of
conservation but could also contribute to his goal of making enough money to
buy a brick house in Park Hill and to open a greenhouse in Cañon City.

While Chapter 9 examines Carhart's development as a writer through the
end of the 1920s, this chapter looks at his conservation advocacy, his work as a
landscape architect, and the Carhart/Van Sickle family business venture—the
Colorado Floral Company. These aspects of his life spread into each other as he
rode the perilous riptides of the 1920s to financial and professional success. At
the end of the 1920s all the tides receded at once, and Carhart learned the old

saw about being careful what you wish for. He got to "go fishing," embarking on the phase of his career during which he became America's premier outdoors writer.

However bitter he might have been at times about the Forest Service, Carhart almost always tried to imagine a better agency. He was less sanguine about the Bureau of Biological Survey (BBS), notwithstanding his friendship with BBS employees Olaus Murie, Stanley P. Young, and Howard Zahniser. Like Aldo Leopold and Olaus Murie, Carhart remained ambivalent about predators, especially the wolf. He knew firsthand that wolves still roamed the Boundary Waters area in the 1920s and 1930s. But he learned to dislike the methods of the wolfers—especially the use of poison, which he attacked in *Sports Afield* in 1929.[3] Carhart also knew anti-predator grazing interests wielded great power in both the BBS and the Forest Service. As a Coloradoan, he was all too familiar with the power of local congressman Edward Taylor, whose 1934 Taylor Grazing Act not only signaled the closing of the frontier but also delivered the open range to ranchers who quickly claimed that predator-free public lands grazing was a right rather than a privilege. This was the sort of special interest favoritism Carhart despised, whether the beneficiaries were tourists or ranchers or sportsmen or loggers. He thought public lands ought to be for the public good.

BOUNDARY WATERS: TO HELL WITH CARHART AND HIS COMICAL IDEAS

If readers today retain any image of Arthur Carhart, they know the classic Boundary Waters photo of 1921, showing a handsome young man about to embark on a canoe trip, delightedly hefting an eighty-pound muslin bag of food stuffed into a Zenith backpack. This is the photo the Forest Service used to promote its Arthur Carhart National Wilderness Training Center in Missoula, Montana.[4]

Carhart did not meet Paul Riis in person until he had left the Forest Service, but on his 1921 trip he did encounter Sigurd Olson and Will Dilg. Carhart already knew Dilg from Denver, where Dilg had helped connect him to *Outdoor Life* magazine, which later published many of Carhart's conservation-oriented fishing and hunting articles. Dilg was also organizing the Izaak Walton League of America,[5] and he was looking for a crusader's cause to spark his efforts. He found it in the Superior National Forest, where he had a powerful ally in Carhart.

At the end of the summer of 1923, Carhart published an article on the Superior that tried to draw the public's attention to a looming catastrophe.[6] The Forest Service, he felt, was about to sacrifice the recreation potential of Boundary Waters to private timber interests. Weyerhaeuser was cutting heavily on the Superior in the early 1920s, thanks to a new system of Forest Service–designed and constructed roads that allowed access to previously uncut parcels. Part of the justification for the cutting was the danger of fire. A Forest Service map of the Superior and a supporting booklet from 1925 elaborated on this problem: "Fire is the forest's worst enemy."

With Carhart's recreation plan for the Superior in hand, opponents like Riis took an increasingly militant stand against the logging. Carhart supported them, especially through his recreation-related business connections. In Denver, Carhart was very active in the Kiwanis and the Masons, speaking on behalf of conservation. Carhart and Riis conducted a correspondence about how to save Boundary Waters. Hectoring Carl Stahl, Carhart submitted formal objections to the Forest Service at the end of 1923, using his new vantage point as a landscape architect in private practice. He was also looking for a chance to meet Riis in person: "Reasons? Too numerous to mention. Brothers-in-arms sort of an idea I guess." He added:

> Have in mind a pollution story titled something like this, "Man the Polluter." Can hit all kinds of defilement of the outdoors, and then swing into a practical application of the deal in showing how it must be that we plan and provide for man's occupancy of the wild life places such as state parks, forests, etc. Take a crack at that threadbare theory of "leave nature alone." Can't be done when man invades. Must protect her so far as possible and protection against pollution one of the most important moves.
>
> Do you ever have any "consultation" on your park system? Got any "famous" landscape architects in there to aid you? Suppose you do all the designing yourself and from reports I have do it mighty well too. What I'm flirting with of course is a chance to get back and meet you in person. We've been retained in a consulting capacity in this city.[7]

In Carhart, Riis found someone with an insider's touch for Forest Service sensitivities—and with access to Forest Service information that Riis did not hesitate to use. Carhart also corresponded with Will Dilg during this time. Their goal became to set up a meeting with Edward A. Sherman—a move that would go over the heads of the Superior supervisor, the much-reviled Richey, and Carl Stahl himself. The primary problem was the Forest Service's wooing of Weyerhaeuser and the auto-borne tourist. Carhart told Dilg, "I hold that seeing the Forest from the seat of the auto is like seeing Venice from a streetcar."[8]

Carhart's departure from the Forest Service allowed him to speak more freely to Sherman. In response, Sherman proposed circulating to all the district foresters Carhart's letter of the summer of 1922, in which he had detailed the reasons for his unhappiness with the Forest Service. It had been a personal letter, so Sherman sought Carhart's permission. Carhart replied:

Would it do anything constructive? I feel that they would read it, rare back, squat on their haunches, show their teeth, expose the whites of their eyes, probably give voice to the classic that has been used on occasions, viz. "To Hell with Carhart and his comical ideas," initial the letter and send it files. Or would they really do a little probing into their approach to recreation problems to find if they consider human service or other work first and get some good out of it? I'll say honestly that I believe that such a letter to them would only thicken the passive resistance to constructive recreation planning rather than swing our men to a critical, self analysis viewpoint.[9]

For better or worse, the letter never went out. The two men could never agree on how much of it should be made public.[10] As the battle for Boundary Waters went on and on, Carhart used his connections in the agency to make it clear that the Forest Service was inflating its case for roading, dams, and timber harvest as antidotes to fire danger. Supervisor Richey was especially culpable, according to Carhart and Riis, and they pummeled him mercilessly.

In the meantime, Carhart and Riis were trying to turn the endless war between the Forest Service and the Park Service to their advantage. Carhart was particularly incensed at the Forest Service's habit of trying to capture or subvert its private conservation partners like the Superior National Forest Recreation Association (SNFRA) and the San Isabel Protection and Recreation Association (SIPRA). Honest Al Hamel was the exception, not the rule, among forest supervisors. Writing to Riis in 1926, Carhart summed up his feelings:

As much as I think of the F.S. [Forest Service] as an institution I must confess I see some faults—or rather some tricky bits of unofficial policy which I do not like. I have seen just the thing they are trying to put over on us happen too often to not recognize it.

The F.S. recognized us at time of formation of Assn. because they felt that we had enough force back of us to do something to them at Washington if necessary. So they played with us, saying to themselves, "Well, let them rave, and after they have had their blow then we'll do what we think is best." They think it is time to sink the SNFRA without a ripple.

Now here is a trump card to hold against the F.S. at all times. The mere suggestion that the Superior be made a National Park IN ORDER TO GET PROPER CONSIDERATION OF THE RECREATIONAL RESOURCE THERE will make them duck for cover. Always remember that. And remember too that if you cannot get cooperation from the F.S. even by strong persuasion, you will always find a ready ally on the part of the Park Service to block any move on the part of the F.S. which does not consider the recreation feature. If the F.S. cannot get their heads above localism and economicism and see that potential wealth in recreation in the Superior perhaps we must turn to the one governmental agency which concerns itself primarily with recreation and ask their aid to take the Superior out of the hands of the men who will not consider that recreation value and put it in hands which will consider that value [emphasis in the original].[11]

Carhart became quite ill in February 1926, suffering from the same amount of overwork that afflicted Riis.[12] Carhart also felt deeply conflicted about having to side with the National Park Service against the Forest Service. So he tried to take a break from Boundary Waters issues while he spent March in Salt Lake City, Utah, on business. However, that break meant he and Riis were out of touch at a critical time. Riis was becoming increasingly desperate, particularly when the Forest Service replaced Carl Stahl with a man named Tinker who lacked Stahl's vision. As Riis told Carhart: "[Stephen] Mather in a public speech or in his annual report made reference to the Superior as a National Park. . . . Mather may promise all sorts of things to begin with and then later cave in to popular demands for roads. I am against the National Park idea and have been consistently because they more than anyone else will motorize the area, in fact make a motor camp of it."[13]

Carhart and Stahl had their differences, but Carhart knew no one could easily replace Stahl—except Hamel, who was more valuable as a forest supervisor. Hamel had the kind of touch with the public that made compromises possible. Carhart had in mind a deal for the cutting of the remaining timber if it did not include too many roads and dams. Carhart told Riis:

> Do not believe that we can expect any real vision on recreation value and its preservation on part of any of USFS except in individual cases and their ponderous policies will muffle them as they did me. . . . Can't give the Park Service much more. They seem to think if they jam greater numbers through the parks they have fulfilled their function.
>
> I think we would be farther ahead to keep this land in Forest hands if we can bludgeon some recreation sense into their heads. And by forming alliance with timber and mine people outside we may have these interests working with us instead of having the FS pit them against us. This is typical FS trick, this playing of one interest against another and then throwing the balance of power in hands of the FS itself to side it wants to win. . . . Am afraid of Park Service putting in a bunch of high powered auto roads and equally high powered hotels.[14]

Heretofore silent on the Boundary Waters issue (but right next door in Wisconsin) was Aldo Leopold. Leopold visited the contested areas in June and July 1926, producing his long memo, "Report on D-1 Trip June 15–July 23, 1926. Aldo Leopold, Associate Director, Forest Products Laboratory."[15] Leopold came down hard on the effects of getting the timber out:

Driving wastes not only timber, but other forest values. It deteriorates the recreational value of streams, especially where splash dams are used. It means dams on lakes and partial to complete deterioration of their recreational value. Streams and lakes are the heart of any country, and their sacrifice, even for the sake of getting out timber, is ultimately a matter of consequence. This region has not yet felt the effects of crowding in the use of recreational resources. Possibly this question strikes very near the heart of our present problem. Possibly the inevitable pre-occupation of products men with the immediate job of analyzing economic conditions prevents us from thinking far ahead in terms of management plans.

Riis and Carhart bolstered each other's spirits. Their goal was to get rid of the hated Richey, hoping Hamel would then be assigned to the Superior.[16] Carhart and Riis played a "good cop/bad cop" duet, with Riis writing directly to Richey: "I found the Forest Service floundering badly in a problem in which you Mr. Richey nor your predecessor nor any other Supervisor in the Service has ample experience, save perhaps your Mr. Hamel of Pike National Forest. This is a hard pill for you and the Service to swallow. As long as you are bent on destroying the Superior, why not let the Park Service do it?"[17]

Soon thereafter, Richey died while on a trip back to Washington to meet with the chief forester. Meanwhile, Carhart was in direct touch with Hamel, who was eager to take on the Superior. Hamel wrote to Carhart that fall, requesting a briefing on the Superior.[18] Carhart reminded his old friend that the model for the Superior came from the San Isabel: "As you know, the first move of the scrap against making the Superior Forest a cut and dried type of National Forest came when the road program was projected for slicing thru the wilderness areas without regard for recreation values."[19] With Hamel in place, Carhart resorted to an extensive letter-writing campaign that lasted from 1927 through 1928. There was one welcome break. Carhart and his Mapleton boyhood friend "Judge" Whiting spent a few weeks in Boundary Waters in August 1927 on a rare relaxing trip that included wolf serenades during their evening campfires.

Then it was back to the fray. The main focus was Park Service vs. Forest Service administration, with Carhart praising Hamel's ability to forge a compromise. By this time, many other parties had entered the ring on behalf of the Superior's conservation values, including the Quetico-Superior Council, which affiliated with the Izaak Walton League in July 1928. Ernest Oberholtzer wrote to Carhart at that time, asking whether Carhart's 1921 Forest Service report could be used for the cause. In return for Carhart's cooperation, Oberholtzer made him one of the conservation effort's national advisers in August 1928. Carhart was working on his first Forest Service–based novel, *The Ordeal of*

Brad Ogden, and he told Oberholtzer that his next novel, called *Big Plunder,* would be about the "Superior Forest conservation-power." Carhart planned an indictment of a powerful lumber baron's proposal to make storage reservoirs out of a string of superlative lakes. Although Carhart never wrote *Big Plunder,* he did write an article for *Holiday* magazine that appeared in 1930.[20]

MCCRARY, CULLEY, & CARHART

Carhart's business partners knew his high profile would be valuable for their new venture. In contrast to the aloof Leopold, who returned to the Forest Service after a short stint with the Albuquerque Chamber of Commerce, Carhart thrived on his connections with businesspeople. He also found private practice refreshing after his immersion in a large federal bureaucracy.

While he was getting his feet on the ground in early 1923, he found that, thanks to his publications, his professional fame had spread. He received a letter from landscape architect Tsuyoshi Tamura, doctor of forestry, requesting a consultation: "I am on a trip in the service of the Japanese Government for the inspection of recreation work in your country and Europe."[21] Tamura was in charge of all recreation planning for Japan. Carhart promptly dashed off a press release announcing the internationally significant meeting—in advance, and booming his connection with McCrary, Culley, & Carhart (MCC).

Irvin McCrary was a Denver native who had personally witnessed the repeated, watershed-wide blunders made by planners and developers along the Front Range.[22] Both McCrary and Carhart felt Denver should seek to rehabilitate its watersheds rather than opt for federally financed and designed engineering solutions such as large dams.[23] Carhart served as front man for the new firm, traveling extensively, often accompanied by Vee. These business-related travels exposed the Carharts to New York, Chicago, Mexico, Utah, and New Mexico.

It was in this context that Denver's ambitious city fathers formed the Denver City Planning Association. After addressing a gathering at the Daniels and Fisher Tower in July 1923, Carhart sold the association on the need for a new city plan. The group invited MCC to take one year to do the appropriate studies and then to draft a new city plan that would keep Denver abreast of its competitors in Colorado Springs and Pueblo. The essence of the plan lay in providing adequate traffic channels to serve the central district. This included an early version of the Valley Highway (today's I-25) that tried to make sense of Denver as the confluence of the watersheds of the mountains and the plains: the South Platte River and Cherry Creek.[24]

The relationship became so close that MCC "loaned" Carhart to the association for a few years as executive secretary. This job suited Carhart's salesmanship and people skills. He could draw on his many connections in the business community through the Kiwanis and Masons. And he cultivated the federal bureaucracies that formed an important part of downtown Denver's economy. While he was doing this work, Carhart got to know Stanley Young, his future writing partner, who was running the federal BBS. He also formed many acquaintances in the federal Bureau of Reclamation, his future nemesis.

Carhart's task was to plan for Denver's growth for the next twenty-five years, projecting a population of 500,000 by 1950. Carhart's stamp is clearest in the document MCC produced for the association in April 1924:

> Denver has accomplished much in city planning in the last twenty years. The embankment of Cherry Creek has been built through the city and Speer Boulevard created alongside. Two great viaducts have been constructed, Broadway has been extended north at a width of one hundred feet through an old section of the city, and the Civic Center has become a reality. A very considerable extension of the park and boulevard system has been made; also a unique system of mountain parks and highways has been developed.
>
> Nevertheless, Denver has not been proceeding along the lines of a comprehensive city plan such as the great number of American cities have prepared. It has no city planning commission, and the need of an official plan is becoming yearly more apparent as the city increases in size and complexity of organization.[25]

Noting a present population of 300,000, Carhart said it was time to provide for growth. There was still a chance to put in the inexpensive structural changes that would make such growth tolerable and even lucrative for the business community. MCC reported on the area immediately around the increasingly congested downtown business section. Congestion hurts business, Carhart told the association, forcing customers to patronize suburban competitors. Good planning meant business should remain concentrated downtown. But bigger buildings meant more congestion. In the retail and financial district, MCC found, 15 percent of the buildings were already more than four stories tall, and there were threats to exceed the present height limit of twelve stories. The demand for skyscrapers would bring disastrous overcrowding. Carhart also noted: "Denver has the distinction of housing more branches of the federal government than any city except Washington. At the present time, there are thirty bureaus which rent space in various office buildings. The Reclamation Service has already indicated its plan to move a part of its organization to Denver."[26]

MCC recommended consolidating all these scattered bureaus into a federal center building. They also suggested a site south of the Civic Center for a new art museum and library, noting that the present library building was becoming crowded. Very emphatically, they endorsed height limits on any hotel planned north of the Civic Center, pointing out that the city should avoid dwarfing its civic presence just below the state capitol buildings. Carhart wrote, "The rather severe arrangement of the open ground on the Civic Center is capable of great enrichment." Summing up, he claimed such improvements would not cost taxpayers much, compared to the costs of waiting. He added that MCC could produce maps that would show land values, population, transport time, public property, industrial zones, and much more. He endorsed the formation of a Denver zoning commission, also recommending a city planning bureau.

Thanks to Carhart's draft of a plan for downtown, MCC had a hand in the Civic Center Park landscaping job. They also did consulting work and landscape design for around thirty-five of the campuses springing up throughout the region, including the University of Denver, the University of Colorado in Boulder, St. Thomas Seminary in Denver, campuses in Utah (the University of Utah and Westminster College), and the New Mexico Military Institute in Roswell. Country clubs were another specialty. Ultimately, MCC worked as far afield as Sunrise, Wyoming, a Colorado Fuel & Iron company town they learned of through Carhart's connections in Pueblo. In Colorado Springs, they landscaped the Broadmoor Hotel and the Myron Stratton Home.[27] North of Denver, they designed the YMCA camp at Estes Park. And there were zoning plans for such places as the rebuilding Pueblo, Cañon City, and Enid, Oklahoma.

Carhart explained to his parents on January 1, 1928, that MCC was again loaning him to the Denver Planning Association. While on loan, he made $4,800 per year as executive secretary for the association. He told George and Ella that the position involved "publicity, education, organization, administration. Busy as the devil." By the end of 1928, Carhart was writing a city planning amendment into the Colorado Constitution.

As MCC's front man, Carhart was everywhere during this huge spate of activity, including Santa Fe, where he met his most valuable writing contact, Mary Austin. She told him, "I also agree with you in what you said to Mr. Meem about planning to save Santa Fe."[28] Carhart's friendship with Austin was one of the main factors in his later decision to leave landscape architecture and commit himself to writing about landscapes—especially the increasingly dry landscape of the American Southwest, which was entering one of its great periodic droughts. Carhart left MCC in the early fall of 1930, cutting back to about three afternoons a week until he felt ready to go it alone on his writing fees at the start of the next year.

All throughout the 1920s, Carhart maintained an active membership in the American Society of Landscape Architects (ASLA) through its National Parks and Forests Committee, where from Carhart's point of view an unacceptable gentlemen's agreement on a stalemate prevailed. After one particularly frustrating meeting with Stephen Mather and Frederick Law Olmsted Jr., he wrote to James Pray, "It is ghastly being a member of such a dead entity."[29] Carhart continued:

> To the public at large, it is my firm belief, the ASLA does not mean any more than one whoop more or less cut loose in a Texas cyclone. Nor does that *profession* as a profession mean much more than that.
>
> You who teach might as well close up shop unless better marketing methods for the profession are devised. There is no use putting out trained men if there is no market for them.
>
> But speaking purely personally and confidentially for the moment, I made almost as much from two nights a week and Sunday morning writing, marketing in the year in excess of 35 manuscripts, [as] I did from eight to twelve hours a day in the landscape office. . . . I'm just as much interested in the field of landscape architecture as I ever was. But I'm plumb fed up on the market.

Threatening to quit ASLA within a year, Carhart ranted on: "Now to prescribe. I believe that the ASLA should be a militant, aggressive, forward moving body. As aggressive as the Chiropractors if need be. I know this is heresy." As late as 1930, Carhart was reappointed to the ASLA Standing Committee on National Parks and Forests. But this was an empty victory for him. When he left MCC on September 1, 1930, he knew he would soon drop his membership in ASLA. Carhart could be as impatient as he was genial. If landscape architecture failed to produce either sufficient money or significant change in conservation policies, he would simply move on.

SIT TIGHT AND PRAY LIKE SIN

George Carhart was proud of his son's accomplishments, praising Arthur for "[s]caling the highest peaks of the mountains and being received and listened to by the most influential men in the cities where you have business. Well, we are proud of you and your dear little wife."[30] This parental pride extended to a wish to join Arthur and Vee in Colorado. Perhaps George and Ella simply shared the Carhart yen for "pioneering," but they were also certainly drawn by Arthur's glowing accounts of potential business ventures in Colorado. Around 1923, George began to write about finding a buyer for the store in Mapleton.[31] For her part, Ella expressed strong affection for Vee, together with her typically effusive way of reminding her son of his religious origins: "The very best and greatest prize is the dear daughter you brought us. We dearly love her and are very proud of her. You have made a name for yourself there in your past and present business and your written articles reach out and help folks see the God sent beauty and goodness of His great outdoors."[32]

George and Ella Carhart moved to Cañon City, Colorado, in the summer of 1924. George was seventy-one; Ella was fifty-five. The main reason for the move, Ella wrote to her son, was to be closer to him and Vee.[33] The other reason was to help Arthur launch what became known as the Colorado Floral Company. George and Ella had solid business experience behind them. In short order, they bought a house and put part of their savings into the Silver State Building and Loan Association, where they also became employees, working on commission and doing very well. George became the Cañon City manager for Silver State, and the formerly withdrawn Ella blossomed into one of the firm's top producers.[34] The rest of their money was invested in the Colorado Floral Company, where they worked in their spare time, joined by the younger Carharts—and by Vee's parents, the Van Sickles. Other investors included various Iowa friends (not the Whitings) and members of the Carhart extended family. Carhart even sold shares to Stanley Young.

It is no wonder Carhart became ill in early 1926, during this intensely active time in his life when he was also deeply involved in the fight over Boundary Waters. In addition to selling shares in the Colorado Floral Company, Carhart supported the new business through his increasingly lucrative writing. The salary from his work with McCrary, Culley, & Carhart went to fulfill the Carharts' longtime dream: owning a house in Park Hill, at 2591 Eudora Street. Carhart supplied his own construction and landscape design for the brick structure, which featured a south-facing garden and a basement big enough for an office. Work began in early 1926, and the Carharts moved into their new home on June 10 that year.

Carhart was also involved in various political causes during this period. As usual, he showed a fiercely independent streak, supporting Democrat Billy Adams's successful gubernatorial bid. He wrote: "Colorado elected not a democratic candidate but Billy Adams. Dirty fight against him by Denver Post. I'm a Republican by inclination myself. My Dad is 73 and it is the first time he ever voted for a Democratic governor."[35]

Whenever possible, Carhart took Vee with him on landscape architecture trips that also doubled as opportunities to market shares in the Colorado Floral Company and to visit urban-based editors who were interested in his tales about wolves. In the fall of 1925, the couple visited New York. In 1927 they traveled to Chicago, visiting relatives in Nebraska along the way.[36]

In the late 1920s, many small investors were cashing out the ten-year Liberty Bonds they had bought during World War I and seeking higher returns in ventures like the Colorado Floral Company.[37] In spite of all the worry and work, the late 1920s were happy times for Arthur and Vee. They loved traveling together. In March 1928 their old Forest Service friend Tibo Gallegos took them to the Holy Week Penitente ceremonies at a secret site in northern New Mexico. And in July–August they took a ten-day pack trip with Forest Service friends into the White River National Forest Game Refuge, which included Trappers Lake.

The mercurial fortunes of the Colorado Floral Company were probably typical of the times. Carhart's juggling act often got him into trouble. He wrote to his parents: "Mother Van's letter came yesterday. Now keep your shirts on. No one is going $50,000 in debt, and furthermore we are not going to quit with that one try."[38] He explained to his parents and parents-in-law that the Colorado Floral Company had lost out on this particular deal (marketing cucumbers to Denver) by being too conservative about the price of cucumbers: "So sit tight, don't sell the house unless you get some real money for it and pray like sin!" Just two months later the company's 75,000-square-foot greenhouse was again thriving, and Carhart estimated it was worth $105,000.[39]

The stock market crash of 1929 did not immediately affect small enterprises like the Colorado Floral Company or even regional financial institutions like Silver State S&L. An ominous note sounded in the summer of 1930, when both George and Ella Carhart became seriously ill, leaving Arthur and Vee and the Van Sickles shorthanded at a time when they were trying to harvest a critical crop. Clearly, something would have to go. The greenhouse might or might not pay off. But Carhart had succeeded as a writer without putting his full force into serious work. He was ready to devote himself full-time to his writing. He would get the chance sooner than he thought.

Carhart always corresponded very frankly with his editors. He wrote to Donald Kennicott of a thriller magazine called *Blue Book* in midsummer 1930, asking for enough advance money to bail the greenhouse out from its latest problems: "Am writing about half time now. Results indicate will be putting full time on it before end of year. Have opened two new markets for novelets, action type, one for every month, another 25,000 words quarterly."[40]

Kennicott replied that the money would flow when Carhart took the time to improve his writing. Carhart, in responding, hoped to tickle his editor's funny bone:

> Well, I'm going on the supposition that you want white-man's language instead of that dam' garbled stuff that is supposed to be cow puncher talk. And I'll work hard, Donald, for the good of my soul. As for plain bad grammer, gosh, I'm the worse speller in America and my grammer's the thing that's *worser* than my seplling. So I'm entirely grateful for your corrections. Guess I'll have to hire me a tame gramarian.
>
> I think a lot of the trouble with my work since the wolves has been that I've had so gawshawful much on my hands I've not had the chance to

WORK at the writing; not the opportunity to grind and grind that puts the polish on such a thing. Greenhouse, landscape, city planning, and now I'm down here harvesting a tomato crop that will run about 100,000 pounds of selected graded table toms.[41]

Unable to afford adequate skilled help, the Colorado Floral Company lost money on its late-summer tomatoes: "Market went haywire."[42] The business also ran into trouble with one of its other staples, carnations for the autumn market. As of December, Carhart was trying to grow cucumbers again, hoping to take advantage of the greenhouse's ability to provide a winter vegetable to nearby Front Range markets. The situation was grim enough that Carhart spent a dreary New Year's Eve writing from Cañon City to his investors, admitting that he could not pay a dividend that year:

> But I'm planning on jumping over the side in toto this fall, face the breadline for a while if I have to, give my entire and primary time to writing. At least for enough of a period to count. The greenhouse business will probably pull out of the hole this fall and winter so it'll bring a right good income within two years but the landscape business has not paid expenses for the past two years. Most money made out of landscape has come from articles on how to grow sweet Williams in an ash heap or how to beautify the kitchenette apartment on the fifth floor.
>
> Vee and I have been down here for nearly three weeks now. My father has been critically ill. Didn't expect him to live. . . . With sickness in family I can use all cash available to pay bills etc.[43]

It was leap or be pushed. Carhart took the leap—and became a full-time writer. His subject was expressed most fully in the novel *Brad Ogden* and in *Last Stand of the Pack*: "That Threadbare Theory of 'Leave Nature Alone.'"

NOTES

1. Letter from Carhart to Riis, February 22, 1926, Carhart Collection, Denver Public Library (hereafter CC, DPL).

2. Letter from Carhart to Donald Kennicott, July 5, 1930, CC, DPL.

3. Arthur Carhart, "Poison in Our Wildlife?" *Sports Afield* (November 1929).

4. See http://carhart.wilderness.net/.

5. The Izaak Walton League was founded in Chicago on January 14, 1922, by Dilg and others.

6. Arthur Carhart, "The Superior Forest: Why It Is Important in the National Recreation System," *Parks and Recreation* (July–August 1923).

7. Letter from Carhart to Riis, December 12, 1923, CC, DPL.

8. Undated letter from the fall of 1923, CC, DPL.

9. Letter from Carhart to Sherman, February 27, 1923, CC, DPL.

10. Letter from Sherman to Carhart, March 6, 1923, CC, DPL.

11. Letter from Carhart to Riis, February 22, 1926, CC, DPL.

12. "Sorry to learn that you are not so well. But remember, you cannot burn the candle at both ends and get away with it. I realize that money is a fine thing. I too earned most of it in my spare time. Take my advice and let up. Money is not everything." Letter from Riis to Carhart, February 16, 1926, CC, DPL.

13. Letter from Riis to Carhart, March 13, 1926, CC, DPL.

14. Letter from Carhart to Riis, April 2, 1926, CC, DPL.

15. This nineteen-page memo is in the CC, DPL. The quote is from pp. 7–8.

16. Letter from Carhart to Riis, June 25, 1926, CC, DPL.

17. Letter from Riis to Richey, July 8, 1926, CC, DPL.

18. Letter from Hamel to Carhart, October 26, 1926, CC, DPL.

19. Letter from Carhart to Hamel, November 15, 1926, CC, DPL.

20. Arthur Carhart, "The Superior National Forest," *Holiday* (December 1930). He did produce a 30,000-word fictional manuscript about the Superior, but it was never published.

21. Letter from Tamura to Carhart, June 19, 1923, CC, DPL.

22. McCrary lived from 1885 to 1971. Carhart and McCrary were still corresponding as late as September 1963. The Denver Public Library has 653 architectural drawings done by McCrary and his various partners, including landscape plans for residences, schools, universities, parks, public buildings, St. John's Cathedral; the residences of John Evans, L. C. Phipps, and George Cranmer; and entire country club–based subdivisions such as Wellshire.

23. Floods regularly devastated cities like Denver and Pueblo. Cherry Creek flooded again in 1933. The U.S. Army Corps of Engineers built Cherry Creek Dam in 1950.

24. Carhart reviewed his role in Denver's history in an August 6, 1954, letter to a Mr. Feucht of the American National Bank, who was trying to rehabilitate the downtown without building skyscrapers. In the 1950s, after much local resistance, the Murchisons of Dallas built skyscrapers in downtown Denver, such as the twenty-two-story, $6.5 million Denver Club and the twenty-eight-story, $10 million First National Bank Building. Although Carhart did not like these buildings, he was not above approaching John Murchison, who also owned *Field and Stream*, for writing plums—and for a chance to bend the Texan's ears about Denver's future. Their correspondence took place on January 20 and January 27, 1958. Although he was friendly to Carhart, Murchison was openly scornful of Denver's "hicks" in a January 19, 1958, letter to *The Denver Post*: "The old leaders of 17th St. couldn't see the opportunities here; they were asleep and liked things as they were. It took an outsider to sense Denver's destiny" (CC, DPL).

25. "Street Traffic and the Business District," a Report to the City Planning Association, Denver, Colorado, April 1924, McCrary, Culley, & Carhart, City Planners, Denver.

26. MCC's proposed solutions defined the downtown area as a sector a mile by a half mile in area, where 80-foot-wide streets included 38 feet of sidewalk. However,

none of these older streets had been planned with autos or trolleys in mind. Present conditions allowed parking to take up 8 feet on either side, leaving a mere 32 feet for moving vehicles. MCC recommended setbacks at least on 15th and 17th streets, following the good example of already having major thoroughfares like Broadway and Colfax at 100 feet. Because of the expense of widening yet more streets beyond this minimum, MCC proposed a 120-foot-wide thoroughfare belt surrounding the business section, working out from the Colfax/Broadway intersection to 20th Street on the north, to Larimer on the west, and to Speer Boulevard on the south. MCC's studies showed that 80–90 percent of people came downtown by tram. In spite of this, many people also chose to drive downtown. For example, 11,509 vehicles passed Blake and 14th streets during an eight-hour day in 1923—the most congested site in the city. Outside the business district, especially to the fast-growing east, they proposed a direct route from Park Hill to north of City Park—today's 26th Avenue. They also wanted to see 17th Avenue widened. And they wanted to connect Montclair and University Park boulevards by another great 120-foot-wide circumferential concourse. Arterials would lead past the parks but not through them.

27. In 1998 the Trust for Public Land, assisting the local Cheyenne Commons Alliance, acquired the 306-acre tract. See Trust for Public Land, "Colorado Springs Community Rallies to Save Urban Refuge," *On the Land* (Summer-Fall 1998).

28. Letter from Mary Austin to Carhart, November 6, 1929, CC, DPL.

29. Letter from Carhart to Pray, December 26, 1925, CC, DPL.

30. Letter from George Carhart to Arthur Carhart, September 12, 1922, CC, DPL.

31. Letter from George Carhart to Arthur Carhart, September 6, 1923, CC, DPL.

32. Letter from Ella Carhart to Arthur Carhart, September 15, 1923, CC, DPL.

33. Ella's September 18, 1924, letter is from Cañon City (CC, DPL).

34. George's annual birthday letter of September 15, 1926, is on the letterhead of the Silver State Building & Loan Association.

35. Letter from Carhart to *Sunset* magazine editor, February 20, 1926, CC, DPL.

36. Letter from Carhart to Mrs. Gretta Carhart, Wayne, Nebraska, February 4, 1927, CC, DPL. Carhart family members still operate a successful lumber business in Nebraska.

37. Whenever he could get his hands on extra money beyond the business's demands, Carhart also invested in property. In addition to his holdings in Minnesota and New Mexico, this included $1,000 for five acres along Colorado Boulevard near City Park. In November 1927 he bought land along the railroad right-of-way in Cañon City.

38. Letter from Carhart to his parents, September 4, 1927, CC, DPL.

39. Letter from Carhart to his parents, November 12, 1929, CC, DPL.

40. Letter from Carhart to Kennicott, July 5, 1930, CC, DPL.

41. Letter from Carhart to Kennicott, August 14, 1930, CC, DPL.

42. Letter from Carhart to Kennicott, September 23, 1930, CC, DPL.

43. Letter from Carhart to investors, December 31, 1930, CC, DPL.

CHAPTER NINE

A GOOD BAD BOOK

Bureaus working in the West—the presentation in fiction form of the great harm that the "bureau" does in some sections of our western states. The good and the bad of the bureau system worked out through conflict.

—CARHART DESCRIBING HIS PROPOSED NOVEL *BUREAUCRAT*[1]

INTRODUCTION: IN HIS SPARE TIME

Arthur Carhart wrote because he had to write, both as compulsion and as compensation. As a free-thinking reformer, he was too busy to distinguish between the two. As a populist, he knew the importance of maintaining a well-informed electorate. He was too good-natured and egalitarian to be a snob, especially when it came to plain English versus professional jargon.[2] George Orwell was referring to writers like Carhart when he wrote that there was such a thing as a "good bad book" that "has no literary pretensions but remains readable when more serious productions have perished."[3] By the time he left McCrary, Culley, & Carhart (MCC) in 1930, Carhart had published more than 200 articles and three books in his "spare time."

On his way to national prominence, Carhart first became a regional writer. And like his friend Bernard DeVoto, he meant to defend the Rocky Mountain West against overzealous federal bureaucrats and eastern cultural imperialists.[4]

By 1928, Carhart and others had formed the Colorado Authors League.[5] Carhart published his own history of Colorado in that popular format, the guidebook.

NONFICTION: THE FACT STUFF READS LIKE ROMANCE

Carhart's four-year writing apprenticeship with the Forest Service led to steady sales of his nonfiction by late 1925.[6] By 1926, the *Christian Science Monitor,* *Sunset,* the *Saturday Evening Post,* and many others were publishing his articles on gardening and wildlife. Carhart's Forest Service and American Society of Landscape Architects (ASLA) credentials stood him in good stead.

While in the midst of the Boundary Waters furor over unnecessary roads, Carhart derided overreliance on auto-based tourism. But he was always friendly to appropriate uses of the auto,[7] submitting a story "The Economics of Scenic Highways" to *The Highway Magazine.* Drawing on his auto-camper–friendly designs for Squirrel Creek Campground, Carhart wrote about "the ideal motor camp" for *Motor Life* magazine in 1927.[8]

Like Leopold, Carhart saw the growing influence of hunters and fishermen. Also like Leopold, he accepted equipment from gun and ammunition manufacturers and from fishing tackle makers. In October 1926, Carhart began writing for *Field and Stream,* which remained one of his most important outlets for decades, along with *Sports Afield* and *Outdoor Life.* Reaction to "Our Superior Forest" in *Field and Stream* was so intense that Carhart's editor worried about libel suits, but Carhart backed up every word—much to the satisfaction of Horace Albright, who was on the magazine's Conservation Council. Encouraged and vindicated, Carhart produced a series on "the present zero hour for western game."[9]

In winter of 1926–1927, Carhart was also writing for *American Forests* and *Forest Life,* both publications of the American Forestry Association. Wallace Hutchinson kept Carhart in this loop, introducing him to Associate Editor Tom Gill. Even more important, in 1923 Hutchinson had introduced Carhart to Stanley Young, a brilliant and ambitious biologist with the Bureau of Biological Survey. Ultimately, their collaboration would produce *Last Stand of the Pack.* Carhart's relationship with Young led in 1927 to "The Trail to the Arctic Willow" in *Nature Magazine,* whose editorial board consisted of many prominent names at the Bureau of Biological Survey and the Audubon Society. However, Carhart and Young were often at odds about predators, as Carhart discovered when he proposed a sympathetic article about coyotes to *Nature Magazine.* He found a better venue at *Outdoor Life,* where he published a confrontational article titled "Mutton—or Game?" Explaining the conflicts between sheep and wildlife, stockmen and hunters, this article provoked the kind of passionate feedback Carhart's editors learned to love.[10]

By the end of 1928, *Sunset* was commissioning gardening articles from Carhart. Then Des Moines–based *Better Homes & Gardens*, with its huge circulation of 1.15 million, offered him its garden editor position at $5,000 per year, which he had to decline because of his many other commitments. Carhart's partners in the landscape architecture firm were not only aware of his moonlighting, but they actually encouraged it because it was good for a business that was flagging as the decade wore on. The partners even contributed illustrations for an article in *Ladies Home Journal*. Carhart had a fruitful professional relationship with Lou Richardson, his editor at *Better Homes & Gardens*, before she left to edit him at *Sunset*. He told her he made about $5,000 per year in 1928 from his writing alone.

FICTION: AND HAVE BASED A VIOLENT COVER ON IT

While editors were quick to accept his nonfiction, they were slower to strike at his fiction. Then he found the right balance between his brand of individualism and his plots, which often involved the Forest Service. The specific twist was to imagine the Forest Service not as it really was but as it ought to be—and to imagine the national forests as a last frontier where individualism had to be of the rugged variety. Carhart told an editor at Doubleday, Page: "It is my belief that the Forest Service has almost as colorful a history as the much-heralded 'Mounted' and I hope I may be able to put some of it on paper in such a way as to command interest. It is also a fact that what remains of the 'old west' is located in the western National Forests."[11]

And so, after a few years of struggling against heavy odds (much like his heroes), Carhart finally broke through. Around Christmas 1925 he heard from Editor Donald Kennicott, who would champion his work for the next decade: "We are keeping 'The Lunkhead' for the Blue Book and a check for $150 will proceed in your direction before long. We are using 'Through the Red Dusk' in the March Blue Book and have based a violent cover on it. We are also buying 'The Greater Loyalty' and 'A Crisis and Friendship.'"[12]

Carhart relished the pulp fiction market. *Blue Book* sold for fifteen cents in 1925 (twenty-five cents by 1929). *Red Book* sold for more and featured longer stories. One of Carhart's fellow contributors was Edgar Rice Burroughs. Before long, Carhart's name began to appear on the covers, identified as a former forest ranger. The March 1926 *Blue Book* featured "Through the Red Dusk," set in the Flat Tops area near Trappers Lake. It starred rangers who fought fires and ranchers with equal dedication. The editors described it as "[a] short novel of swift adventure in one of our National Forests—by the author of 'Two-Fisted Administration' and 'The Race of Forest Men.'"

Carhart's production was remarkable. And no wonder—many of his editors paid by the word. At the beginning of 1927, an editor wrote: "NORTH WEST STORIES, as you know, wants woman interest, or else pardner for pardner stuff, with lots of outdoor tang and color. Please keep our hero young and dashing if possible."[13] This same editor liked Carhart's Forest Service stories, noting, "Such stories are more redolent of the modern West instead of the West of longhorns and mesquite."[14]

Editor Kennicott saw what Carhart was after in terms of treating public lands as a last frontier. Attaching a check for $500, Kennicott wrote to the author: "'Bridges over Purgatory' strikes me as a very good story indeed— the sort of thing I've been contending could and should be written—namely: a thoroughly dramatic and engrossing story of the modern West, without the anachronistic 'bunk' of which one sees so much."[15] A serialization of stories called "The Forest Legion" was sold to *Blue Book* for $1,800 in 1928. Carhart wrote to Kennicott: "At times have yen to get into writing exclusively."[16]

Carhart became so popular that by 1929 *Blue Book* was serializing all the Carhart-Young wolf stories, then known as "Renegades of the Rangelands," ignoring their nonfiction status but valuing Carhart's own appraisal: "The fact stuff reads like romance." The money from articles and stories was good. But Carhart was not satisfied with fame and money. He knew he was writing good bad books, and he wanted to do better. He wanted to become an artist, a writer of major novels. Far from being only a reformer, he wanted to become what Mary Austin and Ernest Thompson Seton (and Ella Carhart) thought he could be: a serious artist.[17]

IF YOU INSIST ON KEEPING WITHIN THE AUTO

In mid-1928, Carhart was looking for an agent to market his considerable output. He contacted Brandt & Brandt, a prestigious New York firm that specialized in selling western writers to eastern audiences. Carl Brandt replied that Carhart's work did not need representation, as it was strictly for "the pulp papers."[18] This curt dismissal bothered Carhart. He fought back through his continued commercial success, through the Colorado Authors League, and through his growing dislike of condescending easterners.

He also turned to the relatively new medium of radio. His constant theme was the necessity for civic and regional pride. If the West was to develop its own positive identity, Carhart would celebrate it as a place of energy and promise. He began to broadcast a weekly radio show called *Writing in the Western Scene*, in which he defended western writers against eastern critics.[19] Gradually,

Carhart began to see himself not as the adversary of easterners but as their guide to a more authentic view of the West.[20]

Carhart was working on the book he hoped would establish him as an interpreter of the West. That was his guidebook, *Colorado*, which appeared in 1932, published in New York by Coward-McCann.[21] In a concluding chapter about the Trappers Lake area called "BIG WEST," Carhart told his readers:

> Listen to the east-of-the-Hudson prophets. But don't always believe them. They nurse a delusion that there is no place left where men ride ponies with brands on their hides, where the riders wear wide hats, leather pants, and feel that they are only half dressed if they do not have a gun and cartridge belt on them, except, of course, in rodeos and Hollywood. . . . You will never see the West except as a gigantic canvas of color and form bordering the motor highway, if you insist on keeping within the auto.
>
> I'm darin' yuh, mister, tuh straddle a cayuse and ride into romance country. Shore yuh'll git saddle sore but there ain't never been nobody died of it yet. . . .
>
> So we dedicate this country to the fellow who wants to straddle saddle leather, who has dreamed of the day when he would ride high trails on a pinto cayuse, hear the whisper of unfettered breezes telling of some distant country beyond the horizon, and for a time get so far from our mechanical today that he will know he is in the real West of his dreams.
>
> So do not listen to the prophets of the Hudson and east. The old West is not dead by a long shot.[22]

The "western" slang might put some readers' teeth on edge, but Carhart knew what he was doing. He knew easterners needed a mythology of the West just as much as westerners did. He knew that mythology should celebrate energy and patriotism. But who would write it? Carhart hoped he would. Gearing up for his labors, he described himself in 1929:

> My ambition is to write the best compelling conservation novels of the next few years, design three gardens, a genuine naturalistic garden, a garden-of-the-night in which electric lighting makes the garden a fairy like place, and a "jazz" or futuristic garden, and be the best cook in the bunch when I go on pack trips. Also own a ranch down in the 'dobe-house district and have a big string of chili peppers hanging over the wall and Navaho rugs on the floor—lot of 'em.[23]

THE ORDEAL OF BRAD OGDEN: TOO FAT, THIN, BLOND, TALKY, SILLY, MANISH, ILLOGICAL, BEAUTIFUL, UGLY, OR WHAT?

Carhart knew *Brad Ogden* was hardly the first Forest Service novel, but he thought it was the best. Published in 1910, Zane Grey's *The Young Forester* portrayed forest rangers as earnest, reliable, and progressive. That same year, Hamlin Garland dedicated *Cavanagh, Forest Ranger: A Romance of the Mountain West* "To the Forest Ranger, whose lonely vigil on the heights safeguards the Public Heritage."

Written without firsthand experience, these books were full of half-truths. Could Carhart do better? Forest Service friends like Wallace Hutchinson knew Carhart could do better than the party line they had to churn out. Fresh from World War I, they knew how deadly propaganda is to the imagination. Yet they also knew the Forest Service had to sell itself to Congress and the taxpayers. Jeff LaLande described the public relations setting in which Carhart found himself:

> Speeches, pamphlets, commentaries in national magazines, and letters to regional newspaper editors all sought to legitimize the new Forest Service in the eyes of the American public. Perhaps the more effective path to public acceptance, even outright admiration, of the forest ranger, however, proved to be through the pages of popular fiction.
>
> Beginning in 1910, several authors used the forest ranger as protagonist in their Western novels, boys' books, and other fiction. Such publications typically had the blessing of [Gifford] Pinchot and later Forest Service leaders, who sometimes contributed glowing forewards [sic] and prefaces. Although the literary merit of most of these works is debatable, they fulfilled a very practical function. Growing in popularity after World War I and continuing through the Great Depression, such stories created for readers a positive, often romantic, image of the ranger and his mission.[24]

Donald Kennicott was always pushing Carhart to go beyond stereotypes. Early versions of the women in *Brad Ogden* did not pass muster. Carhart wrote to Kennicott: "Now I'm going to ask you direct to tell me wherein the females are wrong. You've asserted several times that they are sour but never been specific. Are they too fat, thin, blond, talky, silly, manish, illogical, beautiful, ugly, or what? Wherein do they not click?"[25]

Carhart's problem, his editor told him, was that he did not yield to his imagination enough. From the point of view of his critics in the Forest Service, his problem was the opposite—he had too much imagination and of the wrong kind. One of the leaders of the Forest Service's public relations campaign was Edward A. Sherman, who knew exactly how he wanted the Forest Service portrayed. In 1924, Irving Crump published *The Boys' Book of Forest Rangers*,[26]

> a collection of brief stories about personal challenges faced by various young rangers, interspersed with chapters explaining relevant aspects of the Forest Service's mission. Giving official endorsement to author Crump's fictional ranger tales is a foreword by the Forest Service's assistant chief forester

Edward A. Sherman. Invoking the ranger's image as "watchful guardian of Uncle Sam's domain," Sherman stresses that "this keen-eyed, sunburned forest dweller" is the "keystone of the Forest Service arch—a picturesque and romantic figure."[27]

As he tried to imagine a better Forest Service, the artistic problem for Carhart was to progress beyond stereotypes; specifically, to learn characterization rather than idealization or vilification. The practical problem was to avoid libel suits. His solution was to invent a character named Caverley, who closely resembled his once and future nemesis, Leon Kneipp. As if Brad Ogden did not have enough troubles, his most painful ordeal involved the devious Caverley, who misused the weapons of bureaucratic procedure.

While Brad Ogden was busy battling predators, fire, and ranchers, Carhart had to be sure not to stereotype Ogden's enemies. Most of all, he had to strike a balance. He had to be sure to get the facts straight by accurately portraying the agency's sometimes deadly, procedure-bound side. Then the progressive Brad Ogden and his supporters could show how the job ought to be done: by the book, to be sure, but with spirit. *Brad Ogden* stands above other novels of its type because Carhart cast a critical eye on some glaring faults within Forest Service "burocracy."[28] Naively, Carhart did not see how far he had strayed from the thinking of the entrenched, old-school progressives who now ran agencies like the Forest Service and the Bureau of Biological Survey.

Sherman immediately discerned and disliked what others in the Forest Service saw and liked. Brad Ogden was devoted to the resource first and then to the agency. As Sherman perceived, Brad Ogden was a devotee of conservation in the abstract, "serving her and her alone."[29] After many long delays related to fears of libel suits and to the worsening financial condition of the publishing business in the late 1920s, Carhart asked advance readers for blurbs. He proudly sent an advance copy to Sherman: "I have a hope that this will be the start of a whole group of books dealing with the service. . . . With this book I send my best wishes. Perhaps this opens a new field in which I can help conservation and the forest work even more than if I were still in the service! And for this opportunity as well as others I have you largely to thank."[30]

Carhart soon received a crushing five-page reply:[31]

> You asked for a statement regarding this volume. You will perhaps be a little surprised that I should say that in my opinion no Forest Officer will ever refer to your book with a thrill of pride as giving a fair picture of the Forest Service. It does give a fine picture of Ogden and his followers and Ogden happens to be a forest officer when this scene is laid. But the ideals depicted have their origin in Ogden's own splendid personality and the others follow him, not the Service. It—the Service—is only a handicap to Ogden.

How do I get that way? Well, I read the book and on page 124 I found the following: "It is an easy thing to 'get' a man in the Forest Service." . . .

There is no suggestion that Caverley is an exception. In fact, the inference is the other way.

I am sorry not to find in your book something of the reflection of the courage and square dealing of Pinchot, Price, and Olmsted, who took Roosevelt as their model, loved the outdoors, and fought always for a square deal for everyone. Ogden is a devotee of conservation in the abstract, serves her and her alone. . . .

No, Carhart, I am sorry but am forced to admit that in my opinion no forest officer will read the "Brad Ogden" story with a thrill of personal pride or ever say to his boy, "Son, I want you to read this work by Carhart and learn from its pages the kind of an outfit your dad belonged to."

Finally, I want you to know and understand that I opened the pages of the book expecting to like it as I had always liked the author. I was disappointed. I am sorry to say it but am going to express myself to avoid an explosion. Your book isn't merely bad; it's worse than that. It's poor. I think you could write a good one if you tried. Why don't you?

P.S.: I don't believe it would be wise to use any part of this statement for publicity purposes. It was written for you and not for your publisher or the public.

Carhart must have been devastated, but he rallied:

Of all the men who may read "The Ordeal of Brad Ogden" you are one from whom I had expected a judicial approach. But I can see after reading your letter that was impossible. All these years through which you have battled so valiantly and effectively for the U.S.F.S. [U.S. Forest Service] just wouldn't permit you. . . . You lost sight of the fact that Ogden, Tillamook and Hannum *are* the Forest Service; that Caverley is the untrue, unhealthy thing which for want of a better name we call bureaucracy.

I suppose I might develop a small caliber peeve over your letter if I were so constituted. But I'll not. I thoroughly enjoyed it. I'm mighty glad you wrote as you did.

Some six years away from the Service has not lessened my loyalty to the true things in the Service one particle. But it has permitted me to get far enough away from the work to have a somewhat different viewpoint than is possible when one is right in the midst of it and is giving it the unquestioning, unswerving loyalty which [is] so aptly called "the Forest Service viewpoint." If Caverley helps one whit in shaking any forest executives out of their groove, makes them hyperanalytical, even irritates them to a point where they stamp out faint traces of "bureaucracy" which inevitably sometimes lift their heads, then Caverley is justified.

And as to your suggestion that you "think you could write a good one if you tried," I'll reply, I'm going to write another, and a good one, so help me. And I'll approach it with just the same love for the Service, just as much devotion to good conservation, with just as high a regard for the men and women of the F.S. as I have always had. Yes, I plan to continue my writing, more than ever. I plan to write about the U.S. Forest Service to some considerable extent. And I intend to be constructive and helpful at all times.

I'm so well initiated in this writing game now that a lambasting by someone who disagrees is often more helpful than evasive commendation. Only a good friend would write as frankly as you have to me and I am glad to have your letter. Write me again.[32]

Sherman cooled off for a few months. Then he replied:

One: How do you know that your book did not get from me a judicial approach? It is possible for you to realize that I am so wrapped up in the Forest Service that such an approach was impossible. But it is not possible for you to realize that you in turn are so wrapped up in "The Ordeal of Brad Ogden," your own brain child, that you are unable to recognize the results of a richly deserved and really genuine "judicial approach," even though you should see it lying mangled in the roadway or receive a word picture of it in a letter from an ancient but not yet decrepit friend.

Two: No, Carhart, I didn't go a long way to smack at the book for taking license with the verities. I merely wished to show you that even in this regard your work lacked the painstaking exactitude of Pepys, and consequently if it was not granted a crown of immortality based on its merit as fiction, it couldn't claim special consideration on its merit as history.

Your letter, on the whole, has strengthened the personal esteem I have always had for the writer. I particularly appreciate the ring of the last paragraph. You got me right in that I wouldn't have written you as I did if I was not really interested in your advancement.[33]

Sherman skewered Carhart for not being factual enough. His choice of the diarist Pepys seems peculiar, however, for *Brad Ogden* is fiction rather than diary or history. And it was imaginative fiction Sherman could not abide. Meanwhile, Carhart did receive an endorsement from former district forester Allen Peck, who welcomed the portrayal of Caverley: "I'm glad everyone does despise him. After all he is the element in the yarn which shows up the real forest men, Brad, Tillamook, and Hannum."[34]

Fred Morrell, Peck's replacement, wrote Carhart in a way that confirmed Carhart's sense that the Forest Service was often too beholden to ranchers:

I have enjoyed reading it. I am sorry that I can not give you any comment on the book with permission to use it, and this is the reason.

Stockmen who may read the book will, I think, be hurt and offended. As a member of the Forest Service I could not afford to say anything in favor of a book that would hurt or offend stockmen.[35]

Since *Brad Ogden* is now a rare book, readers might have difficulty locating it. This excerpt allows them to judge the characterization of Caverley for themselves:

Caverley was a District Forest Inspector, a man with some authority and some power in the District Office at Denver. He was generally disliked by most of the field men.

Brad Ogden had never had any particular love for Caverley. In Brad's mind, he had come to classify Caverley as the typical bureaucrat; the man who puts the Bureau, regulations, rulings of the Comptroller, exactness according to the prescribed way of doing things, before human service and the practice of true forestry. Caverley worshipped at the shrine of precedent, could do nothing whatever without consulting the Forest Service manual and the files where the actions of other bureaucrats before him gave him his cue as to what lines to follow.

Caverley raised his colorless brows a little. He was more accustomed to a sort of easy-going knuckling among most of the field men because he could do them injury in spite of the protection of any Civil Service. Caverley liked to be looked up to, feared a little. It gave his small soul satisfaction.

It is an easy thing to "get" a man in the Forest Service although legislators, Civil Service enthusiasts and even the bureaucratic inner circle of the Service will loudly protest that it is not so. Once incur the dislike or personal animosity of a man higher up, and he can shear a service employee and leave his official "hide" drying in the sun. There are enough rules, regulations and precedent to break a man if a superior officer starts out to do it. Caverley was one of the relatively limited group of bureaucrats who would do this sort of thing. Brad had heard of several men in the Service that had been crushed by bureaucratic manipulations of Caverley.

"I've never liked your policy, Ogden. I've spoken to you several times about it in the past. You go at things too direct. You should use more tact. . . . You know that our whole policy is to keep on friendly terms with the cattlemen. Work with them, not cross them. Try to make them friends."

"Well, this bunch of hombres want to rule the forest. I'm not going to let them, not while I'm super."

"You have put the Service in an awkward situation at Washington by your stubbornness, Ogden."

"Oh, to hell with that bunch of musty old pensioners down there. What do they know about what is going on here?"

"They have ways of finding out." Caverley glared severely. "Every time you make a faux pas such as this, it's felt somehow at Washington. We received this telegram two days ago from the Forester's Office about this subject under discussion. The Senator from this District has had a long conference with the Forester about it. Tut, tut, Ogden. You don't seem to realize that when you precipitate a situation like this in the field with such influential men as Banks and Gordon or Moon that you make trouble for us in the District Office and trouble for the Forester. It might have some effect on our appropriations for the next year. You know that Senator Cleeland from this District is on the Appropriations Committee, don't you?"

Brad slumped a little in his chair. Some of the District Office men were upstanding fellows that had won through to their positions because of their courage as well as their work. Caverley had been promoted because of his ability to say yes. Of all District Office men, Brad would have selected Caverley last as the one with whom to discuss the trouble with old Moon and his cohorts. Caverley nursed and cuddled the viewpoint of the Bureau, giving gravest consideration to obtaining support for it, even to the extent of sacrificing much of what the Service is supposed to stand for. . . .

"I'm going to crack down on them, Caverley. I'm going to stand by my guns. Just as soon as I can prove my case. I'll make Christians and believers out of this bunch, so help me!"

"You may find some official backing lacking when you do that," said Caverley sharply.

"Ogden, you're impossible!" exploded Caverley. "You're utterly impossible. I sometimes think that the Service would be far better off without you in it."

"Don't let it worry you, Caverley. Just you do what you think right. I'll do what I think is right. Then both of our consciences will not be troubled; or have you only an office manual where your conscience should be?" . . .

"Right or wrong makes no difference to that bird. He's out to perpetuate the good old pay check that it showers down to him every month. Bureau first. People afterward. Rules and regulations not for forestry but to give those who are good 'yes' men a job for life at the public expense. I'm darned near disgusted; to think that such pin-headed people can hold such positions in this great Service which otherwise is so sound and able." (180–182)

Without any endorsements, *The Ordeal of Brad Ogden: A Romance of the Forest Rangers* finally appeared in 1929. It sold for two dollars. A positive review in the *New York Telegram* said it would make a good movie. Ever optimistic, Carhart tried without success to sell the movie rights to Metro-Goldwyn-Mayer and Warner Brothers. However, the book did not sell. Royalties for *Brad Ogden* in the period July–December 1931 were zero.[36]

NOTES

1. Letter from Carhart to Donald Kennicott, February 12, 1928, Carhart Collection, Denver Public Library (hereafter CC, DPL).

2. Carhart was hard on overly technical writers. On May 24, 1950, he wrote in a review for *The New York Times Book Review*: "The book was hard reading. So many of those who know their subject in such fields, are so saturated with the language of their

profession, they take it for granted all must understand it without having to ponder. It is a basic quarrel I have with those who should most tellingly present these important subjects—that they write inevitably for an audience who is fully trained in such reading. Our schools, teaching technical journalism, seem to have a fixation in their training for such writing; they may have pride in knowing the jargon of the professions!"

3. George Orwell, "A Good Bad Book," *Tribune*, November 2, 1945.

4. My thanks to Richard Eutalain for helping me place Carhart within the regionalist context of Walter Prescott Webb and Bernard DeVoto. When I was a graduate student at Berkeley, Henry Nash Smith taught me how to value "subliterary" works as important parts of myth making. See Henry Nash Smith, *The American West as Symbol and Myth* (Cambridge: Harvard University Press, 1950).

5. Carhart read historian Frederic Paxon, a midwesterner who taught at the University of Colorado from 1903 to 1907. Frederic Paxon, *The Last American Frontier* (New York: Macmillan, 1910) and *History of the American Frontier, 1763–1893* (Boston: Houghton Mifflin, 1924).

6. Subhead from Carhart to *American Forests*, December 26, 1926, regarding *Last Stand of the Pack*.

7. Carhart wrote "Call of the Highlands" in September 1926 for *Motor Life* for thirty-five dollars. The publication also accepted "The Real Tincanners" in May 1926. Carhart wrote for many auto-industry–based publications throughout his life. This relationship culminated in his receiving the American Motors Conservation Award in 1968 on behalf of the Conservation Collection.

8. *Motor Life* (October 1927). The Forest Service made good copy. Carhart's articles and stories about the Superior National Forest were published in a Doubleday, Page & Company imprint called *The Frontier*. He also sold "Forest Fire Fighters" to *Everybody's Magazine*.

9. Letter from Carhart to Holland, October 10, 1926, CC, DPL.

10. Letter from E. A. Holland to Carhart, February 12, 1928, CC, DPL. By 1928, Carhart was selling to *Garden & Home Builder, Frontier, West, Blue Book, Air Stories, Ace High, Action Stories, Red Book, Saturday Evening Post, Outlook, National Geographic, American Forests, Nature, Better Homes & Gardens, House & Garden, Motor Life, Field and Stream, Outdoor Recreation* (now *Outdoor Life*), *Sunset, Everybody's Magazine,* and a dozen or two others.

11. Letter from Carhart to Doubleday, Page editor, February 4, 1924, CC, DPL.

12. Letter from Kennicott to Carhart, December 18, 1925, CC, DPL.

13. Letter from Richard Martinsen to Carhart, January 6, 1927, CC, DPL.

14. Letter from Martinsen to Carhart, January 15, 1927, CC, DPL. There were failures as well. In late 1927, Carhart tried a magazine called *The American Boy* with a story called "Big Footed Lummox." They turned him down. It took another thirty years for Carhart to discover that his best fiction would be written for boys.

15. Letter from Kennicott to Carhart, February 24, 1927, CC, DPL.

16. Letter from Carhart to Kennicott, February 12, 1928, CC, DPL.

17. For another view, see Andrew Glenn Kirk: "For him, writing was a tool for reform; he never really grasped the idea of writing as art." Kirk, *Collecting Nature: The*

American Environmental Movement & the Conservation Library (Lawrence: University of Kansas Press, 2001), 40.

18. Letter from Carhart to Brandt, August 12, 1928; Brandt to Carhart, November 13, 1928, CC, DPL.

19. These transcripts are in the CC, DPL. Carhart started on Denver radio station KLZ, broadcasting on Thursday evenings at 7:15. After a few years he got a better offer and switched to KOA (an NBC network affiliate). This broadcast dates from February 7, 1933. By 1932, Carhart had tried without success to get NBC to broadcast his show nationally. In November 1944 he was back on the air with KFEL, campaigning to save the last fourteen grizzlies in the state of Colorado. (He failed.)

20. Twenty years later, when he finally began to achieve national recognition as a serious writer, Carhart remembered his roots: "There is something too big, too powerful, too dynamic in this western rhythm to allow him [the western writer] to climb a little ladder of superiority and sling muddy ink at his home folk and home and homeland." Letter of June 26, 1953, to a correspondent in the National Park Service, CC, DPL. He continued: "Incidentally, Benny DeVoto had dinner with us last evening, and we blocked out his trip through to Mesa Verde. He shifted it at my urging so his travel would allow him to see the Great Sand Dunes; and he was pleased he could do this."

21. Arthur Carhart, *Colorado: History, Geology, Legend* (New York: Coward-McCann, 1932).

22. Ibid., 203–204.

23. Letter from Carhart to Harriman, December 15, 1929, CC, DPL.

24. Jeff LaLande, "The Making of a New Western Hero: The Forest Ranger in Popular Fiction, 1900–1940," *Journal of Forestry* 98, 11 (November 2000):44.

25. Letter from Carhart to Kennicott, April 12, 1928, CC, DPL, regarding the female characters in what would become *The Ordeal of Brad Ogden*.

26. Irving Crump, *The Boys' Book of Forest Rangers* (New York: Dodd, Mead, 1924).

27. See Jeff LaLande, "The 'Forest Ranger' in Popular Fiction: 1910–2000," *Forest History Today* (Spring-Fall 2003):45. While Crump's work idealized rangers, it did so at the price of racist overtones that Sherman ignored. Even worse was Hunter S. Moles's *Ranger District Number Five* (Boston: Spencerian Press, 1923).

28. Jeff LaLande and I disagree on our interpretation of Carhart's novel. LaLande says: "The 1929 novel *The Ordeal of Brad Ogden: A Romance of the Forest Rangers*, by a Forest Service landscape architect, presents the ranger as a Hollywood demigod. Recently retired from the Forest Service, Arthur C. Carhart (who went on to publish other Western novels during the 1930's under the pseudonym of Hart Thorne) was a committed Progressive conservationist. He portrayed his hero in a manner that provided thrilling reading while popularizing the author's (and the agency's) values." *Journal of Forestry*, 49. In *Forest History Today*, 1, LaLande says Carhart was "recently retired from the Forest Service" and that he "presents the ranger figure as a fully developed Tom Mix–like Hollywood demi-god." One of Carhart's short stories did make it to the silver screen. "Riding On" appeared as a Grade B Western in 1937, directed by Harry Webb and starring Tom Tyler.

29. Carhart set about marketing drafts of *Brad Ogden* and *Last Stand of the Pack* in 1925–1926. In both cases he arranged for serializations that helped him (and Young) recover some of their research and writing costs. But his goal was publication in the most serious national markets. Carhart finally succeeded in selling both books to Karl Harriman at Sears, a New York publisher. Sears's other books were rather daring for the times. They included tales of a young black woman who passes as white and a young Jewish woman who tastes the new freedoms of America. *Brad Ogden* actually appeared before *Last Stand* because of delays caused by the serialization of the wolf stories in magazines.

30. Letter from Carhart to Sherman, February 16, 1929, CC, DPL.

31. Letter from Sherman to Carhart, March 8, 1929, CC, DPL.

32. Letter from Carhart to Sherman, March 16, 1929, CC, DPL.

33. Letter from Sherman to Carhart, June 13, 1929, CC, DPL.

34. Letter from Peck to Carhart, January 28, 1929, CC, DPL.

35. Letter from Morrell to Carhart, March 26, 1929, CC, DPL.

36. Carhart maintained that ordinary Forest Service people liked his book because it "has essential Forest Service regulations as nub of story." Letter from Carhart to Kennicott, July 11, 1929, CC, DPL. Almost as bad, royalties for *Last Stand* in 1931 were $27.25, after Carhart paid his split to Young. This amounted to 109 copies sold.

CHAPTER TEN

I AM GOING TO WRITE A WOLF BOOK

You know yourself that we are rather uncontaminated with the polyglot of the eastern centers. We are farther from the European influence. Writers here are distinctly western stock; pioneer types. They write very much as they see the world and that is through a rather clear, western atmosphere. I believe we are able to get a better perspective of America from here than when hedged with the hectic drive of the stewpots of polyglot cities. And I believe all the factors working together will bring out some outstanding writers of a new regional literature that will set a new and different tempo in our American books.

—ARTHUR CARHART, 1932[1]

INTRODUCTION: TO HELL WITH THE AUDIENCE

Mary Austin was a prominent regional writer in Carhart's time. Born in Illinois in 1868 (a year before Carhart's mother), she and Carhart aspired to share a new regional culture composed of Indian, Hispanic, and Anglo ways of adapting to a harsh environment. When Austin encountered Carhart's book on the ways of the wolf, she was working on her autobiography, in which she described a mystical childhood union with nature very much like Carhart's 1919 experience at Trappers Lake.[2]

Austin settled in Santa Fe in 1923, the year the Bureau of Biological Survey's traps and poisons killed one of the last wolves in Colorado.[3] There she met Ernest Thompson Seton, who in 1898 had portrayed the last wolves in New Mexico as tragic royalty. He grounded his eulogy for "Lobo, King of the Currumpaw" not just in the best science of his time but also in imaginative writing that led some to brand him "a nature faker."[4]

Seton's successor as a wolf authority was Stanley Young, Carhart's collaborator on *Last Stand of the Pack*. One of Young's goals was to eradicate Seton's imaginative, even sympathetic way of portraying predators, such as wolves, and other "vermin," such as crows and ravens. Another of Young's goals was to eradicate the predators themselves—all of them. In a fashion that appealed to Carhart, Seton had worked as an independent wolfer, without the organizational support of a federal agency. In contrast, Young rose swiftly through the ranks of the Bureau of Biological Survey (BBS), leaving Denver for Washington, D.C., in 1928, where he became head of the Division of Predatory Animal and Rodent Control at the BBS.[5]

As the coauthors attempted to market their book, Carhart was turning against poisons and developing mixed feelings about his writing partner, just as his ambivalence was growing about the wolves. As Young moved up in the kind of bureaucracy Carhart reviled, Carhart began to feel his peers might be the ardent Austin and Seton rather than the dour, master bureaucrat Young. Although Carhart was the principal author of their book, he was bound to Young in many ways, not the least of which was Young's status as a stockholder in the Colorado Floral Company.

How did this pair work together? Young provided the facts, which he called "science." Carhart provided the saga. Seton's earlier mix of science and saga had piqued Austin's interest about wolf lore related to Native American cultures. She wanted to know more, and she found it in Carhart and Young's book, where clever wolfers like Big Bill Caywood used their knowledge of wolf lore to kill wolves. But was there something more? What did Austin see in the prosaic Carhart? She was a social theorist who was as interested in wolf behavior as in Indian lifeways. Her considerable political sophistication extended beyond her personal friendship with Herbert Hoover, whom she admired as an efficient humanitarian who saved countless lives after World War I through well-organized relief efforts. Like many American writers in the aftermath of the war, Austin felt there had to be better ways than those of the discredited Europeans to organize society and form good citizens. Like Carhart, Austin thought the public lands of the West might hold an answer.

Austin saw that Carhart was writing a morality tale, driven by the imperatives of survival of the fittest in a setting where wolves and Indians had formerly preyed on bison. In his foreword to *Last Stand*, Carhart wrote: "There was plenty of food for the gray wolves before the white men came. . . . The red brother killed only for necessities; for meat, robes that were needed by that individual hunter and his family, and not for so-called sport which was actually slaughter. . . . The Indians did not make a business of hunting the gray wolf."

Like Carhart, Austin admired the Indians of the Southwest because they seemed to have a sense of scale that allowed them to live on the land. Like wolves, she thought, Indians such as the Utes respected territories under the guidance of the kind of wild spirit Carhart had encountered at Trappers Lake. Austin's death in 1934 at age sixty-six followed all too closely upon the death of Carhart's mother in 1932. This double blow deprived Carhart of the persons most perceptive about his potential as an artist.[6]

SKIMMING THE CREAM OF DELIGHT

Last Stand of the Pack explores the overlapping roles of the noble loner, the rugged individualist, the renegade, the hero. The allure of the book lies in the way it blurs the distinctions that were so clear to Stanley Young. Was the hero the wolf? Or the rancher? Or the federal wolfer? Overtly, the book portrays the workings of a federal government "burocracy." It showcases the efficiency of the methodical men who did what the ranchers could not do: exterminate the last wolves in Colorado, regardless of cost. Covertly, *Last Stand of the Pack* suggests that true nobility perished with the inscrutable wolves. Did the wilderness die when the wild died? Before firsthand memories of the last wolves vanished, could Carhart imagine a wolf's world? Austin wanted to know. She had reviewed his book, after all, for the *Saturday Review of Literature*—not the *Journal of Mammology*. She initiated their correspondence when she sent him her highly favorable review of *Last Stand* in 1929: "I have reviewed your book, which I think should become a permanent asset to nature knowledge of the United States. Ernest Seton has just been here, and I recommended it to him to read. He, you know, has made some wolf studies himself."[7]

Carhart asked Austin for advice about his work.[8] Responding in a graceful hand on exquisite, silvery stationery emblazoned with her name in deep blue, she shared with the typewriter-bound Carhart her sense of what regional writers had to do: "There are almost no modern novelists that I can recommend to you. What we have to do out here is to work out a method and a medium of our own."[9] Carhart replied: "My sympathy too was with the old renegades; and I think the hunters felt somewhat the same way. Personally, I feel that we are floundering dangerously and ridiculously with our wildlife. . . . A lot of so-called conservation is bunk."[10]

Increasingly, Carhart saw, that "bunk" included the work of the growing federal resource management bureaucracies, such as the BBS, the Bureau of Reclamation, and the Forest Service. Could there be effective conservation without these bureaucracies? After all, they were the brainchildren of one of Carhart's heroes, Teddy Roosevelt. But did these bureaucracies still embody progressive ideals? Carhart may have left the Forest Service, but he found it hard to abandon the many friends, such as Wallace Hutchinson and Al Hamel, who stayed in the Forest Service and did not necessarily see things his way. As the Depression deepened, so did Carhart's ambivalence.

Mary Austin was a powerful woman. A friendship flowered from their correspondence. The Carharts visited Austin in Santa Fe on one of their city planning and landscape architecture forays into New Mexico, and she introduced them to architect John Gaw Meem. Carhart kept asking for guidance about his writing. At first, Austin replied laconically: "There are holes in your story where the landscape ought to be."[11] And, "I have a hunch that you could really write if you told everybody to go to hell and wrote what you really think and feel."[12]

Warming to her criticism, Carhart told her he wanted to write about wolves from the wolves' point of view and from a sympathetic hunter's point of view: "I am going to write a wolf book that digs into the rather bloody, merciless warfare America is waging on our four-footed brothers."[13] Austin replied:

> I thought your wolf book might have been truly great if, after mastering all the government reports, you had thrown them all in the fire, called on whatever gods you worship and written the story without a thought of its possible audience. If you are making that mistake, you are not the only writer in America who does so. I do not think it altogether a desire for popularity, or even for making money. A great deal of it comes from that terrible pull of the American notion of democracy. A pull of which you may not at all times be conscious, and [it] is more insidious on that account. I have felt it myself and know exactly what it can do to you and the only thing I have to regret in my literary career are the occasions on which I had yielded to it.
>
> I am sure what you need to say to your soul is, "To hell with the audience."

For good measure, Austin heaped scorn on schools for writers: "There is no such thing as learning to write without writing." Seeking models, Carhart told Austin he admired Willa Cather, but he soon learned that Austin frowned on Cather's denigration of Hispanic culture in *Death Comes for the Archbishop*.[14] Nevertheless, Austin recommended Cather and Sinclair Lewis.[15]

> Just a note to say that I don't believe it is sweating that you need to raise your work to a higher literary level. I think, as a matter of fact, that you sweat too much. One has to do it by way of preparation, but when the sweating period is over, there should come a time of delight and relaxation in the work, which should carry you easily to the desired level. . . . You know I told you this same thing about the Wolf book; that you work the facts too hard.
>
> I am sure that you have it in you to do work of a genuine literary quality. Perhaps you are working too hard on other things and there is a hang-

over of the feeling of hard work. If you look again at my *Land of Little Rain*, you will get an idea perhaps of what I mean by just skimming the cream of delight off your impressions and not using anything else except the bare bones of fact.[16]

Carhart never wrote the second wolf book he promised Austin. For most of his career, he worked the facts too hard. Although he was a loner in many ways, he was also a pack animal. "To hell with the audience" meant breaking with friends and mentors whose approval Carhart craved. To them, the facts said public lands should be as free of predators as they were of wildfires. Long after Austin's death, Carhart finally found a new literary friend in Bernard DeVoto. But for the time being, who was to judge the facts? Some answers can be found in Carhart's prickly collaboration with Stanley Young.

RENEGADES OF THE RANGELANDS

In some ways, Carhart and Young made a good team. Together, they "sweated the facts." Then they turned Carhart loose to "make the fact stuff read like romance." Carhart told their editor at Sears: "Young suggests checking by himself too to be sure no 'nature faking' goes into the book."[17] Sears had libel concerns related to an unfavorable portrayal of a rancher named Stoffel. Carhart tracked the supporting materials down, and Young took them to New York to quiet the publisher's fears.

The notion of predator-free public lands was popular in the 1920s, with hunters, with the general public, and with the ranchers who were the most obvious victims of the predators and the most obvious beneficiaries of federally financed extermination programs. The coauthors' goal was not just to provide the public with a "safe" (i.e., predator-free) recreational and aesthetic experience. Federal homesteading policies had lured numerous families onto lands so dry and agriculturally marginal that they could only support livestock. When market hunting and competition from livestock destroyed the wolves' prey base, such as bison, elk, and deer, the wolves turned to the livestock. Therefore, many in the federal agencies felt the government owed homesteaders additional support in the form of predator eradication programs. One problem with these programs was their high costs, which bore no relationship to the value of the livestock. Without such a commonsense brake, the federal programs skidded out of control to their fanatical end: total extermination, regardless of cost to taxpayers. In other words, as Carhart knew all too well, the self-serving "logic" of the "burocracy" took over. As he described it, the situation was enough to make a man "next door to loco."

At first, both Young and Carhart enthusiastically supported the systematic slaughter. Their collaboration started out in 1923 to celebrate the government's accomplishment of killing the last wolf in Colorado. But in the six years it took their book to reach publication, they had time to reflect on the meaning of what the government had done to the wolves. Ultimately, Carhart came to question his commitment to eradication, thanks to Mary Austin's faith that he could learn to think like a wolf. Young, on the other hand, assumed a position like Sherman's. Early on, Young had learned to "invariably step lucky." He became skilled at thinking like a wolf—but mainly for the purpose of killing wolves. He became the top predator's top predator, a technocrat with no tolerance for amateurs, a bureaucrat with no tolerance for citizen second-guessers. Having hitched the rising star of his career to total and complete eradication of the wolf, Young was betting, correctly, that his association with Carhart would further accelerate his professional progress. He was promoted to chief biologist of the Bureau of Biological Survey just as *Last Stand* appeared in 1929. And when it came out, it had endorsements Young had arranged from the secretary of agriculture and the chief of the BBS.[18]

The raw materials Carhart gathered to quell fears of libel suits may give some idea of Young's devotion to ideals that seem so misbegotten to wolf lovers today. In 1921, in his capacity as predatory animal inspector, Young left Denver and traveled to Las Animas County in southern Colorado in late February to check out reports of "wolf depredations" on livestock at Bear Springs Mesa. He succeeded in trapping a female member of the Thatcher pack. Here are excerpts from his field reports:

> The large male wolf which became known to us as "Old Whitie" that headed this pack, was the main offender in regard to stock killings.
> After I captured the female of the pack, I had several good chances at this old male, but on each visit from him to my traps he would invariably step lucky.[19]

Other duties called Young back to Denver, but he left behind a "blind set" of buried traps that snared Old Whitey. The next thing the Denver-bound Young knew, he was contacted by a man named Stoffel who asked if Young wanted to buy Old Whitey's hide and skull, which Stoffel had sent to Denver to be made into a rug. Skeptical of money-seeking amateurs, Young refused the offer. Claiming he himself had trapped the wolf, Stoffel made the further mistake of stepping into Young's trap by brazenly collecting the twenty-five dollar federal bounty from Young. Furious, Young quickly got to the bottom of the story, thanks to close questioning of one of Stoffel's ranch hands, a Mr. Talbot.

Stoffel had chanced on Old Whitey with a trap on each foot. He sent his cowboy for rope and wire. Young's report continued:

> Mr. Talbot returned from the Stoffel ranch in a short time with a rope and some wire. They hog tied the wolf with the wire—muzzled it—and with the aid of a long pole carried him down to the Stoffel ranch. On reaching the ranch they did not remove the wire muzzle. Because of the fact that this muzzle was put on the wolf's mouth so tight as to partly cut off his breathing facilities, the wolf died the following day.
>
> Naturally, on learning this whole story, I was greatly provoked and for a time decided to bring serious action against Mr. Stoffel. . . . My only reason for not pressing prosecution against Mr. Stoffel is due to the fact that he is a struggling dry farmer in rather destitute circumstances. He has a hard working wife and 3 small children and from my observation could see that they were having a very hard time in making both ends meet.
>
> As to the finis on "Old Whitie" I will state that he has a wicked history. For 12 years he has roamed the Bears Spring Mesa country. In one particular instance, especially as pertains to Mr. J. S. Shaw, this wolf and his band have killed $6,000 worth of stock for this cattle man.[20]

Few writers could resist the chance to work with such extraordinary raw material—and with a man as distinguished as Young.[21] In mid-1926 Carhart told the editor of *ADVENTURE* magazine that he and Young were on their way to Burns Hole in western Colorado "to get some local slants on the background. The life story of any one of the wolves would make a book."[22] By the fall of 1926, Carhart was pursuing publishers, and Sears bought the book in 1927:

> Young got together records, correspondence, wolf lore. I am writing the stories in fiction form. There is conversation, action, description, all-same-short-story. But every vital incident can be proven by U.S. government records. And there is dope there that never has appeared in print; wolf lore that is positively uncanny. Fact is, I'm all steamed up over it and Young is next door to loco. Don't believe there is anything like it in print, anywhere. Guess I better quit before I rave more luridly as I can't talk this stuff without getting that way.[23]

At the end of the year, Carhart wrote to his editor at *American Forests*: "Stanley Young is doing the technical part, I'm doing the writing into fiction form of the fact incidents. And they don't need a lot of dressing up either. Stories of the nine last renegade wolves in Colorado. The fact stuff reads like romance."[24]

At first, Carhart and Young titled their work *Renegades of the Rangelands*. In 1927, Donald Kennicott bought the serial rights, with Carhart and Young splitting the fee of $2,000 for nine stories. Marketing the book itself in 1929–1930 was more problematic, both because of the serialization and because of worsening national financial conditions. Carhart and Young arranged for a traveling, storefront-type exhibit (courtesy of the Bureau of Biological Survey) composed of pelts, skulls, and traps. It toured major cities nationwide for four months.

LAST STAND OF THE PACK: YOUNG IS NEXT DOOR TO LOCO

After 1923, Coloradoans who wanted to see wolves had to rely on the Denver Museum of Natural History's wolf exhibit. There, on the eastern edge of City Park, just a few blocks from Carhart's home in Park Hill, they could marvel at the large female known as Unaweep, or Queen, handsomely mounted for display.[25] Most readers will not have access to a rare book like *Last Stand of the Pack*, so the best approach is to let each reader "get his or her wolf" directly. A photo opposite the title and credits page shows a wolf with its right forepaw caught in a trap. The caption reads: "Come and Get Me!" A page follows that fully expressed Carhart's ambivalence:

> A DEDICATION
>
> They are the heirs of the Mountain Men. They are the followers of the last frontiers. They are the friends of all animals; the compassionate, regretful executioners of animal renegades when such outlaws must die that other wildlings may live.
>
> On far trails, wind swept, snow blanketed, hail pelted, on trails where frost bites or sun bakes, on trails where danger stalks with them as a close companion, these determined men carry on the tradition of the organization to which they belong. They get their wolf!
>
> They have made these true stories with their own acts. It has been our privilege to record them. To these men who live these stories day by day, the predatory animal hunters of the U.S. Biological Survey, this book is dedicated.
>
> Arthur Hawthorne Carhart
>
> Stanley Paul Young

Carhart and Young thought they were writing the final chapter in the story of the wolf. Perhaps that is why Carhart cast their account as a tragedy in the old sense of the word, in which a hero must die because of his or her flawed nature. The foreword is titled "The Day Wanes." It starts as a simple morality tale, driven by the imperatives of survival of the fittest in a setting where wolves and Indians preyed on bison. Then it takes the sort of turn Carhart would pursue for the rest of his life. The root problem was that the Forest Service raised public lands grazing above other interests:

> Stockmen invaded the hills. Cattle herds increased. Wolves followed the mountain migration. Range was cropped until it lost its character and new

forage was not there the following spring. The Forest Service was created and the great National Forests established. Grazing regulations came. Brisk demands arose of this public range at nominal fees. Every good grazing unit was taken over by some rancher and grazed as much as it would carry under the regulations.

The wild things that lived on the range were crowded out. Food for them was taken by domestic stock. Poaching, too, helped to hasten the process; for a certain class of settlers even today do not hesitate to "get a little venison" in defiance of the protective laws. But the most powerful factor in almost smashing the deer, elk and antelope herds has been the over appropriation of their hereditary food supply by the dogies of the ranchers, often under the direction of agencies of the State.

The old world of the wolves now was falling about their heads.

Carhart remembered what Al Hamel had told him about overstocking as a result of war hysteria: "Finally the U.S. Biological Survey and its Predatory Animal Control work stepped in where the bounty hunters had failed. Men were put on the trail of stock-killing wolves. These hunters were on salary. They had only one general instruction. It was 'get your wolf.'"

Carhart knew how to draw his readers into a story. Verisimilitude was important, but so was a final, climactic battle scene, cast as a sporting contest:

Nine of them were thus outstanding. Nine of them were wolves of super training, almost unbelievable intelligence. With the old world of their kind gone forever, they made last defiant stands against man and his death machines. They tested the cunning of the best wolfers that the Biological Survey ever employed.

That the old gray wolf should pass without some record of his exit on the western stage being written seemed likely. He would simply cease to be and his final dramatic defeat would remain unregistered.

All vital incidents of each hunt are true. All wolf lore is positively fact. Those who have worked on this record have tried to make this a book so full of wolf lore that nothing that is true of these old gray, heady, cruel killers was left out.

Man has won. The wilderness killers have lost. They have written their own death warrants in killing, torture, blood lust, almost fiendish cruelty. Civilization of the white man has almost covered the west. And with that nearly accomplished, there was no place left for the gray killers, the renegades of the range lands.

They were great leaders, superb outlaws, these last nine renegades. They deserved and received the profound respect of those men who finally conquered them. Defiant, they were striking back at man, playing a grim losing game but never acknowledging defeat until fate had called the last play.

Like royalty in Shakespeare's tragedies, one by one the renegades of the rangelands lined up to have their "sins" tallied against their noble deeds. It is worth contrasting Carhart's writerly treatment with Young's factual account, for Carhart sees the wolf in the man and the man in the wolf. The next sections discuss six of the nine wolves, with excerpts from the book.

Old Lefty of Burns Hole

Old Lefty's motive for stock killing was simple vengeance against Hegewa, the trapper who tore away his forefoot. The opening scene in which Lefty loses his foot creates admiration and sympathy for Lefty and his peers: "In all of Colorado, only the renegade killer wolves were left. Ordinary traps and ordinary hunting would never stop them in their depredations." Hegewa tries to fool Lefty by using wolf scent and hunting on skis. He is a peculiar sort of backcountry bureaucrat, who sports as his official hide a white, soft-collared dress shirt underneath his rough woods wear. "It's get the wolf or have my own official hide hung up to dry. Lefty's hide'll be dryin' days before mine will." Everyone else has given up, but not the real professional: "Only fate, said the natives, could bring that wolf to his death." Hegewa does not buy such high-sounding talk: "That wolf may be canny, he may be nigh human. I know he is. But he's sentenced to death by the U.S. Government and I'm his executioner." In spite of dire warnings from locals, who sardonically place bets on the action, Hegewa heads out into a spring blizzard:

> Wilderness, stark, challenging, man trying, encompassed him. He gloried in his ability to face it, master it.
>
> Hegewa shot down an open slope, swerved by a tree, pitched down another slope, and then straightened out for the easy sweeping run over a slightly inclined mesa. It was life to get out into unsullied country such as this. He kicked down on the skis exuberantly, his sinewy body swaying. Old Lefty was ahead. Wilderness was around him. Blizzard Gods were preparing to charge from the high country, dashing in leaping wind charges over the country below and scattering harried snow dropping from overladen clouds.

Like Stanley Young at Bear Mesa, Hegewa knows he has to completely understand the wolves' use of their territory before he tries to trap them again. Intent on thinking like a wolf, he stays out too late for a snowy day—and then stumbles across their tracks, less than an hour old, with Old Lefty's stump in the lead:

> Hegewa felt a creepy feeling along his spine. Something hinted at fear of the wilderness, a new, a very new sensation to him.

"Maybe Tex was right," he half murmured. He turned back toward the cow camp. "Maybe it is my pelt against Lefty's." A new idea flashed into his mind. To get Lefty he had to survive the blizzard!

With new fierceness, he fought on. He would get that wolf!

The idea of Lefty clad in Hegewa's short white shirt has a certain subversive appeal. But this perilous night pays off for Hegewa. He and Tex rope Lefty, pole him, and truss his mouth. They use him alive as bait for the rest of the pack. After they slaughter the pack, they kill Old Lefty, grind up the relevant body parts, and bottle his scent, which they will use to fool other wolves.

Whitey of Bear Springs Mesa

Based on Young's account of his visit to Las Animas County, this story takes place in the Huerfano Valley, on the southeastern flank of the Sangre de Cristos and south of Greenhorn Mountain. Carhart sends Young driving through a storm from Denver to answer an urgent call from stockman Jim Shaw. Young tells Shaw he has come in person because the whole bureau is busy with state legislative politics. Like the wolves, men are fighting for bureaucratic territory: "There is a tough fight on. There is a bunch in this state that have been making money from trapping predatory animals for bounty, and they are bringing all the pressure they can to defeat that bill [to appropriate funds for cooperation between the state and the BBS]. If we clean out the animal killers, there'll not be any bounty left for them."

The thoroughly professional Young hates the clumsy bounty hunters, who are desperate for money and resent competition from salaried federal hunters. Carhart recognizes that most of the bounty hunters are marginal homesteaders pitted against established ranchers. But Young follows the law of survival of the fittest, and he is here on behalf of the federal government to see that big ranchers like Shaw survive in a setting where dead predators are the property of the federal government.

Thanks to Hegewa's victory over Old Lefty, Young has a secret weapon: ghost scent in a bottle. As with Lefty, bets are placed, and the game is on. But then a mysterious competitor steals Young's traps and spoils his exquisitely planned sets. Before he can unravel this mystery, a desperate telegram from the BBS's ally, the Colorado Stockmens Association, sends Young back to Denver and the legislative battles.

Meanwhile, Old Lefty's scent proves irresistible to Whitey, who falls prey to Young's cleverness. Taking advantage of Young's absence, a homesteader named Strang (Stoffel in Young's account) steals Whitey out of Young's traps and claims the bounty. Having triumphed in Denver, a wrathful Young returns to Bear Mesa, proclaiming, "Here is where one hungry homesteader finds that it's bad medicine to fool with government property." Strang is convicted as a bounty thief, but he appeals to Young, claiming Shaw has been trying to run him off his homestead. Strang's wife and kids soften Young's heart, so he lets Strang off with a warning.

Rags, the Digger

The scene opens not on the range but in Young's office, where officials of the BBS and the Colorado Stockmens Association are so at ease with each other that they sit smoking cigars and discussing wolfer Bill Caywood. Cattleman and banker Jo Neal[26] says to Young: "I've boasted that whenever we've asked for help from this office, within forty-eight hours there would be a Survey hunter on the trail of any killer wolf. . . . Caywood's the man. He knows more about wolves than they know about themselves. He thinks like a wolf, only more so."

Big Bill Caywood was an independent wolfer in northwestern Colorado before joining the BBS. He appealed to Carhart for many reasons—one being that he grew up along Grape Creek east of the Sangre de Cristos, Carhart's favorite mountain range. In 1912 and 1913, Caywood killed 140 wolves, and local stockmen paid him fifty dollars per head. With the money he bought a ranch, horses, and equipment and supplies. The BBS hired him in 1915, and he retired from federal service in 1935. Carhart interviewed him many times. Before going to work for the BBS, even Caywood had trapped indiscriminately, catching coyotes or whatever else happened along but never snagging the wolf known as Rags. Rags occasionally retreated west to Utah, but he always returned to his territory in the White River watershed below Trappers Lake. Carhart described Caywood: "Big-shouldered, slightly stooped, not quite bow-legged but evidently a rider of cowland trails, Caywood represents the type of frontiersman that put much of the work into the winning of the western wildernesses. Dogged in a hunt, untiring in upbuilding of communities, quiet, high-powered, these men have been the bulwark of western progress."

A cattleman named Coats asks Caywood what he's going to do when all the wolves are gone. Caywood says he doesn't know, but he knows he cannot live in the city:

> "I've just got a lot of love and respect for the gray wolf. He's a real fellow, the big gray is. Lots of brains. I feel sorry for him. It's his way of livin'. He don't know better. And I feel sorry every time I see one of those big fellows thrashin' around in a trap bellowin' bloody murder. . . . Guess I'm too much

a part of this outdoors to hold any grudge against animals. . . . It's part the
way that wolves go after poor defenseless steers, murder does and fawns and
drag down bucks that helps me go out and bring them in."

"Well, you've never been on the trail of a worse killer than this 'Rags,'"
observed Coats. "He's a murderer—straight out animal murderer. I believe
he'd tackle a man if he got the chance, I really do."

"He might," replied Caywood. . . .

"I'm not sayin' what he would do if he got a man cornered. But I'd
rather have it the other man than myself if he ever did decide to eat human
meat."

As he does in each story, Carhart sometimes writes well enough to catch
the interest of literary readers like Mary Austin and Ernest Thompson Seton.
He shifts the scene to the perspective of the wolf. We learn that the stockmen
have killed two of his mates: "Once his heart had known softness, love hunger.
But man had killed that. . . . Rags, the lone wolf, would pad-pad along beside the
trail, alert, watchful, following his creed that it was kill or be killed. He always
struck first, without waiting for adversary to attack. It was his religion."

Rags has a peculiar, visceral reaction to his first sight of Caywood.
"Somehow the man on horseback, quiet, alert, had touched a chord in the heart
of the lonely old wolf that had not been reached even when his last litter of cubs
had rolled in the smelly den on Piceance Creek." The tables turned, curious and
even admiring, predator Rags follows predator Caywood to camp, dragging
one of Caywood's traps. Caywood and Rags face each other: "Caywood, wolfer
supreme, was being stalked by his catch!"

Caywood's gun malfunctions. Then he and Rags lock eyes in a real western
standoff, with Rags inching ever nearer.

> He was still coming in that unhurried, slow walk, so deadly, so like an inevi-
> table Nemesis bearing down on the hunter.
>
> Queer fear leaped through Caywood's heart. There was no real chance
> to fight.
>
> A strange new vision came flashing fleetingly to Caywood. A vision of
> a lonely, heart-hungry old wolf, without a mate, yearning for some fondling
> touch, perhaps the kindly caress of his arch enemy, the trapper. The vision
> came stalking down that trail toward him. Something, something tremen-
> dous, indefinable, about Rags caught his attention and held it for a flash of
> great understanding.

This flash of insight closely resembles Carhart's description of his feelings
at Trappers Lake. Oneness with the wilderness is one thing. But oneness with
the wild, with a fellow predator, is quite another: "With all his understanding
of the wild and its inhabitants Caywood could not tell whether Rags came seek-

ing friendship or was stalking along that trail intent on killing." As Caywood desperately fumbles with his balky gun, Rags gets to within eight feet. Then Caywood fires.

> Almost with his quivering nose touching Caywood's boot he fell, quivered, stiffened.
> "You poor old devil!" cried Bill huskily as he stooped impulsively. "You poor, lonely old murdering devil!"

Unaweep

In Hegewa's return engagement, Carhart presents the Forest Service as the natural ally of the BBS and the stockmen—against the wolf. And this time he pits Hegewa against an unusual foe: "Contrary to wolf law, Unaweep, a she-wolf, would lead them!"

Young and Carhart wanted readers to understand all the weapons in their arsenal. Like Young, Hegewa uses strychnine on a member of Unaweep's pack: "For he had swallowed a full dose of Biological Survey poison, processed strychnine, made purposely for killing predatory animals. He fell in jerking, convulsive writhing."

But even Hegewa can't fool Unaweep, so he calls for help from Young.

Young diagnoses the problem—amateurs. Once he has found Unaweep's den, he tells the cattlemen: "You've got to take off that reward and you've got to get those bounty hunters out of there, pronto. We can't have any amateurs messing up that den, smearing the trails, putting in clumsy trap sets and scaring these wolves."

What follows here and in the "Bigfoot" story is a primer of trapper lore. There are photos of Young setting poison baits. No quarter is asked or given in this war, even when Unaweep's young pups are involved:

> Seldom can a wolf be tamed if captured before they can see. There is no place in today's civilization for the gray wolf except in fur shops, museums, and zoos.
> So the whelps were killed.

Gray Terror

Carhart and Young wanted to be sure readers did not mistake their intentions. They used the story of Gray Terror to drive their point home. Burns Hole in northwestern Colorado was such good wolf country that Old Lefty's successor was soon providing material for lurid descriptions of wolf-killed cattle:

Gray Terror, the butchering wolf of Eagle County, was one of the most fiendish, most heartless killers that ever engaged the attention of Biological Survey hunters. Anyone who can muster sympathy for the genuine killer wolf after knowing of Gray Terror's forays, or who can blame the Government hunters for their unwavering efforts to shoot, poison, snare, trap wolf renegades, after acquaintance with the history of any bad wolf, simply is sentimentally blind, does not see the situation from the side of the game, wild life and stock.

Once he has gotten his wolf, Young makes things perfectly clear: "I wish some of those sentimental fools might see what we've seen here today," he said to ranger William Brown. "There's some that think it's cruel to trap a big gray wolf. I wish they could see the suffering of these cow brutes just for a little while. They'd change their minds."

Caywood is asked if all wolves are bad:

"No, not exactly. Can't truthfully say that all wolves are just blood crazy. Most real renegades are, though. All of them kill game and stock. All are butchers at heart.

"No use talkin', wolves and civilization can't bunk together. Man's too humane a creature, has too much respect down in his heart for other wild things and domestic stock, and squar' dealin' to let such heartless criminals as this big gray I'm after run free."

The Greenhorn Wolf

Carhart brings us face-to-face with an eighteen-year-old "gummer," infamous in the area since before 1915: "Now, in 1923, the Greenhorn Wolf ranged alone. SHE WAS DESTINED TO BE THE LAST NATIVE RENEGADE GRAY WOLF IN COLORADO."

Enter the executioner, Big Bill Caywood:

It was fitting that big Bill Caywood, the craftiest, the most learned of all wolfers in the Rockies, should ring down the curtain on this tragedy of the gray wolf killers. No other man of modern days has ever equaled his knowl- edge of the big gray.

The West was passing. It was falling before the march of the new West of finest auto roads, hydroelectric plants, industry and commerce.

Caywood poisoned the Greenhorn Wolf on Christmas Day, 1923.

AFTERMATH: NO ONE WILL HIRE A CRIPPLED OLD MAN

Carhart and Young included testimonial letters from ranchers at the end of their book. *Last Stand* sold poorly. But the authors had made good money on the earlier serialization, and they declared themselves satisfied.[27] Carhart never finished the wolf book he promised to Mary Austin. But his contacts with others in the BBS, such as Olaus Murie, turned his stomach as if he had swallowed one of Young's poison baits. When Rachel Carson's *Silent Spring* appeared in 1962, Carhart wrote her, asking if she knew about his 1929 anti-poison article in *Sports Afield*.[28]

Increasingly, Carhart found that others shared his doubts—not just about poisons but also about the wisdom of the BBS's wolf extermination program. In 1930, the American Society of Mammalogists held its twelfth annual meeting at the American Museum of Natural History in New York. Previously, the society had functioned as an arm of the BBS, but at this meeting the BBS for the first time came under fire for its predator policies. Young was present to bear the brunt of this attack, which also extended to Carhart. He warned Carhart about their opponents, adding that part of the attack referred to the weakest point in the BBS program—the one Carhart found almost as repellent as the poisons: "excessive expenditure of public funds for drastic reduction of predatory animals."[29]

In response, Carhart wrote Young a letter critical of the agency's predator control policies.[30] Carhart was working, unsuccessfully, on his second wolf book. He was also beginning to learn more about drastic declines in wildlife as a result of the poisons and traps of the BBS's predator programs, especially on public lands grazing allotments. As he had made clear in *Brad Ogden*, the question was: Why should one special interest group's use of public lands and public funds take precedence over other uses? Carhart was particularly critical of "the way stockmen holler bloody murder and get the Survey to spend $100 to save $50 in lambs."[31] Young's response to Carhart went straight for the throat: "The gray wolf has no place in modern civilization. . . . .In my opinion this animal is one hundred percent criminal. . . . Nevertheless, in spite of all that is bad about the wolf I personally consider this animal our greatest quadruped and have often wished that it would change its ways just a little so that the hand of man would not be raised so constantly against this predator."[32]

Young did not stop there. The attack went on in a way certain to further alienate Carhart, who was becoming more and more antagonistic to the government's treatment of Indians. Further, Carhart had become aware of the work of Rosalie Edge, who was beginning her campaign against the BBS's predator programs.[33] Young sniffed around for hints of Edge's influence:

> You state, "Isn't it a just consideration that the cats and wolves and coyotes have a damn sight better basic right to live in the hills and have use of that part of the world that they own than the domestic stock of our stockmen?"

Do you say that also with respect to the American Indian? Your reasoning in this connection would argue that the Indian should have been allowed to "stay put," but advancing civilization has dictated otherwise—and the same holds true for predators. . . .

I agree with the statement that our predators have a right to live in any areas where they do not conflict with any economic endeavor.

I will be quite frank, however, in stating that after reading your questions and turning them over in my mind, I have wondered whether or not you are as ignorant in this matter as you would have me believe. On second thought, I believe you are; but at the same time I can hardly understand why you ask some of the questions in view of the outdoor experience you have had. Has not someone been talking to you and filled you full of opinions. At the present time, opinions are what have raised the present rumpus over our control work. The rumpus is based on what the opposition *thinks* of our work and not on what they *know* in actual facts which will stand up under investigation.[34]

In spite of such profound disagreements, Carhart and Young stayed in touch over the years. When Carhart ran a federal wildlife program in Colorado during the Great Depression, he relied on Young for technical help. In 1947, Carhart acquired the rights to *Last Stand* and *Brad Ogden* from Sears's successor company, hoping to get both books reprinted by Caxton Press. By that time Young was at the U.S. National Museum and Carhart was with the Office of Price Analysis, a federal agency in charge of postwar rationing programs. Ironically, Caxton told Carhart the publisher was too "hard hit by the paper rationing program when it was in effect, and the bureaucrats in Washington hurt us badly with their order for the conservation of strategic materials."[35]

The demise of the wolf also had consequences for the wolfer. Caywood wrote Carhart to say how much he liked *Last Stand*.[36] Their correspondence continued over the years. Carhart alerted Caywood to rumors of a "pack of old buffalo lobos running over toward the Big Salt Wash and the Cathedral Bluffs area. I told him then if they were genuine lobos and you were going to be sent, I wanted to go along if it was OK with you."[37] He also asked for photos of Caywood, who replied after a long delay that the BBS had laid him off: "No one will hire a crippled old man."[38]

NOTES

1. Letter from Carhart to an editor, January 6, 1932, Carhart Collection, Denver Public Library (hereafter CC, DPL).

2. Mary Austin, *Earth Horizon: An Autobiography* (Boston: Houghton Mifflin, 1932). Her only child was a developmentally disabled daughter born the same year as

Carhart, 1892. After much agonizing, she had institutionalized the child to free herself to write.

3. Or so Carhart and Young thought. According to Michael Robinson, there were other lone survivors into the 1940s. See Robinson, *Predatory Bureaucracy* (Boulder: University Press of Colorado, 2005).

4. Ernest Thompson Seton, *Wild Animals I Have Known* (New York: Charles Scribner, 1898). Seton was also an excellent writer of boys' books. John Burroughs slung this mud at Seton. Later, he admitted he was wrong. See Ralph Lutts, *The Nature Fakers: Wildlife, Science and Sentiment* (New York: Fulcrum, 1990).

5. Carhart wrote to congratulate Young on his promotion on February 22, 1928. The original of this letter can be found in Box 325 of the Stanley P. Young Collection, DPL.

6. In 1959, in *The National Forests*, Carhart mentioned *The Land of Little Rain* with sadness and admiration (182).

7. Letter from Austin to Carhart, January 10, 1930, CC, DPL.

8. Letter from Carhart to Austin, September 19, 1929, CC, DPL.

9. Letter from Austin to Carhart, September 29, 1929, CC, DPL.

10. Letter from Carhart to Austin, January 14, 1930, CC, DPL.

11. Letter from Austin to Carhart, September 23, 1930, CC, DPL.

12. Letter from Austin to Carhart, October 31, 1930, CC, DPL.

13. Letter from Carhart to Austin, October 8, 1930, CC, DPL.

14. Letter from Austin to Carhart, October 24, 1930, CC, DPL.

15. Letter from Austin to Carhart, November 2, 1930, CC, DPL.

16. Letter from Austin to Carhart, July 11, 1932, CC, DPL.

17. Letter from Carhart to Karl Harriman, November 25, 1927, CC, DPL.

18. Letter from Young to Carhart, December 21, 1927, CC, DPL.

19. Letter to Dr. A. E. Fisher, In Charge of Economic Investigations, Washington, D.C., from Chief, Bureau of Biological Survey, April 27, 1921, CC, DPL.

20. Report to Dr. A. E. Fisher, In Charge of Economic Investigations, Washington, D.C., April 27, 1921, Copy to Chief, Bureau of Biological Survey, Denver. On June 14, 1926, Young wrote to the BBS to request a copy of this report.

21. Stanley Paul Young (1889–1969) was born in Oregon, the son of a pioneer salmon packer. He got a degree in mining engineering from the University of Oregon in 1911. Although he went to Michigan for graduate work in geology, he received a M.S. in biology and accepted a teaching post in California in 1917. On his way, he stopped in Arizona, where he became a ranger for the U.S. Forest Service for a few months. Then he joined the Bureau of Biological Survey as a hunter of livestock preda-tors. One of his chases led him across the Mexican border. Pancho Villa captured and held him for a week before a rescue could be arranged. In 1919, Young became assistant inspector for Arizona and New Mexico and in 1921 agent-in-control of predatory ani-mal work in the Colorado-Kansas District. He remained there until 1927 when he was assigned to Washington, D.C., as assistant head of the Division of Predatory Animal and Rodent Control. In Washington, Young filled a variety of positions in the BBS: chief of the Division of Economic Operations, 1928–1934; chief of the Division of Game

Management, 1934–1938; and chief of the Division of Predatory Animal and Rodent Control, 1938–1939. When the BBS was transferred to the Department of the Interior in 1939, Young was made senior biologist in the Branch of Wildlife Research. In 1957, when the Bird and Mammal Laboratories were made an independent research unit, Young was named the first director and remained there until his retirement in 1959. Young's chief interests were the predatory mammals of the West: the wolf, coyote, puma, and bobcat. His major publications included *The Wolves of North America*, with Edward Alphonso Goldman (1944), *The Puma, Mysterious American Cat*, with E. A. Goldman (1946), *The Wolf in North American History* (1946), *The Clever Coyote*, with Hartley H. T. Jackson (1951), and *The Bobcat of North America* (1958).

22. Letter from Carhart to editor of *ADVENTURE*, July 24, 1926, CC, DPL.

23. Letter from Carhart to editor Anthony Rud at Doubleday, November 20, 1926, CC, DPL.

24. Letter from Carhart to Tom Gill, December 26, 1926, CC, DPL.

25. November 1926 letter to Carhart from a junior biologist at the museum, CC, DPL.

26. Neal was one of the successful early applicants for a Forest Service lease at Trappers Lake in 1919.

27. Letter from Young to Carhart, July 10, 1927, CC, DPL.

28. Letter from Carhart to Rachel Carson, January 4, 1962, CC, DPL. By November 1959, when another Carhart anti-poison article appeared in *Sports Afield*, his sophisticated understanding of 1080 and DDT helped pave the way for Carson's authoritative treatment. See Carhart, "Poisons: The Creeping Killer," *Sports Afield* (November 1959).

29. Rick McIntyre, ed., *War against the Wolf: America's Campaign to Exterminate the Wolf* (Stillwater, MN: Voyageur, 1995), 297.

30. Ibid., 200.

31. Letter from Carhart to Young, September 4, 1930, CC, DPL.

32. Letter from Young to Carhart, November 24, 1930, CC, DPL.

33. In the 1950s, when Carhart helped lead the opposition to privatization of public grazing lands, he had help from Rosalie Edge and Ira Gabrielson.

34. Letter from Young to Carhart, November 24, 1930, CC, DPL (emphasis in original).

35. Letter from Carhart to Young, October 24, 1947, CC, DPL.

36. Letter from Caywood to Carhart, March 29, 1931, CC, DPL.

37. Letter from Carhart to Caywood, February 2, 1933, CC, DPL.

38. Letter from Caywood to Carhart, April 25, 1935, CC, DPL. Their correspondence continued through 1938, as Carhart prepared a story about Caywood for *Outdoor Life*: "World Champion Wolfer" (September 1939).

CHAPTER ELEVEN

OH, FOR ANOTHER TR

"When you think you've reached the end of your rope, tie a knot in the end and hang on." I had that motto over my desk during the depression when a quarter million dollar enterprise I was mixed up in, had my next-to-last-dollar in, went crashing. It sort of buoyed me up. .

—ARTHUR CARHART[1]

INTRODUCTION: WE'RE ALL HAVING A HARD PULL

During most of the 1930s, Carhart earned his way as a writer. Laboring in the basement office of his home, he pounded out articles about forestry, landscaping, and outdoor sports, especially fishing. Working for one cent per word, he created romance fiction under contracts that required him to produce two stories a month: one 25,000 words long and one 15,000 words long. He also published six books, including some novels that sold moderately well and some books on do-it-yourself landscaping. His production amounted to 1 million words per year during the period 1931–1937, when he finally took a break from his typewriter to work on wildlife restoration projects.

Although Carhart suffered like most people during the Depression, it was a matter of personal pride that he never joined other writers on federal relief. In particular, Carhart did not participate in the Works Progress Administration's (WPA) white-collar relief program, the Federal Writers Project,[2] which started in 1935. One reason was that centralization and bureaucratic delays led to uneven products that did not meet his standards. Another was that project writers operated in an ideological atmosphere that did not suit Carhart. He supported his fellow Iowan, Herbert Hoover, but he was no hidebound ideologue. As the nation neared the 1932 election, he wrote to one of his editors:

> Economic matters seem to be improving here. We usually are lagging about 90 days behind the eastern seaboard but the election may tend to equalize conditions somewhat. Believe Roosevelt did himself harm by his western speaking trip; in this adjacent region at least. Hoover's radio talks have won him friends here. I'm neither one nor 'tother. I think both parties have gone stale, dreadfully so. Oh, for another TR [Theodore Roosevelt] to put some guts and go into this nation.[3]

Carhart thought his stints in the U.S. Army and the Forest Service had been in the service of wider opportunity for all, especially new Americans and working-class Americans. He feared the social consequences of pitting the very rich against the very poor. He wrote to an old army buddy in 1935:

> Yesterday I listened to the wildest revolutionary talk you ever heard; and if that is even a slight barometer, these capitalistic moguls who have the monetary part of America by the throat, will certainly lead us to something pretty terrible unless they find a way to get better distribution of wealth. I'm no socialist or radical, but the blindness of the economic masters of the nation to anything but holding to their boodle and getting more, gets me put out. Well, here's hoping it's evolution instead of something worse.[4]

Things were little better in the Carhart family. Both George and Ella were in precarious health, and their son and his wife had to help support them, sending birthday checks signed "your children."[5] The Colorado Floral Company (CFC) demanded all the spare time and cash Carhart could muster. He suddenly found himself in competition with cucumbers from Texas. He switched to carnations and roses, but his timing was never quite right. He told a friend, "It isn't like the days when there was at least something coming out of the landscape business each month that you could count on."[6]

In October 1931 the IRS billed Carhart for his 1930 taxes. In his reply, he claimed he did not have to file because he was married, made less than $3,500 that year, and had suffered heavy losses from the CFC.[7] In spite of these worries, the Carharts took a month-long trip to the Lake Superior area that fall, paying for it with three stories sold to *Outdoor Life* for $200. It was probably on this trip that they disposed of their Boundary Waters property, selling it to pay back taxes.[8]

Things worsened in the early summer of 1932. As he wrote to a friend: "We're all having a hard pull. Everyone is I guess. . . . Got to mow the yard this afternoon. I'm saving $1.50 per week on that and probably another dollar or so on the care of the garden and feel in better health."[9] George and Ella sold their Silver State stock to pay their medical bills. Ella turned from Methodism to Christian Science. George took long walks, doing "a little missionary work every time I go out," and taught Sunday School at a Methodist church in Cañon City.[10] In letters to his beleaguered parents, Carhart tried a dose of humor: "Keep your bowels open and trust in the Lord. . . . We'll get out of this economic nightmare one of these days and swing away toward better times."[11]

In spite of such tonics, Ella Hawthorne Carhart died suddenly at age sixty-three on June 9, 1932, in Cañon City, before Arthur and Vee could reach her. A letter of condolence came from "Judge" Whiting, who also sent the death notice he had placed in the Mapleton paper: "They [the Carharts] represent the sturdy pioneer type upon which the very foundation of this Nation is builded.— The embodiment of truth, an inherent desire at all times to see the principles of the Golden Rule prevail. She lived to see her son, Arthur Hawthorne Carhart, become a credit to her as one of the foremost writers of Colorado."

Arthur turned forty in the fall of 1932. After Ella's death, the Carharts took George into their home, where he remained until his death in 1941. With Ella gone, there was no further mention of children for Arthur and Vee. By October 1932, some of Carhart's magazine outlets started defaulting on their debts to him. As a consequence, he had to borrow against his personal shares of CFC stock: "And besides that, the old greenhouse, which has been Job's trials all rolled into one for the past 3 years, appears about to bust loose with a handsome crop and reasonable profit. That will not fully materialize until next June. With over $100,000 tied up there's been hard grunting to keep it from getting one down."[12]

Carhart's investors in the CFC began to demand payment. He replied with a detailed review of the situation: he had mortgaged his house and was running on about $100/month. Both he and Vee had been sick during much of 1933. Meanwhile, by 1934 the value of the CFC had fallen to $85,000. Its liabilities of loans and preferred stock were $83,000: "Now about the writing. It's made us a living. I sold the landscape business and was lucky to do it. The little cash I got there was a slim margin that saved the Colorado Floral Co in one tight moment. In the landscape business, my two partners haven't even made expenses, let alone the salary they should have. They both have been on government work." He added that he and Vee had been down to as little as $20 cash on hand. All he could offer his investors was stock in lieu of cash.[13] More rewarding was Vee's business of buying and selling Indian artifacts and wares.

STOCK INTERESTS DICTATE THE POLICY

Carhart did better than most writers during the Depression. One reason was his ability to write for the automobile-borne tourist trade. Another was his growing outrage, rubbed raw by worsening range conditions on public lands. Hunters and wildlife were getting the short end of an already stunted stick. The Forest Service was betraying Teddy Roosevelt and the "common man" hunters Roosevelt had in mind when he established many national forests as game preserves. At a time when many hunters had to "shoot for the pot," Carhart expressed these concerns in a controversial series of *Outdoor Life* articles about conflicts between grazing and game. He knew such conflicts resulted from the Forest Service's failure to plan comprehensively. When stockmen retaliated and tried to intimidate his editor, Carhart responded:

> THE FACTS ARE THAT THE STOCK INTERESTS DOMINATE THE FORAGE AREAS OF THE NATIONAL FORESTS, THE US FOREST SERVICE CONNIVES IN THAT DOMINA-TION. THE US FOREST SERVICE WORKS HAND AND GLOVE WITH STOCK INTERESTS IN GETTING THROUGH LEGISLATIVE APPROPRIATIONS FOR THE BUREAU AND THE STOCK INTERESTS GET THEIR REWARD FOR THEIR "INDEPENDENT PRESSURE" BY THE RANGE ALLOTMENTS THEY GET AND IN THE APPROPRIATIONS SPENT IN RANGE MANAGEMENT. *IN NO SMALL MEASURE* THE STOCK INTERESTS DICTATE THE POLICY OF FOREST GRAZING AND IN THAT POLICY THE GAME GETS MIGHTY SMALL *ACTUAL* CONSIDERATION [emphasis in the original].[14]

Carhart expressed his continuing interest in the people's forests in his 1931 guide to Colorado and its national forests, which he aimed specifically at the automobile-borne tourist. He was especially interested in the "Americanizing" effects of public lands. He wrote for automobile owners seeing their country for the first time.

Carhart had plenty of competition, beginning with the postwar "See America First" series. In 1918, Lacy Mae Baggs had published *Colorado: Queen Jewel of the Rockies.* She idealized Indians as noble savages, connecting her readers to the wild and the free. And she celebrated nature as a resource to be used, emphasizing engineering feats such as road and dam building.[15] Carhart went Baggs one better, working the connections between tourism and nationalism. He reinforced a national identity, based on public lands as a shared territory with a shared history, both of which were open to a mobile citizenship. Carhart dedicated *Colorado* "To my Father and Mother: In their hearts always has beaten the rhythm of pioneer blood." The cover page illustration shows a horse rider in the sky, racing westward over a swift automobile.

Much of Carhart's guide pointed auto-mounted visitors to the Sangre de Cristo Mountains by way of routes such as the Old Santa Fe Trail. Or he directed readers to the Front Range by way of the old Lincoln Highway (today's I-80). Using wolves and Indians as his witnesses, he related a spirited history of Colorado's succeeding waves of settlement (including a defense of the Sand Creek Massacre). He rarely used the term "wilderness," and he consistently stressed his notion that wilderness is where you find it. He did not disparage the tamer offering of the National Park Service, but he said the national forests should be everyone's ultimate goal. Carhart wrote with an intimate, folksy touch. The foreword opens with "BETWEEN YOU AND ME." Then he shifted to the Walt Whitman approach: "I want you to come with me to Colorado, The Silver State. This is no stereotyped guidebook. We'll just ramble and jaunt and loiter, picking up whatever may be interesting, not bound by precedent nor the demands of some devotee of detail."

Carhart insisted that his visitors see cities, but he led them off the beaten track to places of topographic as well as historical interest, such as the confluence of the South Platte River and Cherry Creek in old Denver. Pueblo, the "Pittsburgh of the West," got lots of attention, including an account of the 1921 flood. He enticed readers: "Directly west from Pueblo is the scenic San Isabel National Forest; one of the most spectacular and least spoiled of all Colorado's national playgrounds." Carhart thought the Sangre de Cristos were the perfect national forest setting for auto-borne tourists who wanted to drive to key points, preferably dude ranches, and take off on foot or horseback from there. He knew dude ranches were a key element in preserving the best of the Old West and encouraging ranchers to manage their grazing allotments in ways that benefited wildlife.

Carhart found value in worked land, even in the mountains, for he believed it was the key to a robust regional literature. He carried this tone into aggressive promotion of sustained-yield timber harvest:

> Colorado's forests are about 1% of the timber wealth of the United States.
> At present her annual cut of timber is from 55,000,000 to 75,000,000 board
> feet, no more than a sixth of what could be cut to keep pace with the scien-
> tifically nursed annual increase. In other words, Colorado is growing timber
> about six times as fast as she is using it. The United States as a whole is
> using wood from four to six times as fast as the annual growth is replacing
> it. Few states are in Colorado's position.

He saved his most loving descriptions for his beloved Sangre de Cristos, where he fleshed out his comprehensive recreation plan done ten years ago— imagining it for his readers as if it existed on the land rather than simply on paper. He took his readers west into the Wet Mountains over today's Frontier Pathways Scenic and Historic Byway:

Squirrel Creek out from Beulah has shelter houses and camp equipment of all kinds. Most of the development here is due to the efforts of the San Isabel Recreation Association.

Do not miss the Cascade Trail!

There is nothing exactly like it in the western mountains—a foot trail following up a very ordinary little canon, but so deftly designed by professional landscape architects and executed under the direction of Frank Hamilton Culley, landscape architect, that it presents every bit of the best this little canon can offer. No other place will show you what can be done through good rural park landscape design for human use of naturalistic features as will the Squirrel Creek Canon.

The Sangres conjured up the Pike Expedition:

It's a great mountain range, this Sangre de Cristo. After being all over the state I'm frank to admit it is one of my favorite ranges. Scenically, from the standpoint of personality and the varied treasures in its canons and on its ridges, it is positive first grade as tourist country.

It's a great mountain range. Today we can visit it in comfort. But Pike, when he crossed it, played tag with death.

Carhart does not spare those who devastated wildlife populations and reduced watersheds to gullies. But he uses up-to-date information about remnant populations to create in his readers a sense that wildlife, especially beaver, has a future in his great recreation picture of healthy watersheds.

DRUM UP THE DAWN

In 1953, Carhart tried (in vain) to get the name Mount Herard in the Sangre de Cristos (east of Great Sand Dunes National Monument, which became a national park in 2000) changed to Bill Meek Peak.[16] "I just didn't figure Ulysses (Useless) Herard (Hear-hard, for he was deaf) rated such a monument—he was a cantankerous old cuss."[17] Rancher Herard was singlehandedly responsible for butchering more wildlife and abusing more public land than anyone else in local history. In Bill Meek, Carhart had a man to match the mountain.

Carhart knew fiction could take his readers farther into legend, into the real meaning of the wilderness experience, than any guidebook. He had always been fascinated with Pike's foray up the Arkansas River, over the Sangre de Cristo Mountains, and down into the San Luis Valley of southern Colorado. He had designed his comprehensive recreation plan for the Sangres to help visitors appreciate Pike's expedition. Rather than focus on Pike himself, Carhart wrote from the point of view of Bill Meek, a handsome, plain-spoken sergeant. When the Spanish captured Pike and his men in 1807 near the Conejos River in the San Luis Valley, they took the officers south to Mexico for questioning. The enlisted men remained under a kind of house arrest in Santa Fe, where they had ample opportunity to observe the differences between Spanish and American ways of colonizing the land—and treating women.

Bill Meek is a homespun philosopher of the frontier. He sees Spain as the oppressor of New Mexicans of all races. If Meek has his way, New Mexicans will rise up. It is the duty of the U.S. Army, Meek feels, to help New Mexicans become Americans. A courageous woman, Liseta, tells Meek: "It is the women who will finally claim this land for the Americans. They are different from the Spanish ladies. They stand shoulder to shoulder with their men."

Like most of Carhart's heroes, Bill Meek does not hesitate to manhandle a woman. The book's lovemaking scenes are fast and furious. Various women desire Meek, whom they see as a savior from the double tyranny they suffer under the Spanish king and Spanish men. When they speak, regardless of the language, Meek listens: "They were foreign sounds to an American; and yet human, and therefore holding a common ground-level quality that was no different anywhere."

Bill Meek learns that the Spanish monopoly over trade goods favors the few and punishes ordinary people. This insight alerts him to a group of women who are not only involved in clandestine trade but also plotting a rebellion. Inspired by these strong women, Meek drums up a dawn of freedom from tyranny:

> It had something to do with man's cruelty to man, the sort of oppression suffered by colonists of New Spain, the eternal fight for freedom from tyranny, the war free men must wage to stay free from any man, or class or gang that tried to dictate the way of life of the people. That was the spirit that had made the new nation of the States. . . . Democracy, the rule of the people, could be preserved only by preservation of the spirit that had made the nation and formed the new Constitution.

SADDLEMEN OF THE C BIT BRAND

Carhart published three books in 1937, two under pseudonyms Hart Thorne and V. A. Van Sickle. Once these books had been published, he looked for a new opportunity to work on behalf of Colorado's wildlife. Would he be working for or against ranchers? In 1938 he found out when he took a position working for Colorado governor Teller Ammons as coordinator of the Federal Aid in Wildlife Restoration Program.[18]

195

Carhart distinguished between the frontier spirit of the ranchers he admired and the cynical exploiters of public lands he disdained. In the political battles of the next thirty years, he maintained this distinction, which he articulated best in *Saddlemen of the C Bit Brand*. This book is a mystery as much as an action novel. But it is also a book about private property and personal liberty, especially for women. By setting the book in the San Luis Valley, Carhart pitted the custom and culture of the Spanish and Mexican land grants versus the laws of the United States. For the hero, Sam Clay, the C Bit Brand is portable property: the herd and the cowboys, not the land. Sam believes in the code of the old range—friendship and law.

Carhart paints a scene from the closing frontier, where once again Colorado serves as an exception to a depressing western-wide federal policy of breaking watershed-wide landholdings into parcels so small they become meaningless for wildlife and cattle. The Clays were originally from Texas. They had settled in the Black Hills when herds were still trailing:

> The keystone of their grazing plan had been a lease on an Indian reservation. That lease of government land had been held by them so long they thought of it as a vested right. Perennial talk of opening these lands to homestead settlement had been disturbing at times but had never materialized. Now Washington officials had ordered the change. The Clays either had to be content with a one-horse outfit on restricted lands or move west, to where plowed furrows and barbed wire would not hedge them so closely. So long as there was a Clay man to ride the lead, and a new location to be found, the only decision would be to find other lands of ample spread and start anew.

Desperate, the Clays buy into an old Spanish land grant called "Buenos Posos Baca Grant" in the San Luis Valley. Sam Clay soon discovers that title is one thing and possession another. Arrayed for and against the Clays is a complex and shifting alliance of Spanish and Mexican American ranchers who want to escape the old patriarchal land grant system Carhart describes as "feudal." Sam starts out calling his neighbors "greasers," but he soon learns to respect some of them as peers.

Sam falls in love with a mestiza named Carmen Little, who at twenty-one years of age is nominally the owner of the biggest property in the valley, the 80,000-acre ranch known as Le Marquez that borders on the Clays' contested land. As always, Carhart is adept at describing women, especially the color and cut of their clothing. In the short time since her father's death, Carmen's uncle, who plays by the old feudal rules, has asserted his guardianship and arranged a marriage for her that forfeits her land and her freedom. Victorino offends Sam's notions of free thinking and personal liberty.

THE WILDERNESS SOCIETY: WE WANT NO STRADDLERS

Carhart realized that most westerners were urbanites like him. Many were so deracinated that they needed help with the practical realities of gardening and landscaping to put food on the table. In 1934, Doubleday Page asked Carhart to do a series of do-it-yourself books appropriate to the common lot of reduced circumstances. Homeowners needed to learn the practical art of cultivating vegetable gardens and fruit trees.[19]

By 1934, it was a long stretch from such plebian realities to the privileged realm of the founders of the Wilderness Society. As Carhart voiced the common person's stake in public lands, especially through hunting and fishing, his ideas about a peopled wilderness distinguished him from those who saw wilderness not as a home but as a federally designated place where people might visit but to which they could never belong. Carhart's exposure to Indian, Spanish, and Mexican land uses reinforced his commitment to an active landscape architecture that sought to open and improve public lands for all the people.

Wilderness Society founder Robert Marshall (1901–1939) stood in sharp contrast to Carhart. Like Aldo Leopold, Marshall had trained as a forester at Yale. Coming from a wealthy family, he was an aesthete of a stripe that set Carhart's teeth grinding.

> It thrilled Marshall to witness a landscape never before seen by any human. "Views from summits were deep spiritual experiences," his brother George wrote. "His joy was complete when, standing on some peak, never before climbed, he beheld the magnificence of a wild timeless world extending to the limit of sight filled with countless mountains and deep valleys previously unmapped, unnamed, and unknown."[20]

Marshall was also a society socialist who lacked Carhart's direct experience with the needs of industrial workers in gritty places like Pueblo, Colorado. Whereas Carhart believed in the Americanizing effects of public lands recreation, based on public-private partnerships such as the San Isabel Protection and Recreation Association (SIPRA), Marshall opted for a much stronger role for the central government in recreation. Whereas Carhart believed in the public virtue of private forestry, even on a small scale, Marshall wrote: "Neither the crutch of subsidy nor the whip of regulation can restore [private forestry]."[21] True to his socialist principles, he advocated federal acquisition of private lands, whether for forestry, recreation, or both. This solution did not appeal to the author of *Saddlemen of the C Bit Brand*.

In 1934, when Marshall sent out invitations to the founding meeting of the Wilderness Society in Knoxville, Tennessee (held under the auspices of the American Forestry Association), his list did not include Arthur Carhart.

Marshall wrote in the invitations: "We want no straddlers." In Marshall's mind, that description must have fit Carhart, who always found a place for the automobile and the common man in his wildlands planning.

An argument can be made that Carhart's resignation from the Forest Service in 1922 set the stage for the founding of the Wilderness Society in 1934.[22] The struggle over Boundary Waters provides some context for understanding Carhart's lack of a role in the genesis of the Wilderness Society. Superior National Forest supervisor Al Hamel's boss, Northern District forester Fred Morrell, was of a different, more complex state of mind on the subject of roads and wilderness than Bob Marshall or Ernest Oberholtzer. Like the San Isabel, the Superior had to serve a local population that included industrial workers. Morrell valued Hamel's work with SIPRA and his humane way of dealing with workers' recreation needs in Colorado. Morrell and Hamel looked askance at blanket proposals to add more land to the federal estate. They knew an expanding federal presence would create more roads, even if it also created more wildernesses. Was this a good tradeoff?

Such questions sharpened as the Depression deepened, bringing calls for federal action on any and all levels of land-use management. Morrell praised *The Ordeal of Brad Ogden* in 1929 because he knew firsthand how good Carhart was at guiding readers through the paradoxes of the wilderness and the wild. In 1927, Morrell wrote Carhart, asking for input on roading issues at Trappers Lake and within Quetico-Superior. Carhart replied: "I assure you one of my virtues, which some other people I am sure think are flaring faults, is a tendency to be what might be called non-conformist. So you may find my stuff a little off the usual beaten path."[23]

Carhart explained to Morrell why a forest like the San Isabel is best suited to auto touring, unlike the Medicine Bow National Forest in Wyoming—or even most parts of the Superior National Forest. Wilderness preservation required intensive management rather than a hands-off approach. Carhart knew from experience that simply drawing lines and leaving wilderness areas alone does not preserve natural processes in the face of encroaching civilization. He realized that visitor access and distribution are vital issues that require a well-designed road and trail system. Carhart's middle way ran into opposition from both sides, even within the Forest Service. While some wanted no roads at all in certain areas, others wanted more roads than Carhart thought proper. After the federal Bureau of Biological Survey's "victory" over predators, those who desired more roads saw the prevention and suppression of wildfires as the single most important concern of forestry. And that meant more roads that would quickly take firefighters to their targets.

Carhart told Morrell:

If it produces better recreation through the fact that the road is there, then put in the road. If it does not, and roads have to go in anyway for economic and fire reasons, then put those roads where they will serve the practical uses ONLY. The argument that the lack of a road is preventing people from seeing some [scenic areas] is bunk. There are too darned many places reached easily by auto now. They are cheapened and worse, desecrated thereby. Put your economic and protection roads where they will serve all these needs in such a territory but KEEP THEM AWAY FROM THE SCENIC FOCAL POINTS. Designedly prevent people from getting to areas which should have a type of human use that does not depend on the auto.

Auto roads that are trunks are a different matter. The auto is an express carrier, taking people quickly, economically to the edge of places they wish to go. But outdoors is outdoors and outdoors in an auto is outdoors with a mechanical barrier between it and the user. To get the full benefit of outdoors there must be physical contact. So roads that serve recreation in the forest should not be an end. They should be a means. Take people there quickly[,] set them down in the midst of it, and then say, go to it kid!

In the long run up to the Wilderness Act of 1964, perhaps it is true that extremists on both sides prevailed, pitting the Leon Kneipps against the Robert Marshalls. But there was always a moderate, middle way best represented by Carhart. He knew that planning for wilderness should occur within the larger context of planning for wildlands. But the opportunity for such comprehensive, basin-wide planning would not arrive until the 1960s with the Outdoor Recreation Resources Review Commission (ORRRC). A wilderness bill also had to wait that long. Perhaps it is true that the single-minded drive for wilderness subverted or at least postponed the larger goal of comprehensive planning for recreation. Carhart had learned this once again in 1928, when he read "Recreational Resources on Federal Lands" by Arthur Ringland, secretary of the National Conference on Outdoor Recreation. Did Ringland's report represent progress? Carhart wrote Ringland:

> You may not know that the Wilderness idea was partially evolved in my office when I was Recreation Engineer of the USFS [U.S. Forest Service]. Leopold gets full credit I see by the report for giving birth to the idea. Actually he should get a lot of it—but perhaps some others were in on the development of this idea of classifying lands for recreational use on the basis of types of play they can give. The theory I advanced was that a recreational area should be developed to serve the "typical play" and that wilderness was one form which offered "typical play" while the San Isabel for example was a "typical" auto forest.
>
> And that leads me to remark that whoever designated the Sangre de Cristo division of the San Isabel for a "wilderness area" was wetter than the ocean. It is no more than six miles wide, has auto roads to the base of that 6

mile strip on both sides at many places, offers no chance whatever to "lose" yourself, is strictly an element in a typical automobile–dude hotel recreation scheme. Location, topography, resources all brand it as that type of recreation unit.

He ended on a resigned note: "May the breed of Leopold, Riis and their kind wax strong, become numerous and become a power in the land."[24]

Conferences and reports came and went. Frustrated by the combination of empty rhetoric and inappropriate action, Carhart turned to his writing. How could he push his ideas about recreation forward? As Carhart's *Colorado* showed, the Forest Service should build road systems to serve many kinds of recreationists, as well as other users of public lands. What Carhart disliked was the use of public funds to favor special uses that monopolized public lands. Carhart took his readers west into Colorado by way of the Lincoln Highway, which was funded by auto manufacturers. He lived near Denver's Overland Park, a 160-acre auto camp, which had opened with 800 lots in 1915. Overland Park was the largest and most famous auto park in the nation, and it was free of charge—sponsored by local merchants and governments. As ways of funding highways evolved, however, more-or-less private initiatives like the Lincoln Highway and Overland Park gave way to a system of federal camps and roads vast beyond the imagination of early planners.

Although funding for comprehensive recreation planning was forever lacking, there was always money for more roads. The years leading up to the New Deal were a flush time for other items in the budgets of the National Park Service and the Forest Service. The Federal Aid Highway Act of 1916 had generated $75 million over ten years for roads, with the Forest Service alone spending $1 million per year for new roads. Further legislation produced yet more roads in the national forests. In 1916 there were a few thousand miles of roads in those forests. By 1935 that figure had increased to 90,000 miles. The Park Service was not denied its share of the boodle, as Paul Riis well understood when he and Carhart opposed turning Boundary Waters over to the National Park Service.

The New Deal's solutions to the problems of the Depression brought more, not fewer, roads. By 1933 there were 200,000 Civilian Conservation Corps workers in forestry camps, many involved in building roads on federal lands— without the guidance of recreation planners or landscape architects. The Forest Service still did not use or trust landscape architects. It was not until 1935 that the Forest Service hired a landscape architect and created a Division of Recreation and Lands.

The resulting ugliness and resource damage were perhaps inevitable, given the choice—made by Congress but endorsed by the Forest Service—to proceed helter-skelter in "developing" recreation while grinding ahead systematically in developing fire suppression, grazing, and timber harvest. It can be argued that Carhart's departure from the Forest Service made room for a new generation of agency people, such as Robert Marshall, and their allies. These newcomers were wilderness lovers first. They felt wilderness was where the federal government said it should be. And they believed the federal government should be everywhere.

Meanwhile, more reports materialized. And Carhart was not alone in writing about recreation for a popular audience. Robert Marshall's *The People's Forests*[25] appeared at about the same time as the Copeland Report on recreation, which embodied Marshall's thinking. The Copeland Report was titled *A National Plan for American Forestry*. The report looked at all forested lands—not just federal lands—with the eventual aim of federal acquisition. The *Journal of Forestry* criticized Marshall's book as totalitarian.

Readers can imagine how different things might have been had Arthur Carhart rather than Robert Marshall written the portion of the Copeland Report on recreation. Marshall's twenty-five-page section, "The Forest for Recreation," set auto use against wilderness in stark terms. Like many conservationists of his time, Carhart preferred Teddy Roosevelt to Franklin Roosevelt, and he must have been disturbed to see former TR stalwarts embrace FDR's very different agenda. For example, in an orchestrated series of events, President Franklin Roosevelt requested a letter from TR's Forest Service chief, Gifford Pinchot, concerning the Copeland Report's recommendations for sweeping federal action. Marshall ghostwrote Pinchot's letter, supporting "large scale public acquisition of private forest lands."[26] What good did it do to acquire new lands when there was no money to properly manage either the new acquisitions or the present federal estate?

Although Congress under the New Deal was willing to acquire more public lands, it ignored the Copeland Report in the traditional way, denying funds for a Forest Service recreation planner. Biding his time, Marshall became head of the forestry division at the Bureau of Indian Affairs. John Collier, the commissioner of Indian Affairs, hired Marshall (and diplomatically refused Marshall's invitation to help found the Wilderness Society). With Collier's support, Marshall was free to experiment with his ideas, setting parts of Indian reservations aside as unroaded wilderness. Collier approved this experiment, saying there should be no roads in Indian wilderness "unless the requirements of fire protection, commercial use for the Indians' benefit or actual needs of the Indians clearly demand otherwise."[27] Perhaps misled by his own fervor, Marshall mistook Indian tribalism for an idealized organic socialism. He assumed Native Americans were single-minded avatars of his socialist critique of modern, capitalist America. Marshall did not ask the Indians what they wanted; he told them what he thought they should have. By 1962, only two of these wilderness areas were left—the Indians asked that the others be revoked.

Perhaps out of Depression-bred desperation, Congress finally decided to fund Forest Service recreation. In 1937 Forest Service chief Ferdinand Silcox hired Marshall as head of the new Division of Recreation and Lands. Marshall then wrote the "U Regulations" that would guide wilderness management until the 1960s. This approach ignored the Forest Service's traditional line of authority, which respected the judgment of those in the field. It put power in the hands of the chief and the secretary of agriculture, although it did allow for public hearings if major changes were proposed. Marshall died in 1939, just after the regulations were passed.

A wealthy man, Marshall had paid Robert Sterling Yard to run the Wilderness Society since its inception in 1934. After Marshall died, the society hired an executive secretary, Howard Zahniser, and a director, Olaus Murie.[28] Most of the money came from the Robert Marshall Wilderness Trust. Preferring, as always, to work on a personal basis wherever possible, Carhart was an intimate friend and a political ally of both Zahniser and the Muries. Apparently, he held no grudge against Marshall or the Wilderness Society, although he did not like some of Marshall's socialist ideas.

It would be a mistake to draw too hard a line between Carhart and the Wilderness Society. He may not have been comfortable with the organization's narrow focus on the value of wilderness, but he was too dedicated to wilderness and too genial a soul to force an issue so central to good land-use planning. Wilderness was a spiritual experience for Carhart, just as it was for Marshall. Both men knew wilderness also had to be a political goal. In the long years of struggle leading to ORRRC and the Wilderness Act of 1964, Carhart remained ambivalent about formal wilderness designations and strict definitions of wilderness. When Carhart and Marshall used phrases like "the people's forests," they meant very different things. With his penchant for outliving his opponents, Carhart watched and waited as the Depression ground on and on. Another world war would once again postpone his drive toward comprehensive planning for recreation.

NOTES

1. Letter from Carhart to Bill Robbins, November 22, 1950, Carhart Collection, Denver Public Library (hereafter CC, DPL).

2. The WPA's American Guide Series was designed to promote travel at home. More than 6,500 writers participated in this part of the program alone. During the years

1935–1943, 10,000 writers participated in all aspects of the program. The Colorado guide appeared in 1941.

3. Letter from Carhart to one of his editors, October 16, 1932, CC, DPL.

4. Letter from Carhart to army buddy, February 26, 1935, CC, DPL.

5. Letter from Carhart to his parents, April 11, 1931, CC, DPL.

6. Letter from Carhart to a friend, April 8, 1932, CC, DPL.

7. Letter from Carhart to the IRS, October 27, 1931, CC, DPL.

8. Starting in 1931, Carhart kept his royalty statements on accountant's sheets. He averaged about $500/month from his writing in 1931. By 1936, he was grossing $4,333 a year.

9. Letter from Carhart to a friend, May 26, 1932, CC, DPL.

10. Letter from George Carhart to Arthur Carhart, June 1, 1932, CC, DPL.

11. Letter from Carhart to his parents, June 7, 1932, CC, DPL.

12. Letter from Carhart to an investor, October 12, 1932, CC, DPL.

13. Letter from Carhart to investors, November 6, 1934, CC, DPL.

14. Letter from Carhart to P. K. Whipple, editor at *Outdoor Life*, April 28, 1931, CC, DPL.

15. Lacy Mae Baggs, *Colorado: Queen Jewel of the Rockies* (Boston: Page, 1918), 215. See also Hal Rothman, *Devil's Bargains: Tourism in the Twentieth-Century American West* (Lawrence: University Press of Kansas, 1998).

16. Arthur Carhart, *Drum up the Dawn* (New York: Dodd, Mead, 1937).

17. June 26, 1953, letter to the National Park Service, CC, DPL. See my discussion of Herard's wholesale slaughter of wildlife and abuse of grazing in *Colorado's Sangre de Cristo Mountains* (Boulder: University Press of Colorado, 1995).

18. Wildlife management remained an important and lucrative part of Carhart's writing, keeping him current with the profession. For example, he received $500 from *The Saturday Evening Post* in 1936 for "What Makes Wild Life Wild?"

19. Letter from Doubleday Page to Carhart, June 5, 1934, CC, DPL. Carhart wrote *Trees and Shrubs for the Small Place.*

20. From the Wilderness Society's Web page biography of Marshall: http://www.wilderness.org/AboutUs/Marshall_Bio.

21. This is from a letter Marshall wrote for Gifford Pinchot. See discussion later in this chapter.

22. Paul Sutter, *Driven Wild: How the Fight against Automobiles Launched the Modern Environmental Movement* (Seattle: University of Washington Press, 2002), 65ff.

23. Letter from Morrell to Carhart, February 28, 1927. Carhart replied on March 5, 1927; both in CC, DPL.

24. Letter from Carhart to Ringland, September 4, 1928, CC, DPL.

25. Robert Marshall, *The People's Forests* (New York: Smith and Haas, 1933).

26. Sutter, *Driven Wild*, 225ff.

27. Ibid., 229.

28. Ibid., 248.

CHAPTER TWELVE

GETTING TOWARD HALF A CENTURY

I'd consider federal work, but I'd want to have a spot where
imagination and initiative are not stifled. (Is there such?)

—CARHART TO DING DARLING[1]

INTRODUCTION: *THE OUTDOORSMAN'S COOKBOOK*

Carhart developed a sure sportsman's touch after he left the Forest Service.
He became an expert hunter and fisherman, capping his authority with practical research on game management from 1937 to 1942. Through his writing,
he turned the ardor of sportsmen toward the cause of conservation. Carhart
pushed a conservation credo, but (like any good campfire cook) he made his
lean and gamy message palatable by wrapping it in the bacon of lore and legend. Throughout the 1930s and 1940s, Carhart had his own radio shows on
various Denver-based stations, where he mixed politics and practicalities as
deftly as he whipped up tasty fireside meals from his most popular book of the
period, *The Outdoorsman's Cookbook* (1943).

Although he was working for federal agencies during this time, Carhart did not hesitate to confront anyone on conservation issues. He drew on the rich store of experiences he had accumulated as he worked on Colorado wildlife restoration projects. For example, Carhart started a new series on August 23, 1944, on radio station KFEL at 8:00 p.m. on Wednesdays and Saturdays: "I feel a degree of humbleness as we begin these meetings around the campfire of the airwaves." His subject was the plight of the sage chicken, a species in serious decline in Colorado. He explained their biology and nesting problems related to badgers and ravens and trampling livestock, depicted the Colorado Division of Wildlife's efforts to stabilize sage chicken populations, and described not only how to hunt them but how to prepare and cook them.

As these shows developed over the years, Carhart took strong stands against anti-hunting and anti-gun groups. To prove his points, he read letters from his former field staff then at war in the Pacific, including testimony about the importance of early marksmanship training and an exciting "hunting" series from a sailor whose fieldwork under Carhart helped him spot and destroy Japanese planes attacking under cover of night.

The popular shows came to an end in October 1945, when Carhart fell from a ladder while picking apples in his yard and broke some ribs. He was still working in a public relations position at the Office of Price Administration (OPA) and making increasing use of the Denver Public Library,[2] where he was researching his book *Hunting North American Deer*. Carhart's Park Hill neighbor, Dr. Malcolm Weyer, encouraged him to start using the library to buttress his often controversial conservation writing. Weyer was head of the Denver Public Library. During this time, Carhart also served off and on as an associate editor of *American Forests* and wrote a column called "Conservation Comments" for the Colorado Division of Wildlife.

To the disappointment of war-weary Americans, the end of World War II did not mean the end of government price controls and rationing. Carhart's job was to explain why they continued. The OPA position came thanks to his friendship with fellow Republican Joseph Penfold, the Denver-based staffer for the Izaak Walton League. Together, in their spare time, they founded a small company, Sport-LORE, that marketed game calls. After 1948, the *Sport-LORE Bulletin* picked up where Carhart's personal radio series had left off. It was popular enough to be nationally syndicated—part of the promotional wave Carhart rode to national prominence around 1950, when he emerged as one of the country's most popular and important conservationists. In April 1951, Carhart was asked to deliver the keynote address at the Izaak Walton League's National Convention in Cincinnati—a perfect springboard for publicizing his new book, *Water or Your Life*.

PITTMAN-ROBERTSON: TO GET RESPITE FROM THE TYPEWRITER

On September 15, 1938, the forty-six-year-old Carhart applied for a job with the Colorado Game and Fish Commission, which administered a program set up under the 1937 Pittman-Robertson Act for Federal Aid to States for Wildlife Restoration. Through this program, sportsmen paid a special tax on arms and ammunition. The money went back to the states for wildlife conservation and research.[3]

Times were tough throughout the conservation community. In 1937, Aldo Leopold was conducting Pittman-Robertson training for wildlife managers and researchers. Officially, the research was to be directed toward the management of all species of wildlife. However, in reality it had a special emphasis—how to manage game populations by eliminating predators and substituting hunters and then how to deal through hunting with any resulting increase in prey populations and any carrying capacity problems. Later in his career, when consulting for the National Wildlife Federation and the American Forest Products Institute, Carhart drew on this research to follow the logic of the program. Most hunters want only trophy bucks. As a result, too many deer of the wrong age and sex lead to detrimental browsing effects on forest health. Too many deer also lead to dangerous automobile-deer collisions—an important issue to Carhart, who wrote for automobile-industry publications throughout his life.

Carhart worked for five years as coordinator of the Pittman-Robertson Program, resigning on September 23, 1943. The program's headquarters were in Gunnison in western Colorado. Carhart spent most of his time there, while Vee stayed in Denver. She took care of George Carhart, who died at their home in 1941.[4] Vee also accompanied her husband on some field trips, leaving George in the care of a nurse when she wanted to visit places like Mesa Verde that related to her interest in Indians.

Carhart welcomed the opportunity to escape his typewriter. He was a good choice for the job because he thrived on outdoor living and enjoyed the brotherhood of hunters and fishermen. Most of the work involved taking field crews out to study the habits of Colorado's mule deer, beaver, elk, and antelope. Many years later, Carhart recalled for *Outdoor Life*:[5]

> We got so we could tell at any given time of year just about where the animals were, what they were eating, and from the condition of the range how many of them were there. Later we did some work with turkeys and helped bring them back in areas where they'd been gone for generations. During those years, we learned things that are still being used to answer the anti-hunting crowd: that man has replaced the big cats as predators and has upset

that balance so much that game animals must be managed for their own survival. Hunting has become a matter of animal husbandry.

Carhart also used his position to defeat a proposal to require federal hunting licenses for hunting on federal land, He told *Outdoor Life*:

> It's another part of the anti-hunting thing. From the very beginning states have had prior property rights to wildlife, and now the people who oppose hunting want the federal government to put its grip on wildlife on private as well as public land. Near Hot Sulphur Springs, Colorado, for example, we found that deer were moving onto range that was part private land and part public. You can't draw a line and say to the deer, "We don't want you in there, because Bill Smith owns that land."

Although he had no formal background in wildlife management, Carhart was a quick study. Of course, he also chafed under bureaucratic regimes, as did his friend Ding Darling, who had served as head of the Bureau of Biological Survey in 1934–1935. Neither man had the suppleness of Stanley Young, who knew high-level bureaucrats endure while chiefs and foot soldiers come and go quickly. In 1941, Carhart wrote to Darling:

> The third anniversary of my taking hold of the Pittman-Robertson work in this state has passed. Originally, I took hold here, to get respite from the typewriter and to do a bit for wildlife. My anticipated tenure on the job was about six to twelve months. But the work has led me on, deeper and deeper. I have had the satisfaction of putting some of the boys' ten percent tax into action, and seeing signs pointing toward good production of game.[6]

Carhart gave an account of a study to determine whether sage grouse and sheep can mix without detriment to the grouse. He found that the problem was not sheep but small predators, especially badgers and skunks. Going against his usual practice, his solution was to use poison. He told Darling of other successes and plans for game-bird refuges around the state. Wherever they put in birds, they poisoned predators. Carhart continued in the same letter:

> But now, I am at a point of making some move. If I stay in charge of this work, I will look forward to finishing my life in it. I'm getting toward the half century; just a youngster, I know, but it brings gray hairs. With the governmental set up, where older men are bad risks in social security, the block is somewhat against them, unless it is in an executive or administrative position.

Carhart was at a crossroads in 1941. The $3,600 he was making under Pittman-Robertson was less than he had made from freelancing any year during the Depression. But it was more than anyone else in his department was making by around $600. He told Darling: "I'd consider federal work, but I'd want to have a spot where imagination and initiative are not stifled. (Is there such?)."[7] Darling's response was mixed.[8] Ultimately, he advised Carhart to stay where he was, adding that Carhart's writing was beginning to attract national attention.

Carhart finally quit the Pittman-Robertson job in September 1943, disgusted, as usual, with petty bureaucratic procedures: "I quit the department on Sept. 23, I'd stood up to the battering that was going on for several years and I got a belly full. . . . Nuts to the whole outfit with their ten-cent methods and skunky tactics."[9]

Not all of Carhart's letters were so sour. Darling's sense of humor and cartooning abilities sometimes brought out the best in Carhart, who was returning to writing about wildlife (*Hunting North American Deer*) with renewed vigor. He told his friend: "The book is moving a bit slowly since I stopped to write up the beaver management program here for a back-east magazine. We marketed 12,240 hides last year, all state controlled. Average price, $20. Do you remember I wrote you once that a lot of the wildlife program could be underwritten by this one species well managed? It's being done here."[10]

In 1943, things took a turn for the better for the Carharts. Relieved of the burden of George Carhart's care, they leased a cabin site in western Colorado, taking advantage of a Department of the Interior–administered program available under the Five-Acre Law of 1938. The site was 100 miles west of Denver at 7,200 feet elevation near Hot Sulphur Springs, a place Carhart knew well from his fieldwork. Overlooking the confluence of the Colorado River and Beaver Creek, it also provided excellent backcountry access for hunting.

In 1944, Carhart signed a contract with W. W. Norton to produce a book on Colorado dude ranches called *HI STRANGER!*[11] Research for this book provided Carhart with an important network of conservation-oriented dude ranchers. It also put him on a career-defining collision course with cattle ranchers who wanted to privatize public lands. And that, in turn, led to Carhart's opposition to big dams, which he felt were foolish "solutions" to watershed health problems related to overgrazing.

A REPUBLICAN REGIONAL ADMINISTRATOR

Joe Penfold was deputy administrator and executive officer of the Rocky Mountain region of OPA through August 1945, when he went to China with the United Nations for two years.[12] At OPA, Penfold was in a good position to show sportsmen how to help the war effort. For example, in December 1942, the War Production Board lauded the Izaak Walton League's contributions to the war effort. Members gathered goose and duck down and other materials from their hunting trips for use in sleeping bags made for soldiers fighting on the front lines. Stories like this were perfect for someone with Carhart's connections and promotional abilities. While Penfold was in China, Carhart kept him abreast of conservation affairs. When he returned to Denver, Penfold became the western representative for the Izaak Walton League. Penfold helped Carhart get a position with OPA as regional information executive. The job was a godsend. He made $8,179 per year, and his efficiency ratings were "excellent." Naturally, OPA began to consolidate as wartime rationing became less necessary. Carhart could have retained his position, but he would have had to move to Washington, D.C. Instead, he resigned on July 31, 1946, having served for about two and a half years.

Carhart wrote steadily throughout his employment with Pittman-Robertson and OPA. Finally, he found a way to set his "hook" into a return to full-time writing, but this time on a more lucrative and more prominent national scale. In April 1946, he and Vee drove through New Mexico to the Mexican border. On their way back, they stopped at Dinosaur National Monument along the Green River, where he learned of the Bureau of Reclamation's plans to build a dam at Echo Park. Outraged, Carhart decided to do a series of articles on ill-advised dams for *Holiday*, *Sports Afield*, and *Outdoor Life*: "I proposed that a group of articles should be written on the less publicized monuments." In the process of researching the articles, he refreshed some old contacts in the National Park Service, such as Herb Evison. Evison quickly saw how Carhart could help in the battles to come over dams on the Colorado River and its tributaries. He put Carhart in touch with Park Service information officers and arranged for Carhart to accompany Park Service–sponsored show-me trips, "expeditioning into the canyon with kicker motors."[13]

MANY OTHER PICTURES TROOP OUT OF WILDERNESS MEMORIES

Carhart's hunting-related storytelling reached a new peak in 1946 when Macmillan published *Hunting North American Deer*.[14] He knew from personal experience that returning veterans hungered for ritualized experiences involving weapons and wildlife. He had learned from Mary Austin that New Mexico was rich in hunting lore, especially at the Indian Pueblos along the Rio Grande. He and Vee visited these pueblos many times, and his new hunting book contained an excellent description of the Deer Dance at the Cochiti Pueblo between Santa Fe and Albuquerque. When he opened his book by remarking that "[m]any other pictures troop out of wilderness memories," he was making the point that hunting was a key part of his general myth of an inhabited wilderness. And wilderness was a place where people told stories, often humorous ones:

> It might be worth stopping right here to make the point that most Indians, as tribes and as individuals, have a keen sense of humor. You don't get to know that until you have ridden as trail companions over rough paths and sat beside the same campfire of evening, or have sat on the sunny side of an adobe house in the land of the Pueblos. So let's set aside the idea that an Indian is a dour sort, and have a little laugh with him over some of the deer stories that I have picked up here and there.

As befits Carhart's respect for returning veterans, his tone was man-to-man, direct, no-nonsense. He used the word "wilderness" casually to indicate that wilderness is a companionable place: "I would have to mention the many fine companions of backcountry trails, as we hunted or just packed through wilderness." He hearkened back to Teddy Roosevelt, claiming the national forests were always meant to be the common man's hunting grounds: "Yesterday, now and tomorrow, deer *is* the average huntsman's big game, by spread of habitat, by numbers, by ability to persist, by volume of annual harvestable crop" (emphasis in the original).

Starting with the sixteenth century, Carhart gave his readers a history of hunting in America that helped orient them to the postwar terrain, where habitat loss was the greatest enemy of deer hunters. He knew that in his time, domestic livestock was the deer's greatest competitor, especially when wartime panics allowed ranchers to flood public lands with sheep and cattle. Wavering on the subject of predators, he wrote:

> Some biologists have advanced the theory that war should not be waged so constantly on these big cats, because this is nature's method of removing the crippled, weak, and diseased deer from a herd. This is theoretical bunk. A lion is as good a judge of meat as anyone, and he kills good venison whenever he can get it. He doesn't follow the theory that some people would like to believe, that he kills only culls. . . . The sportsman who goes on a western lion hunt is doing two chores when he gets a lion. He is sure to have one of the most exciting hunts of his life, and he is directly saving the lives of scores of deer.
>
> Wolves formerly preyed on deer. But predator control methods in the interest of domestic livestock protection have reduced the wolf drain on deer herds to almost nil. Formerly the coyote would not drag down many deer. But a curious change in coyotes has taken place within the past few decades. These predators, formerly a plains animal, followed the domestic sheep flocks to the western timber-lines. By a swift adaptation and selection, a greater-boned, rangier, heavier, darker coyote has emerged. These have turned to deer killing.

Carhart treated his readers to highly technical discussions of guns and loads. There was an entire chapter on equipment. Another chapter, "Sweet Meat," gave expert advice on dressing deer meat. Anyone who thinks Carhart was somewhat dainty should work his or her way through his section on how to field dress a deer.

FISHING HALL OF FAME

The end of the war brought prosperity to many, including Carhart, who knew from World War I that there would be a postwar wave of enthusiasm for the outdoors. He produced an astonishing array of books and articles toward the end of the 1940s. In addition to the Colorado Authors League, he was very active in the Outdoor Writers of America. Two major conservation issues motivated him, both high on the agenda of the Izaak Walton League and the National Wildlife Federation: ill-advised dams and proposals to privatize public lands.

At the end of 1948, thinking of postwar Communist scares he had seen before, Carhart circulated a windy "MEMO TO MY FRIENDS,"[15] in which he claimed that the decadence of civilizations comes with

> too much city-type of life. . . . It is the outdoorsman, the pioneer, who builds nations.
>
> Unless we supply the facilities, the opportunities, the "call" of the outdoors, and can get our people to secure to themselves the fiber and sinew which only outdoor life can supply, a force of national decadence will increasingly erode the individuals and therefore the nation.

In 1949, the Sportsmen's Club of America elected Carhart to the Fishing Hall of Fame, placing him among the thirty-eight living honorees. By this time he was editorial director of Better Fishing, Inc. (an industry-sponsored group). He was also writing articles like "Dam Business" for magazines like *The Nation's Business*, detailing the environmental and fiscal folly of Bureau of Reclamation projects such as the Colorado–Big Thompson and the Fryingpan-Arkansas, both of which were trans-basin diversions of a kind that violated Carhart's watershed-wide approach to planning. He sounded the note of the fiscal conservative: "What does our money get us? With the more economical impounding projects for irrigation developed long since, engineers have turned to 1) gigantic and somewhat fantastic 'feats' of high cost, and 2) inclusion of other features such as power to justify the expenditures."[16]

All this activity had side effects. In 1948, both Carharts experienced health problems. Arthur's were related to altitude, prompting him to consider selling his mountain home. For the first time since 1922, Carhart did not go deer hunt-ing, claiming he could no longer haul his own kill out of the backcountry.[17]

DON'T WORRY, I'LL PROBABLY NOT RETIRE

Thanks to his renewed contacts with the National Park Service, Carhart trav-eled to Wyoming to research an article about Jackson Hole National Monument. He coauthored an article for the National Wildlife Federation with Wyoming governor Leslie A. Miller. Carhart also started receiving royalty checks for *Fresh Water Fishing* at the end of 1949.

By the end of 1949, in the face of another regional drought that would persist throughout the 1950s, Carhart was writing about water famines in the West. He had lived through the severe drought of the 1930s. This time he meant to speak his mind about water. His break came in December, when *Atlantic Monthly* commissioned "Turn off That Faucet!" which appeared in February 1950. *Readers Digest* soon reprinted it.[18]

George Stevens, the managing editor of J. P. Lippincott, asked Carhart to write a popular book on water conservation. Carhart and Stevens quickly reached an agreement, with Carhart brashly promising to deliver the manu-script on September 1, 1950.[19] In the meantime, he and Vee proceeded with plans to head south to Mexico, where they would stay until May 1, covering international deep-sea fishing rodeos at the invitation of the Mexican govern-ment. Another reason for the trip, Carhart told Stevens, was that failing health demanded that he and Vee spend more time at lower elevations.

Failing health or not, Carhart felt so buoyed by his sudden success that he wrote all his former book publishers (for nineteen books), demanding that they assign him copyright. This kind of peremptory action was becoming increas-ingly frequent for Carhart. Advancing age and health problems piled on top of concerns about retirement and financial security. Although in retrospect we can see that he was near the apex of his career and his earning power, Carhart never felt financially or professionally secure. Such nagging feelings led him to publish too much and to repeat himself, whether he knew it or not. Every freelance writer knows that recycling is the name of the game. But Carhart's publishers were watching the game closer than he was, as he would discover when bad news from New York caught up with him in Mexico. He had not made things easier when he published a series of thorny articles about writers and editors in the bulletin of the Outdoor Writers of America (OWA). Carhart had joined OWA in 1948,[20] hoping to make crusading conservationists out of the newspaper journalists who wrote for sportsmen. His status as a freelancer was at odds with the editors of publications, who preferred to rely on staffers rather than freelancers.

On their way south to Mexico, the Carharts stopped in Coyote, New Mexico[21]—where they sold their house and property—and Laredo, Texas. The trip to Mexico was fraught with both business and health-related difficulties. But the excursion gave Carhart insight into Mexico and contemporary Communist scares that he shared with an editor, explaining why he did not know enough to write about Mexico:

> Two major things that hit me were, the fact that we do not know the Mexicans. We do come in contact with the laborers. But those who really carry weight are about as fine as any people you can meet. And the other fact is, that the Communists take every chance to disrupt anything they can, particularly blaming everything on Uncle Sam. But that the really solid core of Mexican leaders are terrifically friendly to us as a nation and individuals, are dead against communism as such, and they don't make any petty moves about handling the situation. Time and again they remarked about the communist determination to damage international relationships and honeycomb the country, and how neither would succeed. There's a lot that could be written about the Mexicans that are representative of the middle and upper classes and the general attitude toward the U.S. and the communist activities. But the one to do it would be an intelligent Mexican.[22]

While Carhart was in Mexico, two of his publishers (Barnes and Macmillan) were becoming upset over similarities between his two recent books, *Fresh Water Fishing* (Barnes) and *Fishing Is Fun* (Macmillan). Carhart was fortunate to have an editor at Macmillan with soothing diplomatic skills. Lurton Blassingame seemed to have had the situation under control when Carhart returned from Mexico. So Carhart plowed ahead with the publication of yet another book, *Fishing in the West*, while he hunkered down to work on his authoritative book on the nation's water problems.

WATER OR YOUR LIFE

Carhart's editors squabbled over rights to his increasingly popular books. *Water or Your Life* had been through five printings by January 1954. In 1958, a new and updated edition appeared. The Bureau of Reclamation expressed official disapproval through its employee John Spencer, also a council member for the Wilderness Society. When the *Sierra Club Bulletin* favorably reviewed Carhart's book in December 1952, Spencer demanded that the bulletin print his rebuttal. The favorable review also led to an invitation for Carhart to attend the Third Biennial Wilderness Conference in Berkeley in May 1953, where he was to appear on a panel about "maintenance of the wilderness concept."

Given the condition of his health and his age, Carhart's acceptance of Lippincott's deadline was typically quixotic. Yet he fell to the work in the summer of 1950 with the energy of a younger man. Part of his research involved a flurry of letters to water authorities around the nation. Given his prominence among sportsmen, few could resist Carhart's entreaties. Secretary of the Interior Oscar Chapman (a Coloradoan) told Carhart he would encourage personnel from the Bureau of Reclamation and the U.S. Geological Survey to cooperate, especially as regarded watershed management and soils. As a result, Carhart became especially interested in the relationship between the health of watershed vegetative cover and stream flow.[23] This led him to the grazing issue. Edward Cliff, the regional forester in Denver, did not hesitate to finger grazing as a culprit in watershed degradation.[24] Secretary Chapman replied later in the summer, providing detailed answers to Carhart's questions,[25] which ranged from plans for the Central Arizona Project to the future of oil shale.

As the book progressed, Carhart and Ding Darling exchanged excited letters. Carhart told his friend: "I try to grab the reader and say, 'Look here, you! Have you ever thought of how dependent you and all of us are on water? Have a look. A good one. You'll be in a hell of a spot and so will [we] all, if we don't do a better job of utilizing water wealth than we have.'"

Working out his idea to devolve water authority down to the basin level, Carhart ripped the big dam "burocracy" with his old gusto: "It's screw-ball. And it's terribly costly and uneconomical. The engineer boys have gone loco." He continued proudly about the book: "It's dynamite-loaded. Thank goodness, I'm not tied up with any organization or agencies. I pat on the back, and I also slug."[26]

Darling was impressed. He told Carhart: "Don't ever retire! It's no good."[27] An energized Carhart asked Darling for both a cartoon and an introduction. Remembering a Darling cartoon long past and thinking of a chapter about government waste to be called "Too Many Cooks," Carhart said:

> That old cartoon that stuck so long in my memory was a honey. It was a jab at a very fumbling congress. Congress was standing in the middle of a farm-type kitchen as a bedraggled housewife, midst total confusion, a dripping cooking spoon in one hand, a pot or something in the other that was spilling on the floor, and wiping a worried forehead with the back of the hand, was saying, "Now, what was I going to do next." The pot on the stove was boiling over, the kids which were special interests, were pulling a jar of jam from a shelf, the whole kitchen was in turmoil.
>
> What might be an adaptation of that to show the multiplicity of public agencies scrambling around with water resources could be two figures, one Army Engineers, the other Reclamation. A thought strikes me—why not have this [be] one of those old fashioned country picnics. . . . I'll use the

cock-eyed dam outside of Denver [built] by the Army for one illustration of how wild they have gotten in some instances. . . . Don't worry, I'll probably not retire. The need for keeping on pegging out material so long as I can will keep me at it. I hope I have a decade or two at least to utilize an accumulated background of past years. Seems as though in the past few years, there has come a better sense of man's position in things, and particularly

• with regard to the conservation field. . . .

I don't know that one very small voice can do very much to jolt the rest into getting eyes open and doing some basic thinking. . . .

I must get at this book. Glory, be, it should oughter bin don a fortnight ago. But it's such a terrific subject, Ding. I've never labored so steadily and with all power in any writing.[28]

Darling agreed to provide both the introduction and the cartoon: "All it takes is a request from you and I'll jump over the moon, or try to, and if you really want me to write an introduction, I'll try to do that too."[29] After he had seen the galleys, Darling said:

You have written a great book. I am both delighted and amazed at its comprehensive coverage and the complete conviction which it conveys. . . .

Those last two chapters of yours simply riddle the center of the target. Anyone who reads them cannot help but to enlist in the ranks of the army which is needed to fight the high dam program.[30]

The book opens with a scene of regional drought, resulting in severe water shortages and water quality problems in New York City. Carhart then takes the problem to the familiar contemporary level of national security and national identity, speaking directly to his readers:

In some measure, what has happened to all these communities that have encountered water problems may be sneaking in quietly on you and your neighbors. . . .

The very future of the nation could fall into decadence, fail, even die, if we do not give the consideration we must to the water wealth and the soil wealth so closely linked with it.

That's right—the United States of America might die as a nation because of squandering the basic wealth we have in water.

Other nations, once lusty, have died—just because they suffered a "water shortage."[31]

Drawing on his research in the Denver Public Library, Carhart was far ahead of his time in treating subjects like long-term global climate change and the shrinking of glaciers since 1890. Over the years, he had observed this phenomenon at St. Mary's Glacier on Colorado's Front Range, which he had written about in 1920. In a chapter titled "MORE DEADLY THAN WAR," he chronicled the decline and fall of civilizations, using the ruins at Mesa Verde in Colorado as an example of desertification. He mentioned historian Arnold Toynbee's ideas about the decline of civilizations and also referred to John Wesley Powell. And he talked about his beaver reintroduction successes, pointing out that beaver dams in the upper parts of watersheds were more effective and economical than massive dams in the lower parts, where sediment would soon fill any reservoir, no matter how large.

Bemoaning the mistreatment of public lands grazing allotments, Carhart included a discussion of "the Great Land Grab." He also wrote long sections on soils, as well as a treatment of water quantity and quality related to the paper industry. His point, which caught the attention of industry representatives and later led to consulting work, was that the nation must provide adequate water to keep the wheels of industry moving. Carhart was committed to water-based recreation consistent with a healthy, diversified, industrial economy. A section on irrigation systems and hydropower skewered the Bureau of Reclamation for inflating its hydropower claims. Carhart endorsed coal-fired steam plants as a better power source than hydropower. He frowned on the kind of recreation big dams and their reservoirs provide. Instead, he appealed to trout fishermen, citing the destruction of fisheries that followed the Colorado–Big Thompson Project, especially around Shadow Mountain and Granby at the headwaters of the Colorado River.

Water or Your Life appeared in March 1951, to favorable reviews everywhere except in Arizona, where *The Arizona Republic*'s reviewer called Carhart a liar. When Carhart threatened a libel suit, the newspaper's editor replied, in the best Wild West style, that the erring reviewer had died of a convenient heart attack.[32]

FUTURE COURSE IN WATER MANAGEMENT

By May 1952, Carhart stood at the apex of his career as a writer and conservationist. Between 1949 and 1951, he had published numerous articles[33] and four popular books on water policy. He always linked his policy proposals to sportsmen, for he knew firsthand that Republican businessmen were likely to be hunters and fishermen—and that they made good recruits for moderate conservation groups like the Izaak Walton League. Carhart liked to tally the growing numbers of hunters and fishermen, claiming that the "Fifteen Million Club," if ever organized, would be a potent force for conservation. When Dwight D. Eisenhower became president, he often combined visits to his wife's family in Denver with trout fishing expeditions in the Colorado mountains. Eisenhower and Carhart exchanged friendly correspondence about these expeditions, which included an invitation for Carhart to join Eisenhower on a fishing trip in the summer of 1952.[34]

After three decades as an independent conservationist, Carhart had learned his watershed lessons well. He told would-be conservationists that they had to find the right scale to be successful. In *Fresh Water Fishing* (1949), he warned readers against being too narrow: "As fishermen, we're interested in the whole mechanism."[35]

Carhart's most important water policy statement came on May 6, 1952, in his keynote address to the annual conference of the American Water Works Association in Kansas City. Conservationists were trying to make big dam boondoggles part of the presidential campaign. Carhart knew how to appeal to the fiscal conservatives and anti–big government sympathies of his audience. Looking askance at the various "authorities" (such as the Tennessee Valley Authority), he showed how they made a mockery of basin-wide planning. He asked his listeners:

> Can you support the idea of a presidential-appointed, autocratic board to manage our great water wealth, a corporation beyond the ballot, a corporate entity that could decide what is best for the people and ram it down their necks if that was the decision?
>
> Must we have a valley authority to accomplish basin-wide coordinated water-soil resource management?
>
> God forbid that we become so flaccid about problems that belong to every soul of us that we have to create such a potential monster dictatorship over a region.
>
> No, the responsibility for water management rests in the hands of the fellow who puts a plow-share into the soil, and how he does it. It rests in the hands of the stockman—and he commits a crime against the community if in his greed he so over-grazes his range it becomes a tin roof to produce floods, mud and disaster below. Responsibility for sound water management also lies in the hands of the municipal water division of a community, in the city officials, in the chamber of commerce, in the national bodies of business and industry—it's our job, a job for all of us.[36]

Carhart had seen enough of planning from the top down. He had examined socialist and Communist centralized planning. He had lived through those aspects of the New Deal, such as the Civilian Conservation Corps, the Bureau of Biological Survey, and the Bureau of Reclamation, that did as much harm as good. Now he saw the Forest Service, after decades of restoration work, clear-cutting entire watersheds. The bottom line for Carhart, as for John Wesley Powell, was water—and watershed democracy:

> I propose, now and here, that the organization directing inclusive management of the water wealth, and the soil wealth with it, should not be imposed

from the top, but developed out of the minds and actions of those on the ground and in the field. I propose an organization of what might be termed a water resources planning and policy board, for every minor watershed in the nation—every creek, if you please! . . . Not an imposition of what to do from the top, but a development of policy and broad planning rising up from the grass-roots citizenry.

Where would our governmental bureaus come in? Certainly as counselors and advisors—certainly as organizations to carry out the will of the people. And in that position and in that capacity they would be of great value.

Water management is a peoples' problem—and our water future depends on the people accepting responsibility for solving these problems.[37]

The polite applause that greeted Carhart's proposals did not daunt him. He knew some of the best talk about conservation policy was passed around a campfire, where people discuss what they have experienced firsthand in the field that very day—and where they remember what Carhart told them in books like *Fishing in the West* (1950): "The greatest menace to fishing in the West lies in the rampant program of dam building by the Army Engineers and the Bureau of Reclamation."[38]

Compared with many of his contemporaries, Carhart took a balanced view of dam building, finding some compensation for fishermen in the angling opportunities offered by reservoirs and by the fast, cold tailwaters at the foot of some dams. However, he wanted to see planning for fishing done from the start and not tacked on at the end. If dams do not lead to better habitat for fish, why build them? "When it comes to dams which are projected to secure flood control, isn't it far better to go upstream, make the high watersheds more retentive, prevent floods from forming, than to wait until floods have built to destructive levels and then try to control them far downstream? Common sense should govern in some degree!"[39]

Carhart appealed to the common good and to common sense in conservation politics. His way of bringing out the best in the common person was an important part of the coalition building that led to the great political watershed of the 1960s, when Lyndon Johnson and Richard Nixon judged it in their best interests to support and sign the conservation legislation that still guides us today. By carefully tending his persona as the "curmudgeon of conservation," Carhart led the way.

NOTES

1. Letter from Carhart to his fellow Iowan, J. N. "Ding" Darling, October 12, 1941, Carhart Collection, Denver Public Library (hereafter CC, DPL).

2. In 1935, a Carnegie grant to the Denver Public Library caught Carhart's attention. The grant supported a bibliographic center, built around a brilliant librarian named Eulalia Dougherty Chapman. With her help and Dr. Weyer's guidance, Carhart made extensive use of the library.

3. See "Pittman-Robertson Gang," two boxes of clippings and correspondence exchanged during the period 1942–1945, Colorado Historical Society Library, Denver.

4. *The Mapleton Press,* July 3, 1941: "George Carhart Dies in Denver: Masonic Funeral Services Held Saturday for Former Resident." Masonic funeral services were held in Denver, where he was buried: "George Carhart, 87-year-old Denver, Colo., resident and a former resident of Mapleton and Castana, passed away Wednesday of last week in the home of his son, A.H. Carhart, in Denver, Colo."

5. William Vogt, "Art Carhart: A Man for the Wilderness," *Outdoor Life* (March 1976).

6. Letter from Carhart to Darling, October 15, 1941, CC, DPL.

7. In 1942 Carhart applied unsuccessfully to the National Resources Planning Board.

8. Letter from Darling to Carhart, October 31, 1941, CC, DPL.

9. Letter from Carhart to Henry Spencer, January 5, 1944, CC, DPL.

10. Letter from Carhart to Darling, May 15, 1943, CC, DPL.

11. On February 20, 1947, Carhart and Norton terminated this agreement, and he took the book to Barnes, then to Ziff-Davis.

12. Joseph W. Penfold, *Izaak Walton League Collection,* DPL, Cons 44, AVB 4, Rg 19 B, Sec. 5, Sf 4.

13. Letter from Carhart to Herbert Evison, July 12, 1946, CC, DPL. Carhart told Evison: "Yes, I remember that first meeting at Des Moines, 'way back and the jousting I had with Mr. Mather. I'd not readily forget it."

14. Arthur Carhart, *Hunting North American Deer* (New York: Macmillan, 1946).

15. Memo dated November 25, 1948, CC, DPL.

16. Arthur Carhart, "Dam Business," *The Nation's Business* (Fall 1949).

17. Letter from Carhart to his Christmas list, December 31, 1949, CC, DPL. This promise did not stick. Carhart continued to hunt actively through the mid-1950s.

18. "Turn off That Faucet," *Atlantic Monthly* (February 1950). Reprinted in *Readers Digest* (April 1950).

19. Letter from Carhart to Stevens, January 28, 1950, CC, DPL.

20. OWA was primarily composed of newspaper journalists, so it was not necessarily a good fit for Carhart. Nonetheless, he got an enthusiastic note from the editor of the *Remington News Letter* in April 1948, welcoming him to OWA. And on February 4, 1949, Carhart represented OWA in a public hearing on rivers in Boise relative to dams built by the Corps of Engineers on the Columbia River.

21. The Carharts' trips to New Mexico often included meetings with New Mexico state game warden Elliott Barker. Letter from Barker to Carhart, July 14, 1951, CC, DPL.

22. Letters from Carhart to a magazine editor in New York, May 26 and June 3, 1950, CC, DPL.

23. Letter from Chapman to Carhart, June 20, 1950, CC, DPL.

24. Letter from Cliff to Carhart, June 26, 1950, CC, DPL.

25. Letter from Chapman to Carhart, August 7, 1950, CC, DPL.

26. Letter from Carhart to Darling, September 25, 1950, CC, DPL.

27. Letter from Darling to Carhart, September 16, 1950, CC, DPL.

28. Letter from Carhart to Darling, September 19, 1950, CC, DPL.

29. Letter from Darling to Carhart, October 6, 1950, CC, DPL.

30. Letter from Darling to Carhart, November 22, 1950, CC, DPL.

31. Arthur Carhart, *Water or Your Life* (New York: Lippincott, 1951), 21.

32. Letter from Carhart to editor, April 2, 1951; letter from editor to Carhart, April 5, 1951; both in CC, DPL.

33. For example, "The Menaced Dinosaur Monument" in the January–March 1952 issue of *National Parks Magazine*, with photos by Devereux Butcher.

34. Letter from Eisenhower to Carhart, May 4, 1953, CC, DPL. Carhart's friend Aksel Nielsen arranged the invitation, but Carhart could not attend because of other commitments.

35. Arthur Carhart, *Fresh Water Fishing* (New York: A. S. Barnes, 1949), 230–231.

36. Arthur Carhart, keynote address, annual conference of the American Water Works Association, May 6, 1952, Kansas City, Missouri.

37. Ibid.

38. Arthur Carhart, *Fishing in the West* (New York: Macmillan, 1950), 129.

39. Ibid., 133.

CHAPTER THIRTEEN

A PERVERSE HABIT OF
CALLING THE SHOTS IN ANY DIRECTION

I'm rather flattered at being asked to join in with this group. As you may know, it has been my policy, rather strictly adhered to, to not join up with a number of groups for which I have the highest regard, so I might be an independent individual in a position to pitch in and carry the ball when such groups were prevented from action by various limitations. Being a free agent, I could start slugging without involving [the] organization in embarrassment over what I wrote or said. This looks like a fighting group, well thought out. So I judge it is the exception to the policy I have followed.

—CARHART TO ZAHNISER, 1955[1]

INTRODUCTION: COMPLETE ESCAPE FROM HIGH-VELOCITY LIVING

Shunned by the Wilderness Society, Carhart made a virtue—and a career—of being an increasingly curmudgeonly outsider. In early 1955, Carhart received an invitation to become a director of the Citizens Committee on Natural Resources. After mulling it over for a month, he accepted, joining a prestigious group that included Sigurd Olson, Joe Penfold, Howard Zahniser, Olaus Murie, Alfred Knopf, Ira Gabrielson, Newton Drury, J. N. "Ding" Darling, David Brower, and Horace Albright.

In spite of chronic poor health, Carhart maintained a rigorous writing schedule that kept him both cantankerous and happy.[2] He reveled in the role of curmudgeon. Although the freelance market was somewhat dry, Carhart's books sold well, including his fiction such as *Son of the Forest*, which appeared in 1952, a year when he also spent a short time in the hospital because of heart problems.

Carhart was valuable to the Citizens Committee on Natural Resources because of his high national profile and also because he had excellent connections in the timber, automobile, and pulp industries. As he told his friend Arthur Van Vlissingen, the public relations man for the Pulp and Paper Information Service:

> You don't see why I haven't been thrown out of the "lodge" of the conservationists and outdoor writers? Sometimes I wonder, too. It may be because I've got such a perverse habit of calling the shots in any direction, and the lodge members know it, that they could be a bit leery of tangling [with me]. . . . You can sense honesty; you sorta smell it. . . . And that's why, I guess, you find me as much on "your side" as any.[3]

Carhart wrote positive articles about industries whose support was critical for conservation legislation. During the 1956 political season, Carhart queried *Sports Afield* about an article on the Weyerhaeuser Corporation: "It's a story I've wanted to write; it's on the positive side and it's constructive. I've torn into enough bad situations. It will be swell to crusade a little for . . . 'The Builder-Uppers.'"[4] It was also rewarding to have personal access to the Weyerhaeuser family, which included lucrative consulting contracts and connections to important policy makers in the wood fiber industry. All this led to publication in 1958 of TREES and GAME—*Twin Crops*.

In 1952, national radio personality Arthur Godfrey did a show on Carhart's book *Hunting North American Deer*. When Carhart wrote to thank Godfrey, they developed a relationship based on their shared conviction that "Hunting and Fishing is Big Business," as Carhart had described it in a 1947 article for *Sports Afield*,[5] in which he put dollar figures on outdoor sports. Carhart had obtained his 1947 results working alone. But in late 1950, when he updated his study for the same magazine, he had financial support from Joe Penfold of the Izaak Walton League and Ira Gabrielson of the Wildlife Management Institute, who needed such ammunition as they geared up for the 1952 political season. Carhart and his staff sent out 1,500 questionnaires to readers of the magazine. When the results came in, they confirmed his conviction that the "15 Million Club" of the nation's sportsmen represented an economic force that could be translated into political power—by the right person, of course. Carhart had been dreaming of such power since 1920, when he had proposed a national conference on recreation. Now, after many years of laboring in obscurity, he became a board member for the Izaak Walton League, the American Wildlife Federation, and the Citizens Committee on Natural Resources.

This pace took a continuing toll on both Carharts. They sold their cabin in the mountains in 1955. As Carhart told a Forest Service friend:

Vee is fine. I have been except the middle of July, with Joe Penfold, I tried to skip lightly up to a lake at about 10,000 feet, and that's when the altitude really did hit me. I was sick as a horse; in bed about 10 days. Gosh, I felt lousy! So for the time being I'm staying out of the high country—which bars me from coming to Sulphur much as I wish we could visit over there. This also is added fuel toward our finding a spot [at] or near sea level, maybe so. Calif. Where we might move to anon. No immediate stampede but we seriously contemplate such a move.

Meanwhile, I feel a heap better than a few weeks ago. Feel plumb good most of the time. I'll not try to out-race a 40-year old companion on a 25% trail and at 10,000 elevation. That triggered the mess I am coming out of. Not a heart attack as such; but a severe warning not to mess around that way again. Complicated by too severe adherence to a 1000-calorie diet the doc threw at me. I thought he meant for me to stick right to it; I did. There's where the big backlash came. But with a return to a better fueling of the power plant I do feel probably as well as I have in some years. Still have to move moderately and not let tensions get hold of me.[6]

Concerned about her husband, Vee accompanied him on many of his business-political trips. But from 1955 on, they made a precarious pair. She was afflicted by pre-cancerous symptoms that led to a preemptive operation in 1957 and a full diagnosis of cancer in 1960. Carhart took a long, frustrating road to recovery from his heart attack. Finally, he was able accept the Founder's Award from the Izaak Walton League in April 1956.[7] These tribulations led the Carharts to California, Oregon, Washington, and Arizona, looking for a place to retire. In Arizona, they became acquainted with another genial curmudgeon, Senator Barry Goldwater. The two populists found they shared tastes for fiscal conservatism and a smaller federal government, along with a deep dislike of dictatorships, whether fascist or Communist.

BRANDED A LIAR AND A COMMUNIST

As a lifelong Republican, Carhart did his best to herd other Republicans into the conservation corral. But he also enjoyed productive relations with various mayors, governors, and members of Congress from both parties. These connections included Denver mayor Richard Batterton, a major partner in Sport-LORE.[8] Most important, Carhart cultivated Democratic congressman Wayne Aspinall, who represented western Colorado for many years after World War II and who chaired not just the committees with power over dams and wilderness bills but also the all-important Outdoor Recreation Resources Review Commission (ORRRC). After wandering for the proverbial forty years in the political deserts, advocates for recreation and conservation like Carhart were finally nearing the promised land: the wave of important conservation legislation that passed during the 1960s.

Carhart saw that ORRRC was a good forum for his battles with dam builders and ranchers. One focus was the proposed Bureau of Reclamation dam at Echo Park, part of a much larger drive to complete development of the entire upper Colorado River, known as the Colorado River Storage Project (CRSP). The focus for the grazing battle was a series of proposals from western public lands ranchers to privatize their grazing allotments and sometimes other public lands as well. Fur flew in blizzard proportions when the Wyoming Stockgrowers Association called Carhart a "Communist" in print. When the air cleared, Carhart and his ally Bernard DeVoto had the field to themselves. And when DeVoto died suddenly in 1956, Carhart stood as one of the chief spokespersons for conservation.

Carhart's campaign against monopolizing grazing interests and cynical land grabbers dated all the way back to *The Ordeal of Brad Ogden*. He kept trying to imagine a better Forest Service, especially in his fiction, culminating in the publication of his novel *Son of the Forest* in 1952. Alarmed by plans he saw for massive clear-cutting, he tried to suggest improvements in the Forest Service's land-use planning process, culminating in the publication of TREES *and* GAME (1958), *The National Forests* (1959), and *Planning for America's Wildlands* (1961).

Carhart also monitored the deplorable ecological state of Forest Service grazing allotments. He went after ranchers by appealing to businesspeople and taxpayers. Carhart's job with the Office of Price Administration had given him inside information about war profiteering and fraudulent "resource scarcities" that led the Forest Service to overstock grazing allotments. After the war, adding insult to injury, ranchers reignited their campaign to privatize their grazing allotments. Meanwhile, the Forest Service and the Grazing Service finally summoned the will to begin the stocking reductions that might lead to recovery of damaged watersheds.

The National Cattlemens Association approached the National Chamber of Commerce for a political endorsement of its privatization proposal, based on a common respect for private property rights and a common dislike of federal regulatory agencies. The chamber appointed a committee to study the issue— and then Carhart struck. Hardly a friend of "burocracy," he also refused to trust a special interest such as ranching with the public's land:

> There is a present disposition to class all bureaus with the afflictions we
> have incurred through the New Deal and the war. You know darned well
> I was in the middle of one of them—pitching for all I was worth to get as
> clean as possible [a] job done because it was being done and someone had to
> do it. I've incurred the displeasure, sometimes dislike, of my former associ-

ates in the Forest Service by taking a jab at shortcomings in their operations and I've certainly tangled with the Grazing Service. And I just don't like burocracy as such. But to lump these older bureaus in with the alphabetical bunch, smear good and constructive work they have done, is unfair, blind and will lead to hurtful results.

When the Forest Service is accused of arbitrary action in reducing livestock permits, lambasted as bureaucrats, a general resentment throws sentiment against the dambureaucrats. They've made mistakes; they admit it. One mistake has been to yield to livestock interest pressures for more grazing than the land should carry. But the forest men have not had the understanding of enough people to give them the backing when the force hit them, to insist that livestock reductions must be made for the all-around good of all the community.[9]

Delighted with so powerful an ally, Carhart's sources in the Forest Service were happy to steer him toward information (both public and privileged) that might undermine the stockgrowers' position. One of privatization's chief proponents, Wyoming's senator Robertson, a Republican, had a conflict of interest in the form of numerous permits to graze his sheep on lands managed by the Forest Service. Carhart came out with both guns blazing. *Sports Afield* published "THIS IS YOUR LAND" in early 1947, quickly followed by a rolling broadside of related articles in many different outlets, including and especially *The Atlantic Monthly*.[10]

The cattlemen returned fire in a letter from one of the Arizona members to the editor of *Sports Afield*, in which the writer charged Carhart with being an unsportsmanlike tool of the Forest Service, which he accused of "commissarlike" treatment of ranchers. Thanks to Forest Service sources in Albuquerque, Carhart gleefully skewered the hapless rancher. The range war continued through the summer of 1947, as Carhart worked hard to mobilize opposition to HR 1330, which he termed "the Land Grab bill." Showing considerable courage, Carhart showed up alone in Grand Junction, Colorado, to testify before the House Subcommittee on Public Lands on September 5, 1947. Among his political allies were prominent members of the dude ranching association, such as Charles C. Moore of the CM Ranch in Dubois, Wyoming. Carhart's *Hi Stranger* had won him many friends in this important segment of the recreation industry.

Alva Simpson at the regional office of the Forest Service in Albuquerque provided background for *The Atlantic Monthly* article.[11] He fed Carhart information about threats to Forest Service personnel, where "the 30-30 method" (death by rifle) made riding the range dangerous for dedicated forest rangers. Carhart himself received a letter threatening "the 30-30 method" in the spring of 1948 from a writer in Ogden, Utah.[12] Along with praise from Bernard

DeVoto came a formal letter of congratulations from fellow landscape archi-tect Conrad Wirth, then head of the National Park Service, accompanied by a request to cover similar threats to Park Service lands and personnel.

Attacks on Carhart were especially virulent in Wyoming, where he took up the cause of Dr. E. S. Wengert of the Political Science Department at the University of Wyoming, who had resigned in protest over rancher domination of the university. *Readers Digest* quickly reprinted "Land Grab," much to the consternation of *The Denver Post* and *Cow Country*, the official publication of the Wyoming Stockgrowers Association. In its December 18, 1948, edition, *Cow Country* called Carhart a liar and insinuated that he was a Communist. The publication claimed he had not appeared at the Grand Junction meeting—an obvious lie, since the testimony Carhart gave at the hearing was part of the official record of its findings. Carhart fired off a letter of protest,[13] which *Cow Country* refused to print. Carhart kept up his attack: "The statements that I am a purveyor of untruths and the very direct method of linking my name with the Communists, passes beyond mere controversy, become declarations of record and enter a field in which the law recognizes demonstrable injury may be done. . . . I have no intention of permitting myself to be branded a liar and a Communist by default."[14]

When *Cow Country's* February edition appeared, it contained a note correct-ing the attendance question—but nothing else. By the end of March, Carhart was asking the Sierra Club for help in bringing a libel suit against the publica-tion. This war of words continued over the next few years, as the "land grab" assumed different forms and as Carhart worked on the grazing sections of his books about the national forests:

> I'm citing how this gang has used intimidation as one of their means of try-
> ing to force support for their schemes. I've written into the article that now
> is nearing completion, some of the direct harassment of the forest officials.
> Included is a case of slugging in a stock meeting in Wyoming, where the
> ranger was gotten into a room with apparent premeditated plans to beat him
> up. They did pick a fight and he was hit in the face but cool heads stopped the
> full-scale beating. I have other instances of such attempted intimidation.[15]

TIMBER IN YOUR LIFE

Because he was located in Denver and willing to travel to represent conserva-tion interests, Carhart was a valuable person at a time when the conservation movement was at an important turning point. He served as a bridge between the more traditional hunting and fishing interests and a new breed: educated, urban environmentalists who read magazines like *Harper's* and *The Atlantic*

Monthly. Timber in Your Life was addressed both to Carhart's devoted readers and to this new audience.

Bernard DeVoto wrote the introduction for Carhart's new book. Working through their shared membership in the Outdoor Writers of America (OWA), the two men recruited Senator Eugene McCarthy of Minnesota to their cause. Carhart was the water policy chair for OWA in 1952. Thanks to DeVoto, the 1953 OWA meeting in Missoula was a triumph for Carhart, who presented a proposal for another survey on sportsmen's expenditures. Remington, the arms manufacturer, supplied $6,500 to Carhart to expand the sample to include 25,000 people.[16] Carhart's work with Remington eventually led him to Ed Hilliard, who owned the Redfield Gunsight Company in Denver and who became an important ally in the fight for a wilderness bill and in the founding of the Conservation Library.

DeVoto and Carhart conducted a warm correspondence that lasted from 1950 until DeVoto's death in 1956. DeVoto taught at the famous Bread Loaf writing school, and he generously advised Carhart in ways that improved *Son of the Forest* and other fiction. Carhart kept DeVoto informed about *The Denver Post*, whose editor, Palmer Hoyt, wobbled on conservation issues such as Echo Park and the Colorado River Storage Project.[17]

DeVoto wrote: "So *Timber in Your Life* is a basic handbook of conservation, though its specific subject is trees and wood." A Ding Darling cartoon embellished the back cover, along with DeVoto's ringing endorsement. Thanks to DeVoto, Paul Sears reviewed the book in the *Saturday Review:*

> Thus it is that when an author undertakes to tell, in the words of his publishers, "the full story of the uses and misuses of one of our most crucial natural resources" he is tackling a man-sized job. Bless his soul, Arthur Carhart has brought it off. From now on, whenever I am asked, as often happens, "Where can I find out about forests and forestry in a way I can understand?" there will be no problem. "Timber in Your Life" is the answer. I have caught no important aspect of the subject which has been forgotten, nor have I detected any unfairness, despite the author's strong convictions, in his presentation of hot controversial issues—notably the current attempt to wrest control of grazing on national forests and other public lands from those charged by law with conserving them. Mr. Carhart has done an imposing piece of research and translated it into good readable vernacular.[18]

The book appeared in January 1955 in the midst of a growing controversy over the Forest Service's management of its timber program. Many in the Forest Service thought roading and clear-cutting were right for most of the nation's maturing timber. Others were sure the Forest Service had already built too many roads and that the agency could not be trusted with recreation in general and certainly not with the management of wilderness in particular. Almost everyone agreed on the need for complete suppression of fire, but some were beginning to doubt the wisdom of Forest Service predator policies. Carhart served as defender of the agency's best self. Regional Forester C. J. Olsen wrote Carhart to that effect from Utah, adding that he was having all his forest supervisors read the book,[19] which was subtitled: "The Full Story of the Uses and Misuses of One of Our Most Crucial Natural Resources."

The book encourages knowledge of our public trust heritage. Carhart imagined a better Forest Service by writing of the forest ranger as an executive, much as Herbert Kaufman would do five years later.[20] A patriotic tone to Carhart's prose comes straight out of wartime newsreels. Carhart quotes Teddy Roosevelt in demanding "thoroughly businesslike management" of the national forests. He mocks and vilifies those who would exploit the public domain for private gain. Even Gifford Pinchot gained Carhart's approval when he stood up to his superiors on behalf of conservation: "Absurd as it may be in some instances, anyone who bypasses his superior officer in government service and goes directly to higher levels to get action commits official suicide." Always, the emphasis is on the ideal: "There is no corps of any kind that has a richer, more compelling tradition to live up to, than the members of our United States Forest Service."

Showing the proper role of recreation in comprehensive planning, Carhart recounted the stories of Trappers Lake and Boundary Waters, setting the stage for what he felt should be included in wilderness legislation:

> We need even more such places, well selected and adequately protected. We need a much more positive assurance that they will be perpetuated than the mere administrative action which now establishes them. The administrative order is too easily superseded by another which would wipe out existing values. A law directing the Secretary of Agriculture to establish such areas and protect them against misuse would be a minimum safeguard.
>
> Production of timber and protection of vital watershed areas must be primary objectives in the management of our forests. But are they more vital than the intangible return that lies in the basic need of maintaining healthy perspective and strength of spirit that our forests offer?
>
> Perhaps the rebuilding of body and spirit is the greatest service derivable from our forests, for of what worth are material things if we lost the character and quality of people that are the soul of America?

Carhart explained why he could not support any wilderness bill that "grandfathers in" grazing and other uses that violated his zoning principles. His subsequent refusal to endorse the 1964 Wilderness Act has important roots here.

Other sections of *Timber in Your Life* show Carhart's fascination with what we would now call "appropriate technology." A chapter on new uses for wood endorsed the zoning of forests so the most productive sites can be managed as commercial timber farms. Carhart realized that after fifty years in the role of caretaker, the Forest Service was ready to accelerate its timber harvest program. But he emphatically beat the multiple use drum, disdaining the approach that says every forested acre must be managed for timber. In this, Carhart anticipated the tempests to come, starting with the Multiple Use Sustained Yield Act of 1960. He never let his readers forget Forest Service complicity in under-funding recreation and related interests:

> The funds made available for some divisions of national forest activities are niggardly. There has been no adequate recognition of the gigantic recreational uses of the forests; the 35,000,000 annual visitors merit a lot more consideration than has been given them. Wildlife has been almost completely ignored. Funds for combating diseases and pests, and for vital research have been grievously inadequate. There are inaccessible mature and over-mature stands of timber in our forests that should be harvested; there must be more appropriations for roads to reach these virgin woodlands so they may contribute to current requirements and be put in shape to grow more trees in the future.

The book ends as Carhart ended most of his books—with a direct address to his reader as a fellow citizen for whom watershed-wide management is a critical concern:

> We can not get away from the essential fact that you have a personal stake in the nation's forestry program and the good things it can bring to you in our American way of living.
>
> There's timber in your life. You cannot be indifferent to the fact.
>
> It is entirely natural that those deeply concerned with future timber supplies should pass over lightly the fact that the forest is more than a timber farm; it is a community of values in which every citizen has some interest, minor or of real proportions. It is imperative that the timber industries recognize this truth.

Over his long career, Carhart had seen far too many national plans come and go. Instead, he restated the goal of his book, which was to create responsible citizens:

> The forest of the future of the nation must rest on something more than tables, graphs and the text of reports; it must rest on the belief of the individual that he, personally, has a stake in how our timberlands are handled. Not merely in one phase of it, but in every part of the program—timber

production, watershed protection, and the other values we may derive from the complex forest community. . . . You've got to grow your timber before you can cut it.

TREES AND GAME—TWIN CROPS

Carhart caught the attention of the American Forest Products Institute, which published his booklet *Twin Crops* in 1958, with an introduction by Ernest Swift, executive director of the National Wildlife Federation.[21] Aimed at the non-industrial private forest owner, without whose cooperation watershed management will not work, the book displays the Tree Farm symbol next to a hunter with a dog walking along the edge of a managed forest.

Carhart's commitment to watershed management led him to form alliances with the pulp and paper industry at a time when some of its members were trying to find moderate allies in the conservation movement. The formal name for this effort was the Pulp and Paper Information Service, but Carhart quickly dubbed it "The Grand Conference of Reluctant Polluters and Earnest Conservationists."[22] Carhart insisted that all attendees be aware that the industry was paying some of his expenses.[23] Industry men Art Van Vlissingen and Bernard Orell were active in this effort. Carhart's conservation contacts included Frank Gregg of the Izaak Walton League, which was leading the lobbying effort in Washington on precursor bills to the Clean Water Act.

Walter DeLong, director of public relations for Weyerhaeuser, took a leading role, telling Carhart: "I believe that by the written word alone you could sell a sawmill to the Wilderness Society."[24] But could Carhart sell a deal to the conservationists? He had more luck with the industry side, including meetings with John Philip Weyerhaeuser in Tacoma.[25]

Carhart's correspondence with his friends in the timber industry provides a good index to his thinking about what might make a reasonable wilderness bill. He warned Orell that "extremists among the wilderness folk will rouse people to get a law that will 'freeze' wilderness after it is designated as such, tighter than national parks."[26] As with water issues, Carhart tried to broker meetings of moderates in both the conservation and timber industries over various pieces of legislation. He arranged for Weyerhaeuser to give money to the Izaak Walton League.[27] Orell saw Carhart's value as a moderate, writing to him about a proposed article for *The New York Times* that he hoped would be

an outsider looking in piece. We want men of your caliber to look into the inner workings of our organization to see if we are operating our properties in a manner which would win the approval of conservationists who have a true understanding of what conservation really is. Frankly, I did not expect you to knock yourself out, Art, trying to convince others that the Weyerhaeuser Timber Company took its responsibilities of heritage seriously. I think we have a good story to tell. Naturally we are proud of our company and the job that it is trying to do.[28]

Carhart also successfully pumped his industry friends for writing, speaking, and consulting jobs.[29]

THE NATIONAL FORESTS

Starting in 1954, much to the dismay of some in the Forest Service (who preferred their own budgeting system to earmarked funds), Carhart threw his support behind HR 1952, a bill that would dedicate a large revolving fund to recreation on the national forests.[30] The bill also included a right to appeal forest decisions for all interest groups, thus further undercutting what many like Forest Service chief Richard McArdle saw as time-honored professional prerogatives. Carhart and McArdle corresponded about such subjects, beginning in 1954 and extending through 1957, as Carhart worked on his new book. When the book appeared, Carhart received many letters of praise from regional-level Forest Service friends—but not from the old guard, represented by Leon Kneipp, or from the chief himself. A few years later, faced with the perceived threats to its autonomy represented by the Wilderness Act of 1964 and the National Forest Management Act of 1976, the Forest Service would try to embrace Carhart as a long-lost friend. But for now, many viewed him and his devotion to "conservation first" with suspicion. "The National Forests" indeed! Who was Carhart to presume to tell the history of the Forest Service? Carhart answered with an article in *American Forests* about the first forest ranger.[31]

Alfred Knopf was the foremost publisher of conservation books in the 1950s, including both fiction and nonfiction. For example, Knopf published *This Is Dinosaur: Echo Park Country and Its Magic Rivers* in 1955.[32] After the success of Carhart's Forest Service novel, *Son of the Forest*, Knopf asked Carhart for an auto tour guide to the national forests, published as a way of educating the public about the issues that were leading to the passage of the Multiple Use–Sustained Yield Act in 1960. Carhart's *The National Forests* (1959) includes visits to many forests, including eastern forests like the Monongahela, where he warned his readers of plans for the massive clear-cutting that would soon gain national attention.

Like most of Carhart's conservation books of this period, this one appeared to enthusiastic reviews from all sides, including the Wilderness Society.[33] Joseph Penfold of the Izaak Walton League wrote a generous introduction. Reminding his readers that the restoration period of the Forest Service's work was over, Carhart said many timber stands were now ready to cut, but "the Forest Service has not given watershed management its due consideration. . . . The grazing of privately owned livestock is often grievously detrimental to watershed values." The book's long history of the Forest Service's mismanagement of watershed values leads to the appearance of John Wesley Powell.[34] In that context, Carhart discussed legislation to give legal status to "wildland sanctuaries":

> Good land-use planning would argue for the maintenance of more flexibil-
> ity in shaping these wildland sanctuaries and in determining how, over the
> years, they may best be used. Perhaps "freezing" all the wilderness areas in
> our national forests will be the only way to keep out other damaging uses.
> If a bill with rigid restrictions becomes law and an absolute lock-out of all
> other uses follows, those who cry out against tying up even so much as we
> have in the wilderness reserves can blame only their own schemings to
> "develop" these sanctuaries.
>
> In the last analysis, it is the national forest, generally with acreage suf-
> ficient to throw a protective "buffer zone" around true wilderness, that can
> insure these places of far retreat.

The Carharts traveled by car around the entire country to research the book. They had enthusiastic support from Forest Service people in the field. But Chief McArdle was sensitive to Carhart's criticism of the agency's failures in watershed, recreation, and range management. Carhart asked for an endorsement of his book, but, as he told a friend:

> McArdle wouldn't do it. I suspect that some of the "high priests" that I had
> offended some years back by telling what I thought of some of their actions,
> thought they saw a way to embarrass me by horsing along and then giving
> me the kick. They did make Knopf mad as hell. And I'm saving banana
> peels to throw if anyone, at some time ahead, tries to climb up somewhere.
> It was a struggle to get that book done. The field men helped me much but
> Washington stuck spikes in gears whenever they could. I'm a cross between
> an elephant and an Indian when it comes to remembering some stuff.[35]

BOUNDARY WATERS: A CROSS BETWEEN AN ELEPHANT AND AN INDIAN

Carhart was not the only one with a long memory. After John Tobin of the Izaak Walton League presented him with the league's highest award in the spring of 1956, he wrote to Sigurd Olson, explaining that Tobin had given him too much credit for saving Boundary Waters.[36]

Also interested in the issue of credit were Leon F. Kneipp and Alice Sheffey. Sheffey was a graduate student at the University of Michigan, working on a history of the Superior National Forest. Tough, conscientious, and systematic, she sent a draft of her thesis to both Carhart and Kneipp for comment.[37] Carhart told her she had given him too much credit. For once, Carhart and Kneipp agreed, but not for long. Kneipp did not like Sheffey's thesis. He felt it was both one-sided and anti–Forest Service, and he told her so in no uncertain terms. She refused to be intimidated. Reminding her that A. E. Sherman had been a student of Dr. L. H. Pammel of Iowa State, Kneipp told her she had unfairly "snippeted" Sherman's correspondence. Then he went after Carhart: "Every so often, some specialist became so obsessed with the importance of his particular function as to urge or demand that it be made dominant over all others. If his demands were not acceded to he became rebellious, insurgent, prone to heated denunciation. I had not previously been aware that such situations were acceptable as bases for master's degrees."[38]

Equal to her task, Sheffey told Carhart: "I do not believe Mr. Kneipp has been an 'unbiased reader,' and I think he has not clearly understood what I was attempting to do."[39] She shared Kneipp's objections with Carhart, who responded by reviewing his perspective as a recreation planner on Forest Service history: "I actually had forgotten how bitter the fight was against this old cast-iron viewpoint, this interpretation of the 'greatest good–greatest number' which accepted numbers as measure of worth. . . . The memo recalls it."[40] Carhart refuted Kneipp point by point:

> As for A. E. Sherman, I never lost my affection for that man; he was a great person. He had vision. It was, in fact, with a feeling of outright desertion of Sherman that I quit the USFS [U.S. Forest Service] with real sorrow.
>
> And if you want the flat, sure-fire reason I did quit, it was the utter futility of my staying on, bucking a policy that had switched from reasonable consideration of human uses of wildlands (Sherman, Riley, Morrell) to an over-riding goal of wood, wood and more wood.[41]

Sheffey's husband had received an overseas assignment, and she did not relish spending undue time unraveling the competing wilderness histories of these ancient and bitter enemies. Under pressure to finish her degree, she told both men she was at a loss as to how to do the further research they both recommended, since the materials that would supplement Carhart's version of events were so widely dispersed. This was one of many occasions when Carhart wished for some central place where both his personal conservation library and the papers of organizations such as the Izaak Walton League, the Wilderness Society, and the Forest Service might be available to scholars like Sheffey.

Sheffey asked Kneipp for more material to support his version of events.[42] He told her:

Your ideas and mine move in two widely differing orbits. . . . Since Carhart has had nothing to do with it during the past 35 years, and strongly implies his recommendations were disregarded or ignored, he hardly could be accredited with such improvements as may have occurred. As a matter of fact, Will Dilg is entitled to far more credit than anybody else. To keep the flickering flame of life in the Izaak Walton League he had to have burning issues and for the Lake States Region the Superior National Forest was a sure fire issue; a fact not overlooked by his successors.[43]

After Kneipp dismissed Sheffey's work, Carhart wrote to reassure her. She tried to arrange to interview him in Denver on her way overseas, but the meeting never came to pass. This left the field open for Donald Baldwin.

WILDERNESS AND WATER: ECHO PARK

Early Park Service officials like Stephen Mather had stressed the playground rather than the wilderness sanctuary aspects of the parks. But could that appeal work at Echo Park? Could preservation of such a remote place compete with the pressing needs of the Korean War and anti-Communist campaigns at home? One key to President Eisenhower's 1952 victory had been his ability to balance moderate Republicans like Carhart against anti-Communist crusaders like Senator Joseph McCarthy. Eisenhower wanted to help those in Congress who were standing up against McCarthy's bullying.

If Echo Park could be marketed to Congress and to the people, might it come to pass that the greatest threat to the parks would become not dams but crowds of auto-borne tourists who wanted to visit the heavily publicized wonders in person? The Sierra Club's leaders sensed that Carhart knew how to connect water with wilderness through his emphasis on watershed management. Like Howard Zahniser of the Wilderness Society, the Sierra Club's David Brower was looking for a "hot issue" to breathe life into the flickering flame that was then the tiny Sierra Club. As the founders of the Wilderness Society had done, the Sierra Club omitted Carhart from its critical 1953 wilderness conference. From his perspective, the Sierra Club's snub was doubly insulting, for he felt keenly the contrast between his long labors as a freelancer and what he perceived as the inherited personal wealth of many other conservationists. Carhart was a proud man with a long memory. He regarded himself as an independent whose professional insights and vast experience were valuable to all concerned. After years of obscurity, he now advised everyone involved in conservation that they "better hire Carhart as a consultant." Without Carhart's moderating influence, the wilderness movement proceeded in directions he could not approve. He remained friendly with many in the Sierra Club and the

Wilderness Society (especially Zahniser), but, as he pointedly told the Sierra Club, "We're certainly in a hizzy and brawl over water here in Colorado. The whole thing arises from the segmentary, narrow-interest approach to proposals limited interests are putting forward."[44]

Carhart was also aware that individual grandstanding and interlocking directorates among conservation groups and federal conservation agencies did not promote his populist conservation interests. Through mutual friends, Carhart had access to the intramural conflicts of the Sierra Club that eventually led to Brower's firing and a serious rift within the conservation movement.[45] Like Brower, Carhart understood that CRSP dams and power plants threatened wilderness interests and the national park system itself. Carhart had early schooling in the Park Service's endless scheming to monopolize recreation dollars. His April 1946 visit to Echo Park was part of a series of visits to remote national monuments (such as Big Bend, Texas) that had told him as much about Park Service neglect as about Bureau of Reclamation threats.

Both Carhart and Brower understood that the proposed Bureau of Reclamation dam at Echo Park threatened symbolic as well as intrinsic values. But there they parted ways. Carhart felt it preferable to embrace the more palatable parts of CRSP rather than be forced to accept the less palatable aspects, such as the proposed dam at Glen Canyon, a site almost no one had seen. Through Carhart's access to Wayne Aspinall, he knew they both were interested in proposals to dedicate a large federal trust fund to recreation in ways that would earmark money for planning, maintenance, and upkeep, as well as for acquisition of new lands.[46] Finally, it seemed to Carhart, there was a way to fund comprehensive planning for recreation. Swallowing hard, he temporarily put aside his reservations about federal power and spending. Carhart and Aspinall understood that auto-based tourism would have to drive any large-scale proposals for national recreation if Congress were to fund them. They felt conservationists must accept a major federal presence in dam building and timber harvest in return for a major federal presence in recreation.

Carhart was in a good position to assess such tradeoffs. Thanks to his work at the Office of Price Administration, he knew the war had been good news for the economy of the West, stimulating a boom with a massive influx of federal money. After the war, the end of rationing for gas and rubber meant a rise in auto-based recreation that benefited conservation interests in the West. Carhart also knew the Communist scare and the Korean War were diverting attention and funding from CRSP, giving conservationists time to plan their strategy. And finally, Carhart was acutely aware that the early 1950s had brought drought and dust storms to the West, where people remembered similar Depression-era conditions with dread.

The conflict over Echo Park erupted in the Department of the Interior between the National Park Service (NPS) and the Bureau of Reclamation. It culminated in the resignation of longtime NPS director Newton Drury (a Republican) on April 1, 1951, leaving conservation organizations to carry on the battle until its resolution in 1954. Conservationists like Carhart questioned the need for the dam (especially through a critical analysis of evaporation rates). They also proposed alternate sites.

Carhart knew full well the history of NPS attempts to corner congressional money for recreation. Mark Harvey said, "Yet it must be remembered that the Bureau and the Park Service *cooperated* in planning the use of the upper Colorado River throughout the war years" (emphasis in the original).[47] The Park Service meant to expand its recreation empire to include reservoirs. Early on, this included an agreement for the NPS to manage a reservoir at Echo Park, should the dam be built. Drury had approved this agreement in 1941. The secretary of the interior under President Truman, Denverite Oscar Chapman (a Democrat), was a former Park Service employee. Carhart wrote Chapman in opposition.[48]

Carhart soon learned of a more ominous side to Chapman's decision. Carhart drew the line at nuclear power. Like many conservationists when faced with the choice in the midst of the CRSP battle, Carhart opted for coal-fired plants instead of nuclear plants—or more hydroelectric plants. But there were exceptions. Both Brower and physicist-conservationist Richard Bradley supported a "high" Glen Canyon Dam in lieu of Echo Park. Brower and Bradley were also convinced that nuclear power would replace the need for hydropower.[49] It was against this background that Carhart wrote:

> Perhaps the most significant "inside" story is this: At the time the first hearing was held in Washington, George Marshall, then Secretary of War (Defense), in a closed session, declared that the dam was indispensable in national survival. The reason for the statement was that the big new atomic plant was to be located near the Echo Park power. The location then was shifted to near Gallopois, Ohio, as you know, and that urgency for the dam has been wiped out. It was on this basis that Oscar Chapman was driven into his first support of the dam scheme.[50]

Chapman's approval was one thing. Congressional approval—and money— were another, especially since Chapman acted on the day President Truman decided to commit the nation to the Korean War. The war allowed conservationists precious time. As one of the first conservation writers to visit Echo Park, Carhart had written "The Menaced Dinosaur National Monument" for *National Parks Magazine* in early 1952. He was careful to toe an important Park

Service line: Dinosaur should not be dammed, but it should be developed for tourists.[51]

Adding to the print barrage, although a little late to the fray, Alfred Knopf published *This Is Dinosaur: Echo Park Country and Its Magic Rivers* in 1955 (see note 32). Knopf presented copies to members of Congress. President Eisenhower finally signed the law authorizing CRSP without Echo Park in April 1956. Conservationists had proved unwilling or unable to stop Glen Canyon Dam, but at least the final CRSP legislation of 1956 prohibited dams in any part of the national park system.

Throughout these battles, Carhart felt Brower had a tendency to push a weak hand too far, such as in taking too much personal credit for the point about evaporation rates from a proposed Echo Park reservoir. This important detail probably originated with former Corps of Engineers employee and conservation consultant General Ulysses S. Grant, who preferred a dam site lower down the Green River at Gray's Canyon.[52]

As the conservationist who actually attended many of the key meetings held far from the centers of political power, Carhart was aware that Grant rather than Brower was doing most of the heavy lifting on Echo Park and CRSP. For example, Carhart sent a report directly to Grant about an Echo Park–related meeting in Moffat County in western Colorado.[53] Typically a bridge builder rather than a bridge burner, Carhart remained in close touch with Oscar Chapman and President Eisenhower as the controversy swirled on and on. Carhart wrote to Eisenhower to ask him to reconsider his support for Echo Park Dam. Ike responded by reminding Carhart of their missed fishing trip in the summer of 1952.[54]

Carhart's role contrasts with Brower's tactics. Still, he and Brower served together on the Citizens Committee on Natural Resources, and Brower kindly sent Carhart a condolence letter when Vee died. Ultimately, the Sierra Club board voted not to oppose Glen Canyon Dam in late 1955. In contrast, as Mark Harvey has shown, Carhart's friend Howard Zahniser used the Echo Park controversy as a way to build the Wilderness Society. Was this a pyrrhic victory? When the 1964 Wilderness Bill finally came to President Johnson for his signature, it lacked support from both Carhart and the Park Service. The Park Service opposed including its lands in the Wilderness Act, claiming it managed all its lands outside of developed areas as "wilderness" (following its 1916 Organic Act).

Amid all this turmoil, Carhart showed more signs of flagging. He told Zahniser: "I'm getting very tired, Zahnie."[55] Somehow, Carhart rallied. It would be another twenty years before the curmudgeon gave up his battle on behalf of conservation.

NOTES

1. Letter from Carhart to Zahniser, March 27, 1955, Carhart Collection, Denver Public Library (hereafter CC, DPL).

2. Photos from this period did not flatter him. On March 19, 1951, he wrote to Richard Henry Dana at Lippincott: "In re photograph, they both make me out grumpy. I have my other moments. One reason I avoid photos is they make me out as dyspeptic. . . . For general newspaper use, I'd prefer the less dress-up. Suggest maybe I work at times."

3. Letter from Carhart to Van Vissingen, January 16, 1958, CC, DPL.

4. Letter from Carhart to editor of *Sports Afield*, July 17, 1956, CC, DPL.

5. See Carhart, "Hunting and Fishing Is Big Business," *Sports Afield* (July 1947), and the updates of late 1951 and 1954.

6. Letter from Carhart to Forest Service friend, November 5, 1955, CC, DPL.

7. Gradually, he began to dispose of some of his vast personal library. In 1960, even as he was brainstorming the birth of the Conservation Library in Denver, he offered his papers to the Welder Wildlife Foundation in Texas. For Carhart and the Conservation Library, see Andrew Kirk's excellent books. Carhart had long been interested in the conservation library concept. In August 1957 he tried to sell *The Saturday Evening Post* an article about the Bibliographic Center in the Denver Public Library. In September 1957 he landed an article on Dr. Malcolm Weyer in *Better Homes and Gardens*.

8. Sport-LORE was incorporated in Colorado in January 1948.

9. Letter from Carhart to Paul McCrea, editor of *The Nation's Business*, December 12, 1946, CC, DPL.

10. Arthur Carhart, "Raiders on the Range," *Trail and Timberline* 339 (March 1947):39–43; "Who Says—Sell Our Public Lands in the West?" *American Forests* 53 (April 1947):153–160; "Don't Fence Us In!" *Pacific Spectator* 1, 3 (Summer 1947); "Our Public Lands in Jeopardy," *Journal of Forestry* 46 (June 1948):409–413; "Land Grab: Who Gets Our Public Lands?" *Atlantic Monthly* 182 (July 1948).

11. Letter from Simpson to Carhart, March 31, 1948, CC, DPL.

12. Letter from writer in Ogden, Utah, to Carhart, April 2, 1948, CC, DPL.

13. Letter from Carhart to editor of *Cow Country*, January 31, 1948, CC, DPL.

14. Letter form Carhart to editor of *Cow Country*, February 7, 1949, CC, DPL.

15. Letter from Carhart to Clarence White , October 22, 1953, CC, DPL.

16. Letter from Carhart to Remington, August 3, 1953, CC, DPL.

17. Letter from Carhart to DeVoto, March 1, 1954, CC, DPL.

18. *Saturday Review* January 1955.

19. Letter from Olsen to Carhart, June 21, 1955, CC, DPL.

20. Herbert Kaufman, *The Forest Ranger: A Study in Administrative Behavior* (Baltimore: Johns Hopkins University Press, 1960).

21. Arthur Carhart, TREES and GAME—*Twin Crops* (Washington, DC: American Forest Products Institute, 1958).

22. Letter from Carhart to Art Van Vlissingen, September 5, 1958, CC, DPL.

23. Letter from Carhart to Van Vlissingen, August 22, 1958, CC, DPL.

24. Letter from DeLong to Carhart, October 11, 1956, CC, DPL.

25. Weyerhaeuser admired Carhart and Carhart's books. He died in December 1956, a loss to conservation as great as that of DeVoto. See his correspondence with Carhart of October 26 and November 5, 1956, CC, DPL.

26. Letter from Carhart to Orell, October 29, 1956, CC, DPL.

27. Letter from Carhart to Orell, December 8, 1956, CC, DPL.

28. Letter from Orell to Carhart, October 16, 1956, CC, DPL.

29. Letter from Carhart to Sandvig, January 9, 1958, CC, DPL: "So I've said in a pretty blunt fashion that unless they make coordinated, all-use plans, based on sound study by qualified land-use planners, and make these other values available, the public will demand condemnation of the lands to make state parks, local picnic and community camp grounds, whole basins condemned or hell raised because some politico starts shouting the company's harvest plan jeopardizes local water supply, and the sportsmen are going to hunt and fish—period. You may have seen my article in TIMBERMAN. They better get Carhart on a consultant basis."

30. Arthur Carhart, *The National Forests* (New York: Alfred A. Knopf, 1959).

31. Arthur Carhart, "The First Ranger," *American Forests* 62 (February 1956) on William Kreutzer in Colorado, 1898–1939.

32. Wallace Stegner, ed., *This Is Dinosaur: Echo Park Country and Its Magic Rivers* (New York: Knopf, 1955).

33. See the review by Professor Bernard Frank of Colorado State University in *The Living Wilderness* (July 1960).

34. See pp. 141ff. Wallace Stegner's biography of John Wesley Powell, *Beyond the Hundredth Meridian*, had appeared in the spring of 1954.

35. Letter from Carhart to Earl Sandvig, January 9, 1958, CC, DPL.

36. Letter from Carhart to Sigurd Olson, April 27, 1956, CC, DPL.

37. See Sheffey's and Carhart's correspondence, June 9 and June 25, 1958, CC, DPL.

38. Letter from Kneipp to Sheffey, September 4, 1958, CC, DPL.

39. Letter from Sheffey to Carhart, September 13, 1958, CC, DPL.

40. Letter from Carhart to Sheffey, September 17, 1958, CC, DPL.

41. Ibid.

42. Letter from Sheffey to Kneipp, September 13, 1958, CC, DPL.

43. Letter from Kneipp to Sheffey, September 28, 1958, CC, DPL.

44. Letter from Carhart to Sierra Club, January 7, 1954, CC, DPL.

45. A copy of the minutes of the Sierra Club board meetings is in the CC, DPL.

46. These ideas eventually bore fruit in the Land and Water Conservation Fund. For good or for ill, the fund covers acquisition only, leaving Congress—and the Park Service—in control of funding for other purposes that traditionally remain neglected.

47. Mark Harvey, *A Symbol of Wilderness: Echo Park and the American Conservation Movement* (Albuquerque: University of New Mexico Press, 1994), 31. I thank Professor Harvey for his insights about Carhart's relations with Echo Park and with Zahniser.

48. Letter from Carhart to Chapman, June 30, 1950, CC, DPL: "I'm grieved that you made the decision as you have. . . . [T]hat is the real indication of what lies ahead—

the raiding of the national park system throughout for irrigation and power dams first, any other uses serving commerce on the heels of such dams."

49. See Harvey, *Symbol of Wilderness*, 223.

50. Letter from Carhart to Martin Litton, August 3, 1953, CC, DPL.

51. Arthur Carhart, "The Menaced Dinosaur National Monument," *National Parks Magazine* 26 (January–March 1952): "[T]he canyons within Dinosaur are, in fact, a succession of smashing gorges between amphitheaters, where the serried cliffs sweep back, and bottomlands afford generous locations for tourist accommodations."

52. Letter from DeVoto to Carhart, January 4, 1955, CC, DPL. A copy of this letter is also in Box 6, DeVoto Papers, DPL.

53. Letter from Carhart to Grant, January 17, 1953, CC, DPL.

54. Letter from Carhart to Eisenhower, March 24, 1954; letter from Eisenhower to Carhart, April 7, 1954; both in CC, DPL.

55. Letter from Carhart to Zahniser, January 12, 1957, CC, DPL.

CHAPTER FOURTEEN

AN OLD BUCK, ALWAYS OFF
THE RESERVATION AND HUNTING LONELY

Let someone who might prowl my papers in the Conservation Library
Center some years hence find the facts "hitherto unreported," and gather
stature as a researcher thereby, or tell the facts, as stripped of personality
and impulses as possible, double-stripped with your help, and say, in effect
"This is historical fact of importance" and let the chips fall. Certainly I can't
be accused of any adverse feeling toward NPS [National Park Service] and
the parks; I've fought, sometimes pretty much alone, for Dinosaur, Teton,
against Yellowstone dams, as early as 1920 for the Great Sand Dunes.
So—What's the verdict?

—CARHART TO SAMUEL DANA[1]

INTRODUCTION: I'M A NONCONFORMIST, TOTALLY

Having ridden out the Depression at his typewriter, Carhart retained a vivid
sense of the value of a dollar to the end of his life.[2] Arthur and Vee had inherited their parents' old-fashioned work ethic, and they fully intended to toil as
long as they were able. They had taken George Carhart into their home. They
entered their old age beset by health problems. Carhart gamely "played hurt,"
remaining productive until his stroke in 1966 and then persevering until his
death at age eighty-six in 1978.

Family prevailed. A few months after Vee's death from cancer on January
29, 1966, Arthur suffered a major stroke that left him mute and partially par-
alyzed. During his rehabilitation, he worried over selling his home with its
beloved mature landscaping (apples, grapes, cherries, aspen), and he agonized
over leaving Colorado when there was still so much to be done for conservation.
Although he considered retiring to Mapleton, encouraged by "Judge" Whiting

during a final 1968 visit, he settled on a retirement home in southern California in 1969. Lemon Grove was a poor choice to begin with, and Carhart was difficult to please in an institutional setting. Peace arrived in the form of Joy Carhart Fuenzalida, a cousin once removed. She had been born and raised in Mapleton before marrying and moving to California, where she was widowed. Her capacious house sat in the midst of an avocado grove. There she granted Carhart the dignity of spending the final years of his life.[3] He called his office "the Crow's Nest," and he liked to sit and gaze out over the avocado trees, pondering the meaning of a life that began with a love of trees. There was ample precedent for such a display of family values, as one can see in Carhart's correspondence with family members in the 1960s—especially those who had moved west from Iowa to Nebraska, where they prospered in the lumber business.

Carhart had a touch of drama about him, even as a child holding out his bowl and crying "poor boy!" Yet his needs and fears were real enough. His diminished capacity left him feeling vulnerable when Park Hill went through a period of "white flight" as African Americans arrived, sending the value of his sole significant asset plummeting. The year 1969 was a low point in Park Hill real estate values, but the house on Eudora Street had long since been paid for.[4] Although Arthur had worked at home, except during his stints in government jobs, he collected Social Security. And Sport-LORE provided a small but steady income until 1964. The Carharts had managed to travel extensively, although generally to destinations related to his writing. As they aged, both Carharts became more active in Vee's family faith: the Episcopalian Church, both in their local Park Hill parish, St. Thomas, and at St. John's, Denver's Episcopalian cathedral—the grounds of which McCrary, Culley, & Carhart had landscaped in the 1920s.

Carhart's curmudgeonliness and his nonconformist streak carried a price when he reached the age at which most people retire. He turned sixty-five in 1957. Although his books sold relatively well, he had long since learned that book royalties rarely provide a steady income. These personal financial realities may explain Carhart's constant grasping after money. He relished the freedom of getting paid to do and say as he pleased, especially when it came to his last works: telling his own version of early wilderness history at government expense. The government also paid Carhart $1,000 for his contributions to the Outdoor Recreation Resources Review Commission (ORRRC) report.

Carhart's annual consultant fee from the Conservation Library was $7,200 plus travel and expenses.[5] Because he was receiving Social Security, the Internal Revenue Service billed him for back taxes in 1964, claiming he was exceeding its revenue caps. Battling the zealous bureaucrats, as always, he told them he had no additional sources of income, except for the small Civil Service annuity he had finally wheedled out of a reluctant government.[6] The stakes were relatively small, but with Vee's cancer treatments eating away at their savings, Carhart left no stone unturned. Neither did the IRS, which pursued him again in 1965. During all this turmoil, Carhart managed to keep up payments on two life insurance policies. After Vee's death, he made Joy Carhart Fuenzalida the beneficiary.[7]

Carhart's modest personal finances and humble background may help explain his populist approach to public lands. He did not somehow mysteriously "fail" to support the Wilderness Act of 1964, nor did he duck the battle to kowtow to potential funding sources for the Conservation Library. He wisely stepped aside from the fray because he did not like the way the bill pandered to special interests rather than serve the public interest. After half a century of active participation in public lands politics, he understood that every interest group scrambles to socialize costs but privatize benefits, leaving organizations like the Forest Service and the Park Service with unfunded mandates they sometimes cover with devious budget maneuvers. The agencies were hardly passive participants in the struggle for money and power. The overzealous "burocrats" had their own goals and incentives, which sometimes did not serve the public interest. Although often wavering, Carhart's faith in the public trust lived to see in ORRRC a final chance to put real money into recreation, including wilderness. By Carhart's populist standards, ORRRC may have failed, but it was not for want of Carhart's trying to provide a consistent flow of funds for maintenance and management of wildlands recreation.

In 1958, Congress started the first Outdoor Recreation Resources Review Commission, which reported in 1962 with *Outdoor Recreation for America.* Carhart tried mightily to influence the outcome, mostly through Wayne Aspinall and the Citizens Committee on Outdoor Recreation. As Carhart himself had done on behalf of various sporting magazines, ORRRC conducted surveys. And as Carhart already knew, ORRRC's surveys found that pleasure driving was the most popular form of outdoor recreation. ORRRC also recommended legislation creating wilderness areas, and Carhart timed his final book to influence the wilderness debate by framing it within the larger terms of *Planning for America's Wildlands.* Meanwhile, Carhart tried to help the National Park Service (NPS), both through articles about Echo Park and other, less visible national monuments and also through support for Conrad Wirth's Mission 66, which pumped up NPS budgets, providing $1 billion over ten years.

While Carhart was publishing his books about recreation, forestry, and the history of the Forest Service, the agency was undergoing a radical change. Gone was the relatively passive caretaker role of the first fifty years, as Forest Service timber harvest levels mushroomed from 3 billion board-feet in 1945 to

12 billion in 1970. In a related development, roads to access remote timber and fight fire and pests went from a total of 100,000 miles in 1945 to 160,000 miles in 1960, when the Forest Service released "Operation Multiple Use," calling for an additional 400,000 miles of developed roads by 2000.[8] Beset by critics, top Forest Service personnel began to woo their sometime adversary, who responded by hornswoggling Forest Service historians into letting him write his own history of the idea of wilderness.[9]

FRY-ARK: MR. CARHART IS NOT A CONSERVATIONIST, HE IS A DISTORTIONIST

Politics were such that water and wilderness were forever entangled. And regardless of whether conservationists liked Wayne Aspinall, conservation legislation had to go through him. Carhart learned this the hard way when he discovered that he had outlived all his San Isabel Protection and Recreation Association–era contacts in the Pueblo business community. Around 1950, the Pueblo Chamber of Commerce began to rally support for a Bureau of Reclamation project that would take water from the Western Slope's Fryingpan River and pump it through tunnels under the Continental Divide and down into the Arkansas River. In 1953, Carhart wrote to the Sierra Club: "I was growling about the Arkansas diversion project as much as 6 years ago but nobody got stirred up then about it."[10] Carhart had indeed stood pretty much alone in opposing this project with his usual invective. He met his match when *The Pueblo Star-Journal and Sunday Chieftain* lit into him in an editorial: "Mr. Carhart is not a conservationist, he is a distortionist."[11] Carhart fired back, noting that the publisher, Frank Hoag, was also a director of the Water Development Association of Southeastern Colorado.

The hole card in such rough-and-tumble games was always Echo Park, which rose from the dead each time another project proposal came online. Conservationists would find themselves whipsawed, as when Democratic governor Steve McNichols supported the Fryingpan-Arkansas Project in 1957, claiming it was better for Colorado than Echo Park. Meanwhile, *The Denver Post*'s editorial writers thought Coloradoans should have all these projects, based on the paper's position that the reservoirs associated with dams attract tourists. Conservationists felt beleaguered, as Carhart told the paper's editors:

> Most conservationists have favored Glen Canyon, Flaming Gorge, and emphatically much more attention to watershed protection and management than we have had. As one interested in true conservation and all-use planning and utilization of our natural wealth, I would welcome a chance to plug a bit for the Upper Colorado project program as we all can support it. We

have enough constructive things to do that it can be a disservice to the area to try to puff the breath of life into the quite dead Echo Park dam proposal as a group of our governors have tried recently, and keep controversy in that quarter alive.[12]

OUTDOOR RECREATION RESOURCES REVIEW COMMISSION

One of the plums that fell from Aspinall's ORRRC tree was the assignment for Carhart to write about the history of recreation planning under the direction of Dean Samuel T. Dana of the University of Michigan. As part of his research, Carhart asked Joe Penfold who should get the credit for ORRRC. Penfold's emphatic answer: Aspinall.[13]

In January 1964, Carhart's heart problems prevented him from testifying about the 1964 Wilderness Bill at regional meetings of Aspinall's subcommittee—or at least that is what he told Aspinall.[14] At the same time, Carhart was helping both the Wilderness Society and the Dude Ranchers Association prepare their testimony, so he was certainly as active as circumstances would permit. Carhart supported Aspinall's reelection in 1964, at a time when many conservationists backed Aspinall's Republican opponent. Carhart did not see it that way, nor did Penfold—by then the top figure at the Izaak Walton League's Washington office. Penfold was also chair of the Rockefeller-financed Citizens Committee for the Outdoor Recreation Resources Review Commission Report (CORC). CORC was designed to provide "guidance" to Aspinall's committee as it drafted legislation related to outdoor recreation planning, land acquisition, wilderness, and development. In 1964 this effort finally led to Aspinall's Land and Water Conservation Fund Bill. In 1965 the Izaak Walton League gave Aspinall its Founders Award.

Carhart and Penfold valued Aspinall's ability to deliver on his promises. In his 1964 reelection campaign, Aspinall faced a tough battle in a redrawn district. In an effort to help Aspinall, Carhart turned to friends in the dude ranch industry: "As you well know, I'm a lifetime, registered Republican. But I vote for the man and I suspect you do. You're a conservative, and I guess I am."[15] Carhart also appealed to friends in wildlife management, especially Professor J.V.K. Wagar at Colorado State University: "I don't get into politics much. . . . Anyway, as you probably know, I've been a registered Republican all my life, but I'm not hide-bound about it."[16]

Carhart's final word before the election (which Aspinall won) illustrates his mature political thinking:

> I do not know Wayne's opposition. He's a Republican. But I'd bet a bushel of sheckles [sic] that he is closer tied in with the exploitive bunch than Wayne.

With the segment of the livestock interests who want someone in Congress to "represent them"; the same with mining and related resource users.

The picture in the western states is badly distorted in this respect in this area of Congressional representation. By the donation to campaign expenses and "ties" with livestock and related interests, the stockmen, cow and sheep, lay a foundation for support for their askings and demands and they whoop it up by getting all chamber of commerce members to dress up like cowboys on the slightest provocation. The inclusive effect is, that they create a belief that theirs is the "vote of the west."

The blunt facts are, that we have passed out of the pastoral stage of free range, into the ranching stage, and into the agricultural stage. We're moving out from that. And, we are destroying capital stock in our tourist-recreation industry by continuing to over-use watersheds, fill streams with silt, dry them up, and try to induce tourism which will not come to see a used-up country. I've told you I believe Wayne hauled out as good a bill as he could with a predominantly western membership of his House committee, so far as wilderness goes.[17]

RESOURCES FOR THE FUTURE

Carhart's ties to the Republican Party and the Rockefellers paid off. He contributed to the water portions of the 1960 Republican platform and wrote parts of the 1964 platform. A letter from Horace Albright to Carhart recalls the tenor of the times among conservationists: "I personally like Nixon and think he would make a great President but I agree there are a lot of people who do not like him and who think he cannot win."[18]

As president of Resources for the Future (RFF), a Ford Foundation–funded think tank, Albright tried throughout the 1950s to help Carhart with writing and consulting contracts. Carhart also had help from Wyoming governor Leslie Miller, who was on the board of RFF. Carhart asked Albright to appoint him to an executive position with RFF, adding "Within the past few years I have been offered the executive head position with two national conservation organizations, and the editorship of one of the three top outdoor magazines."[19] Miller told Carhart, "It appears it is just about going to be up to Albright and me to set up the Denver office and we have agreed that you will be on the staff. I am sure it will be an assignment with which you will be pleased."[20] None of these arrangements worked out, however, and by the end of 1953, Carhart was trying (without success) to get RFF to fund *Timber in Your Life*.

Carhart was sensitive about class relations, even as he tried to transcend class through his individualism. In 1960 he told Albright:

Arthur Carhart, 1961. Courtesy, Denver Public Library.

The most bitter aspect for me of Resources for the Future has been that with such a magnificent opportunity to carry this type of terribly, terribly necessary approach to natural resource conservation there has been such a compounding of high-falutin' and high-brow academic and pedagogic repeating of the sort of thing (statistics, "studies," monographs), that never get to the people with their desperate position of having their lives rest on the simple living and management of soil, water, atmosphere and green living things.

I guess, Horace, I'm a non-conformist, totally; an old buck always off the reservation and hunting lonely.[21]

THE CONSERVATION CONSULTANT

Carhart was not much more successful in his efforts to become a "conservation consultant" to the pulp and paper industry. Ding Darling teased him about this, calling him "Counselor-in-Conservation" to the timber and pulp folks.[22] Other conservationists, lacking both Darling's affection for Carhart and respect for his integrity, whispered that Carhart had sold out to industry interests. Stung, Carhart remarked:

> [Ira] Gabrielson was here with Mrs. G for dinner in August. We talked of the visitations I made to your region and Gabe answered a question I put by saying there had been some who remarked I'd sold out to the "lumber interests" by so doing. Subverted, in other words. And Gabe's remark to whoever said it was, "They picked a hell of a poor subject in Carhart to try to buy off if that's what they had in mind!"[23]

Carhart may have failed to ascend to an executive position in the conservation movement, but he did not lack recognition among his peers. In 1958 the Outdoor Writers of America presented him with its highest award through Denver publisher Alan Swallow, then president of the Colorado Authors League. Then he set to work on the book wilderness historian Roderick Nash, writing in the official magazine of the Wilderness Society, called the "first systematic statement of philosophy and policy in the nascent field of Wildland management."[24]

PLANNING FOR AMERICA'S WILDLANDS: I AM A HERETIC

It is a testament to the courage of Carhart's convictions that this volume appeared at all. Amid disappointments and setbacks, an aging Carhart worked on his final book, which took him longer than any other he had written. He was trying to sum up his career as a wildlands recreation planner, but he was also smarting from rejection by conservationists he regarded as fanatics: "It started because of my impatience with the extremists in the wilderness controversy, both the outdoor extremists and the 'practical' people who screamed about 'locking up' material values."[25] He told an industry friend, "To tell the truth, I began writing it because I was irritated by the extremist purists among the 'sanctified wilderness' people."[26]

The fiercely independent Carhart was accustomed to writing for conservation-minded editors like Alfred Knopf. But he made a poor choice when he agreed to accept payment for his book from the very people who might be regarded as extremists and purists. Things got worse when some of his funders reneged on their promises. Carhart accepted an advance of $3,000 from the Wildlife Management Institute in November 1958, telling Pink Gutermuth that this would be his definitive work on planning for dominant use rather than segmented use—or even the multiple use he despised because it was "laminated" rather than integrated. The National Wildlife Federation's Charles Callison was also interested, but he could not come up with the money Carhart felt was due him, leaving the entire effort strapped for cash. The good-natured Gutermuth accelerated payment of another $1,000, but by then Carhart was plainly aggrieved that the Wilderness Society and others had not fulfilled their commitments. In an effort to clear the air, Carhart waived royalties to his book, an unusual step for him.

Although a groundbreaker in many ways, as Roderick Nash correctly perceived, the book suffered from composition by committee. It reflected all the tensions of a conservation community finally nearing the promised land of a wilderness bill that Congress could pass and the president could sign. Further, Carhart encountered his usual stylistic problems when he tried to "write up" to a sophisticated audience.

The more he (and his funders) wrestled with the conundrum of wilderness management, the more it changed shape. The book's tortured logic and category chopping reflect the many changes Carhart had to make in his text, responding to his funders and sponsors, chiefly Zahniser at the Wilderness Society and Gabrielson at the Wildlife Management Institute. Zahniser sent Gabrielson a six-page, single-spaced critique of one of Carhart's drafts in October 1959, mostly objecting to terminology and to Carhart's concept of requiring buffer zones around any designated wilderness. Carhart responded good-naturedly to this critique, admitting, "I let the Wilderness Bill get into this booklet [in draft]. It has no proper place there."[27]

In his introduction, Zahniser emphasized private initiatives, both corporate and individual, in protecting wilderness. Adding to the confusion, he interchanged the terms "wilderness" and "wildness," and then he tried to distinguish something he called "wildlands" from both. Zahniser wrote:

For Mr. Carhart is a landscape architect, a land-use planner who brings to the consideration of the conflicting uses proposed for our wildlands the zoning skills that have become so effectual in dealing with similar conflicts for the use of areas within our cities. To his training in the application of zoning principles he has added long experience in the wildlands. And with all his land-planning objectivity he has the conscience of a conservationist and a love for the wild outdoors. He is in a position to propose a sound orderliness in wildland management that can reasonably meet all needs and yet protect in various zones the quality of wildness and provide also for the preservation of the ultimate form of wilderness.

Zahniser went on to praise Carhart's "central regard for orderliness in accommodating various and conflicting land uses while cherishing always the quality of wildness," adding that "all the wildlands to be cherished need not be subject to wilderness standards."

Seemingly at a loss for his own words, Zahniser simply quoted from the work he was introducing. Carhart wrote:

Physically, wildlands begin wherever we face away from the man-dominated landscape of farm, town, city or any landscape grossly modified by human occupancy maintained for any purpose. From this spot the wildlands extend in graduated degrees of lessening human influence in the natural landscape, outward, to reach their type climax in the wilderness. Thus the term "wildlands" is more than a synonym for the term "wilderness"; wildlands are the wilderness plus all the surrounding lands that lie between genuine wilderness, as exemplified by the totally natural landscape, and those landscapes where man's control and manipulations are immediately evident.

Zahniser finished with strong praise, which showed what the wilderness movement owed Carhart as well as Zahniser's respect for Carhart's influence with both timber and auto industry officials and the Republican Party.

It is an independent appraisal of our wildland needs and opportunities, not necessarily representing the policies, beliefs, or specific recommendations of any of the sponsoring organizations but dealing with some of their distinctive and common concerns in such a way as to be helpful to all. . . .
It is fitting that in the publication of Planning for America's Wildlands Arthur Carhart should have the sponsorship of the National Audubon Society, National Parks Association, Wildlife Management Institute, and the Wilderness Society.

Carhart appealed to the vital link between U.S. concepts of individualism and wilderness. He did not, however, always express that appeal in his usual simple language. He started out high-flown, only hitting his true stride at the end:

It is this implication, of being places of freedom rather than of danger that I would attach to the word wildlands. However, I would regard them as places in which men are challenged—to think, reason, even dare to find and practice techniques of simple survival. . . . These are the acres where Americans can find the fullest freedom that is theirs, and in finding it, knowingly or subconsciously realize that this freedom has as its very core, common self-discipline.

For if there is one lesson sojourning in the wildlands can teach it is the individual's responsibility to the community. . . . You obey the natural law of the wildlands on your own initiative or you get hurt. In a city you are constantly pushed into conformity. In the wildlands you must live as part of that community voluntarily. [Wildlands are] the greatest proof we have of that old expression, "This—is a free country! Ain't it?"

Carhart stung the "We-Gotta-Do-Sompin" tribe of natural resource "managers" who want to "improve" wildlands. But he also struck a note new to the argument: "The persons most likely to destroy the finest qualities of the wildlands will be the unimaginative, insensitive gentry proposing that city-tinkered improvements be installed in rural and wild landscapes."

After long experience, Carhart knew the danger of "the breed of fixed-thinkers in land use planning [who] impose the templated recreational facilities of urban environment on the wildlands." Against these and other threats, he proposed a working definition of wilderness that accounted for human-induced changes in the past. But could he find a way for humans to inhabit wilderness in the present? He tried this version of wilderness: "It is land lacking permanent facilities and conveniences of any kind needed for human occupancy. Its natural attributes remain practically undisturbed by transient and impermanent human visitations."

Carhart knew that in the continental United States there were very few acres "where human beings have not trod." He knew from Trappers Lake that to set wilderness and humans against each other was to erect a false dichotomy. He himself did not fall for the fallacy of uninhabited wilderness, but he had to contend with Zahniser, for whom wilderness and humans seemed antithetical. As a way out of this impasse, Carhart applied his zoning concepts: "Wildland would be a portion of the earth's surface on which it is readily evident that the topography and ecological associations living thereon exist in relationships determined predominantly by natural laws and forces." Such wildlands begin with the belts around suburbs, where a person might face toward the true wilderness. Carhart had to tiptoe around the difficult subject of buffer zones around wilderness. Many wilderness advocates saw buffer zones as political obstacles to designating as much wilderness as possible. However, as a landscape architect, Carhart was interested in anything that blocks out "the feeling of man dominance." In discussing this threshold or transition zone, Carhart relied on his 1919 epiphany at Trappers Lake:

> Too much depends on the individual *experiencing* the entering of wildlands to have that line a fixed one. For each person finds the wildlands at a different point in a trek from urban-town surroundings to wilderness environment. And each person finds his or her wilderness at a different point on the trail from this semi-suburban belt to unmistakable wilderness. . . . The recreational use of the wildlands of any type is an *experience*. These landscapes, what they contain, as physical attributes, the emotions and reactions they generate—the end product is something that comes into being, remains in your recollections, *within your mind* [emphasis in the original].

And then he wandered off into a landscape that was at once therapeutic, political, religious—even millenarian:

> The wildland environment is the one most effective therapy we have to protect Americans against extreme-isms of all kinds. It is the antidote, almost specific, against the dictatorships we have lumped under the term "communism." It is equally the antidote for the dictatorships called "fascism." . . . We need this therapy. We need this re-creation for presidents, chairmen of the boards, policemen, barbers, clothing store clerks and husbands of women who have driven them into politics so social ambitions may be realized. We need it for career women, female executives and mothers who would give to their children understanding of the Omnipotent Entity we speak of fervently as "God." We need it for conservationists! No leadership that has true goals of service to our kind can do without this readjustment after too much city. No nation can do without the leadership that draws wisdom and force from the "Something" that speaks to us only in the great quietude of God's Country. And we've got to preserve enough of this country that can engender that leadership—or we perish!

More of this windy prose followed, in which Carhart addressed his reader as "Mister." The winds calmed in a chapter on "Dominant Use vs. Multiple Use," where Carhart showed that he had listened carefully to those in the Forest Service who work on the ground and who must try to implement the latest fads in resource planning: "In many cases multiple use has degenerated into layering. Each specialist works up a layout for the planning unit as if his specialty were the only one in highest priority."

Earning his keep, Carhart also examined the planning provisions of the Multiple Use–Sustained Yield Act of 1960:

> Even on those areas that have been dedicated to continue as "wilderness," there may be other than wilderness recreation uses that should take prece-

dence there. Nevertheless if the areas are to continue to have a wilderness character the use that takes precedence should be consistent with the preservation of the wilderness character of the area.

Conversely, other acres, threatened with destruction of wilderness-use-values, or already damaged, should have total wilderness reserve status forthwith.

Carhart told his readers that the U.S. political approach to wilderness designation, dominated by interest groups, had served its citizens poorly compared to "a systematic, studied approach to land use planning of wildlands, based on intelligently determined, best sited use and uses for a piece of land, that will avoid impulsive, emotional, dollar-chasing or one-use land management." He portrayed the management of a watershed according to dominant use principles. He knew intimately the Rawah area in northern Colorado on the Roosevelt National Forest, so he could emphasize water collection and delivery as the dominant use for the Roosevelt, with the Rawah's recreation values as a subset. It is worth noting that Carhart did not categorically exclude grazing or reasonable timber harvest at the right elevations as part of wildlands watershed management.

Carhart also suggested that planners develop a sort of "scorecard." This idea resembled the linear programming matrices planners of his time were beginning to adapt from military to natural resource uses. But he did not seem to realize that the demands for quantification inherent in such matrices would give short shrift to recreation—especially to aesthetic and spiritual values. Instead, Carhart returned to one of his main themes: "Remember—planning human use of wildlands for recreational purposes is the reverse of planning for Metropolitan needs. In city planning you manipulate land and what is on it to fit the city dweller routines. In planning wildlands for recreation you plan the use so as to fit the use to Nature's regiments."

When it came to dealing with those he regarded as wilderness extremists and purists, Carhart wanted the last word (even if he could not resist a bewildering array of quotation marks):

> Those who have been lumping all types and concepts of wildlands together and calling them all "wilderness," particularly those who insist that only where the natural environment is absolute, truly virgin, can there be "wilderness," may protest these listings [of wildland recreation zones]. To argue that "wilderness" is anything less than physically "virgin" may be heresy. If so, I am a heretic. I do not argue that there can be any gradations of virginity. I do argue that there may be gradations in the physical attributes representing the wildness of wildlands which, as in other areas of human experience, may be as gratifying to those associating with it as absolute virginity—perhaps even more so.

With all its faults, *Planning for America's Wildlands* did succeed in setting the stage for the 1964 Wilderness Act. Somehow, it helped create consensus, especially by appealing to the better instincts of the timber and auto industries.

I'M STARTING A NEW CAREER AT 70; AS A LIBRARIAN, YET!

As he struggled to finish *Planning for America's Wildlands*, Carhart frequently visited with his friend, City Librarian John Eastlick, who agreed that the Denver Public Library should house a conservation collection, beginning with Carhart's papers. Meanwhile, Carhart experienced increasing frustration as a freelancer. His long-standing ambition to succeed Bernard DeVoto failed when he ran afoul of the new editors at *Harper's*:

> I suppose I lost a market when I wrote Fisher and told him exactly my convictions of the disservice he had performed in this grubby article. But I'm getting along far enough that I don't care to be mealy-mouthed any longer. Benny DeVoto sometimes wrote so emphatically it's a wonder he didn't break out of the envelope and cause consternation in the PO department. And I'm inclined now to use harsh words at times. Seriously, Grace [Naismith], there are some such stupid things being hailed as shining progress in conservation fields that someone must rise up and remark how putrescent they really are.
>
> Stafferism reduces a whole magazine to a one-note melody. Ultimately, it will conformerize the entire magazine field. . . . But under the present staff-and-trained-seal writing, the free-thinking, freelancing scribe is being liquidated. All you have to do is look around the Colo. Authors League, and you can see the trend. As for me, I'm starting a new career at 70; a Librarian, yet![28]

The Conservation Library dominated the rest of Carhart's life. Andrew Kirk has told this story well.[29]

THE WILDERNESS BILL: BOTH JOE
AND I ARE BOTHERED BY THE WHOLE THING

In the later Eisenhower years and the transition to Kennedy's administration, conservationists struggled over whether to focus their wildlands planning efforts on the specific issue of wilderness. Bernard Orell was a key figure in wilderness circles, because of his strong connections with the Rockefellers and his position with Weyerhaeuser. Carhart told Orell:

> A mimeo sheet came in from Sierra Club t'other day that indicates an incli-nation to expand considerably the wilderness reserves, I've had more on the

bill or bills that may be in next Congress, everyone seems to be getting all
whooped up to "write a book" about wilderness and related stuff, and all this
seems to [be] bustin' out all over. Both Joe [Penfold] and I are bothered
by the whole thing; I had a long phone discussion with him yesterday about
it. We both feel there's pressing need for those who are not at the extreme
points of view on this subject to get down to brass tacks and try to pull a
sound, all-resource, "dominant use" sort of land-use planning program out
of the fires.[30]

In 1958, Carhart used the occasion of an interview with *The Denver Post*
to hammer the Wilderness Society for its rigid definition of wilderness.[31]
Members of the Wilderness Society responded by calling him a waffler and
a sellout. Carhart told the *Post*: "I recognize that the bill may be necessary to
protect the wilderness, but it is only a portion of the all-inclusive plan we need
for the recreational use of all our public land."

Carhart's seeming heresies came to the attention of John Oakes of *The
New York Times*, who wrote to Carhart: "I am interested and surprised by your
remarks on the Wilderness bill. When you get a chance, give me the benefit of
your views at greater length."[32] Having consulted with the Muries, Gabrielson,
and Sigurd Olson, Carhart replied to Oakes:

> This must not be taken as opposition to any bill regarding the wilderness
> safeguards that should be passed. [If we tried the dominant use approach]
> we'd have far more wilderness than if the program is to set up some proce-
> dure for the folk who want to protect wilderness to slice out chunks of the
> public lands, tag them for their one particular use without integration and
> correlation of uses on adjacent lands and other important considerations,
> and then say to other interests: "We've stripped out the tenderloin; here's the
> rest of the carcass—you do what you want to do with it."[33]

Carhart told Oakes the "wilderness effect" was also important:

> To grab wilderness, then run for our tepee, on the basis of "this is for this
> and we let you take the rest," may deny us *wilderness effect* recreation in
> many, many more acres of high recreational use. . . . But by golly! If we have
> conservationists doing in *essence* exactly what we so roundly damn when
> other special interests try to grab a chunk of public property for their own,
> one-use purposes, all of us are going to be without one of the most potent
> arguments for *conservation as such* [emphasis in the original].[34]

Carhart was also concerned about the poor quality of many areas proposed
as wilderness, especially those—such as the Sangre de Cristo Mountains in
Colorado and New Mexico's Sandia Mountains—that lacked sufficient buffer zones to protect them from inappropriate adjacent uses. As the wilderness

debate waxed and waned, environmentalists such as Kay Collins, Carhart's fiery choice to head the Conservation Library, found these buffering concepts especially offensive. C. K. Collins, Kay Collins's father, took Carhart's side: "I am also working to block some of the proposed Wilderness Areas. The Wilderness Society is out to grab acreage without regard to quality. . . . The restrictions in the Act prevent restoration programs. The term Wilderness now means just any old piece of beat up country no matter the condition."[35]

I'M WEARY KIDS; SO GOOD NIGHT

During all the turmoil over the Wilderness Bill and the Conservation Collection, Vee Carhart was in and out of the hospital with various illnesses first judged to be influenza. Then in 1965 the diagnosis was changed to stomach cancer. Vee stayed in Denver's Mercy Hospital, where the parishioners of St. Thomas Episcopal Church conducted a laying on of hands ceremony for her on January 12. She died on January 29, 1966.

Vee's death robbed Carhart of the most important nurturing and stabilizing influence in his life. Although he lived twelve more years, the usually genial curmudgeon became increasingly querulous. Without Vee, it was only a matter of time until Carhart suffered a stroke, which he did on May 18, 1966. It sent him first to the hospital and then into rehabilitation. A succession of housekeepers only made things worse. He told his colleagues at the library, "I need steno help to do anything. To write a letter of resignation. . . . I'm weary kids. So Good Night. I'll keep you advised."[36] To his nephew Chuck Carhart in Neligh, Nebraska, he wrote: "I am plodding along a rough trail and more of the like is ahead."[37]

Carhart somehow rallied, as he always did, surviving to give his final interview in 1976 to *Outdoor Life*:

> It was a stroke, and doctors told Carhart he would never walk again. But they didn't know Art Carhart, the self-made man. He would teach himself to walk just as he'd taught himself to play musical instruments well enough to pay for his education at Iowa State College in Ames. In the Army he'd taught himself microbiology and had been awarded a commission for his work as a sanitation engineer. Later he had taught himself to write professionally, and he'd mastered the basics of wildlife biology. This was no different. First, Carhart read up on anatomy to learn about muscles. A young nurse helped him devise some exercises. Almost miraculously, Carhart's health began to return. Once, I offered to help him out of a car. He frowned, and I stepped back. "I have to do it myself," he told me, getting out and onto his feet. "I told you I'm stubborn."[38]

SPECIAL REPORT ON WILDERNESS

Carhart sold his personal library and his home in Colorado in 1969. He stayed in touch with old friends, such as Ed Hilliard's widow, Joy, who sent him a Christmas card in 1974. In the fall of 1975 she was following his wilderness history, telling him how happy she was that he was fleshing out Donald Baldwin's work: "Your book will give substance to Baldwin's book. . . . Don's book lacked color, life, and warmth."[39]

No Carhart work ever lacked color, life, and warmth. When the Forest Service hired a professional historian, Clifford Owsley, he looked into the ranks and found Robert Cermak, formerly the supervisor on Carhart's favorite forest, the San Isabel. Cermak was one of many in the Forest Service who felt the agency should manage Carhart's wilderness memories as carefully as it managed wilderness itself. After reviewing Cermak's history of recreation management on the San Isabel, Owsley told Forest Service chief John McGuire: "This shows Art is a genuine statesman of wilderness and regional planning, and there is not many of those around!"[40] Soon Owsley and Cermak were asking for help from Carhart,[41] who played hard to get until he heard directly from the chief of the Forest Service:

> All of us in the Forest Service owe you much gratitude—for your early
> work in recreation planning on Colorado's San Isabel National Forest, for
> your vision of wilderness in the Trappers Lake area, for your determination
> in establishing the Conservation Library, and for your authorship over the
> years of so many works on resource management. We hope your pen continues to stay active.[42]

Meanwhile, Owsley delivered a paper at Yale to the Western History Conference titled "Opportunities in Forest Service Historical Research," in which he said:

> Stirrings of interest in a better organized history effort in the Forest Service
> began in the 1960s, when Arthur H. Carhart started the Conservation
> Library, and came to Washington to ask that the Forest Service begin to
> send papers and documents to the Conservation Library.
>
> Arthur H. Carhart, as a young landscape architect in 1919, applied the
> first de facto concept of Wilderness on the White Mountain and San Isabel
> National Forests of Colorado. Now a well-known conservation giant, the
> author of twenty-four published books, Carhart is nearing the end of yet
> another one, tentatively called *This Way to Wilderness*—his own personal
> story of how the Wilderness concept was born on the National Forests.
>
> This story—of how the National Forests gave birth to the Wilderness
> concept—has already been done in a doctoral dissertation by Dr. Donald

Baldwin, late of the Denver Public Library, whose untimely death of a heart attack September 25, of this year shocked all who knew him. His book, being published by the Pruett Press, Boulder, Colorado, will be off the presses any day now.[43]

Carhart had somehow convinced Owsley that he practically had a manuscript in hand. Owsley wrote Carhart:

> Regarding the publishing of your book, THIS WAY TO WILDERNESS, have you made any contact with your publisher, Alfred A. Knopf? If not, there is a good chance that the Wilderness Society will want to publish it.
>
> I have talked with Paul Oehser, Treasurer and PR man for the Society, and he said the Society would be most interested in considering the manuscript.[44]

Carhart was working on a chronology, but he knew it was not the narrative Owsley wanted. Nonetheless, the Forest Service paid Carhart to travel to Washington to try to straighten things out. Owsley persisted:

> Art, I understand some of the difficulties under which you labor, but I feel compelled to call attention to the book project which was originally to have been completed in one year, from the date of beginning—March 3, 1971. It has now been two years and four months.
>
> I urge you to please proceed with the work as rapidly as possible, so that we can pay you the remaining $1,900. The Accounting Office is putting pressure on me, and I can only turn to you. Unfortunately, I have not been able to get the original amount raised, with the present tight budget situation the Forest Service is under!
>
> We are counting on you, Art, to finish it, and I know you will.[45]

Carhart kept angling for more time and money. Both were running out. In 1974 the Forest Service organized "Wilderness Appreciation Weeks." Carhart was invited, but he could not attend. Finally, Carhart submitted his chronology in December 1974, along with a cover letter saying this was what he and the Forest Service had agreed on, "to close up the work I had done on a book I had worked on for some time."[46]

But Carhart was not finished. He kept sending bits and pieces to Frank Harmon.[47] Meanwhile Owsley became ill and retired. He died in 1976, giving way to a new historian, David Clary.

Carhart never finished *This Way to Wilderness*. Given the nature of the subject, perhaps no one ever could. Thanks to Joy Carhart Fuenzalida, he stayed active until his death, meeting with his old Pittman-Robertson crew in August 1978 and conducting a lively correspondence with Robert Cermak and Mardy Murie about wilderness and watershed planning.

NOTES

1. Letter from Carhart to Samuel Dana, February 2, 1962, Carhart Collection, Denver Public Library (hereafter CC, DPL).

2. Letter from Carhart to Horace Albright, undated, but probably late April 1960, CC, DPL.

3. Fuenzalida lived at 1386 Oak Hill Drive, Escondido, CA 92027.She accompanied Arthur to a National Wildlife Federation banquet and was mistaken for his wife. Neither she nor Carhart seemed to mind. See her letter of April 30, 1973, with photos, in the CC, DPL.

4. Letter from Carhart to James Irwin, May 17, 1958, CC, DPL: "The house is all paid for! Has been, for years, but in these days it seems an item worth mentioning."

5. Letter from Carhart to the Social Security Administration, March 29, 1963, CC, DPL.

6. See letter from Johnson to Carhart, November 16, 1954, CC, DPL.

7. Carhart had maintained his Iowa State Travelers policy since his marriage. He added a policy with Equitable Life Insurance after World War II. On January 10, 1962, Carhart wrote to his lawyer about changing his will, leaving most of his estate to the Denver Library Foundation. He converted his life insurance to a ten-year annuity in 1968, making the Conservation Library the beneficiary. He changed it again on May 13, 1976, making Joy Carhart Fuenzalida the beneficiary, with the Ding Darling Foundation as backup. No other family members received money from Carhart's estate, but he did divide his belongings among them when he left Denver. There are many family letters in his correspondence file, especially from Chuck Carhart. Joy Fuenzalida sent Carhart a birthday card in 1977: "You are a dear, and I sincerely hope that I'm able to enjoy your company for many more happy years. Joy." Carhart also left money to the Mapleton Library.

8. Forest Service figures from the Federal Budget (Washington, DC: Government Printing Office, various years).

9. See Robert W. Cermak, "In the Beginning: The First National Forest Recreation Plan," *Parks and Recreation* 9, 11 (November 1974):20–24, 29–33.

10. Letter from Carhart to Dick Leonard of the Sierra Club, August 25, 1953, CC, DPL.

11. August 31, 1952.

12. Letter from Carhart to Robert Lucas, editorial page editor, November 24, 1957, CC, DPL.

13. Letter from Penfold to Carhart, February 16, 1962, CC, DPL. On September 11, 1959, Penfold recommended Carhart to Francis Sargent, executive director of ORRRC, for public relations work. Bernard Orell seconded the recommendation.

14. Letter from Carhart to Aspinall, January 7, 1964, CC, DPL.

15. Letter from Carhart to Ralph Jordan, September 22, 1964, CC, DPL.

16. Letter from Carhart to Wagar, October 4, 1964. Wagar replied on October 7, 1964, telling Carhart he thought Aspinall should be replaced—and threatening to give the Colorado Wildlife Federation's papers to the University of Wyoming rather than the Conservation Library. Both letters are in the CC, DPL.

17. Letter from Carhart to Jordan, November 1, 1964, CC, DPL.

18. Letter from Albright to Carhart, April 19, 1960, CC, DPL.

19. Letter from Carhart to Albright, January 10, 1953, CC, DPL.

20. Letter from Albright to Carhart, February 7, 1953, CC, DPL.

21. This undated letter is probably from April 1960. In a July 22, 1959, letter to Penfold, Carhart repeated the details about RFF's Denver office. Both letters are in the CC, DPL.

22. Letter from Darling to Carhart, March 15, 1958, CC, DPL.

23. Letter from Carhart to Robert Beatty, December 28, 1957, CC, DPL.

24. Roderick Nash, "Arthur Carhart: Wilderness Advocate," *Living Wilderness* (December 1980):34.

25. Letter of May 21, 1961, to a fellow OWA member, CC, DPL.

26. Letter from Carhart to Stanton Mead, Consolidated Water Power and Paper Company, May 31, 1961, CC, DPL.

27. Letter from Carhart to Pink Gutermuth, WMI, and Zahniser, October 9, 1959, CC, DPL.

28. Letter from Carhart to Grace Naismith, June 15, 1962, CC, DPL.

29. Andrew Kirk, *The Gentle Science: A History of the Conservation Library* (Denver: Denver Public Library, 1995); Kirk, *Collecting Nature: The American Environmental Movement & the Conservation Library* (Lawrence: University of Kansas Press, 2001).

30. Letter from Carhart to Orell, November 29, 1956, CC, DPL. Carhart was also in direct contact with David Brower during this period. See letter from Carhart to Brower, January 15, 1959. See also Harold K. Steen, *The U.S. Forest Service: A History* (Seattle: University of Washington Press, 1976), 301–307, for a discussion of the grand-fathering issue.

31. Cal Queal, "Ah, Wilderness," *The Denver Post*, December 23, 1958, 18.

32. Letter from Oakes to Carhart, December 19, 1956, CC, DPL.

33. Letter from Carhart to Oakes, December 24, 1956, CC, DPL.

34. Ibid.

35. Letter from C. K. Collins to Carhart, April 8, 1977, CC, DPL.

36. Transcript of a tape Carhart sent to DPL staff, June 1977, CC, DPL.

37. Letter from Carhart to Chuck Carhart, December 9, 1967, CC, DPL.

38. William Vogt, "Art Carhart: A Man for the Wilderness," *Outdoor Life* (March 1976).

39. Letter from Joy Hilliard to Carhart, October 22, 1975, CC, DPL.

40. Letter from Owsley to McGuire, June 15, 1972, CC, DPL.

41. Letter from Owsley and Cermak to Carhart, July 2, 1972, CC, DPL.

42. Letter from McGuire to Carhart, September 18, 1972, CC, DPL.

43. Paper delivered on October 13, 1972.

44. Letter from Owsley to Carhart, October 17, 1972, CC, DPL.

45. Letter from Owsley to Carhart, July 19, 1973, CC, DPL.

46. Letter from Carhart to Owsley, December 16, 1974, CC, DPL.

47. Harmon kept trying to find Forest Service people who could move Carhart along to a finish. This included Regional Forester Craig Rupp, who had been supervi-

sor on the Superior and who told Carhart: "I accept stewardship for this wilderness legacy you established before leaving these mountains and will try to warrant the trust and confidence you have extended." Letter from Rupp to Carhart, July 23, 1976, CC, DPL. Conservationists will remember Rupp for ignoring formal Forest Service plans and ordering the liquidation of much of Colorado's remaining old-growth forests at the behest of the Reagan administration in the 1980s.

NOW A WELL-KNOWN CONSERVATION GIANT

Arthur Carhart knew that every interest group strives to socialize costs and privatize benefits. In contrast, he rose to national prominence as a spokesperson for the public interest, for the common person. He was a voice for moderation in conservation politics. He was never partisan. Whether he was writing about water or wilderness or grazing, his voice was distinctive and contrary, as if he were a twentieth-century Walt Whitman, a kindly curmudgeon of an uncle, appealing to the democratic best in us.

> I happen to be an American citizen, equal owner with you in these public lands, interested in their fullest productive use including proper grazing, and I'm willing to stand up and battle when any small clique cooks up a scheme to deliver my small shred of ownership in these lands, my interest, to a hand-picked group—and you'd feel the same way about it in all probability. The total disregard of other interests, the almost arrogant way in which those promoting this land sale idea have taken a demanding attitude

that if they ask for a thing they should be given it forthwith, is one of the grave errors, one of the most objectionable phases of their activities. The answer lies in cooperative, middle-course land use planning and management, with grazing in its proper position in the plan.[1]

SON OF THE FOREST

Carhart used his fiction to imagine mutually beneficial relations between humans and wildlands. His 1952 novel, *Son of the Forest*, sums up the major concerns of his entire career. Writing for boys and girls freed Carhart to write at his best. All his life he had criticized Forest Service bureaucrats who lacked the courage to oppose the small clique of politically powerful, land-grabbing ranchers who were trying to use mob rule tactics to privatize public grazing lands. Some ranchers had abused their public lands grazing allotments for so long that ecological conditions had declined into what Carhart called "tin roof watersheds."

Not content with the merely negative, Carhart used his novel to imagine better ranchers. His novel is for girls as well as boys, for it matches the daughter of a rancher with the son of a forester. Overseeing this match is a less bureaucratic Forest Service that stands up to interest groups (including narrow wilderness groups) and genuinely serves the people of the small, watershed-based political units he felt were more democratic and also more American than the vast, centrally controlled national forests. Today, watershed-wide conservation efforts are under way throughout the West, just as Carhart prophesied. Some are even experimenting with alternative procedures of governance and funding, especially with regard to recreation.[2]

Son of the Forest presents a richly peopled landscape somewhere along Colorado's Front Range, where the imaginary Shavano National Forest serves as the watershed for Denver. It is the job of the Forest Service to restore the watersheds of the Shavano to health. Young Jim, the would-be son of the forest, is seventeen. Jim is a bureau brat: the son of Glenn Craighead, a forest ranger on the Ragged Hills District, and the grandson of a forest ranger in Montana. Glenn Craighead is a range expert, formerly detailed to the regional office in Denver. Buried deep in Glenn's personnel file at Forest Service headquarters is a secret related to a long history of personal and professional conflicts over grazing. Now Glenn has been assigned to this dangerous district to solve resource abuse problems caused by a minority of local stockmen, who do not care that they are turning Ragged Hills into a tin roof watershed.

Because of the danger, Jim, an Eagle Scout, languishes at East High in Denver. He is safe with his mother near the City Park that gave the neighborhood of Park Hill its name. Meanwhile, his father takes on this sticky new

assignment. Stockmen unhappy about Forest Service attempts to reduce grazing and heal the watershed ran out the previous rangers. Ranger Craighead
tells his son, "Some of the higher-ups in the Forest Service will back me all the
way. Some won't. There are those who believe I speak out too plainly in dealing
with the ranchers." When school is out, Jim travels up to his father's Spartan,
isolated ranger station to spend the summer. But things have taken a turn for
the worse. Will Glenn Craighead have to turn tail and resign before fists and
guns drive him out?

Worthy of Ernest Thompson Seton, the book's frontispiece sports a tanta-
lizing, hand-drawn map of the imaginary Ragged Hills District. Phones exist,
but the party line renders them of dubious value in a hostile setting where it
seems everyone is listening in. Right off, the father gives his boy a man's job,
riding fence; and right off, Jim finds himself in a fistfight, mistaken in his
fresh-from-the-city duds for a greenhorn from a nearby dude ranch. A pretty
girl named Celia complicates things further when she reveals herself as the
daughter of Webb Stone, the leader of the rebellious ranchers.

Initially, Jim hides his true identity from Celia. He makes wise-cracking,
country-clever friends in Pete, the son of a sheep rancher, and Archie, a young
Navaho sheepherder. This triumvirate agrees that a rancher who is a good
steward of the public range is better than self-interested. "He's something
more," said Jim. "A darned good citizen."

The novel has three crises—one over predators, one over grazing, and
another over wildfire. In a setting where federal manpower is short, his father
presses Jim into service to deal with these crises. This crescendos into an
assignment as a fire lookout, where his Eagle Scout's mastery of Morse code
comes in handy. Good resides not in the city but in the forest, where one can
practice the virtues of private land stewardship and ownership possible only in
a watershed-wide setting that mixes private and public ownership but depends
on a general devotion to the public good. In the end, Jim and Celia and Archie
and Pete inherit the public lands and the public trust. The younger set shames
their parents into behavior worthy of real Americans. Daring to risk all by
standing up to Celia's powerful father, Jim says to rancher Webb Stone: "Don't
you think we kids should have something to say about damage to our forest
property? Do you grown-ups want merely to make a big profit now, and leave
us a bunch of beat-up tin roof watersheds? Are you going to give us the job of
trying to heal the injury you did to the range . . . and about break our hearts
doing it? Should we keep still?"

The youngsters become the children of the forest itself. They inherit the
public trust. Can the public lands forester's son win the daughter of a wealthy
private landowner? Only in America. Jim's reward for bravery under fire is that

his family is reunited, and he gets to transfer from East Denver High to nearby Clearwater High for his senior year:

> He let out a shout of sheer happiness. Suddenly it felt great to be a son of the forest. Pete yelled, too, and they jumped their horses into a run on the last bit of trail toward the station.
>
> As they pulled to a stop, Jim looked up to the forest-cloaked hills. He saw them mistily and they were beckoning to him. He stretched his arms wide. This was his country.

A cynical reader who smirks at this ending has forgotten his or her own youth—forgotten the capacity of the young for idealism and service. Perhaps it is the childless curmudgeons like Carhart who retain their ability to learn, to imagine a better world.

ORDINARY YOU-AND-ME WORDS

The testimonies of Carhart's contemporaries and peers provide the best conclusion to his life. In 1932, a reporter in Cañon City wrote:

> Mr. Carhart is one of Colorado's most noted authors and a great favorite with the local high school readers. He talked of his book, "The Last Stand of the Pack" which nearly every student in the school had read. He mentioned the characters of the book, most of them taken from real life, some being relatives of students in the audience.
>
> Mr. Carhart's popularity as a writer with the pupils was brought out when it was stated by the librarian, F. C. Kessler, that although there are seven copies of the book on the library shelves, books must be spoken for ahead to get them. Each of these seven books has been rebound, also testifying to their popularity with the students. . . . Mr. Carhart is a splendid talker and thrilled his young audience as he followed Pike through Colorado and spoke of places familiar to many of his listeners.
>
> One present at this talk said: "Mr. Carhart impressed the students deeply and awakened sympathy and appreciation of the work done by these men with a sense of gratitude."[3]

Roscoe Fleming was a longtime outdoors reporter for *The Denver Post* and *The Rocky Mountain News.* In 1955 he wrote: "Carhart at 49 is a pleasant gentleman, fairly tall and still built like a halfback, who can swing a pack and tramp a trail with any of them. He has brown eyes, dresses quietly, talks quietly, earnestly and sometimes a trifle dogmatically, wants to get back to writing sometime." Of *Timber in Your Life*, Fleming said: "It's a pleasure to read after a man who is so at home with his subject that he can convey its subtlest meaning in ordinary you-and-me words, such as Arthur Carhart of Denver."[4]

IT'S OUR JOB—A JOB FOR ALL OF US

The wisdom of hindsight tells us that Carhart was wrong about predators and wildfire. He never wrote his second wolf book. But his doubts about the Bureau of Biological Survey, the Forest Service, the National Park Service, and the Bureau of Reclamation help us see that we should consider changing the scale of natural resource administration. Instead of repeating the mistakes of the twentieth century, we are more likely to learn from the land if we learn the humility of working watershed by watershed. Carhart was certainly right about watershed health, both ecological and political. And a healthy watershed, we now know, balances humans and the wild, predators and wildfire.

Curmudgeons are idealists grown older and wiser. But they are still idealists in the fervent fashion of Ella Carhart's Methodism. They want to rebuild Jerusalem. Carhart was right to use the figure of an old man to describe his epiphany at Trappers Lake. He was right to cultivate a myth of inhabited wilderness that made him a prophet to the many and a heretic to the few. If we make a place for the human in the wild, we will do much to broaden the appeal of wildlands. But if we make wilderness but another bitterly partisan issue, we rob future generations of Americans of their birthright. Carhart's life shines so brightly because he exemplified the basic principle of all conservation: he showed us how to learn from our mistakes, how to be fair to the future by giving the past a vote.

Carhart lies buried next to Vee at Fairmount Cemetery in east Denver. Nearby runs the High Line Canal, bearing water from the snow-capped mountains to grow trees in the cities on the plain. The tree doctor and recreation engineer lived to see the High Line Canal Greenway, which was finished in 1974. It is part of a much larger greenway design that carries recreationists along canals and natural watercourses, linking open spaces by the use of bicycle and foot trails throughout Metropolitan Denver.[5]

The Carharts' graves are at ground level, marked only by small stones inscribed with their initials. Overhead: the spreading, sheltering branches of a green ash and a silver maple.

NOTES

1. Letter from Carhart to editor of *Sports Afield*, May 6, 1947, Carhart Collection, Denver Public Library.

2. William deBuys and Don Usner, *Valles Caldera: A Vision for New Mexico's National Preserve* (Santa Fe: Museum of New Mexico Press, 2006).

3. *Canon City Daily Record*, February 10, 1932.

4. *The Rocky Mountain News*, December 27, 1941; *The Denver Post*, January 30, 1955.

5. The High Line Canal is sixty-six miles long. It diverts the South Platte River at Waterton Canyon and carries its waters out to the former Rocky Mountain Arsenal, now a wildlife refuge. See http://www.denverwater.org/recreation/highline.html.

Abrams, M. H. *Natural Supernaturalism*. New York: Norton, 1973.

Albright, Horace, and Marian Albright Schenck. *Creating the National Park Service: The Missing Years*. Norman: University of Oklahoma Press, 1999.

———, as told to Robert Cahn. *The Birth of the National Park Service: The Founding Years 1913–1933*. Salt Lake City: Howe Brothers, 1985.

Austin, Mary. *The Land of Journeys' Ending*. New York: Century, 1924.

———. "Last Stand of the Pack." *Saturday Review of Literature*, December 21, 1929, 587.

———. *Earth Horizon: An Autobiography*. Boston: Houghton Mifflin, 1932.

Backes, David. "Wilderness Visions: Arthur Carhart's 1922 Proposal for the Quetico-Superior Wilderness." *Forest and Conservation History* 35 (July 1991): 22–25.

———. *A Wilderness Within: Life of Sigurd Olson*. Minneapolis: University of Minnesota Press, 1997.

Baden, John, and Pete Geddes. "Environmental Entrepreneurs." In *Symposium: Wilderness Act of 1964: Reflections, Applications, and Predictions. Denver University Law Review* 76, 2 (1999):49–51.

Baggs, Lacy Mae. *Colorado: Queen Jewel of the Rockies*. Boston: Page, 1918.

Baldwin, Donald. "Historical Study of the Western Origin, Application and Development of the Wilderness Concept." Ph.D. dissertation, University of Denver, 1965.

———. "Wilderness: Concept and Challenge." *Colorado Magazine* 44 (Summer 1967): 14–15.

———. *The Quiet Revolution: Grass Roots of Today's Wilderness Preservation Movement.* Boulder: Pruett, 1972.

Beveridge, Charles F., and Paul Rocheleau. *Frederick Law Olmsted: Designing the American Landscape.* New York: Rizzoli International, 1995.

Botkin, Daniel B. *Discordant Harmonies: A New Ecology for the Twenty-First Century.* New York: Oxford University Press, 1991.

Brosnan, Kathleen A. *Uniting Mountain and Plain: Cities, Law, and Environmental Change along the Front Range.* Albuquerque: University of New Mexico Press, 2002.

Brown, P. M., and R. Wu. "Climate and Disturbance Forcing of Episodic Tree Recruitment in a Southwestern Ponderosa Pine Landscape." *Ecology* 86 (2004):3030–3038.

Burton, Lloyd. *Worship and Wilderness: Culture, Religion, and Law in Public Lands Management.* Madison: University of Wisconsin Press, 2002.

Bush, Monroe. "Denver's Conservation Library." *American Forests* 77, 4 (April 1971):12–15.

Carhart, Arthur. Papers. Carhart Collection, Denver Public Library, Denver, CO.

Cermak, Robert W. "In the Beginning: The First National Forest Recreation Plan." *Parks and Recreation* 9, 11 (November 1974):20–24, 29–33.

Clepper, Henry. "American Forests: A Magazine of Record in Conservation." *American Forests* 80, 4 (April 1974):55–61.

Cohen, Michael P. "Blues in the Green: Ecocriticism under Critique." *Environmental History* 9, 1 (January 2004):9–10.

Copeland Report. *A National Plan for American Forestry.* Washington, DC: Government Printing Office, 1933.

"Corridor Management Plan." *Frontier Pathways Scenic and Historic Byway.* Pueblo, CO: Pueblo Museum, 1995.

Cox, Jack, "Camping's Birthplace." *The Denver Post,* June 13, 2005.

Cronon, William, ed. *Uncommon Ground: Toward Reinventing Nature.* New York: Norton, 1995.

Crump, Irving. *The Boys' Book of Forest Rangers.* New York: Dodd, Mead, 1924.

Dalbey, Matthew. *Regional Visionaries and Metropolitan Boosters: Decentralization, Regional Planning, and Parkways during the Interwar Years.* Boston: Kluwer Academic, 2002.

Davey, John. *The Tree Doctor: A Book on Tree Culture.* New York: Saalfield, 1904.

deBuys, William. "Uncle Aldo: A Legacy of Learning about Learning." University of New Mexico School of Architecture and Planning, John Gaw Meem Lecture Series/Annual Aldo Leopold Lecture, March 9, 2004.

———, ed. *Seeing Things Whole: The Essential John Wesley Powell.* Washington, DC: Island, 2001.

deBuys, William, and Don Usner. *Valles Caldera: A Vision for New Mexico's National Preserve.* Santa Fe: Museum of New Mexico Press, 2006.

Dusenbury, Mary E. Carhart. *A Genealogical Record of the Descendants of Thomas Carhart of Cornwall, England.* New York: A. S. Barnes, 1880.

Elliott, G. P., and W. L. Baker. "Quaking Aspen (Populus tremuloides Michx.) at Treeline: A Century of Change in the San Juan Mountains, Colorado, USA." *Journal of Biogeography* 31 (2004):733–745.

Etulain, Richard, and Wallace Stegner. *Conversations with Wallace Stegner on Western History and Literature.* Salt Lake City: University of Utah Press, 1983.

———. *Re-imagining the American West: A Century of Fiction, History, and Art.* Tucson: University of Arizona Press, 1996.

———. *Telling Western Stories: From Buffalo Bill to Larry McMurtry.* Albuquerque: University of New Mexico Press, 1999.

Flemming, Roscoe. "The Story of Arthur Carhart." *Rocky Mountain News,* December 29, 1941, 2.

Flippen, J. Brooks. *Nixon and the Environment.* Albuquerque: University of New Mexico Press, 2000.

Friederici, Peter. *Ecological Restoration of Southwestern Ponderosa Pine Forests.* Washington, DC: Island, 2003.

Fromme, Michael. *Battle for the Wilderness.* New York: Praeger, 1974.

Frontier Pathways: A Traveler's Guide to the Scenic and Historic Byway. Pueblo, CO: U.S. Department of Transportation, 2003.

Grese, Robert. *Jens Jensen: Maker of Natural Parks and Gardens (Creating the North American Landscape).* Washington, DC: Johns Hopkins University Press, 1998.

Gulliford, Andrew. *Sacred Objects and Sacred Places: Preserving Tribal Traditions.* Boulder: University Press of Colorado, 2002.

Harvey, Mark. *A Symbol of Wilderness: Echo Park and the American Conservation Movement.* Albuquerque: University of New Mexico Press, 1994.

———. *Wilderness Forever: Howard Zahniser and the Path to the Wilderness Act.* Seattle: University of Washington Press, 2005.

Hazlett, Maril. "'woman vs. man. vs. bugs': Gender and Popular Ecology in Early Reactions to *Silent Spring.*" *Environmental History* 9 (October 2004):17–18.

Hirsch, Jerrold. *Portrait of America: A Cultural History of the Federal Writers' Project.* Chapel Hill: University of North Carolina Press, 2003.

History of Monona County, Iowa. Chicago: National Publishing Company, 1890.

Jones, Stephen R., and Ruth Carol Cushman. *Field Guide to the North American Prairie.* New York: Houghton-Mifflin, 2004.

Kaufman, Herbert. *The Forest Ranger: A Study in Administrative Behavior.* Baltimore: Johns Hopkins University Press, 1960.

Kipling, Rudyard. *American Notes: Rudyard Kipling's West,* ed. A. M. Gibson. Norman: University of Oklahoma Press, 1981.

Kirk, Andrew Glenn. "Conservationists and Wilderness Preservation." M.A. thesis, University of Colorado, Denver, 1992.

———. *The Gentle Science: A History of the Conservation Library.* Denver: Denver Public Library, 1995.

———. *Collecting Nature: The American Environmental Movement and the Conservation Library.* Lawrence: University of Kansas Press, 2001.

Knopf, Arthur. *Publishing Then and Now.* New York: New York Public Library, 1964.

LaLande, Jeff. "The Making of a New Western Hero: The Forest Ranger in Popular Fiction, 1900–1940." *Journal of Forestry* 98, 11 (November 2000):37–41.

———. "The 'Forest Ranger' in Popular Fiction: 1910–2000." *Forest History Today* (Spring-Fall 2003):2–29.

Lanigan, Esther. *Mary Austin: Song of a Maverick.* Tucson: University of Arizona Press, 1997.

Lear, Linda. *Rachel Carson: Witness for Nature.* New York: Henry Holt, 1997.

Lendt, David L. *Ding: The Life of Jay Norman Darling.* Ames: Iowa State University Press, 1989.

Leopold, Aldo. *A Sand County Almanac.* New York: Oxford University Press, 1966.

Lippincott, Joseph Wharton. *The Wahoo Bobcat,* with illustrations by Paul Bransom. New York: Lippincott, 1952.

Lutts, Ralph. *The Nature Fakers: Wildlife, Science and Sentiment.* New York: Fulcrum, 1990.

Marshall, Robert. *The People's Forests.* New York: Smith and Haas, 1933.

Marshall, Robert, and James Sturgis Pray. "The American Society of Landscape Architecture and Our National Parks." *Landscape Architecture* 6, 3 (1932):119–120.

Martin, Erik. "A Voice for Wilderness: Arthur Carhart." *Landscape Architecture* (July–August 1986):71–75.

Matlock, Staci. "Parks in the U.S.: Born to Be Wild?" *The New Mexican,* August 26, 2004.

McClelland, Linda F. *The Historic Landscape Design of the National Park Service, 1916–1942.* Washington, DC: National Park Service, 1998.

McCrary, Irvin J. Architectural Drawings, Denver Public Library, Denver, CO.

McIntyre, Rick. *A Society of Wolves: National Parks and the Battle over the Wolf.* Stillwater, MN: Voyageur, 1993.

———, ed. *War against the Wolf: America's Campaign to Exterminate the Wolf.* Stillwater, MN: Voyageur, 1995.

Meine, Curt. *Aldo Leopold: His Life and Work.* Madison: University of Wisconsin Press, 1988.

———. *Correction Lines: Essays on Land, Leopold, and Conservation.* Washington, DC: Island, 2004.

Melville, McClellan. "A Conservationist Conserves Learning." *American Forests* 79 (January 1973):15, 60–63.

Miller, Char, ed. *American Forests: Nature, Culture, and Politics.* Lawrence: University of Kansas Press, 1997.

Moles, Hunter S. *Ranger District Number Five.* Boston: Spencerian, 1923.

Monona County, Iowa. Dallas: Taylor, 1982.

Mumford, Lewis. "Writers' Project." *The New Republic,* October 20, 1937, 306–308.

Nash, Roderick. "Arthur Carhart: Wilderness Advocate." *Living Wilderness* (December 1980):32–34.

————. *Wilderness and the American Mind.* New Haven: Yale University Press, 2001 [1967].

Noel, Thomas, and Barbara S. Norgren. *Denver: The City Beautiful.* Denver: Historic Denver, 1987.

Oelschlaeger, Max. *The Idea of Wilderness: From Prehistory to the Age of Ecology.* New Haven: Yale University Press, 1991.

Olmsted, Frederick Law, Jr. "The Distinction between National Parks and National Forests." *Landscape Architecture* 6, 3 (April 1916):114–115.

Overpeck, Jonathan. "Keynote Address: Global Climate Change, the West, and What We Can Do about It." San Juan Climate Change Conference, October 11, 2006. Available at http://www.mountainstudies.org/home.asp.

Paxon, Frederic. *The Last American Frontier.* New York: Macmillan, 1910.

————. *History of the American Frontier, 1763–1893.* Boston: Houghton Mifflin, 1924.

Penfold, Joseph W. Izaak Walton League Collection, Denver Public Library, Denver, CO.

Peterson, Jon A. *The Birth of City Planning in the United States, 1840–1917.* Baltimore: Johns Hopkins University Press, 2003.

Pinchot, Gifford. *Breaking New Ground.* New York: Harcourt-Brace, 1947.

Pomeroy, Earl. "Toward a Reorientation of Western History: Continuity and Environment." *Mississippi Valley Historical Review* 41 (March 1955):579–600.

Pray, James Sturgis. "Danger of Over-Exploitation of Our National Parks." *Landscape Architecture* 6(3):11 (n.d.).

"Pueblo to Get All the Forests She Wants Declares Visiting Head of Forests." *Pueblo Chieftain*, August 24, 1919.

Robinson, Jeffrey. *The Walk.* Norman: University of Oklahoma Press, 1989.

Robinson, Michael. *Predatory Bureaucracy.* Boulder: University Press of Colorado, 2005.

Rogers, Kevin. "Resurrecting a Native Conservation Population of Colorado River Cutthroat Trout." M.A. thesis, Colorado State University, 2005.

Rothman, Hal K. "'A Regular Ding-Dong Fight': The Dynamics of Park Service–Forest Service Controversy during the 1920s and 1930s." In Char Miller, ed., *American Forests: Nature, Culture, and Politics.* Lawrence: University of Kansas Press, 1997.

————. *Devil's Bargains: Tourism in the Twentieth-Century American West.* Lawrence: University Press of Kansas, 1998.

Scamehorn, H. Lee, and Lee Scamehorn. *High Altitude Energy: A History of Fossil Fuels in Colorado (Mining the American West).* Boulder: University Press of Colorado, 2002.

Schulte, Steven C. *Wayne Aspinall and the Shaping of the American West.* Boulder: University Press of Colorado, 2002.

Scott, Doug. *The Enduring Wilderness: Protecting Our Natural Heritage through the Wilderness Act.* Boulder: Fulcrum, 2004.

Sears, Paul. "Timber in Your Life." *Saturday Review* (January 1955):88.

Sellars, Richard West. *Preserving Nature in the National Parks.* New Haven: Yale University Press, 1997.

Seton, Ernest Thompson. *Wild Animals I Have Known.* New York: Charles Scribner, 1898.

———. *Two Little Savages.* New York: Doubleday Page, 1903.

Shaffer, Marguerite. *See America First: Tourism and National Identity, 1880–1940.* Washington, DC: Smithsonian Institution Press, 2001.

Simonds, O. C. *Landscape Gardening.* Amherst: University of Massachusetts Press, 1920.

Smith, Henry Nash. *The American West as Symbol and Myth.* Cambridge: Harvard University Press, 1950.

Snyder, Pamela S., and Jane S. Shaw. "PC Oil Drilling in a Wildlife Refuge." *Wall Street Journal,* September 7, 1995.

Stahl, Carl. "The Recreational Policy of the Forest Service." *Trail and Timberline* 17 (January 1920):7.

Steen, Harold K. *The U.S. Forest Service: A History.* Seattle: University of Washington Press, 1976.

Stegner, Wallace. *Beyond the Hundredth Meridian: John Wesley Powell and the Second Opening of the American West.* Lincoln: University of Nebraska Press, 1954.

———. *Angle of Repose.* New York: Penguin, 1971.

———, ed. *This Is Dinosaur: Echo Park Country and Its Magic Rivers.* New York: Knopf, 1955.

Sturgeon. Stephen C. *The Politics of Western Water: The Congressional Career of Wayne Aspinall.* Phoenix: University of Arizona Press, 2002.

Sutter, Paul. "'A Blank Spot on the Map': Aldo Leopold, Wilderness, and U.S Forest Service Recreational Policy, 1909–1924." *Western Historical Quarterly* 29 (Summer 1998):187–214.

———. *Driven Wild: How the Fight against Automobiles Launched the Modern Environmental Movement.* Seattle: University of Washington Press, 2002.

Thelan, David. *Memory and American History.* Bloomington: Indiana University Press, 1990.

Thomas, John L. *A Country of the Mind: Wallace Stegner, Bernard DeVoto, History and the American Land.* New York: Routledge, 2000.

Titus, Glenn. "Arthur Carhart: A Champion for Our Wild Lands." *Wyoming Wildlife* 57 (March 1993):77–78.

Trust for Public Land. "Colorado Springs Community Rallies to Save Urban Refuge." *On the Land* (Summer–Fall 1998):9–10.

Turner, Frederick Jackson. "The Significance of the Frontier in American History." In Martin Ridge, ed., *History, Frontier and Section: Three Essays by Frederick Jackson Turner.* Albuquerque: University of New Mexico Press, 1993.

Tweed, William. *Recreation Site Planning and Improvement in the National Forests, 1891–1942.* Washington, DC: Government Printing Office, 1981.

University of Denver College of Law. *Symposium on the Wilderness Act of 1964.* Denver: *Denver University Law Review* 76, 2 (1999).

U.S. Department of Agriculture, Forest Service. *Report of the Chief of the Forest Service.* Washington, DC: Government Printing Office, 1950, 1964.

U.S. Department of the Interior, National Park Service. *Squirrel Creek Recreational Unit Registration Form.* Denver: Colorado Historical Society, 2004.

Vogt, William. "Art Carhart: A Man for the Wilderness." *Outdoor Life* (March 1976): 27–29.

Waugh, Frank. *Landscape Engineering in the National Forests*. Washington, DC: Government Printing Office, 1918.

———. *Recreation Use on the National Forests*. Washington, DC: Government Printing Office, 1918.

Weber, William, ed. *The American Cockerell: A Naturalist's Life, 1866–1948*. Boulder: University Press of Colorado, 2000.

Wellman, J. Douglas, and Dennis B. Probst. *Wildland Recreation Policy: An Introduction*, 2nd ed. Melbourne, FL: Krieger, 2004.

Whitman, Walt. *Leaves of Grass: His Original Edition*. New York: Viking, 1961.

Wilderness Society. *The Wilderness Act Handbook: 40th Anniversary Edition*. Washington, DC: Wilderness Society, 2004.

Williams, Gerald. *The USDA Forest Service: The First Century*. Washington, DC: USDA Forest Service, 2000.

Witt, Bill. "Iowa's Last Wilderness." *The Iowan* (May–June 2001):30–41.

Wolf, Tom. "Literary Tradition on a Walk in Colorado's Sangre de Cristo Mountains." *The Walking Magazine* (Spring 1986):30–34.

———. *Colorado's Sangre de Cristo Mountains*. Boulder: University Press of Colorado, 1995. Revised paper ed., 1998.

———. *Ice Crusaders: A Memoir of Cold War and Cold Sport*. Boulder: Roberts Rinehart, 1998.

———. "The Real Arthur Carhart." *Forest Magazine* (Summer 2004):26–29.

———. "The Community Forest Restoration Program." *American Forests* (Winter 2007):49–52.

———. "Climate Change and the Rockies." *Inside/Outside* (Spring 2007):14–17.

Worster, Donald. *Nature's Economy: A History of Ecological Ideas*. Cambridge: Cambridge University Press, 1985.

———. *A River Running West: John Wesley Powell*. Cambridge: Cambridge University Press, 2002.

———. "Wild, Tame, and Free: Comparing Canadian and American Views of Nature." In Ken Coates and John Findlay, eds., *On Brotherly Terms: Canadian-American Relations West of the Rockies*. Seattle: University of Washington Press, 2002.

Wrobel, David, and Patrick Long. *Seeing and Being Seen: Tourism in the American West*. Lawrence: University of Kansas Press, 2001.

Wyckoff, William. *Creating Colorado: The Making of a Western American Landscape*. New Haven: Yale University Press, 1999.

Young, Christian C. *In the Absence of Predators: Conservation and Controversy on the Kaibab Plateau*. Lincoln: University of Nebraska Press, 2002.

Young, Stanley Paul. *The Wolf in North American History*. Caldwell, ID: Caxton, 1946.

———. *The Last of the Loners*. New York: Macmillan, 1970.

Young, Stanley Paul. Papers. Denver Public Library, Denver, CO.

922).

stem." *Parks*

1e 1924).

g Associa-
Planners,

l Carhart."

).

).

ARTICLES

men's Home Companion (May 1904).
Bulletin, District 2. Denver: USFS 3 (May 1919).
Forests." *Municipal Facts Monthly* 2 (July 1919).
Bulletin, District 2. Denver: USFS 3 (November 1919).
merican Forestry 26 (May 1920).
merican Forestry 26 (September 1920).
ecreation." *American Forestry* 26 (September 1920).
our National Forests." *American Forestry* 26 (September

Step?" *American Forestry* 26 (October 1920).
eation." *American Forestry* 26 (December 1920).
turing Plant." *Municipal Facts Monthly* 4 (August 1921).
1e *Denver Post* and the *Rocky Mountain News*, August 25,

1947):

"Forest Recreation." *American Forestry* 28 (January 1922).

"Minimum Requirements in Recreation." *American Forestry* 28 (January

"Going to the Glaciers." *Municipal Facts Monthly* (March–April 1922).

"Producing Forest Recreation." *American Forestry* 28 (April 1922).

"Recreation in Forestry." *Journal of Forestry* (January 1923).

"The Superior Forest: Why It Is Important in the National Recreation *
and Recreation* (July–August 1923).

"156,000,000 Acres—Count 'em." *Outdoor America* (October 1923).

"Lure of the Land above the Trees." *American Forests and Forest Life* 30 (

"What Is Conservation?" *Parks and Recreation* (August 1924).

"Street Traffic and the Business District." Report to the City Plan
tion, Denver, Colorado, April 1924. McCrary, Culley, & Carhart, (
Denver.

"Report to the Denver City Planning Association from McCrary, Culley,
July 1924.

"Two-Fisted Administration." *Blue Book Magazine* (February 1925).

"Sanctuary!" *American Forests and Forest Life* 31 (March 1925).

"The Race of Forest Men." *Blue Book Magazine* (May 1925).

"Out-of-Doors: The Tree Stork." *The Saturday Evening Post* (December 1

"Through the Red Dusk." *Blue Book Magazine* (March 1926).

"The Real Tincanners." *Motor Life* (May 1926).

"Call of the Highlands." *Motor Life* (September 1926).

"The Trail to the Arctic Willow." *Nature Magazine* (May 1927).

"Our Superior National Forest." *Field & Stream* (June 1927).

"Mutton—or Game?" *Outdoor Life* (July 1927).

"The Ideal Motor Camp." *Motor Life* (October 1927).

"The Economics of Scenic Highways." *The Highway Magazine* (November

"Poison in our Wildlife?" *Sports Afield* (November 1929).

"The Superior National Forest." *Holiday* (December 1930).

"The Sacrifice of Centipede Ranch." *Five Novels Monthly* (June 1931).

"What Makes Wild Life Wild?" *Saturday Evening Post* (January 1936).

"World Champion Wolfer." *Outdoor Life* (September 1939).

"Down Went Communism." *Family Circle* (November 1944).

"THIS IS YOUR LAND." *Sports Afield* (January 1947).

"Raiders on the Range." *Trail and Timberline* 339 (March 1947):39–43.

"Who Says—Sell Our Public Lands in the West?" *American Forests* 53
153–160.

"Don't Fence Us In!" *Pacific Spectator* 1, 3 (Summer 1947).

"Hunting and Fishing Is Big Business." *Sports Afield* (July 1947).

"Blue Rhythm." *Nature* (March 1948).

"Our Public Lands in Jeopardy." *Journal of Forestry* 46 (June 1948):409–4

"Land Grab: Who Gets Our Public Lands?" *Atlantic Monthly* 182 (July 194

"Forests in the Rockies." *American Forests* 54 (September 1948).

"Golden Anniversary." *American Forests* 54 (September 1948).

"Mass Murder in the Spruce Belt." *American Forests* 55 (March 1949).

"Dam Business." *The Nation's Business* (Fall 1949).

"Turn off That Faucet." *Atlantic Monthly* (February 1950). Reprinted in *Readers Digest* (April 1950).

"Western Land and Water Use." *The New York Times Book Review*, May 24, 1950.

"Go West to Hunt Elk." *Sports Afield* (December 1951).

"The Menaced Dinosaur National Monument." *National Parks Magazine* 26 (January–March 1952).

"Granby Dam." *Sports Afield* (March 1952).

"Bad-Man's Last Hangout." *Denver Westerner's Brand Book* (October 1952).

"They Still Covet Our Lands." *American Forests* (April 1953).

"State Must Not Toss Away Scenic Dinosaur Park." *The Denver Post*, April 7, 1954.

"Drought and Fire." *Hunting and Fishing* (Spring 1954).

"Forest Beacon in Michigan." *American Forests* 61 (April 1955).

"The First Ranger." *American Forests* 62 (February 1956).

"Poisons: The Creeping Killer." *Sports Afield* (November 1959).

"Shelterbelts, a 'Failure' That Didn't Happen." *Harper's* 221 (October 1960).

"Historical Development of Outdoor Recreation." *Outdoor Recreation Literature: A Survey.* ORRRC Study Report 27. Washington, DC: U.S. Government Printing Office, 1962.

"New Conservation Center." *Izaak Walton Magazine* (November 1962).

"The Lore and Learning of Conservation." *American Forests* (January 1963).

"The Conservation Library Center of North America." *Green Thumb* (January 1964).

"This Way to Wilderness." Unpublished manuscript, 1974.

BOOKS

The Ordeal of Brad Ogden: A Romance of the Forest Rangers. New York: J. H. Sears, 1929.

In collaboration with Stanley P. Young. *The Last Stand of the Pack.* New York: J. H. Sears, 1929.

Colorado: History, Geology, Legend. New York: Coward-McCann, 1931. With nine illustrations by Paul Bringle.

Trees and Shrubs for the Small Place. New York: Doubleday, 1935. Illustrated by the author.

How to Plan the Home Landscape. New York: Doubleday, 1936. Illustrated by the author.

[Hart Thorne.] *Bronc Twister.* New York: Dodd, Mead, 1937.

[Hart Thorne.] *Saddlemen of the C Bit Brand.* New York: Dodd, Mead, 1937.

Drum up the Dawn. New York: Dodd, Mead, 1937.

[V. A. Van Sickle.] *The Wrong Body.* New York: Knopf, 1937.

The Outdoorsman's Cookbook. New York: Macmillan, 1943.

Hunting North American Deer. New York: Macmillan, 1946.

Fresh Water Fishing. New York: A. S. Barnes, 1949.

HI STRANGER! The Complete Guide to Dude Ranches. Chicago: Ziff-Davis, 1949.

Conservation, Please! Questions and Answers on Conservation Topics. New York: Garden Club of America, 1950.

Fishing in the West. New York: Macmillan, 1950.

Fishing Is Fun. New York: Macmillan, 1950.

Water or Your Life. New York: Lippincott, 1951.

The Adventures of Pinto, the Cowboy Pony. Denver: Nifty Novelties, 1952.

Son of the Forest. New York: Lippincott, 1952.

Timber in Your Life. Philadelphia: Lippincott, 1955.

TREES and GAME—Twin Crops. Washington, DC: American Forest Products Institute, 1958.

The National Forests. New York: Alfred A. Knopf, 1959.

Planning for America's Wildlands. Harrisburg: Telegraph, 1961.

INDEX

283